VCs
OF THE FIRST WORLD WAR
PASSCHENDAELE
1917

VCs

OF THE FIRST WORLD WAR

PASSCHENDAELE
1917

STEPHEN SNELLING

First published 1998
This edition published 2012

The History Press
The Mill, Brimscombe Port
Stroud, Gloucestershire, GL5 2QG
www.thehistorypress.co.uk

British Library Cataloguing in Publication Data.
A catalogue record for this book is available from the British Library.

ISBN 978 0 7524 7666 7

Typesetting and origination by The History Press
Printed in Great Britain

Contents

ACKNOWLEDGEMENTS

Looking back through my files of correspondence as I prepared the final draft of this volume brought home to me what a long road I had travelled. I started my research in the summer of 1991, long before this series was even envisaged, and since then my Passchendaele odyssey has taken me as far afield as Australia, Canada, New Zealand and South Africa, not to mention Eire and all the home nations.

One of the great joys of writing a book such as this is making contact with so many people in so many places; over the last six years I have been grateful for the assistance, moral and practical, from a small army of supporters. The pleasure of research, with all its thrill of the hunt, is, however, tempered by the sense of responsibility felt towards all those who have given so freely of their time. To have incorporated everything sent to me would have required another volume at least, but I hope that I have been able to do justice both to their efforts and to the memory of the sixty-one gallant men featured in this book.

With the help of numerous appeals published in newspapers around the world, I have been able to make contact with a large number of relatives of the men who won their Victoria Crosses during the Passchendaele campaign. It has proved one of the most fruitful avenues of research and I would like to place on record my thanks to the following for supplying me with a wealth of biographical material and previously unpublished family photographs: Don Andrew, Major-General the Viscount Monckton of Brenchley CB, OBE, MC, DL, William Harrison, Marjorie Giles, Joe and Kathy Edwards, Grace McIntosh, S. Davies, Mary Moody, G. Armstrong, Edward Malet de Carteret, Dr Christopher Ackroyd, Arnold Loosemore, Joyce Lockier, Harry Cooper, William Ireland, Alisdair Skinner, Nicholas de Silva, Philippa Feeney, Jessie Rogers, Mollie Goggins, Barbara Newman, Gordon McGee, Shirley Kuo, Ivy Wrankmore, Christopher Evans, Reginald Hutt, James Ockendon, Fanny Brown, Ann Risley, Frank Bromley and Marjory Thompson.

Of the many fellow enthusiasts and researchers who have contributed greatly to my research, I would particularly like to thank Anthony Staunton, Ron Praite and Esme Smith, for assistance in Australia, Phillip O'Shea for his expert guidance and support in New Zealand, and W. James MacDonald, Terry Macdonald and Albert Hobson Thorn in Canada. I am also indebted to Donald C. Jennings of Gainesville, Florida, for generously allowing me access to what must be an unrivalled collection of photographs of VC graves and memorials. Nearer to home, my thanks go to Frank Gordon for checking my manuscript as well as offering suggestions on how it might be sensitively edited, to my colleagues Simon Finlay and Annette Hudson for their advice and practical assistance and to the ever-generous Dick Rayner for his support. As always the staff at Sutton Publishing have been a pleasure to work with and in Jonathan Falconer I found a most patient, considerate and enthusiastic ally in all my endeavours. Gerald Gliddon, fellow author and the man responsible for turning the idea of this series into reality, added support and much useful counselling whenever I seemed to become bogged down in the quagmire of research.

None of this, however, would have been possible but for the help given by the staff at countless regimental museums, local libraries and county record offices. To all of them, I shall be eternally grateful. In particular, I must thank Dennis Pillinger, the Military Historical Society's Custodian of the Lummis VC files at the National Army Museum, Nigel Steel at the Imperial War Museum's Department of Documents, the staffs at the Public Record Office, Kew, and the National Library of Wales in Aberystwyth, and Chris Lloyd, assistant curator of social history at Queensland Museum, for sending me complete copies of Patrick Bugden's wartime correspondence and family papers not once but twice after the first set had been lost in the post.

Lastly, there is a group of people who must be singled out as deserving my undying gratitude – my wife Sandra and daughters Katie and Holly. Together, they have made the greatest sacrifices, given the greatest support and shown the greatest tolerance. To them, therefore, must go the greatest thanks of all.

PREFACE TO THE 2012 EDITION

As most writers of military history will readily acknowledge, research rarely ever ends. In my experience, publication usually serves as a stimulus for discovering new sources of information and opening up new lines of enquiry. Of course, it can be also be a frustration, even an irritation, to suddenly find a vital clue to unlocking some hidden detail or to unearthing a previously unseen record within months of your book hitting the shelves. But that's the way it usually is, and certainly was so far as Passchendaele 1917 was concerned.

It's hardly surprising. Since it first appeared in 1998, there has been a technological revolution so far as historical research is concerned. At the heart of it is, of course, the internet. Its reach has become enormous and the opportunities for tracking down 'lost' families or undiscovered sources have multiplied a thousand-fold, and more.

Coupled with the rapid advances in technology has been the release of important documents by official archives. The opening up of many of those service records to have survived the damaging results of a Second World War has been a boon to researchers. Though frequently disappointing, every so often they yield unimagined treasure troves. Meanwhile, in Australia and Canada, a benevolent approach to the custodianship of public records has made accessible much new material and rendered long-distance research a joy rather than a chore.

But, as ever, the most memorable sources of fresh information about the Victoria Cross recipients of the 1917 Ypres campaign have been the relatives who have generously opened their private archives to furnish me with anecdotes and letters, diaries and photographs, which add fresh layers of knowledge and interest to the biographical portraits of their brave ancestors.

In particular, I must thank Ian Robertson for allowing me access to papers and photographs relating to his great uncle, Clement Robertson, the Tank Corps' first VC; Pam Colvin, daughter of William Hewitt, for her photographs and personal recollections; Anne Walsh for biographical information and photographs relating to her grandfather, Alfred Knight; Hazel Greaves for a wealth of material and memories about her father, Fred Greaves; and, lastly, Charles and John Moore, son and grandson respectively of 'Monty' Moore, for their generous assistance and candour in discussing one of the campaign's more colourful heroes. They alone have made the hours of work spent writing this revised and expanded edition worthwhile.

I am grateful, yet again, to the ever-supportive team at The History Press, Jo de Vries, senior commissioning editor, and Paul Baillie-Lane, military history editor; to Gerald Gliddon, my chief collaborator in the *VCs of the First World War* series; to Dick Rayner, my knowledgeable and most generous-spirited of fellow researchers; and to Brian Best, founder of the Victoria Cross Society, whose regular journals continue to inform and inspire. Most of all, though, I have my wife, Sandra, to thank not just for her unswerving support and myriad sacrifices but for miraculously managing to never quite tire of a husband with a strange obsession that continues to defy rational comprehension.

INTRODUCTION

The sufferings, privations and exertions which the soldiers had to bear were inexpressible. Terrible was the spiritual burden on the lonely man in the shell hole, and terrible the strain on the nerves during the bombardment which continued day and night. The 'Hell of Verdun' was exceeded by Flanders. The Battle of Flanders has been called 'The greatest martyrdom of the First World War' ... Looking back it seems that what was borne here was superhuman ...

These words were written about the German experience of Passchendaele by General Hermann von Kuhl, historian and former Chief of the German General Staff; they might, with minor adjustments, be said to apply equally to the ordeal endured by the thousands of British and Commonwealth soldiers who struggled in vain to achieve Field Marshal Sir Douglas Haig's much-vaunted breakthrough. The misery was universal. Eighty years on, Passchendaele, the soldiers' name for the Third Battle of Ypres, remains synonymous with desolation and despair, a potent symbol of the folly and futility of war. Haunting images of men toiling through a sea of mud have, rightly or wrongly, come to define the popular conception of the conflict that raged across the fields of Belgium and France between 1914 and 1918. Never before and, mercifully, never since have British soldiers been forced to endure such prolonged horrors.

It is, however, one of the great ironies that the campaign which has come to most represent the war's attritional stagnation was originally intended to break the deadlock. The Ypres offensive, launched in the summer of 1917, was designed not merely to drive the Germans off the commanding heights from where they had dominated the salient for more than two years, but to bring about a great strategic victory. With the help of an amphibious landing and a strike along the coast, Haig aimed to sweep the Kaiser's army of occupation clean out of Belgium, thus removing the U-boat menace from the Channel ports. It was a grand, over-ambitious plan destined to be fatally undermined by the weather and the tenacity of the German defenders.

Passchendaele followed General Sir Herbert Plumer's successful operations to secure the Messines Ridge. It was a tragedy in eight parts, eight distinct battles fought in varying conditions with varying degrees of success: Pilckem Ridge (31 July–2 August), Langemarck (16–18 August), Menin Road (20–25 September), Polygon Wood (26 September–3 October), Broodseinde (4 October), Poelcappelle (9 October), First Passchendaele (12 October) and Second Passchendaele (26 October–10 November).

Such neat delineation, however, was not always apparent to the fighting men. To them, Passchendaele was one long struggle amid squalid conditions which frequently beggared belief. In circumstances such as these, merely to have endured was a form of heroism hard enough to comprehend. Yet there were men whose courage conquered all; men who overcame cold, drenching rain, fear and weariness to win the nation's supreme award for valour.

This book sets out to tell the story of the sixty-one men awarded the Victoria Cross for feats of outstanding gallantry performed during the Passchendaele campaign. In keeping with the democratic traditions of this most coveted decoration, there were no distinctions of class or rank among the recipients. They ranged from humble private to brigadier-general and included men from big city slums as well as sons of the landed gentry. They ranged also in age, from 19-year-old Thomas Holmes, a Canadian private from Owen Sound, Ontario, to 47-year-old Clifford Coffin, the first brigadier-general to win the VC.

Not all, however, were model soldiers. Cecil Kinross was probably one of the scruffiest and most unruly individuals ever to don a uniform, yet it did not stop him being one of Canada's finest fighting soldiers. Thomas Whitham was serving a sentence for 'disobeying a lawful command' when he won his award. Nor were all recipients necessarily much loved or admired: Bertram Best-Dunkley, the 26-year-old commanding officer of the 2/5th Lancashire Fusiliers, was roundly hated by virtually every officer in his unit. Every member of this elite band of men was linked by a common thread of valour.

Their acts of courage reflected the nature of the fighting. All but a handful of the VCs were won for 'offensive' acts. More than two-thirds were connected with daring assaults on enemy machine-gun posts, most of them pillboxes and fortified farms, upon which so much of the German defensive system was based and which gave the campaign its unique character. In contrast, only seven awards directly involved the saving of lives. Two of these went to medical officers and another two to men who smothered live grenades with their own bodies. Strangely, while the two former were posthumous awards, the latter pair both miraculously survived.

Although the overwhelming majority of the VCs were won by British troops, the Commonwealth nations were also represented. Nine went to Canadians (including one serving in a British county regiment), seven to Australians and one each to a New Zealander and a South African.

Closer scrutiny of the awards shows that eighteen were won by officers, twenty-nine by non-commissioned officers (or acting NCOs) and fourteen by privates. Of these, none appears to have been won by conscripts. A breakdown of the recipients' recruitment details reveals that forty-seven were volunteers, many of whom had answered Kitchener's call to arms, five had been serving in the Territorial Forces at the outbreak of war and nine were professional soldiers (including one officer, Thomas Colyer-Fergusson, who was given a permanent commission during the war and two officers, Denis Hewitt and Montague Moore, straight from Sandhurst). Roughly a quarter (fifteen) of the awards were made posthumously while another five recipients did not survive the war. Others, such as Arnold Loosemore and Frederick Room, never fully recovered from the conflict, their short lives reduced to a grim struggle against ill-health.

The campaign provided its share of VC records: 31 July 1917 yielded the highest number of Crosses won on a single day in the course of the war – fourteen awards. This figure can be compared with the twelve won on the first day of the Gallipoli landings, nine in the opening 24 hours of the Somme offensive and the same number on the first day of Ludendorff's 1918 Spring Offensive. The Passchendaele awards also included the war's only double VC winner (Noel Chavasse), the first Welsh Guards' VC (Robert Bye), the first VC in the fledgling Tank Corps (Clement Robertson) and the youngest New Zealander to win the Cross (Leslie Andrew).

For those who lived long enough, winning the Victoria Cross brought with it a measure of fame. Some went on to achieve great things. Major George Pearkes, the former Mountie who had enlisted as a trooper in a Canadian cavalry unit, rose to become a general, a Cabinet minister and finally Lieutenant-Governor of British Columbia. John Dwyer, who won his Cross as a sergeant in the Australian Machine-Gun Corps, held high office in the government of Tasmania. But for many, the instant fame which followed the announcement of their awards was short-lived and they quickly slipped back into the obscurity whence they came. Far from returning to a 'land fit for heroes', all too many came home to the dole queue and a life of struggle. Yet each of these men deserves to be remembered. For in a campaign dominated by artillery, mud and formidable fixed defences, theirs was, indeed, the highest form of valour.

L.W. ANDREW
La Basse Ville, 31 July 1917

A light rain was falling as the New Zealanders trudged eastwards along one of countless trails criss-crossing Ploegsteert Wood. Once renowned as a shooting reserve for Belgium's ruling classes, by the fourth summer of the war the sprawling Flanders forest had become simply another haunted landmark, a staging post on the way from the catacombed shelters of Hill 63 to the front line.

Night masked the worst disfigurements as 8 officers and 328 men of the 2nd Wellington Regiment filed through in the early hours of 31 July 1917. Their trek took them past the ruins of St Yves, along the duckboards of St Yves Avenue towards their assembly points at Le Truie Sap and Cabaret Road. By 3 am, they were in position. Zero hour was 50 minutes away and the Kiwis steeled themselves for the attack. They represented the extreme right wing of Haig's grand offensive, designed not merely to eject the enemy from the ridges overlooking Ypres, but to free the Channel ports and, ultimately, to drive the Germans back across the Belgian border. In the tragic drama about to unfold, the 2nd Wellingtons were to play a supporting role, though one not without its hazards. Their task was to capture the village of La Basse Ville, a place they had captured and lost four days previously, in order to help draw enemy reserves away from the main thrust to the north.

The small hamlet of La Basse Ville, built beside a loop in the River Lys, formed part of a screen of outposts barring the way to the Warneton Line, west of the Ypres–Comines Canal. Much of the ground was wired and studded with machine-guns, but the most potent defensive position was housed in the Estaminet, an undistinguished two-storey building standing in splendid isolation at the northern end of the village, alongside the Warneton road. A machine-gun post sited in its upper floor was credited with having turned the tide against the New Zealanders in their first attempt to capture the hamlet.

For the second assault, therefore, not only was a larger force to be employed but special attention was to be paid to the capture of this strongpoint. The task was given to two sections of the Wellington-West Coast Company, 2nd Wellingtons, commanded by Corporal Les Andrew, a 20-year-old railway clerk from Wanganui. The orders for the fifteen-strong party were to follow close behind the barrage, avoiding trouble if possible, and knock out the machine-gun post in a 'commando-style' operation.

The attack went in at 3.50 am, the rising sun blotted out by mist and low cloud. Supported by machine-gun fire and a rapid mortar bombardment, the Ruahine Company dashed across the low-lying flats towards the Armentières–Warneton railway which cut between the lines. Almost immediately, they hit trouble. A machine-gun, hidden in a fence, tore gaps in the leading section of No. 15 Platoon, bringing the advance to a halt. As the survivors took cover in shell-holes, the platoon commander, Lt H.R. Biss, moved forward but before he could devise a plan for overcoming the obstacle, the issue was settled by Cpl Andrew.

Spotting the danger, Andrew diverted his party along the railway and charged it from the flank, killing a number of the enemy and capturing the gun. According to war correspondent Malcolm Ross, Andrew lost eleven men wounded in wiping out the entire gun team. Strangely, however, neither the unit diarist nor the official New Zealand historian mention any casualties suffered by Andrew's party. Colonel H. Stewart credits Andrew entirely with the success, while the history of the Wellington Regiment offers contradictory versions. One states that the approach of Andrew's party caused the Germans to waver, allowing Lt Biss to capture two machine-guns, while the other version refers to only one gun being seized by the two sections of the Wellington-West Coast Company led by Andrew.

All, however, agree that the gallant corporal's handling of the situation prevented a critical delay. The danger removed, Andrew and his depleted party sprinted after the barrage. While heavy fighting continued in a system of outposts known as the Hedgerows, the main force fought their way into La Basse Ville. There, as expected, the Estaminet proved one of the biggest obstacles. Machine-gunners fired continuously as Andrew's group closed in. Ross recorded:

> To attempt to attack the post from the front clearly meant that he and his little remaining band [sic] would be wiped out altogether ... Coolly sizing up the situation, he led his little party round for a quarter of a mile on their stomachs through some thistles and attacked the German position from the

rear. As soon as they got close enough the intrepid quartet threw bombs at the crew and rushed, killed four of the enemy and put the rest to flight, and captured the gun and the position.

According to Ross, all four members of the attacking party suffered slight wounds while their equipment showed signs of numerous near misses. Andrew was grazed by a bullet wound in the back and had his rifle smashed in his hand.

After a struggle lasting about half an hour, La Basse Ville was once again in New Zealand hands. As the garrison's survivors fled, preparations were made to meet the inevitable German counter-attack. Andrew, however, had not quite finished his day's work. Taking advantage of the confusion and the garrison's precipitate retreat, he ordered two of his men to carry the captured machine-gun back while he and Pte Laurie Ritchie set off in pursuit. Andrew's intentions were apparently to reconnoitre towards Warneton but they had not gone far when they encountered another enemy outpost. Stewart recorded:

> 300 yards along the road, on the very threshold of the village, was a wayside inn, In Der Rooster Cabaret, and in its cellars some of the hunted Germans sought refuge. A machine-gun post was in an open trench beside it. The post was rushed, the cellars and adjoining dugouts were thoroughly bombed, and only then did the 2 men turn their faces towards our line.

Precise details of how many Germans had been accounted for by Andrew's various attacks are unclear. Years later, he put his personal tally at eight killed, six of them with the bayonet. Ross also credited Andrew and Ritchie (who was later awarded the Distinguished Conduct Medal) with bringing back 'most valuable information' about the German dispositions. They may even have supplied the earliest warning of the first enemy counter-attack around 5 am: enemy soldiers were observed forming up at the In Der Rooster and were effectively smashed by artillery fire.

The battle for La Basse Ville raged throughout the day and this time the New Zealanders held on at a cost to the 2nd Wellingtons of 134 casualties – roughly 40 per cent of the attacking force – including thirty-seven men killed. Despite all their efforts, there is no evidence of the action diverting any significant enemy reserves from the main front. However, the considerable courage displayed did not go unnoticed. According to Major William Cunningham, the Wellingtons' commanding officer, 'GHQ attached a great deal of importance to the ... operation and as it was quite successful they were very liberal in the matter of awards'. In a letter written on 18 August, he added:

So far we have received 14 Military Medals, 1 bar to Military Medal, 3 DCMs and 4 Military Crosses, and there is still a chance for a VC. Young Andrew who used to be in Charlie Mackay's office is the man recommended. He was in charge of a couple of sections in the attack and captured two machine guns and brought them both in, killing a good many of the Bosch [sic] crews and putting the others to flight. His work was very fine and he displayed great gallantry and splendid leadership. If he gets it, it will be a great thing for the Battalion and I am particularly pleased that it will be a Wanganui boy to earn the coveted distinction.

Major Cunningham's hope was fulfilled on 6 September when the *London Gazette* announced the award of a Victoria Cross to No. 11795 Cpl Leslie Andrew.

Leslie Wilton Andrew, the youngest New Zealander to win the VC in the First World War, was born on 23 March 1897 at Ashhurst, Palmerston North, on the North Island. He was the eldest son of William Jeffrey Andrew, headmaster of the Wanganui East primary school, and his wife Frances Hannah. He was educated at Ashhurst primary school, Wanganui East District High School and Wanganui Collegiate, a prestigious private school for boys.

On leaving school in 1913, he worked in a solicitor's office before joining the New Zealand Railways Department as a head office clerk. He served in the Avenue School Cadets, a unit in which his father was a company commander, and the local Territorial force. He is said to have lied about his age in order to serve overseas, enlisting in the NZ Expeditionary Force on 26 October 1915. He embarked for Egypt with the 12th Reinforcements on 1 May 1916 as a 19-year-old sergeant credited with being the best shot in his company and having already passed exams for a commission.

Although he reverted to private in order to be posted to the 2nd Wellington Regiment, Andrew's maturity was clearly marked. Sailing for England in July 1916, he joined his unit in France the following month. During his fighting career on the Western Front he was wounded twice – the first time on the Somme in September 1916 – and survived being buried by shells on three occasions. Made corporal on 12 January 1917, Andrew took part in the Messines operations in June. The day after his exploits at La Basse Ville he was promoted sergeant and shortly afterwards sent for officer training while one of the machine-guns he captured was sent back as a trophy to New Zealand (now housed in the Wanganui Regional Museum). Commissioned second lieutenant on 1 March 1918, he remained in England until August the following year. During this time, he met Bessie Mead Ball, of Brinsley, Nottingham, whom he married 24 hours after Armistice Day.

Andrew made the Army his career. After leading a Victory Day contingent through London, he returned to New Zealand in the summer of 1919 as a lieutenant in his country's small permanent military forces. A captain by the age of 27, he held various staff appointments before being posted for two years, on an officer exchange scheme, to a battalion of the Highland Light Infantry in India. Back in New Zealand, he served as adjutant of the 1st Wellington Regiment. In 1937, still a captain in the Staff Corps, he led a fifty-strong New Zealand contingent, including two other VC holders, to England for the coronation of King George VI, and commanded the Kiwi party which mounted guard on Buckingham Palace on 11 May 1937.

By the outbreak of the Second World War he was a major and on 29 January 1940 he joined the 2nd New Zealand Expeditionary Force as a lieutenant-colonel, commanding the newly formed 22nd Wellington Battalion. He was then aged 42 and had a reputation as a tough taskmaster. Keith Elliott, one of the volunteer soldiers who would go on to win a Victoria Cross in North Africa, wrote of his CO:

> Some thought him to be too much of a disciplinarian, but he'd been schooled through the hardest experiences of life and knew that if we were to be properly prepared for our task, any weaknesses would have to be hammered out through rigorous training and self-discipline.

An upright man, Andrew was intolerant of slackness and inefficiency. Once described as a 'walking encylopaedia on all matters military', the same writer described him as a 'natural leader': 'Perhaps his greatest characteristic is that he demands the best, that things be done in the right way. But he will always give first the help and then the reason for his demand and indicate how it later affects battle performance.'

On taking command of the 22nd Wellington Battalion, he urged his men to be 'second to none in whatever we achieve or undertake to do', and his words were adopted as the unit's unofficial motto. Under his leadership, the battalion served in Britain (where it helped to guard the Kent coast during the invasion scare of 1940), Greece, Crete and North Africa. He proved a resourceful and courageous commander, as evidenced during the British Crusader offensive fought in the Libyan desert in late 1941. For fourteen difficult days, he commanded the remnants of the 5th New Zealand Brigade, defeating a series of enemy attacks, after the headquarters staff had been overrun and captured. His gallant stand at Menastir was later recognised by the award of a DSO. But that success was overshadowed by controversy surrounding his actions during the Crete débâcle seven months earlier. At the height of the German airborne assault on 20 May 1941, Andrew had withdrawn his hard-pressed battalion from a vital hill feature overlooking the strategically important airfield at Maleme upon which the fate of the defence hinged. There were mitigating circumstances. Such was the ferocity of the air and ground attack on his battalion, he later insisted that 'the Somme, Messines and Passchendaele were mere picnics' by comparison. Having held out for the best part of a day without relief, Andrew felt he had no option but to withdraw his depleted command or risk being overrun. The Germans seized the airfield and, in a matter of days, Crete fell.

Andrew accepted responsibility for his actions, but the real fault at Maleme had lain with those senior officers in the 5th NZ Brigade who had denied support to the 22nd until it was too late. Significantly, the island's commander, Major-General Bernard Freyberg, another New Zealand-born VC of the First World War, never blamed him. When Andrew was ordered home in February 1942 to command the Fortress Area, Wellington, Freyberg thanked him for his fine work and concluded: 'I need hardly add that I should be delighted to take you back in the Division at any time should the CGS be able to let you go.'

Andrew never again held an operational command. Promoted colonel, he ceased service with the Expeditionary Force in October 1943, resuming service in the regular army. At the end of the war, Colonel Andrew returned to Britain in command of the New Zealand contingent for the 1946 victory parade. That same year he was appointed ADC to the Governor-General of New Zealand, Sir Cyril Newell.

Les Andrew soldiered on into the peace, attending the Imperial Defence College in London before being promoted brigadier in 1948. By then, it was his proud boast that he had held every rank from private to brigadier, bar that of quartermaster-sergeant. He remained in command of the Central Military District until his retirement in 1952. The last seventeen years of his life were spent peacefully with his wife Bess and their family. They had five children, three boys, one of whom died in infancy, and two daughters. His son, Don Andrew, recalled: 'He was a strict disciplinarian with himself as well as others, but still modest. I remember him cooking breakfast for us children before we went to school, and doing the laundry at the weekends ... He was very much a family man.' After retiring from the Army, Andrew was courted by politicians and invited to stand for the national parliament but he rebuffed all approaches. Don recalled: 'He said that it wouldn't fit in with his honesty, although what he said was more direct.'

After a short illness Les Andrew died at Palmerston North Hospital on 8 January 1969, and was buried with military honours in the Returned

Services Lawn cemetery, Levin. Veterans of the 22nd Battalion acted as pall-bearers and three of the country's nine surviving VC holders attended. The Revd Keith Elliott VC, who had served with him in North Africa, read one of the lessons.

Almost forty years later, Les Andrew's valour was headline news again, albeit in unhappy circumstances. On 2 December 2007 it was reported that his Victoria Cross group was one of nine VCs among ninety-six medals stolen from the Queen Elizabeth II Army Memorial Museum at Waiouru, where it was on display. The heist sparked international revulsion and a nationwide hunt for the thieves. Following the offer of a NZ$300,000 reward by VC collector Lord Ashcroft and Nelson businessman Tom Sturgess the New Zealand Police announced on 16 February 2008 that all the medals had been recovered.

T.R. COLYER-FERGUSSON AND C. COFFIN

Bellewaarde Ridge and Westhoek Ridge, 31 July and 16 August 1917

The night of 30/31 July was dark and cloudy with the threat of rain as the men of the 2nd Northamptonshires shuffled towards their assembly positions in front of Bellewaarde Ridge. B Company was last to arrive, led by the boyish-looking Old Harrovian 'Riv' Colyer-Fergusson, a veteran at 21. Two of his platoons formed part of the battalion's third wave in the coming attack, the remainder being employed as mopping-up teams. The Northants had been allotted stretches of the Kingsway and Kingsway Support trenches, but shortly after midnight Colyer-Fergusson, anxious to avoid any retaliatory bombardment, moved his men, together with a supporting section of machine-gunners, 100yd forward.

By 2 am they were in position. The night was quiet, with little shelling or rifle fire. 'We lay there quite happily to wait for the off,' observed

A/Capt. T.R. Colyer-Fergusson

2/Lt Leslie Walkinton, the young officer in command of the machine-gunners of the 24th Machine-Gun Company. 'One of the men handed round humbugs which he had just received from home.' That morning the men of II Corps, of which the 2nd Northants were part, faced the most important task to be undertaken by General Sir Hubert Gough's Fifth Army. Operating south of the Ypres–Roulers railway, three divisions, the 8th, 30th and 24th, were to capture the entire Gheluvelt plateau, the most heavily defended enemy sector along the Ypres front. Three main defence zones and no fewer than seven lines of fortifications ran across the high ground. Once freckled with woods, the plateau had

20

become a 'wilderness of fallen trees' masking a lethal network of pillboxes and machine-gun nests that had survived intact the British bombardment. The Northants were the left-hand battalion of the 24th Brigade, and their task was to capture Bellewaarde Ridge, one of the enemy's key observation posts. They had spent days rehearsing the attack through fields of standing corn near Bomy. Now it was the real thing.

At 3.50 am the barrage came down with a 'tremendous roar' and the battalion advanced under its cover. Perfect order prevailed, the battalion keeping its formations just as if they were still in the practice trenches back at Bomy. 2/Lt Hubert Essame, the acting adjutant, recorded:

A/Brig. Gen. C. Coffin

> The blast was so deafening that we jammed our fingers in our ears; the ground shook. We could see the flashes of the barrage in the murk ahead ... The swish of the 18 pdr shells tempted us to crouch down. In fact, although we could not see them, the two leading companies advancing on compass bearings were clinging to the barrage and moving forward each time it jumped a further 25yds ...

A and D Companies led the advance, followed by Colyer-Fergusson's B Company ready to push on to the battalion's main objective on the ridge. Little remained of the enemy wire or their forward trenches. According to the Northants' war diarist, the defenders were 'too dazed to put up a fight'. As the leading waves occupied Ignis Trench and Ignorance Support, mopping-up parties netted sixty prisoners from the craters around Hooge and scattered outposts along the Menin road. B and C Companies, meanwhile, skirted Bellewaarde Lake and a line of smouldering dugouts treated to a barrage of Thermite (incendiary mortar bombs). 2/Lt Essame, who had moved forward with Lt-Col C.G. Buckle DSO, MC, the 2nd Northants' 26-year-old CO, saw them 'ploughing through the mud' on their way towards the crest of Bellewaarde Ridge.

Forming up for the final approach, however, proved difficult. Colyer-Fergusson realised his company was in danger of losing the barrage. Ahead lay Jacob Trench, covered by a machine-gun in a wired strongpoint missed by the bombardment. Knowing a delay could prove disastrous, Colyer-Fergusson collected ten men, including Sgt W.G. Boulding and his orderly

Pte B. Ellis, and dashed forward under cover of the shelling. Just as they gained a footing in the enemy position, a German company was spotted advancing en masse barely 100yd away. The regimental historian recorded:

> Captain Colyer-Fergusson and his picked men knocked out 20 or 30 of them with rifle fire, and the remainder put up their hands. The men of his company were beginning to come up, when the German machine-gun came into action. Leaving his company to hold the trench, and assisted by his orderly alone, Captain Colyer-Fergusson attacked and captured the gun. He then turned it on to another group of the enemy, killing a large number of them and driving the remainder into the hands of another British unit. Later, assisted only by Sgt Boulding and Pte Ellis (both later awarded DCMs), he attacked and captured a second machine-gun ...

At around 5.30 am, when the young company commander reported to his CO, consolidation was under way. Buckle, who had signalled the ridge's capture to a patrolling scout plane, ordered B and C Companies to push on 100–200yd to establish a line of outposts, and it was while directing this operation, shortly afterwards, that 'Riv' Colyer-Fergusson was hit in the head by a sniper's bullet, dying instantly. It was a tragic blow. No one had done more to ensure the success of the operation. As the unit war diarist recorded: 'He had done magnificently. The capture of Jacob Trench was largely due to his courage and initiative.'

While the Northants dug in, fresh battalions drove on to the 24th Brigade's final objective on the forward slopes of Westhoek ridge. But it quickly became apparent that these positions were untenable. The attack of the neighbouring 30th Division had stalled, leaving the right flank open and the men of the 24th and 23rd Brigades were vulnerable to enfilading fire from the direction of Nonne Boschen and Glencourse Woods. It was a grim augury.

Further back, near Jacob Trench, 2/Lt Essame saw a 'mass of troops' coming up from Hellfire Corner. These were units of the 25th Brigade, who had the task of carrying the advance from Westhoek ridge to a line beyond the Hanebeek, within 2 miles of Passchendaele. Their commander was Brig.-Gen. Clifford Coffin DSO, a 37-year-old Royal Engineers officer who had been promoted to command the brigade in March. Coffin was the antithesis of the popular and much-misrepresented image of the First World War general. When news reached him that Westhoek ridge had fallen, Coffin immediately set off to reconnoitre the ground with an advance party. He found not only his right flank wide open, with heavy fire coming from Glencourse Wood, but the enemy still occupying Westhoek crossroads and neighbouring houses. A message was sent back to Divisional HQ stating that more time was needed to clear up the situation and that 'a fresh attack would have to be planned behind a new barrage'. Then, with Brigade HQ set up in Jaffa Avenue, Coffin made his way back to 23rd Brigade HQ at Ziel House to get a clearer picture. The 25th Brigade war diary states:

> It was reported that only a few snipers and one or two machine-guns were holding out and that it was hoped to be able to deal with these before the next advance began. As it was doubtful whether the message asking for a postponement would get through in time, it was decided to carry out the attack as originally laid down ...

Coffin had grave misgivings but he realised that a delay could prove yet more disastrous. However, the gamble did not come off. Although he directed a company to protect the right flank, it was not enough.

The attack went in at 10.10 am. At first the three assault battalions appeared to be 'going strong'. On the left, parties of the 2nd Rifle Brigade broke through to Hanebeek Wood, but in the centre and on the right the 1st Royal Irish Rifles and 2nd Lincolnshires were decimated by enfilade and reverse fire from Glencourse and Nonne Boschen Woods. Only one company reached the Hanebeek, a few men actually crossing it, but they were too few and were soon in retreat. By midday the shattered remains of the three battalions were back on Westhoek ridge, manning a ragged line cut along the reverse slopes with Lewis gunners guarding the crest.

Enemy reaction was not slow in coming. Large numbers of troops were seen arriving in lorries, and far from striking out beyond the Hanebeek the question now was whether the badly shaken units of the 25th Brigade could hold Westhoek ridge. Failure to do so would undoubtedly have jeopardised gains to the north and might even have proved fatal to the operation as a whole. Aware of the desperate state of affairs, Coffin set out to tour his command. The divisional historian wrote:

> He went about from shell-hole to shell-hole, organising the defence ... and urging on his troops to new and willing efforts. Walking about in the open, with supreme disregard of the fact that he was at all times under fire, he seemed to bear a charmed life. His control was everywhere and his spirit irresistible. During the afternoon he himself carried up ammunition to the front line. No spot was too exposed for him to visit, no task too laborious for him to share ...

The ridge was under more or less continuous fire from the right and around midday began the counter-attacks which continued into the late afternoon. Around 2.30 pm, the Lincolnshires were forced to give ground, which was swiftly recaptured. Shortly afterwards, Coffin received orders to hold the line 'at all costs'. Heading towards the left flank, he found the 2nd Rifle Brigade 'very exposed'. Calling for help from 23rd Brigade, he managed to seal a potentially dangerous gap.

Enemy troops continued to threaten, massing within 200yd of the ridge, inside the protective barrage called down by Coffin. 'There is no doubt that a strong attack would have materialised,' he wrote, 'but for the tenacity with which our men held their ground ...' Their ordeal continued until reliefs arrived around 9 pm. Two days later, Coffin appended a personal note to his official report of the ill-starred operation:

On arrival behind the Westhoek ridge the situation which met the Brigade was not quite the one which had been anticipated, but all ranks acted up to the changed conditions. The line reached was held against numerous enemy counter-attacks and was handed over intact upon relief. These enemy attacks were taken full advantage of by the Brigade and the enemy's casualties must have been very heavy.

The remnants of the 25th Brigade had little time to recover from their ordeal. On 12–13 August they returned to the line of shell-holes they had fought desperately to hold to lead a renewed attack towards the Hanebeek. A deluge of rain had turned the battlefield into a quagmire. 2/Lt Essame, of the 2nd Northants attached to Coffin's brigade, wrote: 'Conditions had been bad when we left; they were even worse now. All the holes were full to the brim with water. Everywhere it was hard going through the mud. In some places duckboard tracks sank out of sight almost as soon as they were laid.'

Glencourse and Nonne Boschen Woods remained in enemy hands, and it was clear that if the 56th Division on the right failed to capture them, a repetition of the near catastrophic reverse on 31 July was certain. Tragically, that was what transpired.

At 4.45 am on 16 August, 25th Brigade, comprising the 2nd Royal Berkshires, 1st Royal Irish Rifles and 2nd Lincolnshires, made swift inroads. Troops crossed the swollen Hanebeek, penetrated Hanebeek Wood and captured a number of redoubts. Some units even approached close to Zonnebeke. But it was to no avail. The 56th Division failed where 30th Division had failed before them, with appalling consequences for the 8th Division.

By 8 am a counter-attack was in full swing. Anzac redoubt was retaken by the Germans and a thrust from the south threatened to cut off the greater part of 8th Division. Coffin's brigade was most immediately affected. The Berkshires, fighting desperately, were almost overwhelmed. The CO of the embattled 1st Royal Irish Rifles stumbled wounded and exhausted into Brigade HQ to report that his men were retreating.

Shortly after 9 am Coffin set out to find the Berkshires, arriving just as a powerful counter-attack broke around them. It was pandemonium. The line on the right had broken and men were streaming back in disorder. Coffin took charge, stopped the retirement by dint of personal example and succeeded temporarily in checking the enemy advance. Then, returning to his HQ, he ordered his reserves forward.

The first of two companies of the 2nd Northants arrived on Westhoek ridge at about 11 am. By then, the brigade strength was estimated at about 500 men. Coffin's brigade was being shot to pieces. Around 3.45 pm an enemy attack pressed his depleted units back to the foot of the ridge. It was 31 July all over again. The divisional historian recorded: 'So menacing ... did the situation become that General Coffin, whose energy, resource and daring had once more become the soul of the defence, decided to put Brigade Headquarters personnel into the line.' Having averted one crisis, Coffin then led the Northants in a counter-attack that succeeded in restoring the position on the forward slopes. Shortly afterwards, the remainder of the Northants arrived to reinforce his hard-pressed command.

It was a hellish scene on the ridge. 2/Lt Essame wrote:

> ... we found Coffin standing upright in the open. He welcomed us with a smile: 'Those two companies of yours are a fine lot. They got here just in time.' We then discovered that he had led the counter-attack with them and halted the Germans about 150yd ahead. He ... then took the rest of the battalion forward and patched up some sort of line with Royal Berkshire survivors and filled the gap between the right flank and what was left of 167th Brigade [56th Division]. Neither Coffin nor Latham [CO of the Northants] for that matter showed the slightest inclination to take cover or indeed of being in any way perturbed.

A final counter-attack was destroyed by a combination of artillery and massed machine-guns, so that by 5 pm an eerie quiet settled across the battlefield. Essame observed:

> It seemed that both sides had had enough for the time being. The sun made a fitful appearance. Three of Coffin's battalions had lost half their strength – the Royal Irish Rifles had only one officer and 60 men left. They were still, however, a disciplined body prepared to fight on. So long as Coffin remained with them they would have gone on to the last man.

The attack had become a fiasco, but an even greater catastrophe had been averted. Twice in the space of a fortnight, Coffin's personal intervention had prevented routs. It was an extraordinary display of resolute and inspirational leadership justly crowned by the first award of a Victoria Cross to an officer of general rank. Strangely, his citation, published on 14 September, made no mention of his performance on 16 August, but there was no question it had contributed to his award. The 8th Division historian described it as a reward for his 'consistent gallantry and skill' in both actions. The official announcement came eight days after the *London Gazette* reported that the same honour had been posthumously conferred on 2/Lt (Acting Captain) 'Riv' Colyer-Fergusson.

Thomas Riversdale Colyer-Fergusson was born at 13 Lower Berkeley Street, London, on 18 February 1896, the third and youngest son of Thomas Colyer-Fergusson, a former High Sheriff of Kent, and his wife Beatrice (née Muller).

His father was a Kentish squire with homes at Wombwell Hall, Gravesend, and Ightham Mote, and he was a grandson of the Rt Hon. Professor Max Muller, a distinguished oriental scholar, and Sir James Fergusson. He inherited the name Riversdale, with its Irish connections, from his maternal grandmother, a daughter of Riversdale Grenfell. The name Colyer came to the family through Sir James Fergusson's first wife, Mary Soames, elder daughter of Thomas Colyer of Wombwell Hall.

'Riv', as he was known in the family, was taught at Summer Fields, Oxford, and then went on to Harrow in 1909. As a youngster, he developed a passion for country sports. A keen follower of the hounds, he was also an accomplished shot. In the summer of 1914 he was due to take his place at Oriel College, Oxford, but the war intervened. He enlisted in the Public Schools Battalion in September, and the following February was granted a temporary commission in the Northamptonshire Regiment. He went to France in November 1915, and was wounded in action at Contalmaison on the Somme in July 1916. After recovering from his injuries, he returned to his unit in November and the following month was given a permanent commission.

In January 1917, aged 20, he was promoted to acting captain and given command of B Company. The following month, as the Germans pulled back to the Hindenburg Line, he led his men in a dashing attack on the ridge overlooking Bouchavesnes. Sweeping across two lines of enemy trenches, they burst into the third line, captured a machine-gun and bombed a dugout before realising they had advanced beyond their objective. Pulling back, they helped consolidate their newly won position and held it against five counter-attacks. The action cost the Northants almost 250 casualties, but Colyer-Fergusson emerged unscathed with his reputation enhanced.

A contemporary account described the young officer as 'a fine type of healthy English boyhood'. His high-spirited behaviour and cherubic appearance, however, belied his mature leadership qualities: 'He was a general favourite and had a peculiarly frank and open manner which gained him the affection of all classes with whom he came in contact. One of his commanding officers speaks of his adroitness in managing the men under him.' Leslie Walkinton, the machine-gun officer who came to know him shortly before the Ypres offensive, described him as a 'keen young regular ... obviously greatly liked by his men'.

'Riv' Colyer-Fergusson was buried in the Menin Road South military cemetery. The inscription on his headstone reads: 'My son, my son. No reward can be too great'.

Writing of him, Col Buckle, only five years his senior, declared: 'I think his death was more keenly felt in the Regiment than any other I have known. To my mind, he was the most promising officer under my command. I cannot hope ever to replace him. He was, besides being such a first-rate officer, a thorough sportsman and the cheeriest of companions.'

Clifford Coffin was born at Blackheath on 10 February 1870, the youngest son of Lt-Gen. Sir Isaac Campbell Coffin KCSI and his wife Catherine Eliza (née Shepherd). He was educated at Haileybury College and the Royal Military Academy, Woolwich, and joined the Army on 17 February 1888, following his brother into the Royal Engineers as a second lieutenant, a week after his 18th birthday.

His first spell of foreign service was with the Submarine Miners in Jamaica, from December 1891 to March 1894. Five months after his return, he married Helen Douglas, elder daughter of Admiral Sir Thomas Sturges Jackson KCVO, and the couple had four children.

After a three-year spell in Ireland as a member of the 1st Fortress Company, Cork Harbour, he was promoted captain on 17 February 1899 and appointed to the Staff College, at Camberley. Employed as assistant to the CRE of the 6th and 10th Divisions, he saw considerable service during the South African War, taking part in the relief of Kimberley, the operations at Paardeberg and the actions at Poplar Grove, Driefontein and Zillikat's Nek. In July 1900 Coffin led a composite force made up of men of the 9th and 7th (Field) Companies as part of Sir Ian Hamilton's column pursuing the Boer leader De Wet. His work was recognised by a Mention in Despatches in November.

After serving as CRE Standerton, he returned to England in 1904 as staff captain in the Intelligence Department of the War Office. Promoted major in 1907, he was given command of 56 Field Company RE at Bulford, only to return to staff duties four years later as a GSO2 in Sierra Leone.

At the outbreak of war, Coffin was appointed CRE of the 21st Division. Promoted temporary lieutenant-colonel on 9 June 1915, his rank was confirmed thirteen days later. During the fighting at Loos and on the Somme, he acquired a fearsome reputation as a taskmaster with an explosive temperament that belied a gentle appearance. His adjutant, Stephen Foot, described him as a 'sort of mixture of Cromwell, Savonarola, and St George':

> With a quiet voice, a pleasant smile, and a mild manner, Coffin at first sight appeared to a young subaltern as quite a kindly old gentleman.; but when roused he was fiercer than Vesuvius in eruption. The voice took on a rasping tone, the smile vanished, and with heightened colour the colonel would proceed to demolish his victim with a storm of invective that was completely shattering. The medical officer, who lived in the mess, was much less frightened of the Germans than he was of the colonel.

According to Foot, Coffin, a deeply religious man, went nowhere without his Bible and was 'always ready to pour out his wrath on the sins of extravagance and idleness'. Foot, however, found him far from the ogre many of his divisional colleagues thought him to be. As well as admiring his courage and sangfroid in the heat of battle, he was struck by his humility. By way of example, he recalled:

> The day after I joined (him), he wrote out some orders for the Field Companies, and when he had finished he handed them over to me with the remark: 'Read this and tell me if it is quite clear.' I was staggered! – a senior lieutenant-colonel asking the opinion of a junior subaltern; it was not at all the kind of thing that I expected.

Coffin enjoyed remarkable good fortune during his front-line service. On one occasion a shell came close enough to him to 'feel the heat of it as it passed', yet he escaped with nothing worse than a mud-spattered uniform. Another time, while sitting on the fire-step of a trench during an intense bombardment, he came through unharmed though shells fell all around, in the bays either side of him and on the parapet above his head, and it seemed, to his adjutant, that 'each moment threatened to be our last'.

His courageous leadership was recognised by the award of a DSO in the 1917 New Year's Honours List. This was followed, on 11 January, by promotion to temporary brigadier-general. Two months later he was selected to command the 25th Brigade, 8th Division. In the wake of his heroic performance during the opening days of the Ypres offensive, Coffin was conspicuous again for his gallantry during the March retreat of 1918 and the subsequent fighting around Villers-Bretonneux. For a time, command of all the infantry in his division devolved upon him, and his firm handling of the crisis was rewarded with a Bar to his DSO (*London Gazette*, 26 July 1918):

For conspicuous gallantry and devotion to duty during a long period of active operations, when he handled his brigade with great skill, especially when covering the withdrawal of the remainder of the division. On one occasion he commanded for a time the infantry of the division with marked success, and his personal courage and example at all times inspired all ranks with him.

Following stabilisation of the line, Coffin was promoted major-general and on 6 May he was given command of the 36th (Ulster) Division, which he led during the advance to victory. After the Armistice, he commanded a brigade in the Rhine Army of Occupation and in September went to Ireland in charge of the 16th Brigade. In June 1920 Coffin was made commander of British troops in Ceylon, and the following month he was appointed an ADC to King George V.

Clifford Coffin returned to England and retired from the Army with the honorary rank of major-general in November 1924, settling in Forest Row, Sussex. In 1936 he came to public prominence when newspapers reported that a Dutch Bible he had brought back at the end of the Boer War had been returned to its previous owner, who was traced by a name in the fly-leaf. For the most part, however, the retired general busied himself with work for ex-servicemen. Appointed Colonel Commandant of the Royal Engineers from 1936 to 1940, he devoted himself to the British Commonwealth Ex-Service League, serving as chairman of the executive throughout the Second World War. Sir Ernest Hartson CBE, secretary of the league, wrote:

> In whatever he did he excelled because he put his whole heart in the job without worrying about himself – on the Staff, in the field and in civil life afterwards it was the same, as the BCEL, the Diocese of Chichester, the Society of St George and many another worthy cause can abundantly testify. Yet he used to look me sternly in the eye and say that most of the harm in the world was caused by people trying to do good! – something which he never stopped doing.

As loyal as he was courageous, Clifford Coffin combined a cool, analytical mind with a taciturn manner. Hartson acknowledged that 'he could say say less with more effect than anyone I knew'. Maj.-Gen. Clifford Coffin VC, CB, DSO and Bar, the most senior ranking VC of the Passchendaele campaign, died at Torquay on 4 February 1959, within a week of his 89th birthday. A memorial service was held for him in the Garrison Church, Chatham, and his many honours and awards, including the French Croix de Guerre and the Belgian Order of the Crown, were presented to the Royal Engineers Museum for display.

The hero of Westhoek ridge was buried in Holy Trinity churchyard, Coleman's Hatch, Hartfield, in East Sussex, a modest memorial stone bearing the inscription: 'God be merciful to me a sinner'.

B. BEST-DUNKLEY, T.F. MAYSON AND N.G. CHAVASSE

Near Wieltje, 31 July–2 August 1917

The unexpected difficulties which beset General Coffin's advance beyond Westhoek Ridge on the first morning were mirrored in the experiences of the 164th Brigade amid the barren expanse of shell-holes forming Pilckem Ridge. As reserve brigade of the 55th Division, their task was to follow through the assault units ranged along the lower slopes and push on almost a mile towards the Gravenstafel Spur, barely 4,000yd from Passchendaele. The initial attack went broadly to plan. After some stiff fighting, a foothold east of the Steenbeek was established from Pommern Redoubt to within 600yd of St Julien. By 9 am mopping-up operations were under way but, as at Westhoek, early reports proved overly optimistic. Not only were key strongpoints within the Black Line holding out, but the barrage made little impact on a cluster of concrete blockhouses, gun emplacements and fortified farms straddling the 164th Brigade's line of advance.

None of this was known as the brigade's four battalions left their assembly trenches at Congreve Walk and Liverpool Trench, close to Wieltje, to begin their march to the Black Line, more than a mile away. The mood was cheery. Even the 26-year-old CO of the 2/5th Lancashire Fusiliers, a man renowned for his fragile temper, seemed in good spirits. A school-teacher before the war, Lt-Col Bertram Best-Dunkley had a reputation as an arrogant, overbearing, self-seeking martinet. Yet as they waited to go over, 2/Lt Thomas Floyd saw him 'walking along the line, his face lit up by smiles more pleasant than I have ever seen before'. They had the briefest of conversations. 'Good morning, Floyd; best of luck,' said the colonel, before passing on to greet his other officers. 'Everybody', observed Floyd, 'was wishing everybody else good luck.' The portents did indeed appear promising. A steady flow of German prisoners straggled back as they pushed on across ground strewn with bodies and wreckage towards the Steenbeek. There was little enemy fire, but once across the stream it mounted steadily.

The 2/5th Lancashire Fusiliers, the left leading battalion, was 200–300yd short of the Black Line when a hail of fire burst around them from strongpoints at Wine House, Spree Farm and Capricorn Support, supposed to have been captured along with the second objective, and from the enemy fortifications at Pond Farm and Hindu Cottage. Attempts to shake into extended order were unavailing as men went down and confusion reigned.

It was a shattering moment and provided the first test for Best-Dunkley. Until then, he had shown little sign of inspirational leadership. Now, he was a man transformed. Officers and NCOs displayed much gallantry in trying to rally the shaken remnants of companies and platoons, but none more so than Best-Dunkley. Minutes earlier, 2/Lt Floyd had seen him 'complacently advancing, with a walking stick in his hand, as calmly as if he were walking across a parade ground'. Realising all the officers in C Company were dead or wounded, he ran forward, took command of the leading wave and led them through a storm of fire.

At great cost, small parties captured Wine House, Spree Farm (where Best-Dunkley set up his battalion HQ) and Capricorn Support. The 2/5th had lost half its strength and was in poor shape to launch its attack. According to the second-in-command, Major George Brighten, the battalion was 'in a very weak and disorganised state' and still under heavy fire. But there was no time to reorganise: delay would mean losing the barrage. 'The advance', wrote Brighten, 'had to continue and quickly.' By then, the 2/5th had all but merged with the 1/8th Liverpool Regiment. They went on in mixed, widely dispersed parties. 2/Lt Floyd was one of them:

We left St Julien close on our left. Suddenly we were rained with bullets from rifles and machine-guns. We extended. Men were being hit everywhere. My servant … was the first in my platoon to be hit. We lay down flat for a while, as it was impossible for anyone to survive standing up. Then I determined to go forward. It was no use sticking here for ever, and we would be wanted further on; so we might as well try and dash through it. 'Come along – advance!' I shouted, and leapt forward. I was just stepping over some barbed wire defences – I think it must have been in front of Schuler Farm – when the inevitable happened. I felt a sharp sting through my leg. I was hit by a bullet. So I dashed to the nearest shell-hole … My platoon seemed to have vanished just before I was hit. Whether they were in shell-holes or whether they had found some passage through the wire, I cannot say …'

Despite appalling losses, some parties reached their final objectives. Pond Farm and Hindu Cottage were captured and a few men managed to establish outposts along the Gravenstafel Spur. One of the deepest incursions saw

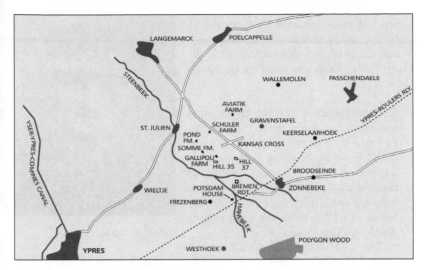

The Pilckem Ridge, scene of heavy fighting on the first day of the offensive

Capt. J.R. Bodington take Wurst Farm with ten men. But they were too few to resist the enemy onslaught when it came in the early afternoon. Isolated platoons were steam-rollered and the dazed survivors streamed back via the Winnipeg Farm–Kansas Crossroads and Jew Hill, east of St Julien. What took hours to capture and would take several weeks more to regain was abandoned in less than 30 minutes. Of the 130 men of the 2/5th Lancashire Fusiliers and 1/8th Liverpools holding a strongpoint near Schuler Farm, barely a dozen came back. Orders to form a new line stretching from Hill 35 via Somme Farm to Border House were overtaken by the rapid advance.

The panic and confusion, combined with heavy losses, threatened even the Black Line. Best-Dunkley's HQ at Spree Farm was almost overrun before he realised what was happening. He and his staff beat a hasty retreat, but once more he refused to cave in. Having withdrawn a short distance, he gathered every man available, and led a sharp counter-attack, recapturing Spree Farm. Shortly afterwards, a heavy barrage brought the enemy attack to a standstill. Sporadic fighting continued into the evening, and around 8 pm, while still directing the defence of the Black Line, Best-Dunkley was mortally wounded – the last of eighteen casualties among the nineteen officers who had started out a little less than 12 hours earlier.

Evacuated to the main dressing station, the dying colonel was visited the next day by the Revd James Coop DSO, the divisional chaplain. Best-Dunkley whispered that he hoped his general had not been disappointed with his battalion. When Coop relayed this to Maj.-Gen. Sir Hugh 'Judy' Jeudwine, the 55th Division's GOC replied:

T/Lt-Col B. Best-Dunkley

> Disappointed! I should think not, indeed. I am more proud of having you and your battalion under my command than of anything that has ever happened to me. It was a magnificent fight, and your officers and men behaved splendidly, fighting with their heads as well as with the most superb pluck and determination.
>
> The 31st July should for all time be remembered by your battalion and regiment and observed with more reverence even than Minden Day. It was no garden of roses you fought in. I have heard some of the stories of your battalion's doings and they are glorious. And I have heard of your doings too, and the close shave you had.

Bertram Best-Dunkley succumbed to his wounds on 5 August, two days after his 27th birthday. He was buried at Proven in a service attended by a number of senior officers and at which General Jeudwine was heard to remark: 'We are burying one of Britain's bravest soldiers.'

Smoother progress had been made to the Black Line by units on the right of the 164th Brigade front. 2/Lt C.H. Newbold, commanding No. 10 Platoon, C Company, the 1/4th King's Own Royal Lancaster Regiment, reported suffering only one casualty despite passing through 'a barrage of HE and shrapnel'. Following close behind the 1/4th Loyals, each platoon of the King's Own had specially designated objectives. Newbold's task was to mop up Somme Farm and the strongpoints between Hill 35 and Pond Farm. Morale among his men was high. According to L/Sgt Tom Mayson, a 23-year-old Cumbrian, the 'boys' were in 'fine fettle'. Advancing with what one man described as 'clockwork motion', they reached the Black Line according to plan before running into heavy opposition. A tank, identified as F19, rumbled forward to their aid. It was almost immediately knocked out, but not before it had silenced a machine-gun barring their way. Newbold's platoon, however, was still in trouble. Mayson recorded:

> Another gun … opened fire from half-left, so I crawled to a flank for about 150 yards and got behind a mound and then found cover in a ditch.

I approached to within 20 yards of the gun when I threw a bomb, putting the gun out of action and wounding 4 of the team. The remainder of the team bolted into a dugout near by. I went into the dugout after them, but found only 3 of them there, whom I slew with the bayonet. My platoon then came up and pushed on with me. For a time there was some mixed fighting in shell-holes. Then we came across some dugouts near the WIELTJE ROAD which we cleared, capturing 16 prisoners. Next we went across to POND FARM (which we were not supposed to touch, but there was no one else at hand) where we captured from 100 to 150 prisoners. We were literally surrounded by them, and not one of them resisted [Newbold's own report described them as 'poor specimens and very scared' and noted that 'very strangely most of them had haversacks on but no other equipment except gas masks'. In the meantime, the platoon for which we were mopping up had gone ahead. I then reconnoitred the SOMME, where I found the Brigade Forward Station. Finally, my platoon started to dig in near the WIELTJE ROAD ...

Newbold's platoon had been greatly assisted in clearing the dugouts by another tank, F16, directed by an unnamed officer 'who walked in front although he was under heavy MG fire'. Having gained Pond Farm at around 11.15 am, Newbold formed a defensive position. By then, the platoon consisted of twelve men, including four stragglers from other units, with two Lewis guns. They resisted enemy counter-attacks until 4 pm, when, having run out of ammunition, they reluctantly withdrew to avoid being cut off. 'If we had had more SAA and if the troops on the flanks had not gone back, we could have held out easily,' Mayson later complained. Newbold brought his men, including the belligerent Mayson, into the Black Line:

My party immediately joined in the defence of the trenches. I found that the fire of the Lewis guns in the trench was masked by the line of outposts, so I took charge of half a dozen Lewis guns and put them in position on top of the dugouts behind the trench. From there they were able to bring very effective fire to bear on the Germans as they appeared on the ridge of Hill 35 ...

According to Mayson, they 'held the Black Line all night – at times under heavy shell fire – and at 11.30 am next morning received orders to withdraw to our original front line, which we did with the loss of one man wounded'. By midday only 150 men remained out of the 420 who had started the attack. Yet heavy as their losses were, they were less than those suffered by the 2/5th Lancashire Fusiliers. Out of a fighting strength of nineteen officers and 593 men, only one officer and 120 men reported for duty.

Few men better appreciated the sacrifices made by the 'poor bloody infantry' than the overstretched medical officers forced to contend with the flood of wounded pouring back from the front line. Throughout 31 July and in the days following, they worked unceasingly, recovering and treating the injured, despite the constant danger from enemy shelling. Theirs was a measured and selfless courage exemplified by Captain Noel Chavasse VC, MC, who over three days performed prodigious acts of heroism, recognised in the posthumous award of a Bar to his Victoria Cross won almost a year earlier on the Somme.

By the summer of 1917, this 32-year-old medical officer of the 10th Battalion, the King's (Liverpool) Regiment, the Liverpool Scottish, had a reputation for unstinting devotion to duty. He had even declined offers of less dangerous appointments in order to stay with the regiment he had accompanied overseas in November 1914.

On 31 July the Liverpool Scottish, part of the 166th Brigade, had supported the first wave of the attack east of Wieltje, pushing on across the Steenbeek to reach the 55th Division's second objective, destined to become the scene of bitter fighting later in the day. Most of the battalion's goals had been achieved by 7.45 am, although casualties were severe.

Chavasse, as was his custom, took up position close to the front line. Leaving the relative security of the Wieltje dugout near the start line, he set up a regimental aid post in a captured enemy dugout near Setques Farm, close to Battalion HQ, 500yd west of the Steenbeek. Not long after arriving, the area was so heavily shelled that HQ found it necessary to move. Chavasse chose to stay, working in cramped conditions, the sound of battle reverberating all around. He was wounded early on by a shell splinter which struck him in the head. According to the unit history, he was in the process of carrying an injured man into the dugout, but Ann Clayton's masterly biography states that he was waving to some men to indicate the location of the aid post. Although some believed the wound may have fractured his skull, he was able to walk back unaided to the Wieltje dugout for treatment. Despite being implored to seek further attention, he returned to his post with his head bandaged.

Acting L/Sgt T.F. Mayson

Throughout the rest of the day he continued to treat the never-ending flow of wounded, even as the German counter-attack threatened to overwhelm the line. Then, when darkness fell and with rain filling the shell-holes, he set out to search the churned ground for more wounded. Early the next day, having had little sleep for more than 24 hours, he was still working at his post when a shell struck the dugout. One patient was killed instantly, and Chavasse may have been wounded a second time. Precise details of his injuries are unclear, but it would appear that at some point on 1 August he was hit on the left side of his head. Again, it seemed to make no difference to his work. His unit historian wrote:

> Still he insisted on carrying out his duties and he did not confine his work to those men who were brought to the dressing-station ... He repeatedly went out with stretcher-parties to the firing line in search of wounded and to dress those lying out, and he personally assisted in carrying in under heavy fire a number of badly wounded men who were found in the open. Though suffering intense pain he continued for two days to attend the casualties, and during this time he had no rest and very little food ...

Around 3 am on 2 August, while he was trying to snatch some sleep, another shell landed in the dugout. Every man inside was either killed or knocked out except Chavasse. He was hit by splinters in four or five places, the most serious injury being to his abdomen. Yet somehow he managed to crawl or stagger back towards Wieltje. Picked up along the way, he was taken back to Casualty Clearing Station No. 32 at Brandhoek, which specialised in treating abdominal wounds.

Chavasse survived the initial operation, and surgeons were cautiously optimistic that he might pull through. He was said to be weak but cheerful and was anxious to get back 'to his boys'. But in the early hours of 4 August, his condition worsened. He asked a nursing sister to write a letter home to his fiancée. 'Tell her Duty called and called me to obey,' he said. At 1 pm, still dazed from morphia to deaden the pain, Noel Chavasse passed away.

Noel Godfrey Chavasse, the only man to win two Victoria Crosses in the First World War, was born at the Rectory of St Peter-le-Bailey, Oxford, on 9 November 1884, one of identical twin sons, to the Revd Francis James Chavasse and his wife Edith Jane (née Maude). He grew up in a large family with three sisters and two younger brothers as well as his twin, Christopher, who was destined to become the Bishop of Rochester. Their father was the Principal of Wycliffe Hall, a theological college, and later became Bishop of Liverpool.

Noel was educated at Magdalen College School and, following the family's move to Merseyside, at Liverpool College. An outstanding scholar and athlete, he went to Trinity College, Oxford, in 1904 to study natural sciences. A double blue, he was selected, along with his twin brother who was also a student at the university, to run the 400m in the London Olympics of 1908, but was eliminated in the first round. Having gained a first in physiology, he undertook his clinical studies at Liverpool's Royal Southern Hospital. He qualified BM, BCh, in 1912, having acquired a reputation as a 'muscular Christian', organising Bible classes, sporting events and annual camps for deprived children in Liverpool.

Capt. N.G. Chavasse

He would carry his social conscience and religious convictions with him into the Territorial Army in 1913. Commissioned as a lieutenant and medical officer, the Royal Southern house physician was attached to the 10th King's (Liverpool) Regiment. Mobilised with his battalion on 4 August 1914, he went to France in November when the Liverpool Scottish became one of the first Territorial units to be sent into action.

It was during their first major action at Hooge on 16 June, an attack launched in conjunction with operations around Givenchy and Vimy Ridge, that Chavasse, known as 'the Doc', won his first award.The casualties suffered by the Liverpool Scottish were out of all proportion to their gains. Of twenty-three officers and 519 men, only two officers and 140 returned unharmed. More than 200 men were wounded and Chavasse, together with his stretcher-bearers, braved enemy fire to comb the battlefield for injured survivors. According to the unit historian, it was due to his 'untiring efforts in personally searching the ground between our line and the enemy's many of the wounded owed their lives'. Chavasse was awarded the Military Cross.

Promoted captain in August 1915, Chavasse proved as enlightened in ministering to his men's welfare and hygiene as he was to treating their battlefield injuries, establishing a bath house, a laundry and, initially at his own cost, a dry canteen. The unit historian noted:

> The Doctor had a genius for picking out those men who were near a breakdown, either in nerve or general health, but not yet run so down as to be hospital cases. Rather than send them into the trenches, where their collapse sooner or later was inevitable, he kept them at his aid post as

light-duty men, where in comparative comfort they had a chance to rest and recover.

The Liverpool Scottish were not involved in the early fighting on the Somme, but on 9 August 1916 were hurriedly thrown into a disastrous attack against the heavily fortified village of Guillemont. It was Hooge all over again, only worse. Blasted by a counter-barrage, mown down in droves by machine-guns, only a handful of men reached the enemy trenches and they were quickly overwhelmed. The rest retreated, leaving dozens of wounded behind. It was the signal for Chavasse to mount another rescue operation which resulted in his being awarded the Victoria Cross while four of his men received DCMs. His citation in the *London Gazette* on 26 October read:

> For most conspicuous bravery and devotion to duty. During an attack he tended the wounded in the open all day, under heavy fire, frequently in view of the enemy. During the ensuing night he searched for wounded on the ground in front of the enemy's lines for four hours.
>
> Next day he took one stretcher-bearer to the advanced trenches, and under heavy shell-fire carried an urgent case 500yd into safety, being wounded in the side by a shell splinter during the journey. The same night he took up a party of 20 volunteers, rescued three unwounded men from a shell-hole 25yd from the enemy's trench, buried the bodies of two officers, and collected many identity discs, although fired on by bombs and machine guns. Altogether he saved the lives of some 20 badly wounded men, besides the ordinary cases which passed through his hands. His courage and self-sacrifice were beyond praise.

He received his award from King George V at Buckingham Palace in February 1917. Among those accompanying him was his first cousin Gladys, with whom he had fallen in love. They had become secretly engaged and hoped to be married by the year's end. His fiancée was anxious for the wedding to be sooner rather than later. But all their dreams were crushed on the battlefield east of Wieltje.

His death was mourned throughout the division. The unit historian declared:

> It is difficult to find words to express all that the Doc's life and example had meant to the Liverpool Scottish. There never was a man who was better loved by officers and men alike; there never was a man who gave himself more unsparingly in the service of others. His bravery was not of the reckless or flamboyant type but the far finer bravery that sprang

from his determination that nothing should stand in the way of whatever he considered his duty.

For a time, his medals were displayed on the staircase at St Peter's College, Oxford, which his twin brother Christopher, a wartime chaplain and MC winner, had founded. Later they were placed for security reasons in a bank vault before being presented to the Imperial War Museum on loan in 1990. Almost twenty years later Lord Ashcroft paid almost £1.5 million for the outstanding medal group and they are now displayed in the new Victoria Cross and George Cross gallery at the IWM which the Conservative peer helped establish with a £5 million donation.

Nearly a century after he marched away to war never to return, Chavasse's extraordinary story continues to inspire. In August 2009, a magnificent bronze statue, depicting him helping a wounded soldier with the assistance of a Liverpool Scottish stretcher bearer, was unveiled in Liverpool's Abercromby Square. Dedicated to all the city's VC recipients, it was commissioned by the Noel Chavasse VC Memorial Association in which his biographer Ann Clayton played a leading role. Three years later a further monument, of a more contemporary nature, took root in Chavasse Park to keep his memory alive. There are myriad other smaller tributes to the most highly decorated medical officer of the First World War. But the main focal point for remembrance remains the simplest memorial of all. The unique Commonwealth War Graves Commission headstone in New Brandhoek military cemetery with its twin VC engravings continues to draw battlefield pilgrims moved by an epic saga of sacrifice summed up by the apt inscription: 'Greater love hath no man than this, that a man lay down his life for his friend.'

Bertram Best-Dunkley was born in York on 3 August 1890. Educated in Germany, he joined the 4th Lancashire Fusiliers (TF) as a second lieutenant in 1907 and was promoted lieutenant the following year. A school-teacher, he was working as an assistant master at Tientsin Grammar School in China when war broke out. He immediately returned to England to join his Territorial unit.

Posted to Barrow as part of the 'fortress' garrison guarding the shipbuilding works, he immediately ran foul of the Army Council over a letter he wrote to an American friend in Sweden. According to a letter, dated 30 September, in his personal file, 'he was employed on duty at works of Messrs Vickers and gave particulars of His Majesty's ships then with that firm, as well as information regarding the state of completion of the ships, the members of the guard affording protection to the works and other matters ...' Though a breach of regulations, it was regarded as an act of naivety rather than anything more serious.

In May 1915 he was posted to the 2nd Battalion, which had suffered heavy losses during the Second Battle of Ypres. He was transferred to the King's Own Lancaster Regiment and then to the 2/5th Battalion of his own regiment, serving as claims officer before being made adjutant. On 6 July 1916 Best-Dunkley was promoted temporary captain and later that same month he saw action on the Somme, where the 55th Division was heavily engaged until late September. The next month he was gazetted captain, and then assumed command of the battalion on 20 October following an accidental injury sustained by the colonel only days after arriving in the Ypres sector. Best-Dunkley was granted the temporary rank of lieutenant-colonel. That same year he married Marjorie Kate Pettigrew, the daughter of Mr and Mrs W.F. Pettigrew, of Barrow-in-Furness. A dedicated, hard-driving commanding officer, Best-Dunkley did nothing to endear himself to his fellow officers. He possessed little charm and his brusqueness combined with unpredictable mood swings were legendary.

In an unusually candid memoir, Thomas Hope Floyd, who joined the 2/5th Lancashire Fusiliers as a second lieutenant in June 1917, provided a vivid portrait of Best-Dunkley. He described him as 'brilliant young man, endowed with a remarkable personality', an imperfect hero, 'a petty tyrant' who would surprise everyone by his fearless leadership. Writing home on 12 June Floyd recounted his first impressions:

> He is small, clean-shaven with a crooked nose and a noticeable blink. He looks harmless enough; but I noticed something about his eyes which did not look exactly pleasant. He looks more than twenty-seven [in fact, he was 26] ... It is interesting to note that he was educated at a military school in Germany! (And he had travelled a good deal in the Far East. 'When I was in China' was one of his favourite topics of conversation) ... an officer observed in the mess this morning that there were some people who liked the Kaiser, but he was sure that there was not a single soul who liked Best-Dunkley! That is rather strong ...

Best-Dunkley had a twitch to go along with his blink. Both were thought to be legacies of shell-shock suffered on the Somme. For all Best-Dunkley's flaws, Floyd refused to condemn him, although he did list a number of 'faults', which included being endowed with 'a very bad temper and a most vile tongue' and showing 'an inordinate desire to be in the good graces of the Brigadier-General'. Floyd's memoir, published in 1920, charted the unit's preparations for the 'big push' at Ypres, and the extraordinary highs and lows of their commander, including a training march which ended with all but sixteen of his men falling out from exhaustion and Best-Dunkley being bawled out by his general. According to Floyd, there was a suggestion, shortly before the battle, that the colonel, together with other battalion commanders, would be left in reserve during the initial assault. Best-Dunkley, however, pleaded and protested until the general relented. Floyd observed:

> Throughout the whole summer of 1917 his whole heart and soul were absorbed in preparation for the coming push; never did a man give his mind more completely, more unstintingly, and whole-heartedly to a project than Best-Dunkley did to the Ypres offensive ... He was determined to associate his name indelibly with the field of Ypres; he was determined to win the highest possible decoration on July 31 ... And I think – there was that in his bearing the nearer the day became which suggested it, everybody who had known him of old declaring that they noticed a certain change in him during the last two months of his life – that he felt that his glory would be purchased at the cost of his life.

A few days before the attack in which he would achieve his ambition, and receive his fatal wound, news reached him of the birth of his son. Some weeks later, King George V would pin the Victoria Cross, gazetted on 6 September 1917, to the shawl of the baby boy who never knew his heroic father.

Bertram Best-Dunkley's valour was recognised by a memorial tablet in Tientsin Grammar School, which survived the Communist take-over. It was still on display quite recently in what is now No. 20 Tianjin High School although the inscription was defaced by Red Guards during the Cultural Revolution. His Victoria Cross and other medals were reportedly sold during the late 1970s and the VC is now thought to be in a private collection.

Tom Fletcher Mayson was born in the coastal village of Silecroft, near Millom, Cumberland, on 3 November 1893, the third son of William Mayson, a pit worker at Hodbarrow iron ore mine, and his wife Ann (née Kneebone). His mother died while Tom was young, and his father remarried. Educated at Whicham School, he left to work as a labourer on a nearby farm at Gutterby.

He enlisted as a private (No. 200717) in the King's Own Royal Lancaster Regiment on 16 November 1914, and served throughout the war in the 1/4th Battalion. The unit moved to France in May 1915, and in the following month suffered more than 150 casualties in its first major action at Festubert. By early 1917, Mayson had been twice wounded and promoted to corporal. Shortly before the Ypres offensive, he was made lance-sergeant.

The recommendation for Tom Mayson's VC was made on 11 August. Ten days later Gen. Jeudwine signed a card congratulating him which

Mayson posted to his stepmother at the John Bull Inn, Silecroft. He wrote:

> I have been recommended for a great honour, as you will see by the card, but I have not got it yet. It will be a surprise to a good few if I get it, which I think I will, but I will not tell you what it is because I have not got it yet, but you might be able to guess what it is. I expect to be at home in a few weeks if this decoration comes through.

The solution to his cryptic puzzle came with the announcement in the *London Gazette* of 14 September (in the same list that included the Bar to Noel Chavasse's VC). But Mayson had to wait until December before he got his leave. The people of Millon and Silecroft gave him a grand welcome home. A public subscription had raised more than £200, and a large crowd turned out in Millom's market-square to see the young hero presented with £169-worth of war loans certificates. A shy man, Mayson found the celebrations an ordeal. 'I am no good at this sort of work,' he admitted, 'but I think it is my duty to thank you all. I am sorry I can't say any more but I thank you all who are present now.'

After the war, he returned to Silecroft, living a quiet life in the shadow of the towering mass of Black Combe, working on the land and then for a time as greenkeeper of the local golf course. He married Sarah Eleanor, who died in 1946, and was a regular worshipper at St Mary's church, Whicham. In 1956 Mayson attended the Victoria Cross centenary celebrations in London. By then he was living at the Miners Arms, Silecroft, and was employed by the Atomic Energy Authority at Sellafield. The last three years of his life were a constant battle against illness, which, his family believed, stemmed from an undisclosed accident at the Sellafield power station. At the end of 1957 his health deteriorated and he was compelled to give up work. He was taken to North Lonsdale Hospital, in Barrow, where he died on 21 February 1958, aged 64.

Tom Mayson was described as 'a kindly man whom everybody loved and respected'. He was also a man of considerable determination. 'When he said "no", it was "no",' his local vicar remarked. He was laid to rest with full military honours in St Mary's churchyard. The tiny church was packed and a blinding snowstorm swirled around Black Combe as three volleys were fired over his grave. Among a distinguished band of mourners from his old regiment was Harry Christian, who had won his Victoria Cross at Cuinchy in October 1915.

Tom Mayson's medals are displayed in the King's Own Royal Lancaster Regiment Museum but minus the original VC, which he bequeathed to his local church. A small display in Millom's museum bears mute testimony to the pride felt in Silecroft's unassuming hero.

D.G.W. HEWITT

Near St Julien, 31 July 1917

The 39th Division, aided and abetted by effective tank support, scored one of the spectacular successes of the first morning's attack. By 8 am, the 116th and 117th Brigades had swarmed across a swathe of enemy territory, capturing the ruins of St Julien and crossing the Steenbeek all along the divisional front. During those early hours, when it appeared fleetingly possible that the long-awaited breakthrough might be within Gough's grasp, the attackers' determination was splendidly highlighted by the gallantry of one of the British army's youngest officers – 2/Lt Denis Hewitt of the 14th Hampshires, who at 19 found himself commanding a company in one of the most important actions of the war.

His battalion, part of the 116th Brigade, was to leapfrog the first wave and push on 200yd beyond the Steenbeek. The initial advance went without a hitch. The bombardment had almost obliterated the enemy's front line and the 11th Royal Sussex, advancing within 40yd of the barrage, encountered negligible opposition. The advance was then taken up by the 13th Royal Sussex and the 17th Sherwood Foresters, with the 14th Hampshires sandwiched in between.

Resistance stiffened almost immediately. The second objective facing the Hampshires, 'Black Line', ran along the Pilckem ridge, with the third objective, 'Black Dotted Line', 200yd further on, along a slope overlooking the Steenbeek. Most of the ground was covered by pillboxes and fortified farms unmarked by the bombardment. Fighting past strongpoints at Hampshire, Mousetrap and Juliet Farms, the advance splintered into a series of small-scale actions. Position after position had to be stormed, sometimes with the aid of tanks and mortars and always with the infantry's guts and determination. Casualties, delays and loss of cohesion ensued.

In the midst of the chaos, 2/Lt Hewitt tried to reorganise his company. They were on the Black Line, waiting for the barrage to move on. All of a sudden, a shell exploded nearby, scattering shards of red-hot splinters in all directions. Some cut through Hewitt's haversack, igniting signal flares and setting light to his clothing. Only by desperate efforts were the flames extinguished and by then the wounded officer was terribly burned. Given his condition and the intense pain, Hewitt might have been expected to retire for treatment, but he refused. It is not known why.

The advance to the next objective was a short one, but most of it was under intense machine-gun fire. According to the Hampshires' historian, Hewitt 'led his men resolutely ... and played a big part in capturing the Black Dotted Line'. From there, at around 7.10 am, small groups of the battalion pressed on down the slope and, despite much difficulty at the defended locality known as Alberta, they mastered the Green Dotted Line on the opposite bank of the Steenbeek. Hewitt, however, was not among them. The youngster who had done so much to inspire his depleted company had fallen victim, like Colyer-Fergusson, to a sniper while superintending consolidation of the Black Dotted Line.

Later in the morning the advance was extended as far as the third line defences near Gravenstafel spur. But taking ground was one thing, holding it was quite another. The rest of the day followed the same wretched pattern as that endured by the 8th and 55th Divisions. Counter-attacks drove the scattered troops back across the Steenbeek and out of St Julien until they stabilised on the ground Denis Hewitt had won at the cost of his life. Six weeks later, with the British line little further forward than the deepest advance made on that opening morning, the *London Gazette* of 14 September carried news of the posthumous award of the Victoria Cross to the 19-year-old subaltern. The closing sentence of his citation reinforced his achievement: 'This gallant officer set a magnificent example of coolness and contempt of danger to the whole battalion and it was due to his splendid leading that the final objective of his battalion was gained.'

Denis George Wyldbore Hewitt was born in Mayfair, London, on 18 December 1897, the eldest son of Hon. George Wyldbore Hewitt and his wife Elizabeth Mary (née Rampini), daughter of Charles Rampini, a deputy lieutenant of Hampshire. On his father's side, he could trace his lineage back to James Hewitt, the 1st Viscount Lifford, a former Lord Chancellor of Ireland during the eighteenth century, who was elevated to the Peerage of Ireland in 1768 as Baron Lifford, of Lifford, County Donegal, and created a viscount thirteen years later.

Hewitt's early years were spent at the family home, Field House, in Hursley, near Winchester. He attended prep school at The Old Malthouse, Swanage, and then went on to Winchester College in 1911, joining Culverlea House. He left in 1915, at the age of 17, for Sandhurst. Hewitt was gazetted a second lieutenant in the Hampshire Regiment on 1 April 1916 and joined the 14th Battalion in France in September, taking part in the later stages of the Battle of the Somme.

Denis Hewitt has no known grave and is commemorated on the Menin Gate Memorial. His name is also engraved in the War Memorial Cloister at Winchester College, in honour of all those Wykehamists who died during the conflict.

His younger brother, Alan William Wingfield Hewitt, followed him into the Hampshire Regiment by way of Winchester and Sandhurst. He retired from soldiering in the 1920s and took up farming. In 1954 he succeeded his cousin as the 8th Viscount Lifford. The title was then inherited by his son, Edward, who still resides at Field House, Hursley, and now holds the Victoria Cross that his uncle won eighty years ago.

A. EDWARDS AND G.I. McINTOSH

Macdonald's Wood and the Steenbeek north-east of Ypres, 31 July 1917

The stream of visitors to Lilac Cottage seemed endless. It was as though everyone in the close-knit fishing community wanted to congratulate Lossiemouth's local hero. Sandy Edwards coped well enough, but after more than a day of relentless back-slapping he had to escape. With his brother John and a friend, he headed for the nearby golf course, on the shore of the Moray Firth. There, where he had caddied as a boy, he found relief from the adulation.

Returning home, he found a journalist waiting and an awkward interview ensued. Only after much gentle persuasion did Sandy speak. 'There is nothing to beat the Jocks,' he finally declared. 'If an English regiment is told to take an objective and find it can't be done, the men have sense enough to turn back, but the Jocks are too thick-headed and on they go.' Self-mocking or not, it was the nearest Sandy Edwards ever came to explaining his extraordinary actions on 31 July 1917.

That day, he was acting company sergeant-major of C Company, the 6th (Morayshire) Seaforth Highlanders, part of the 152nd Brigade of the 51st Highland Division. The battalion formed the left wing of the second wave intended to drive forward from the Black Line down the shallow slopes of the Pilckem Ridge to the final objective straddling the Steenbeek. C Company, led by the dashing Capt. James Biss MC and Bar, was detailed to establish a bridgehead across the stream. They set off from their assembly positions near Muller Cottage almost 3 hours after the attack began. It was hoped they might steer clear of trouble until the Black Line. But gradually, the going became harder, the mud deeper, and the advance slowed. Around Macdonald's Farm, on the fringes of Macdonald's Wood, straddling the Black Line, C Company became embroiled in trying to clear a maze of concrete machine-gun emplacements hidden in the shells of ruined buildings amid a clutter of shattered trees. A tank, G50, one of eight assigned to the division, helped to batter the farm into submission. The Seaforths stumbled on, taking heavy casualties as machine-guns spluttered through the tangle of roots and branches. Edwards recorded:

> One gun in particular was very troublesome ... The officer in charge of the company was knocked out of action, so I went out to locate it. I got round behind, and hid in a shell-hole which commanded a good view of the gun. I could see right into the door of the pill-box. I had two revolvers in my belt, and a bullet stopped the career of the man who was firing the gun, and what a kick he gave. The other nine of the crew will trouble our boys no more ...

But Edwards' assault had not gone undetected. He went on: 'I then made back the way I had come to ask the men to come on, when I was hit on the right arm by a sniper's bullet. I thought we could be doing without him, and with a bite of luck I attended to him. He is quiet enough now.' His under-stated account gave little hint of the true drama. According to his unit's historian, the sniper had been causing 'havoc' among the Seaforths and Edwards, despite his wound, had stalked him 'across the open and along his very line of fire'.

Although bleeding heavily, Edwards insisted on staying with the company as they fought their way to the Green Line. Nearing the Steenbeek, they came under heavy fire from enemy positions on the opposite bank. Covered by Lewis gunners, they inched their way forward to within 100yd of the stream where, protected by a tank, they dug a shallow trench. C Company had lost all but one of its officers, and the strength of the opposition persuaded the survivors to delay forcing a crossing. Machine-gun fire spraying through the 'hideously riven stumps' lining the banks hampered consolidation, but Edwards remained undaunted. The unit historian wrote:

> Along the line he moved, only a gunshot from the nearest Germans, cheerily exhorting his men by Christian name and nickname. Sergeant Edwards was bent on one thing: he was determined that his company should cross the Steenbeek and reach their objective.

But for now, he bided his time. One man from the 152nd Brigade did, however, succeed in crossing the Steenbeek that morning. His name was Pte George McIntosh and his astonishing single-handed foray won him the Victoria Cross. McIntosh, a 20-year-old pre-war Territorial, belonged to C Company, the 6th (Banff and Donside) Battalion, the Gordon Highlanders. His unit were on the right of the 6th Seaforths. The unit's task was to secure the Green Line in front of the stream and link up with the 16th Rifle Brigade from the neighbouring 39th Division.

Since 6.30 am, progress across 3,000yd of shell-torn ground had been largely unimpeded. Brushing aside pockets of resistance, the Gordons of C Company, ably led by Capt. J. Hutcheson MC (whose efforts here won him a DSO), reached the Green Line around 7.50 am and dug in about 200yd short of the Steenbeek. While consolidating, they came under savage fire from two machine-guns in a concrete emplacement on the opposite bank. The Gordons dived for cover as a hail of bullets cut the ground. All except George McIntosh who, without a word and armed only with a revolver and a single grenade, sprinted towards a narrow bridge spanning the stream. His charge took everyone by surprise but before he reached the bridge, the Germans had recovered from their shock and were sending a stream of fire towards him. At least two bullets hit his haversack, another struck his mess-tin and others shredded his kilt. McIntosh, however, was unharmed and ran on, dodging from shell-hole to shell-hole as he worked his way up a slight rise towards the blockhouse. An account of the action that McIntosh himself helped to compile recorded the climax:

When he arrived near the dugout [sic] some of the Germans – there were about 20 in it – threw up their hands, but he threw a bomb amongst them, killing two and wounding another. The remaining Germans, said McIntosh with a smile, flew in disorder, probably considering discretion the better part of valour. He then entered the dugout and seized the two machine-guns of a light pattern, which had been causing the mischief, and with one on his shoulder and the other under his arm he returned to his own lines, a Rifle Brigade comrade assisting him with the booty part of the way back.

Asked years later why he made his lone attack, he reportedly replied: 'Somebody had to gae forrit!' To a sergeant in the same battalion, he said that he felt it his duty 'knowing that he could throw a Mills bomb farther and more accurately than anyone else of the bomb squad'. However, when asked by an old comrade to explain why he had not despatched the remaining gunner inside the smoke-filled emplacement, McIntosh 'blew his top': 'He ... asked me if I thought he was going to shoot a defenceless and wounded man lying on the ground! On the right was an English regiment [16th Rifle Brigade] and he waved them to come on and they carried away the wounded German ...'

By 8.30 am the men of Capt. Hutcheson's company were securely established. Knowing they had been detected, Hutcheson had switched his original positions, pushing one trench 100yd forward and the other the same distance back, his foresight paying off when the enemy artillery opened a furious bombardment on the recently vacated ground.

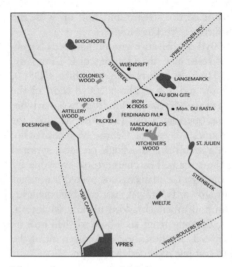

The northern sector on 31 July

The position on the left was less certain. Throughout the morning, the Seaforths' line, dominated by the enemy strongpoints across the Steenbeek at Maison du Rasta and Maison Bulgare, remained uncomfortable. The strength of opposition was underlined when a squadron of the 1/1st King Edward's Horse tried to comply with orders to exploit a reported crossing of the Steenbeek. They were cut to ribbons 150yd west of the stream. Among the many casualties was the commanding officer, Major Swan, thus signalling the next episode in Sandy Edwards' epic saga of courage.

The unit historian noted:

> The news ran along the troops that a major of a cavalry unit ... had been left out in the open badly wounded. Without a moment's hesitation, Edwards crept out, and through a hail of bullets darted from shell-hole to shell-hole, until he reached the wounded officer. Lifting him up, he carried him back to our line, while the fire increased in intensity.

By early afternoon, heavy rain had turned the shallow trenches into water-filled channels and the sluggish stream into a muddy torrent. But despite the precariousness of their position, the Seaforths had destroyed a powerful German thrust, part of the massive counter-attack which proved so effective elsewhere along the line. Then, exploiting the enemy's failure, the Seaforths turned defence into attack. In spite of his wound, Edwards led the rush across the surviving bridges and captured Maison du Rasta and Maison Bulgare. But just when it seemed victory was complete, they were ordered, much to their displeasure, to withdraw, their hard-won bridgehead having been rendered untenable by the enemy's success further south.

Edwards remained with his men throughout the night despite a shrapnel wound to his right knee. When he eventually reported to Battalion HQ the following morning, the doctor decreed he should go 'forthwith to hospital'. Edwards said nothing. His arm was stiff with bandages, and his only complaint was about the 'awfu' weather'. Told to follow an orderly back, he walked away and promptly turned in the opposite direction. He was still with his company when they were finally relieved. Edwards later remarked:

> If I had not gone on, it would not have given the boys much encouragement … The wound on my arm was worst. I was in too big a mess to think of the others. The sleeve was cut from my tunic, my hosetops were down over my boots, and I was covered with mud. Oh, what a game …

A month later, the *London Gazette* of 6 September 1917 announced the award of the Victoria Cross to No. 265579 Pte George McIntosh. The next list of VCs carried the name of No. 265473 Sgt Alexander Edwards. The citation spoke of Edwards' 'complete disregard for personal safety', 'conspicuous bravery' and 'high example', yet still scarcely did justice to his outstanding feat of sustained valour.

Alexander Edwards was born at Stotfield, Lossiemouth, Scotland, on 4 November 1885, the son of Alexander Edwards, a fisherman, and his wife Jessie (née Smith). He was one of four brothers, one of whom, James, was lost at sea; he also had four sisters. Sandy was educated at Lossiemouth School and as a youngster, brought up alongside the Moray golf club, he caddied for the gentry who came to play on the new course.

Leaving school, he trained as a cooper, making barrels for the fishing industry. Apprenticed to Thomas Jenkins, a fish-curer of Burghead, he followed the herring fleet around the Moray coast. He worked with James Gerry of Buckie and, shortly before the war, he was employed by Thomas Davidson of Aberdeen. Edwards was among the first of Lossiemouth's men to answer the call of King and Country. He enlisted at Elgin as a private in the 6th Battalion, the Seaforth Highlanders, on 1 September 1914. After training in England the battalion proceeded to France on 1 May 1915 and eighteen days later went into the line at Richebourg St Vaast. Edwards was already a lance-corporal,

A/CSM A. Edwards, left, with his brothers, CSM John Edwards MM and William Edwards

and the following month he came through the battalion's first serious fight at Festubert. Edwards proved an excellent front-line soldier, and was soon promoted to sergeant.

He survived the Somme fighting unharmed but was evacuated in October 1916 suffering from a throat infection. After six weeks in hospital and two weeks leave in Lossiemouth, he was posted to a reserve battalion training in England. Edwards missed the heavy fighting at Arras, but when a draft for his old battalion fell short of an NCO in June 1917, he immediately volunteered. His very next action resulted in his Victoria Cross.

It was the third distinction won by a member of his family. His younger brother John, a company sergeant-major in another Seaforths battalion, had won a Military Medal in July 1916, and his cousin George, a lieutenant in the 6th Seaforths, had won a DSO for capturing over 200 Germans by a daring ruse at Beaumont Hamel the previous November – an action some thought worthy of a VC. Edwards spent the weeks after his gallant action at a base hospital recovering from his wounds, but was fit enough to rejoin his battalion when they paraded in his honour on 18 September. The following day, he set off on leave, arriving to a hero's reception at Elgin's Great North station on 22 September. He had to fight his way through the cheering crowds with shouts of 'Good auld Lossie' and 'Good auld Seaforths' ringing in his ears. To a few friends, he joked: 'What is all the fuss about? I've been here before.' The scenes were repeated ten-fold at Lossiemouth where, according to one report, 'practically the whole population turned out to meet him'. After a greeting from civic dignitaries, Edwards was carried shoulder-high to a waiting car before being driven to his family's home at Lilac Cottage behind a procession of pipers and volunteers.

Four days later, he travelled to Buckingham Palace to receive his medal from King George V. Observers watching the open-air investiture noted that the kilted Edwards was limping slightly. Returning to Lossiemouth, he was fêted all over again. At a proud ceremony, civic leaders presented him with gifts in recognition of his bravery, including a gold watch and £100-worth of war bonds.

The honours continued to flow in. In November he was made an honorary member of the Veterans' Club, and the following month the Seaforth Highlanders Association awarded him an 'address of appreciation'. It is not known whether he ever received this last distinction. Four months later, the 6th Seaforths were embroiled in the struggle to stem the German Spring Offensive. During five days of bitter fighting the battalion sustained almost 400 casualties. Most notable among them was Sgt Alexander Edwards VC, who was reported wounded and missing in action on 24 March 1918 in the vicinity of Loupart Wood, near Bapaume. As the days passed, hopes that he might have been taken prisoner faded and Edwards, who had become engaged to Bella Christie of Aberdeen, was officially listed as killed.

Sandy Edwards has no known grave. His name is recorded on the Arras Memorial. His Victoria Cross and 1914–15 Star are displayed with his New Testament Bible in the museum of the Queen's Own Highlanders at Fort George, having been loaned to the regiment by the family. A few miles east along the coast, the man who became a folk hero among the people of Lossiemouth is still proudly remembered. A display of photographs in the town's Fisheries and Community Museum honours his gallant sacrifice. But perhaps the most poignant memorial of all is the ornate sundial situated alongside the last green on the Moray golf course, where Sandy Edwards had retreated to escape all the public attention eighty years ago. Unveiled amid much pomp in August 1931, the memorial was dedicated to Alexander Edwards VC and his cousin George Edwards DSO, who was also killed in action. The inscription on the plinth reads: 'In their boyhood they "carried" on the Moray Links.' Around the dial are the words: 'Sunshine after shadow.'

George Imlach McIntosh was born at 80 Portessie, Rathven, Banffshire, on 22 April 1897, the son of Alexander McIntosh, a fisherman, and his wife Mary Jane (née Reid). McIntosh lived during his early years in Shore Street, Fraserburgh, and was educated at Fraserburgh Academy. In 1910 the family moved west along the coast to Buckie, where he joined local wood merchants Tom Jones & Son as an apprentice, and worked on the Cluny Dock extension to Buckie harbour. A keen footballer, he played for Buckie Thistle FC.

He joined D Company, the 6th Gordon Highlanders, in 1913. When war broke out the following year, he was still employed at Tom Jones' sawmill. Aged only 17, McIntosh was mobilised with his unit on 4 August. The 6th Gordons were one of only twenty-three Territorial units selected to go to France before the end of 1914. They arrived in France in November and went into the line on 6 December. In the months that followed they took their places in a series of ill-starred British attacks, including Neuve Chapelle, Festubert, Givenchy and Loos. Little is known of McIntosh's involvement. Some weeks after arriving in France, he was evacuated suffering from trench-foot but was soon back with his unit, and survived the following year's fighting on the Somme.

Shortly after his brave action on the opening day of Third Ypres, McIntosh received a congratulatory card from the GOC 51st Highland Division, Maj.-Gen. G.M. Harper. At that time he had no idea he had been recommended for a VC.

McIntosh left his unit to go on leave on 12 September, six days after his Cross was gazetted, and he arrived unannounced at his parents' home in Seaview Road, Buckie, the following day. News of his return quickly spread, and on 15 September he was presented with a purse of fifty gold sovereigns given by his pre-war employer. More gifts followed and a few days later came McIntosh's proudest moment when he received his VC from King George V at an investiture held at Ibrox Park, Glasgow – an appropriate setting for a member of the 6th Gordons' football team! McIntosh was then appointed batman to a senior field officer, almost certainly in an attempt to preserve the young VC winner from exposing himself to further danger. But, as one of his colleagues later put it, the 'easy life' did not suit him and he went back to the 6th Gordons.

At the end of the war, McIntosh returned to Buckie and took a job as a 'herring runner' for Thomson & Brown, a local fish sales company. In July 1919 his work took him back to Fraserburgh.

The 'Buckie VC', as he was known, married Alexanderina Sutherland on 27 April 1923, and they had two children (George, born in 1924, and Grace, born in 1929). Like countless other ex-servicemen, McIntosh suffered his share of hardship during the post-war depression. With the fishing industry shedding jobs, he was forced to try his hand at a variety of jobs, including acting as greenkeeper at the Buckie bowls club before taking the post of janitor and groundsman at Buckie High School on 1 July 1939.

Two months later he found temporary new employment in the Royal Air Force. As a reservist, he was called up on 26 August, eight days before the outbreak of the Second World War. Although based mainly in Britain, McIntosh enjoyed another escape from death every bit as miraculous, and gained another Mention in Despatches to his list of honours. During 1940–41 he was the flight-sergeant in charge of ground defences at RAF St Eval in Cornwall. On one occasion, a 100lb bomb was said to have grazed him on the shoulder, but failed to explode. He merely looked down at it for a moment and then went on working until the next morning, putting out fires. Of this 'difficult time', his former commander, Air Cdre A.P. Revington CB, CBE, wrote: 'We were subject to very heavy air attack … and "Mac" was in his element – an inspiration and example to everybody. He matched up to every situation, however hazardous, and seemed to welcome danger, and was indeed a very brave man of great resource.'

In September 1941 he was posted to Reykjavik, Iceland, as station warrant officer. There he took charge of the young RAF ground crews and, according to Revington, 'improved the morale by 100 per cent'. Revington wrote: 'Mac had his faults but these were far outweighed by his splendid character, considerable personality and his very great courage.' Later, McIntosh served as a disciplinary warrant officer at a number of fighter stations in southern and eastern England, including Manston and Coltishall, before being demobbed at Ludham in July 1945.

McIntosh returned to his janitor's job, a post he held to the end of his life. A modest man, McIntosh was popular and widely respected in Buckie. The first honorary president of the town's British Legion branch, he also served as president of the bowls club and was kirk elder for Buckie North church. His outstanding record in two world wars, combined with his many public services, were recognised in 1955 when he was made a Freeman of the Royal Burgh of Buckie.

The following year he attended the VC centenary celebrations in London, and in February 1960, McIntosh took a day off school to become the first and only ranker in the history of the Gordons to take the salute at a passing out parade. One of the two platoons was called 'McIntosh' in his honour. It was his 'last hurrah'. After a series of heart attacks and two operations, McIntosh died on 20 June 1960 in Woodend Hospital, Aberdeen. In Buckie, flags were flown at half-mast. Hundreds turned out to pay their last respects as the Gordons' VC was buried with full military honours in New Cemetery.

McIntosh Avenue and a memorial plaque unveiled in 2004 perpetuate his memory in Buckie, while visitors to the Imperial War Museum in London can view his remarkable group of medals in the Lord Ashcroft Gallery as part of a magnificent celebration of courage in war and peace.

J.L. DAVIES AND I. REES

Pilckem and Au Bon Gîte, 31 July 1917

The big push was imminent and Cpl James Davies' thoughts were of home and family. Before leaving for the assembly trenches east of the Yser Canal, the 31-year-old non-commissioned officer, a Welsh miner from the coal-rich Ogmore Vale, wrote:

> Dear Wife,
>   You will see by the address that I have been made a corporal – two stripes instead of one. If I am spared I hope to be made a sergeant soon. I am glad to hear that Priscilla Maud is a good girl and going to school. Tell her that daddy thinks of her often. We are about going over. Don't vex, as I hope to go through it all right, and if I do not you will know that I died for my wife and children and for my King and country.

James Davies was a member of the 13th Royal Welch Fusiliers, a New Army unit formed at Rhyl in October 1914, and part of the 113th Brigade of the 38th (Welsh) Division. On 31 July the 13th RWF were the right-hand leading battalion, attacking south of the Ypres–Staden railway. The ground leading up towards the remains of Pilckem was churned by artillery and flecked with blockhouses which the Welshmen were encountering for the first time. The outline of a road cut across the divisional front. It ran from the railway, via Corner House, an enemy strongpoint, passed north of Pilckem and crossed the Steenbeek on its way to Langemarck, one of the first day's objectives, 3,000yd distant.

Following a fiery deluge of thermite shells and oil drums, the leading companies of the 13th RWF carried the enemy's front line ('Blue Line') with little trouble, hampered only by the darkness and the lack of obvious landmarks. Stumbling on, through a weak and erratic counter-bombardment, they took the first objective by 4.50 am. Then, it was the turn of C and D Companies to carry the advance past Pilckem to the 'Black Line'.

Opposition increased as the light improved and the Welshmen found themselves in the midst of a strongly fortified network of pillboxes and dugouts.

Later estimates put the number of enemy strongpoints facing the division at 280. Corner House, sited at a barely discernible crossroads near Pilckem, was one such bastion. Near it lay a traditional pillbox, where the 13th RWF met their first check. The regimental historian recorded:

> Several attempts had been made to outflank it, but its flanks were protected and each effort resulted in the men being shot down. There was no long pause in front of the pillbox – these events happened quickly – but the assaulting line had dropped into the protecting cavities of shell-holes …

Not everyone, however, sought cover. With the protective barrage falling around them, Cpl Davies dashed out alone and made straight for the pillbox. Braving a storm of fire, he burst among the garrison, bayoneted one man, captured another and returned carrying the gun as a trophy. The advance was resumed, but not for long. Fire from Corner House drove the Welshmen to ground again. Davies, however, was like a man possessed. He had already been wounded, although not badly enough to stop him. Now, within yards of the spitting machine-guns, he gathered a bombing party and led them in a charge that destroyed the garrison, allowing the battalion to push through Pilckem to the 'Black Line' by 6 am.

All objectives were secured and in good time but machine-guns along the railway and snipers sheltering in the profusion of shell craters hampered consolidation. One sniper, however, met his match in the redoubtable Davies. Although labouring with a second wound, he crept out and stalked his quarry, finishing him off with a well-aimed shot. It was his last act. According to the regimental history, Davies 'died on the field of his wounds' after killing the sniper. But questions about his death persist. In a letter to his widow, Davies' platoon commander 2/Lt C.W. Coulter claimed that the gallant NCO had been mortally wounded after attacking the machine-gun posts around Corner House and had died the following day, not on the battlefield but behind the lines after being evacuated. Coulter stated:

> He entered the attack with the others, and having passed through the most violent stage had the ill-luck to be struck by a bullet in the side. He was conveyed to hospital where all possible aid was rendered, but unfortunately he passed away next day. Before he was wounded he did some wonderful work which consisted in capturing single-handed an enemy gun which … others had been shot attempting to reach. He was easily the best non-commissioned officer in the platoon. He was buried at Canada Farm Cemetery, near Ypres.

The location of his grave points to the veracity of Coulter's account. The cemetery, near Elverdinghe, took its name from a farm used as a casualty clearing station throughout the offensive. If correct, it means the date of Davies' death given in official records and inscribed on his headstone is wrong. Those fatal wounds robbed Davies of the third stripe that would undoubtedly have been his had he survived, but his exploits did not go unrecognised. On 6 September 1917 the *London Gazette* announced the posthumous award of the Victoria Cross to James Davies for 'most conspicuous bravery'.

Hard fighting followed the seizure of the 'Black Line' as support units extended the advance towards the third objective along a slight rise designated Iron Cross ridge. The barrage, so influential in the early stages, drifted away, and the infantry were raked by machine-guns sited in Battery Copse and in ruined houses and pillboxes around the railway crossing on the left. The positions were still resisting fiercely when the 11th South Wales Borderers approached the ridge at about 8.50 am. Part of the reserve 115th Brigade, they had started their advance 100 minutes after zero hour with the aim of exploiting the gains across the Steenbeek, securing bridgeheads and pushing out towards Langemarck. The battalion suffered a number of casualties, including two company commanders wounded, but the men fought their way over the ridge and then, spreading into attack formation, surged down towards the Steenbeek. They had lost the barrage and were under intense close-range fire from both sides of the stream but their advance proved irresistible. One by one the posts were stormed with a degree of skill and courage that reached a peak of valour in the performance of a 23-year-old pre-war steelworker from Llanelli, Sgt Ivor Rees.

By 10 am the Steenbeek had been reached, but the east bank was covered by powerful enemy defences lodged in an old roadside inn called Au Bon Gîte, barely 100yd from the water's edge. Within its ruined walls the Germans had constructed a formidable blockhouse, supported by two large pillboxes. The remains of A and C Companies, together with a party from D Company, made it across the stream, but the approach to Au Bon Gîte drew an automatic response. Close-range machine-gun fire inflicted many casualties and was threatening to halt consolidation of the bridgehead until Sgt Rees took a hand.

Leading his platoon forward in short rushes, he worked his way round to the rear of the strongpoint. Then, when he was within 20yd of the nearest position, he charged ahead of his men, shot one of the machine-gunners dead, bayoneted a second and captured the gun. From there, he scarcely paused before launching a bombing attack on the main blockhouse. Five men died in the confined interior and the remainder, two officers and thirty men, came out as prisoners.

Cpl J.L. Davies

Largely as a result of his intervention, several bridgeheads were established, two by the 11th SWB and one by the 17th RWF. These positions should have provided a valuable springboard for the next stage of the advance, but the enemy reacted quickly. Shelling, weak at first, grew in intensity, destroying all communications. Aircraft followed up, bombing and strafing. By 3 pm, with no reinforcements in sight, enemy infantry, almost certainly units of the 229th Reserve Regiment, were seen marching through Langemarck. Shortly after, a grey tide burst around the Welsh outposts. An SOS signal went unanswered with predictable consequences. After heavy fighting, the 17th RWF fell back across the Steenbeek, leaving the 11th SWB at Au Bon Gîte exposed. By 4.30 pm they too were forced to withdraw to avoid being cut off. Before leaving, however, the Welshmen had inflicted 633 enemy casualties. It would take the British sixteen more days and a specially mounted attack by two companies to recapture the position that had fallen to a single stout-hearted Welsh sergeant. Ivor Rees' outstanding individual action may have been in vain, but it was not forgotten. In a letter to his parents on 2 September, he wrote:

I am very pleased to say that I came out of the last 'push' quite safe and sound, and I have been recommended for the VC. I hope I shall get it, mother. What do you say? It will mean some weeks leave for me, and possibly a commission in the Army. How would you like to see me an officer. What hopes! What do you say?

James Llewellyn Davies was born in Lethbridge Terrace, Victoria, Ebbw Vale, Monmouthshire, on 16 March 1886, the third of nine children, to John Davies, a steelworker turned collier, and his wife Martha (née Llewellyn). He grew up in Fronwen in the Ogmore valley district of Glamorgan where his family moved after his father took a job at the Wyndham Colliery around 1889. Educated at Ogmore Vale and Nant-y-Moel Formal Education Council Schools, he followed his father into the coal mines at Wyndham and became a member of the South Wales Miners' Federation. Four days after his 20th birthday, he married Elizabeth Ann Richards, the daughter of a colliery timberman, at Bridgend Register Office. They settled in Nant-y-Moel Row, Nant-y-Moel, a few doors away from Elizabeth's parents, and had three sons and a daughter, all born in the space of six years.

As a miner, Davies could have chosen to avoid military service, but he enlisted in the Royal Garrison Artillery (No. 44304) at Bridgend on 12 October 1914. After undergoing basic training, he was transferred on 5 June 1915 to the 3rd (Reserve) Battalion, the Royal Welch Fusiliers. Given a new army number (No. 31161), he continued his training in Lancashire and became a machine-gun specialist before being posted to the 8th (Service) Battalion, serving as part of the 13th (Western) Division in Gallipoli. His service on the peninsula was cut short in December by a bout of enteric fever which resulted in him being hospitalised in Alexandria. Invalided home in January 1916, he spent several months recovering at Stobhill Military Hospital in Glasgow. In October, following a spell of convalescence, he was posted as a reinforcement to the 13th Royal Welch Fusiliers, then serving in Belgium after a summer of hard fighting and heavy losses on the Somme.

James Davies was described in a contemporary account as 'a steady, good-living man'. In peacetime, he and his family had regularly attended the Mount Zion English congregational church in Nant-y-Moel. His widow and eldest son attended a Buckingham Palace investiture on 20 October 1917 to receive his Victoria Cross from King George V. A memorial fund had been established in Ogmore Vale to assist Davies' widow and young family, and when they returned crowds gathered at the station, with a band playing them back through the narrow streets to their home in Nant-y-Moel Row.

Elizabeth Davies later remarried, and her husband's Victoria Cross is now among the regimental treasures at the Royal Welch Fusiliers Museum in Caernarfon Castle. James Davies VC is commemorated on the Nant-y-Moel War Memorial where his name heads a list of sixty men who died during the First World War. Ogmore Vale's only VC winner is also remembered in the Berwyn Centre, where there hangs a fine portrait painted twenty-five years after his death and where relatives and senior army officers gathered in 1977 to mark the sixtieth anniversary of his heroism. One of the most poignant tributes was provided by Welsh poet, Mogg Williams. His work, entitled 'Elegy', concludes with the lines:

> Oh Soldier
> You were a Christian;
> The poet is not.
> James Llewellyn Davies, Victoria Cross.
> Sincerely,
> The poet hopes you found your God.
> Would it be if we could meet,

Would it be as strangers?
I think not.

Ivor Rees was born in Union Street, Felinfoel, Llanelli, Carmarthenshire, on 18 October 1893, the son of David Rees and his wife Ann (née Bowen). He was educated at Pwll Council School and Old Road School. After living for a time in Mount Pleasant, Llanelli, the family went back to Pwll. On leaving school, he went to work at the Llanelli Steel Works, where his father was an electrical engineer. When war broke out, he was working as a crane driver at the South Wales Steel Works.

Rees enlisted in the South Wales Borderers as a private (No. 20002) on 9 November 1914, and went overseas on 4 December 1915, three days after being promoted corporal. He came through the heavy fighting at Mametz Wood without injury, but was invalided home in February 1917, with a severe bout of trench fever. Rees, who had been made sergeant the previous September, spent seven weeks at the Cardiff Red Cross Hospital and, having made a full recovery, returned home for a day before returning to France.

His Victoria Cross was gazetted on 14 September 1917, and as the villagers of Pwll and the citizens of Llanelli prepared to celebrate his triumph the young hero arrived home unannounced. On 26 September he was at Buckingham Palace to receive his VC from King George V and four days later he married Mattie Jenkins. In between, Rees was fêted by his home town: around 20,000 people lined the streets to cheer the VC cavalcade. Among the civic dignitaries hailing his achievement was one of the nation's senior VC holders, Sir James Hills-Johnes, who had won his Cross as a subaltern during the Indian Mutiny. Rees received a cheque of £156, raised by public subscription, a cheque of £100 having been pledged by the late chairman of the South Wales Works to the first company employee to win a VC; later, at a party organised by the Pwll Reception Committee, he was greeted by the village male voice choir before being presented with an inscribed gold watch.

Ivor Rees proved a popular attraction wherever he went. At his wedding, Trinity Chapel was filled to overflowing by people seeking a glimpse of the hero and his bride. He bore the adulation well, but drew the line at recounting his exploits. 'I am not a speaker, but a soldier,' he declared. Even in letters home he made no reference to his gallantry. During one leave, however, he had described one narrow escape when he was among a party of men surprised by a number of Germans. In the close-quarter fight, his bayonet had broken off and he was compelled to club his way out of the mêlée using his rifle butt. It was left to his father to do most of the talking: 'Ivor seems to have been specially cut out for soldiering. In fact, he is a born soldier ... Hardships do not seem to interfere with his work – he was always a patient little fellow – and there is no doubt about it, he did all that was expected of him.'

Described on his service record as 'an excellent leader of men', Rees, who had been promoted CSM on 5 September, qualified as an instructor. Posted to the 53rd SWB, Rees spent most of the remainder of the war training new recruits. He was transferred to the Reserve on 21 March 1919. Unlike so many of his fellow VC holders who came home broken in health, he ended the war with a medical rating of A1.

Even heroes, however, suffered in the post-war depression. Rees trained as a barber but was unemployed for two years. He was eventually employed by Llanelli Borough Council in the Public Health Department as a water inspector and cleansing superintendent. It was a post he held for thirty-eight years until his retirement in 1959. He served briefly in the 4th Welch Regiment, a Territorial unit, during the 1920s, and during the Second World War he served as a CSM in the 2nd Carmarthenshire Home Guard.

A peaceable man, who counted sea fishing and bowls among his pastimes, he led a quiet life in Llanelli. He attended the VC centenary celebrations in 1956 and maintained close ties with his former regiment. One of his last appearances at the Welsh Brigade Depot was in July 1966, at an event to mark the fiftieth anniversary of the Battle of the Somme. By then, he was beginning to suffer from bronchial trouble.

Ivor Rees died at his home, 5 Craddock Street, Llanelli, on 11 March 1967 aged 73. He left a widow, two sons and three daughters. His funeral service was attended by soldiers from the Welsh Brigade, former members of the South Wales Borderers and many townspeople.

In 1969 his VC group was presented on loan to the SWB Museum at Brecon, and a few years later the regiment purchased them from his widow. They now feature among an impressive display of Victoria Cross exhibits including the illuminated address presented to him in October 1917 by the people of Pwll, Llanelli. His home town, meanwhile, honours his memory with a brass tablet on the wall of the town tall's entrance hall, a proud salute to a former council worker remembered by his obituarist as 'one of the bravest and most respected soldiers' to wear the insignia of the South Wales Borderers.

Sgt I. Rees

R.J. BYE AND T. WHITHAM

Wood 15 and near Captain's Farm, 31 July 1917

> The sight was one never to be forgotten. During the night, for 6 hours incessantly, the enemy batteries and lines were dealt with by gas shells. Never for one moment did other shelling cease, and when the actual Zero hour came, boiling oil was poured on the enemy and the place became a perfect inferno.

So wrote Lt-Col Douglas Gordon, commanding officer of the 1st Welsh Guards. Yet for all the bombardment's fury, with its chilling echoes of medieval warfare, nagging doubts persisted about the attack east of the Yser Canal. The Welshmen, part of the 3rd Guards Brigade, marked the left wing of the vast British effort north of the Ypres–Staden railway. In unison with French troops on their left, the Guards Division was to begin its advance towards the Steenbeek at 4.28 am – exactly 38 minutes after the main assault had been launched. During the wait, the guardsmen, sheltering in their thinly protected assembly positions, would be exposed to any counter barrage. 'This was inclined to make me nervous,' confessed Col Gordon. In the event, enemy retaliation was so muted as to allow the attack to proceed unhindered, with units of the 3rd and 2nd Guards Brigades following the barrage's inexorable march at a rate of 25yd a minute.

Attacking from Baboon Trench, the 1st Welsh Guards' objectives were to capture and consolidate as far as the 'Black Line' some 1,700yd distant, roughly halfway towards the division's final goal. Weeks of heavy shelling had destroyed the network of channels which drained the low-lying ground, making the conditions some of the worst in the Ypres sector. The Welshmen would also have to negotiate the remains of a small wood known as Wood 15 and a phalanx of pillboxes, a type of fortification they had not previously encountered.

The initial outpost lines fell easily enough. The frontal zone had been all but obliterated, leading Colonel Gordon to comment: 'The havoc caused by our artillery in Wood 15 and elsewhere beggars description.' But the bombardment had not been as successful everywhere. As two platoons of No. 2 Company, in the van of the attack on the right, neared Wood 15 in the grey dawn, they were met by heavy fire from a large pillbox, untouched by the barrage, which lay amid a tangle of tree stumps and mangled branches. As the barrage had moved on the advance thereabouts was checked. All those who escaped the opening bursts dived for cover with the exception of one man, who now began a series of remarkable exploits destined to become the stuff of regimental legend.

Sgt Robert Bye, aged 27, was a heavily built miner from the small village of Penrhiwceibr, deep in the Welsh valleys. Although not a soldier by profession, he came of a fighting family. Three brothers had taken up arms in the war, and his own fighting experience stretched back to the battalion's baptism of fire at Loos in 1915. With his comrades pinned down, Bye squirmed from shell-hole to shell-hole to outflank the strongpoint. Having got within striking distance, he then rushed forward across the final few yards, disappearing behind the concrete structure where he proceeded to put the garrison out of action with bombs. Shortly after, he rejoined his platoon and they pushed on to the first objective. Despite the delay, the Welshmen were still on schedule.

The advance carried the Guards past Wood 16, on the left, from where they were again assailed by fire from pillboxes missed by the barrage. Parties on the right succeeded in reaching the second objective, where volunteers, led by Bye, were hastily assembled to deal with the menace. There followed a succession of gallant attacks in which the pillboxes were stormed one by one, with Sgt Bye making the single most outstanding contribution. He led the way with a lone assault on the first strongpoint. The Welsh Guards' historian recorded: 'Sgt Bye, who was truly inspired that day, went forward at a steady amble, stumbling over the uneven ground, so that with each fall he was thought to be dead, and again got behind the blockhouse and bombed the machine-gunners.'

One after another the posts fell in similar manner until by the end all had been bombed into submission, the redoubtable Bye having accounted for no fewer than seventy men dead, wounded or captured. The threat of Wood 16's defences thus removed, the whole of the 'Black Line', the battalion's final objective, was in Welsh hands by 8 am. Casualties were remarkably light by Western Front standards: twenty-five dead, ninety-one wounded and twenty-two missing. Bye's platoon, however, had suffered more than most. At the end of the day, only eight men were still in action. Estimates of German losses in the same sector were put at between 100 and 160 men. Colonel Gordon was delighted. 'The way the men consolidated the points ordered is quite one of the outstanding features of the attack,' he wrote. 'The battalion did quite splendidly in every way and no words of praise can be too high for all ranks.'

The enemy positions along the right of the 'Black Line' had been taken by the 1st Scots Guards and 2nd Irish Guards of the 2nd Guards Brigade. Behind them came the 3rd Grenadier Guards and the 1st Coldstream Guards. As the Coldstreamers steadied themselves for the next bound on the left, the ground 200yd in front writhed beneath a swirling cloud created by the covering barrage. For almost an hour the guns thundered, before extending their range to signal the advance to the 'Green Line' 1,100yd further on.

With Nos 3 and 4 Companies leading in two waves on a four-platoon front, the 1st Coldstreams set off, following the creeping barrage as closely as they dared. Successive waves followed with each section ready to meet all contingencies. This was well illustrated on the left flank. With units of the 3rd Brigade held up amid the concrete emplacements in Abri Wood, the Coldstreamers extended their front and assisted in clearing the position. Resistance was stiffening everywhere, but the Guards proved irresistible. The 'Green Line' was reached around Fourche and Captain's Farms and the position consolidated despite intense shelling. Outposts were pushed forward, and it was at this point that the Coldstreamers discovered an unlikely hero in their midst.

The Grenadiers advancing alongside were coming under enfilading fire from an enemy machine-gun post that had survived the barrage. It was one of many strongpoints studding the line of the Ypres-Staden railway which dogged the advance. Its precise location is not clear, but it was certainly identified by Pte Thomas Whitham, who took it upon himself to do something about it.

Whitham was scarcely a model soldier. His record sheet was sprinkled with misdemeanours. Less than a month before the Ypres offensive, a Field General Court Martial had convicted the 29-year-old guardsman of 'disobeying a lawful command'. His sentence of fifty-six days field punishment No. 1 had been interrupted by the battle. Yet, unruly as he may have been out of action, Whitham proved thoroughly reliable when it came to fighting, although quite what stirred this previously unexceptional soldier into such heroic action is unclear. Shells from the British barrage were falling all around as he set off alone.

The machine-gun was about 50–60yd away on the right flank. According to the Guards Division history, it was sited in a 'concrete emplacement'. But neither Whitham nor the subsequent citation for his Victoria Cross makes any mention of a pillbox. As elsewhere on the battlefield, it may be that the gun was located near a shelter that served as protection until the assault began. What is certain is that it was situated in one of the many shell-holes that scarred the battlefield. And it was these that Whitham used as cover as he crept from shell-hole to shell-hole to the rear of the post from where he could see two men were operating the gun under the command of a single officer. In an interview with a reporter from the *Burnley News*, he described the hand-to-hand struggle that followed:

I got into this shell-hole before the Germans were aware of my presence. Immediately I tackled the officer, who was in the act of turning a revolver on me, but before he could do so I seized his wrist and wrenched the revolver from his hand, putting him out of action by putting my knee in his stomach. On jumping into the shell-hole where the machine gun was, I was too near the officer to use my rifle. I had no trouble with the two Germans working the gun. They put up their hands at once and surrendered.

There was an alarming moment for friend and foe when Whitham picked up the officer's automatic revolver. His finger accidentally touched the trigger and before he knew it six shots were fired, fortunately without harming anyone. He then set about putting the machine-gun 'out of action', although, subsequently, it was brought back as a trophy.

Whitham's bold action, undertaken entirely on his own initiative, had undoubtedly saved many lives and was instrumental in allowing the whole line on the right to reach its final objective, near the banks of the Steenbeek. The 1st Coldstreams' advance, conducted with what its historian called 'great regularity and determination', had achieved all its goals for the loss of forty-two men killed and 124 wounded.

Lt-Gen. Lord Cavan, the XIV Corps commander, hailed the Guards Division's attack as 'a great success'; heading a long list of awards for that first day were two Victoria Crosses gazetted on 6 September to No. 939 Sgt Robert Bye, 1st Welsh Guards, and No. 15067 Pte Thomas Whitham, 1st Coldstream Guards. It is not known whether the gallant Whitham ever completed his sentence!

Thomas Whitham was born in the village of Worsthorne, near Burnley, on 11 May 1888, one of eight children and the youngest of four sons, to John and Catherine Whitham. Originally from Scotland, his parents had lived for a time in Embsay, near Skipton, where Tom's father worked as a stonemason in the local quarry, before moving to Gorple Road, Worsthorne.

Tom attended Worsthorne Church School, but his education appears to have been brief. The 1901 Census shows the family having moved again, to 4 Acre Street in Briercliffe, and lists Tom, aged 12, as working in a cotton mill. Later, he followed his father and gained employment as a bricklayer and mason with the local firm of Simpson Brothers and he also worked for his eldest brother, William, a builder based in Fulledge.

He married Fedora Bennett in Burnley on 1 May 1909. She was expecting their first child, a boy, at the time. By the outbreak of war, Tom was living with his young family at 111 Barden Lane.

He enlisted as a private in the Coldstream Guards at Burnley on 25 January 1915 and, in time, all four Whitham brothers would serve in the Army; William in the Royal Engineers, John, a Boer War veteran also in the Coldstreams, and Harry in the Royal Field Artillery. Joining at Caterham, Tom underwent basic training, spending the next ten months with the 4th and 5th Battalions in England. His record was not a happy one. He was reported absent without leave on 1 April, turning up six days later, and then on 8 July went absent again. Hauled before the commanding officer, he was given fourteen days Field Punishment No. 2.

On 26 October 1915 he was posted as a reinforcement to the 1st Battalion, already serving in France. Little is known of his service between his arrival on the Western Front and his VC action, although newspaper reports published at the time of his award state that he had come through all his unit's engagements 'without a scratch' and having enjoyed some 'miraculous' escapes. On one occasion, he was officially reported missing after being cut-off and 'lost' in a shell-hole in no-man's-land. He was eventually found and rescued three days later by a party of Irish guardsmen who stumbled across him. Another time, he set off to search for a missing sergeant when a shell-burst precisely in the spot he had just left, blowing his kit-bag to smithereens. During all his time at the front, he only had one spell of home leave and that was in October 1916, following his eldest son's death.

He appears to have stayed out of trouble until the summer of 1917. His record sheet lists him as awaiting trial on 26 June. Seven days later, he was convicted by a Field General Court Martial of disobeying a lawful command and sentenced to fifty-six days Field Punishment No. 1. No further details of his case have been found, but the severity of the sentence points to a serious breach of discipline. Field General Court Martials dealt with offences that carried the death sentence. Tom Whitham could only have served a maximum of twenty-seven days of his sentence, however, before moving up the line in readiness for the attack on 31 July.

His actions that day transformed him instantly from reprobate to hero. According to his brother, John, who was serving in the same unit, Tom was the talk of the battalion. In a letter home, John declared:

He is splendidly mentioned. I have made full inquiries of the matter, in fact, I was speaking to the Sergeant today who drew the attention of four officers, one of whom declared that he had earned more than one VC. I have spoken to several sergeants of his battalion, and also to men, and they all declare the matter to be certain. He has told me all about the affair, and I pressed him to give me the details, but he is like myself, he will not tell. It is not expected that he will do. But I myself cannot speak too highly of him, and if he does not receive the Victoria Cross it is well understood that he deserves it ... All his battalion is with him in praise, and all declare that he well deserves it for what he has done.

Though aware of the rumours that his name had been put in for some 'great distinction', Tom remained reticent in his correspondence home. Eventually, he wrote telling his wife he had been recommended for the VC. 'Everybody says I am sure to get it, but I am not,' he commented. He gave no further details of his exploit and said that the only reason he had mentioned it at all was because his brother was 'making such a fuss about it'. His scepticism continued until the award was confirmed in General Orders. Shortly afterwards, on 8 September, an impromptu ceremony was staged at a camp behind the lines, where his company commander presented him with the ribbon of the Victoria Cross. 'There was not much in the nature of a parade or anything of that sort for the camp was under shell-fire at the time,' Tom later recalled, 'and bombs from hostile aeroplanes were dropped during the time I was there.'

Granted ten days' leave, he returned to Burnley on 30 September. His family, now including two sons and a daughter all below the age of 6, were living at 4 Board Street, Burnley Lane, which became a focal point for celebrations. Among those beating a path to his door was a reporter from the *Burnley News* who found him a 'picture of health'. Describing him as 'modest' and 'unassuming', he nevertheless thought Tom 'cheery' and 'affable' and saw in him a personality that 'commands admiration'. From him, he gleaned that his company included five more men from Burnley, two of whom had earned Military Medals on the same day as his VC action. Initially reluctant to speak about his exploit, he was eventually persuaded to add a little more detail to the citation published in the *London Gazette*.

Shortly after the reporter's visit, on 6 October, Tom was treated to a grand civic reception in front of the town hall. Escorted by the National Reserve Band, he was driven in style through streets thick with cheering people. Eulogising about the event, the *Burnley Express & Advertiser* reported:

> The town was marked by scenes reminiscent of the day when Boyle and his merry men brought home the English Cup they had won after a strenuous football campaign. It was like a gala day, there being a brave display of flags and bunting in the main streets ...

So vast was the crowd that Tom was compelled to complete the journey on foot, wading through the throng with his daughter tottering on his shoulders. To a mighty cheer, the mayor presented him with a gold watch and chain. Clearly embarrassed at such attention, Tom struggled to reply. At one point, he appeared to dry up, before declaring: 'I must say this is worse than being at Ypres.'

More public engagements followed. During one, at his home village of Worsthorne, the platform set up on the green collapsed, but it didn't prevent the proud citizens presenting him with a large carriage clock, a silver rose bowl and a pair of bronze ornaments. The celebrations culminated on 20 October with his attendance at a Buckingham Palace investiture, where he received his Victoria Cross from King George V. Ten days later, he reported for duty with the 5th Battalion, Coldstream Guards.

He continued to serve in England until he was demobilised on 7 March 1919. During his four years in the Coldstream Guards, he appears to have been promoted only once, to acting lance-corporal on 30 September 1918.

His short military career had been a chequered one, but his post-war experience would prove far worse. Early indications of his prospects were not good. Before leaving the Army, and perhaps hoping to make the most of his celebrity status, he wrote to Burnley Corporation, seeking a job as a builder. The response from the civic authority that had so recently feted him was negative. Replying to his request for work on 3 January 1919, the mayor of Burnley stated: 'I very much regret to say, however, that owing to the large number of former employees of the Corporation who are at present serving in the Army and who have been promised employment on their return, it is not possible to guarantee that a position would be found for you under the Corporation.' It was the beginning of a long and hard road that Tom Whitham would have to travel. With the 'land fit for heroes' in the grip of an economic depression, he soon found himself among an army of unemployed. Without a job and with now five children to support, he was forced to pawn his proudest possession, his Victoria Cross, along with his campaign medals and the many gifts he had received.

Eventually, he found work as a bricklayer on a housing scheme at Egremont in the Lake District. His family followed him there, but when the project was completed in 1924 he was thrown out of work again. In desperation, he began touring the district on his bicycle in search of jobs. But misery was piled on misfortune when, during one expedition through Windermere, he crashed into a wall and suffered head injuries. A local doctor who treated him advised him to stop and rest, but being short of money Tom decided to carry on. According to contemporary newspaper reports, his injuries caused him to lose his memory and shortly afterwards he disappeared. With her husband missing and two of their children suffering from pneumonia, Fedora moved the family back to live with her father in Burnley. Finally, after appeals were published in the press, Tom was traced to lodgings in Liverpool.

Having recovered from his accident, he found work in Gatley, near Manchester, from where he wrote to his wife. Tom's plight, however, took another turn for the worse and contact was again lost. By October 1924 he was living in extreme poverty in lodgings in Hollins Green, Middleton. His health, once so robust, was failing. Admitted to the Oldham Royal Infirmary, he died of a perforated gastric ulcer complicated by peritonitis on 22 October. He was 36.

Tom Whitham VC was buried with full military honours in the Inghamite Burial Ground, Wheatley Lane, in Nelson, Lancashire. Thousands turned out to watch the funeral cortège pass by. Twenty-eight years later a headstone paid for by the North-east Lancashire Branch of the Coldstream Guards Association was dedicated. After falling into disrepair, it was eventually restored to its original state in 1988.

His hard-earned medals remained in a Burnley pawnbroker's shop until 1931 when they were bought for £50 by the same corporation that had turned down his application for a job. Along with the gold watch that had been presented to him in front of the town hall in the autumn of 1917, his VC and Victory Medal were put on display in Towneley Hall Art Gallery and Museum, close to a portrait of him by the artist Ivan Cooke which had been commissioned by the local authority.

In 1994, his son, William Whitham, unsuccessfully petitioned Parliament to have the medals removed to join a display of similar awards to Coldstreamers. Today, they remain on public view in Burnley, where Tom has recently received further posthumous recognition with the decision, in 2008, to name a new sixth-form school after him. Three years after his tragic life story featured in the *Not Forgotten* television series, Burnley's unlikely hero was hailed a role model for a new generation. Stuart Smith, principal of Thomas Whitham Sixth Form, explained: 'Thomas' story demonstrates that everyone has in them the potential to achieve something significant in their life. It illustrates perfectly the ethos of the sixth form, which is high achievement for people from whatever background.'

Robert James Bye, the first Welsh Guardsman to be awarded the Victoria Cross, was born at 13 Maritime Street, Pontypridd, on 12 December 1889, the son of Martin Bye, a coal miner, and his wife Sarah Jane (née Edwards). The family moved to Woodfield Street, Penrhiwceibr when he was 4 and he was educated at Penrhiwceibr boys' school. Following his father down the pit, he worked at the coalface at Deep Duffryn Colliery, Mountain Ash and other local mines. He married Mabel Lloyd at Pontypridd on 14 October 1912, and they had four children (Robert

Edward, born in 1913, Jenny in 1915, Desmond James in 1922 and Mary in 1928).

Bye was living in Church Street, Penrhiwceibr, when he enlisted as a private in the newly raised Welsh Guards at Mountain Ash on 3 April 1915. Although he had no military background, two of his brothers were already serving in the Army; David, a regular, was with the 18th Hussars and Vivian, who had enlisted shortly after the outbreak of war, was in the Royal Welch Fusiliers. A third brother, Donald, had enlisted and gone to France despite being only 14. When his age was discovered, he was sent home, but subsequently re-enlisted at the age of 17. A brother-in-law was also serving and went on to win the DCM.

On 17 August 1915 Bye moved to France with his unit, barely two weeks after the regiment had received its colours from King George V. Their first major action followed in September at Loos. Bye, a robust character and a member of the battalion boxing team, proved a fine soldier and his war service was marked by steady promotion: to lance-corporal on 13 March 1916, to corporal on 21 September 1916, and to sergeant on 4 April 1917.

Following the announcement of his Victoria Cross, Bye, who had also been awarded the Legion of Honour by the French Government, returned to England on leave. He received his Cross from King George V at Buckingham Palace on 26 September and then travelled home where he was fêted in the towns and villages lining the Aberdare Valley. Concerts were staged in his honour at Penrhiwceibr and Aberdare and he was showered with gifts, including a gold watch, a silver cigarette case and an illuminated address. A fund was also launched with the local colliery levying sixpence from men and threepence from boys. During his stay, Bye attended numerous official functions, at one of which he declared: 'I am proud of the honour conferred upon me, but I only went out to France to do what millions of others are doing – my duty. In honouring me you are honouring my comrades out in France, for they all did well that day.'

Bye served with the Welsh Guards until the end of the war. He was discharged on 1 February 1919 but re-enlisted in the Sherwood Foresters six months later on 22 August. After a short spell at the regimental depot, Normanton Barracks in Derby, he joined the 1st Battalion on 5 November 1919 when he was promoted to his former wartime rank of sergeant. He served with the unit in Germany during the Plebiscite of 1920, but was discharged on medical grounds on 2 July 1921. His family was still living in Penrhiwceibr and unemployment was high in the Welsh valleys. His daughter, Mary Moody, recalled: 'My father saw a lot of poverty in his life and I remember him saying that when he came home from the war to more poverty, he thought about what Lloyd George had said about coming back to "a land fit for heroes to live in".'

With prospects of work bleak, Bye moved to Warsop in Nottinghamshire, where he returned to pit work as a miner at Warsop Main, Firbeck and Wellbeck collieries. For a time, he also worked as a temporary police constable at Mansfield. His chief recreations were sport and listening to Welsh choirs. He also took an active role in a number of ex-service organisations, being a member of the Warsop, Spion Kop and Wellbeck Abbey branches of the British Legion. His daughter recalled him serving as parade marshal for Remembrance Day parades throughout the 1930s: 'He was a very straight-talking man and did not suffer fools gladly. He was a popular and kind man who was very modest about his Victoria Cross. In fact, I can hardly ever remember hearing him speak about it.'

When the Second World War started, Bye joined the National Defence Corps. He served as a sergeant-major in the Sherwood Foresters and helped guard a prisoner-of-war camp in Derbyshire before being discharged, once again on medical grounds, in 1941. He was then 51. He returned to work in the mines, where the effects of prolonged exposure to coal-dust took an increasing toll on his health. When he retired in 1955, he was already showing signs of suffering from pneumoconiosis. By the summer of 1962, when he was living at 120a Sherwood Street, Warsop, he was having great difficulty in breathing. His daughter recalled:

He had been ill for some time and on the doctor's advice, it was suggested he come to stay at my house, because it was on a hill and was thought to be more airy. He had only been there a few days when he suffered a heart attack, which I think was brought on by the coal-dust.

Robert Bye died at his daughter's house in Hammerwater Drive, Warsop, on 23 August 1962. He was buried with full military honours at Warsop cemetery. His death was followed by a second family tragedy when one of his brothers died of a heart attack during the funeral.

Eighty years after his VC action, Bye is remembered proudly by his old regiment. His VC group of medals are displayed at the Guards Museum, Wellington Barracks, in London and in 1988 a painting of his action by the artist David Rowlands, commissioned by the Warrant Officers' and Sergeants' Mess of the 1st Welsh Guards, was unveiled by Bye's great granddaughter Claire Armstrong and his grandson, Paul Bye, then a 23-year-old Welsh guardsman. It was a fitting tribute to a superb fighting soldier.

H. ACKROYD

North-west of Clapham Junction,
31 July–1 August 1917

Harold Ackroyd scarcely conformed to the popular image of heroic manhood. He was 40 years old, grey-haired, wore thick-lensed spectacles and walked with a slight stoop. Yet in the space of thirteen months this highly sensitive man, a research scientist before the war, was twice recommended for the nation's highest military honour. By general consent, the middle-aged medical officer of the 6th Berkshires, who already wore the purple and white ribbon of the Military Cross, was the most courageous member of the battalion. His commanding officer, Lt-Col B.E. Clay, considered him 'the most gallant man I have ever met'. In the shell-torn fields west of Glencourse Wood between 31 July and 1 August, that opinion was repeatedly borne out as the Berkshires' doctor scaled the supreme heights of valour.

The 6th Berkshires formed part of the 53rd Brigade (18th Division), attached to the 30th Division, with the task of carrying the advance through to its final objective in Polygon Wood on the eastern end of the Gheluvelt plateau. Their attack astride the Menin Road, through a tangled mass of shattered woods strewn with barbed wire and a multitude of pillboxes, was recognised as one of the most important and hazardous operations on the first day. But attempts to adjust the timetable for the barrage, taking into account the difficulties, were disregarded with fatal consequences. After initial success, the attack was checked almost everywhere along the 30th Division front. Enemy guns rained shells on Sanctuary and Château Woods. Casualties soared, communications were wrecked and confusion reigned. Units became intermixed. One battalion, assigned the task of taking Glencourse Wood, blundered into Château Wood, where, oblivious to the error, they proceeded to report the capture of their real objective. It was a shambles that proved costly for the 6th Berkshires, one of the units designated to continue an advance which had never been made.

Few units of the 30th Division had advanced beyond the first objective. The Berkshires, their progress slowed by heavy shelling, missed the barrage which had switched to the third objective even before they could struggle through to the first at around 8 am. Instead of forming up in Glencourse Wood, they found themselves having to negotiate their way around the Menin Road over ground which was alive with machine-guns that should have been silenced. By 10 am Clay's battalion had toiled – at considerable cost – across approximately 400yd of pitted ground west of Glencourse, finishing short even of their planned start line. By the end of the disastrous day the Berkshires' casualties amounted to forty-four officers and men killed, 182 wounded and twenty-eight missing.

One of the worst features of the operation now presented itself in the suffering of the wounded. Many lay out in the open at the mercy of enemy fire of every description. The heavy rain which began to fall at midday quickly turned the churned ground to muddy slush, and as shell-holes began to fill with water the peril of drowning was added to the anguish of the wounded. It was amid 'that hellish turmoil', as the 18th Division historian called it, that the selfless efforts of Captain Ackroyd shone out:

> He seemed to be everywhere; he tended and bandaged scores of men, for to him fell the rush of cases round Clapham Junction and towards Hooge. But no wounded man was treated hurriedly or unskilfully. Ackroyd worked as stoically as if he were in the quiet of an operating theatre ... When it was all over and the reports came in, it was found that there were twenty-three separate recommendations of his name for the Victoria Cross ...

Ackroyd, who had taken to wearing large shaded goggles because of his failing sight, did not remain at his dressing station. Like Noel Chavasse, he toiled long into the night, trawling the ground for injured men, careless of his own safety. His forays often took him beyond the shell-hole line consolidated by the Berkshires around Jargon Switch and were invariably carried out in the face of heavy machine-gun, rifle and shell fire. His citation recorded: 'He carried a wounded officer to a place of safety under very heavy fire. On another occasion he went some way in front of our advanced line and brought in a wounded man under continuous sniping and machine-gun fire.'

The Berkshires came out of the line on 1 August. Ackroyd, despite being under fire for hours at a time, emerged unscathed. In the days that followed, recommendations for him to be awarded the supreme honour began to work their way through the system.

By the time the 6th Berkshires returned to the front, Ackroyd was aware he had been put in for the VC. Tragically, however, he would not live to see its confirmation. Around 7.20 pm on 10 August, the battalion received orders to move forward. Following a failed attack on Glencourse Wood, the 7th Bedfords had withdrawn to Jargon Trench and were being counter-attacked. Advancing through a heavy bombardment, the Berkshires found themselves moving across the same ground they had fought over ten days earlier. The line had barely advanced, but conditions had worsened. The relief completed, the Berkshires remained to beat off an enemy attack the next day.

During a lull following the enemy's repulse on 11 August, Ackroyd set off from his advanced dressing station to search for casualties behind the firing line. Normally, he was accompanied on these ventures by his orderly, Pte A. Scriven. But on this occasion he went alone, leaving his orderly in charge of the dressing station.

Scriven later wrote:

He was visiting each company about 150yd in front of us, to see whether there were any wounded to attend to ... he had to go from one shell-hole to another, and in so doing was shot through the head by a sniper. Immediately I heard the news I took a party of stretcher bearers, but on arrival found he was dead. There were six other poor fellows in the same shell-hole who had met the same fate, it was a perfect death trap.

According to Sgt Maurice Butter, Ackroyd had gone out to treat a wounded man lying in a crater actually in the front line: 'He reached the shell-hole, dressed the man, and as he got up to fetch the stretcher bearers a sniper shot him.' Ackroyd's death came as a terrible blow to the 6th Berkshires. On 19 August Capt. J.N. Richardson, one of his closest friends, wrote to his widow:

It's the biggest loss this battalion has ever suffered and it's nothing more or less than a tragedy for us all. As you have probably heard before he was the most fearless man imaginable and to see him in his cool way picking up wounded and sending them off was a sight no one can ever forget. The hottest shell fire never stopped him going to a wounded man and the men used to simply stare in wonderment at his bravery. In all fights he was worth a hundred men to us for morale's sake ...

Less than three weeks later, the *London Gazette* of 6 September carried the announcement of the posthumous award of the Victoria Cross to Temporary Captain Harold Ackroyd MC. The citation concluded: 'His heroism was the means of saving many lives, and provided a magnificent example of courage, cheerfulness and determination to the fighting men in whose midst he was carrying out his splendid work.'

Harold Ackroyd was born on 13 July 1877 in Southport, Lancashire, the younger son of Edward Ackroyd, chairman of the Cheshire Lines & Southport Extension Railway Company, and his wife Ellen. A gifted scholar, Harold was educated at Mintholme College, Southport, and Shrewsbury School, from where he gained entrance to Gonville and Caius College, Cambridge. He completed his BA degree in 1899. Around this time, he was reputed to have travelled widely around the world, setting off alone to explore distant parts. Back in England, he continued his studies at Guy's Hospital, London, achieving his MB (Cambridge) in 1904 and his MD six years later. He held house appointments at Guy's, the General Hospital in Birmingham and the David Lewis Northern Hospital in Liverpool. Ackroyd, who was never in private practice, then secured a BMA research scholarship at Downing College Laboratory, Cambridge, where he helped pioneer research into human metabolism. It was during this period that he met Mabel Robina Smythe, a matron at Strangeways Hospital, Cambridge. They were married on 1 August 1908 and had three children.

Ackroyd was working in Cambridge and living at Brooklands, an imposing house in Kneesworth Road, Royston, when war broke out. He was commissioned a temporary lieutenant in the Royal Army Medical Corps on 15 February 1916 and was attached to the 6th Royal Berkshires as medical officer. The battalion proceeded to France in July 1915 and went into the line a month later opposite Fricourt on the Somme.

Prior to going into action, Ackroyd had been less than popular in the training camps. It was said that he could tell a malingerer by instinct and, according to his divisional historian, 'he did not suffer weaklings patiently'. At the front, however, he soon made his mark, his own selfless courage being matched only by the pride he took in the battalion's achievements. The 6th Berkshires took part in the attack towards Montauban ridge on 1 July 1916, one of the few successes on the first day on the Somme. Eight days later, in a letter to his daughter Ursula, he declared: 'The battalion ... did splendidly ... I can tell you I was very proud of the officers and men I have known so long. Now we rest ... and we are all very happy and contented sleeping on the ground while at last the sun shines and it does not rain.'

After Montauban came the horrors of Delville Wood on 19 July. The 53rd Brigade was decimated during the three-day struggle to capture and hold one of the enemy's strongest positions. The fearful casualties included more than 700 wounded. Medical teams were stretched to breaking point. The divisional historian recorded: 'The fighting was so confused and the wood so hard to search that the difficulties of evacuating the wounded seemed unconquerable. But Captain Ackroyd ... was so cool, purposeful and methodical that he cleared the whole wood of wounded, British and Boche as well.' Much of this work was carried out in the face of snipers and heavy shelling. Such was his courage that no fewer than eleven reports were filed by officers outside the 6th Berkshires. A recommendation for the Victoria Cross followed, but this was down-graded to a Military Cross (*London Gazette*, 20 October 1916).

Ackroyd came through the fighting physically unscathed, but the strain took its toll. At one point, he had been 'blown up' and it appears that fellow officers feared he was on the point of cracking up. According to the Berkshires' history, he suffered a 'breakdown' after Delville Wood. To his young daughter Ursula, he gave only the vaguest hints of his ordeal. In a note written on 23 July, one day after his brigade was relieved, he said: 'The places I have been in lately are so very noisy but now it is all quiet and peaceful and perhaps I may get leave to come home before long so as to see you.'

Ackroyd was invalided home on 11 August, suffering from nervous exhaustion. However, he felt a short rest was all he needed, and was dismayed when a medical board gave him six weeks' leave. Writing to his brother Edward on 4 September, he declared: 'I argued with them that 10–14 days would be quite enough with the result that they got shirty and said I must take what the board gave me; an awful lot of fossils.'

Ackroyd considered himself 'quite well' and 'really quite fit to return to duty'. His main concern was to get back to his battalion. It was not a view easily understood by his wife. Family legend has it that attempts were made to persuade him to accept safer employment. Some comrades also felt he had done enough. Writing to Mabel after his death, Alfred Clark, an officer at 18th Division HQ, confessed: 'We were all half sorry when he returned after getting blown up last July, for we knew that, if he came back, he would go on taking appalling risks, and that the end was almost a certainty ...' Ackroyd appeared torn between his sense of duty and his family. But for a man who abhorred any kind of shirking, it was perhaps inevitable that duty should win out. Passed fit by a medical board on 3 October, he was back in France the following month, although it was not until December that he rejoined the 6th Berkshires.

During the bitter winter of 1916–17, the Berkshires were engaged in sharp fighting around Miraumont as the Germans prepared to withdraw to the Hindenburg Line. Most of the spring and early summer were spent preparing for the Flanders offensive. Ackroyd enjoyed a leave with his family and on 19 July, shortly before his 40th birthday, wrote to Ursula urging her to 'Tell mother that a year ago today we were in Delville Wood; it was a most dreadful place and now a year later all is quiet and peaceful'. This may well have been his last letter to his daughter. A little over three weeks later, Mabel Ackroyd received the news she had dreaded and which her husband's closest colleagues feared was inevitable.

Harold Ackroyd's body was brought out and buried behind the lines. His headstone in Birr Crossroads cemetery, Zillebeke, carries the inscription: 'Believed to be buried in this cemetery.' Memorials to his gallantry abound. They include a plaque at Cambridge University and a painting of his VC action at the RAMC Officers HQ in Millbank, London. Ackroyd Troop of the RAMC perpetuates his memory in military circles. In Royston, where he was living at the outbreak of war, there is a road bearing his name and a commemorative plaque on the wall of his former home. His VC and MC, which were presented by King George V to Mabel and her 5-year-old son Stephen on 26 September 1917, were acquired by Lord Ashcroft in 2004 and are now displayed in the Imperial War Museum. 'All of our medical officers are wonderfully brave,' Alfred Clark had written to Mabel, 'but your husband was quite in a class by himself.'

A. LOOSEMORE

Wellington Farm, near the Steenbeek,
11 August 1917

By 4 August, following four days of unremitting rain, the battlefield had dissolved into a bog, delaying but not stopping offensive operations. Trenches became miniature watercourses and shell-holes overflowed to form slimy lakes. Across many parts of the battlefield, a fragile web of wooden duckboards provided the only means of crossing the swamp. During those four days almost 41mm of rain was recorded, more than half the total August average, and the misery was compounded by persistent German shelling. Planning for the resumption of the attack, however, continued unabated. Along most of the line, fresh battalions ploughed through the mire to relieve the exhausted units that had spearheaded the assault. Among the last to leave was the 51st Highland Division, replaced on the night of 7 August by the 11th Division.

One of the new battalions was the 8th West Ridings, of the 32nd Brigade. Their route to the front, via Poperinghe, Elverdinghe and Flamatinghe, had provided a harsh initiation with rain and shells plaguing their steps. The next few days spent 'holding the line' brought scant relief. As the second week of the offensive opened, British activity focused on an attempt to clear the Gheluvelt plateau. On the northern flank, where the Steenbeek separated the two front lines, operations were limited to small-scale attacks to establish outposts along the east bank in readiness for the next push towards Langemarck. The 8th West Ridings' contribution was a minor one, memorable only for the exceptional courage displayed by a 21-year-old private soldier. Details of the action fought on 11 August are sparse. The only apparent reference to it in the unit's original war diary is a brief pencilled note, erroneously entered under 10 August. It reads: 'Attack by Y and Z Coys on strongpoints west of Steenbeck (Langemarck). Positions held to 4 pm but forced to withdraw owing to heavy MG fire, a large superior force of enemy and strength of their positions.'

The central figure in this otherwise inglorious affair was Pte Arnold Loosemore, a Lewis gunner in No. 12 Platoon and one of fifty men from Y Company assigned the task of capturing a German blockhouse known as Wellington Farm. The attack went in at daybreak, after a night spent sheltering in shell-holes, up to their knees in mud. CSM E. Miles described it, no doubt with a degree of irony, as 'one of the prettiest little stunts you can imagine':

> We advanced on the farm in extended order, but went too far ahead, and had to retire to keep in touch with the companies [sic] on our left and right. It was then that a very brave act was committed by a Lewis gunner of ours named Loosemore; he certainly saved a very awkward situation. He stayed in a shell-hole and covered our retirement with a Lewis gun. Well, this gun got put out of action, but Loosemore hung on and kept the advancing Germans at bay with his revolver. When that gave out, he threw his disabled gun at the remaining German and fled back to where we had consolidated, a truly brave act ...

Miles reported the young soldier's gallantry to his company officer, 2/Lt E. Wood, a Sheffield man like Loosemore, who gathered eyewitness statements to support the VC recommendation. Included among them was the testimony of Sgt S.L. Ridgeway, another member of 12 Platoon, who described how Loosemore held off 'a great number' of the enemy, enabling the company to consolidate 'in front of the Boche wire':

> He displayed great courage when attacked by a party of German bombers who put his Lewis gun out of action. He then threw two German stick bombs at the said bombers and, using his revolver, he killed four Germans and when he came in to where our company had dug in under heavy machine [gun] fire he brought out a wounded comrade. During the day, while we still held to our new position, he sniped off five of the enemy's men.

To Loosemore's parents Ridgeway wrote: 'He wrought havoc amongst them, scattering them right and left, saving many of our lives ... Not only has he proved himself a soldier, but one of England's bravest soldiers ...' The sergeant was not alone in believing that Loosemore's stand had averted disaster. Sgt A. Rossiter wrote:

> The work which he did after having his machine-gun blown up, and the number of men he has been able to account for, is simply marvellous ... everybody is extremely delighted with him. The officers from the commanding officer cannot praise him enough, and officers of other companies also think the world of him.

It was a view confirmed by 2/Lt Wood in a letter to Loosemore's parents, in which he described their son as 'the bravest lad I have ever seen' and said 'his magnificent gallantry undoubtedly saved the whole of his company'. Such claims were not exaggerated. After two members of his section had been killed beside him, Loosemore had fought with every means at his disposal – machine-gun, bomb, rifle and revolver – to thwart a determined counter-attack which appeared to many as though it must succeed. He accounted for about twenty of the enemy, as well as a number of snipers. Almost as miraculous as his Herculean feat of arms was the fact that he emerged unscathed. Indeed, the youngster appeared in more danger from his grateful comrades. Ridgeway recorded: 'Arnold is in the best of health and almost shaken to pieces with officers and men who are left, shaking hands and wishing him the best of everything.'

The first reward for his exploit followed a few days later when he was promoted to corporal. In letters home to his parents, however, he confined himself to a single oblique reference in which he commented: 'You will be having a great surprise one of these days.' The prophecy was fulfilled on 14 September 1917, when the *London Gazette* announced the award of the Victoria Cross to No. 15805 Pte Arnold Loosemore. The 8th West Ridings were out of the line, living in billets in Poperinghe, when news of the award came through. CSM Miles excitedly recorded: '... Loosemore gets the VC. Hurray! He is only a young fellow and I hope it won't turn his head.'

Arnold Loosemore was born at Sharrow, a district of Sheffield, on 7 June 1896, the second youngest of seven sons to George and Mary Loosemore. His father worked as a gardener at the city's central cemetery and all of the boys were educated at Clifford School. Arnold's first job was on a farm at Fulwood, where he was working when war broke out. His elder brothers soon enlisted and he followed them, after being initially turned away. Some accounts claim that he was rejected as being under age, but it seems more likely that he was turned down on account of his frail physique. According to his son, in order to be accepted by the Army, he took a job with a coal merchant to build up his strength.

Whatever the truth, by 1915 he was serving with the York & Lancasters. Aged 19, he saw action at Suvla Bay during the Gallipoli campaign. He remained on the peninsula until December 1915, when the northern sectors were evacuated. Back in England, he was transferred to the 8th West Ridings and proceeded to France in 1916. Trained to operate the new Lewis machine-gun, he was reputed to have shot down an enemy aircraft as it chased a British fighter low over his unit's camp. A keen and efficient soldier, Loosemore celebrated his 21st birthday at home during a ten-day leave. Barely two months later came the action for which he was awarded the VC.

He was decorated by King George V at Buckingham Palace on 2 January 1918, and the following day it was the turn of the people of Sheffield to honour him. A crowd of 2,000 gathered to watch the ceremonies on the town tall steps. Although there was much cheering, the signs of war-weariness were apparent. There were neither bands nor parades. Loosemore, by then a sergeant, was accompanied by his father and two of his six serving brothers. Two other brothers were in France, while the other two were with their units in Italy.

The 'slim, modest-looking' hero was congratulated by a succession of civic dignitaries who used the occasion to shame 'shirkers' who 'had gone into the munition factories for the purpose of avoiding military service' and to urge perseverance in the nation's struggle. Loosemore merely called on the crowd to 'give three cheers for the wounded and our fellows at the front'.

His service with the 8th West Ridings was almost over. A few weeks later the battalion was disbanded as part of a major reorganisation and at the end of April Loosemore was posted to the 1/4th West Ridings. In June, after weeks of training new drafts, the battalion returned to the front, taking over a stretch of line in the Zillebeke sector. Within days, Loosemore had distinguished himself again. During a well-planned raid carried out on the night of 19–20 June more than 350 men had rushed the enemy positions, bringing back eleven prisoners and a light machine-gun. The operation, carried out at the cost of three killed, seventeen wounded and one man missing, resulted in twenty-one gallantry awards, including a DCM for Loosemore. The citation read:

When out with a fighting patrol he displayed conspicuous gallantry and powers of leadership when his officer was wounded and the platoon scattered by hostile bombs. He rallied the men and brought them back in order with all the wounded to our lines. On a subsequent occasion he handled his platoon with great skill and a complete disregard of his own danger under heavy machine-gun fire, and it was owing to his determination and powers of leadership that the platoon eventually captured the enemy post which they were attacking.

The 1/4th West Ridings remained in the Ypres sector until the end of August when the unit was ordered south. Weeks of inactivity came to an end on 11 October when the battalion was assigned the task of capturing a ridge in front of Villers-en-Cauchies. So fast was the advance that the West Ridings broke through their own barrage. The Germans retaliated by raking the crest with machine-gun fire. Among many casualties was Sgt Loosemore, seriously wounded in both legs.

Medical staff saved his life, but surgeons were forced to amputate his left leg. It was a cruel end to an outstanding war record. He was still undergoing treatment when the Armistice was signed. The people of Sheffield did what they could to alleviate his suffering. A public fund launched by the Lord Mayor raised £1,000 to be invested on his behalf. Other efforts were also made to help ease him back into civilian life. His son recorded:

> He was sent on a chicken farm course, but this proved too physically demanding so he took up photography ... To help him get about he was bought a pony and trap with a helper-driver to assist him. Our house was a court house, three-up, but the stairs were too much for him, so Sheffield's Rotary Club supplied him with a large hut, which was built on to the back of the house. It was there that he slept and did his photography work.

Arnold Loosemore married Amy Morton, of the Lescar Hotel, Sharrow Vale Road, on 24 August 1920 and their only son was born a year later. By 1924, however, Loosemore's health, undermined by the war, was failing. He contracted tuberculosis and, after several weeks battling against the disease, succumbed at his Stannington home on 10 April 1924. He was 27.

In accordance with his wishes, he was buried at Ecclesall church with full military honours; crowds lined the streets as a gun-carriage carrying his coffin made its sombre procession. Fifteen months later, Loosemore's former CO, Lt-Col A.L. Mowat DSO, MC, unveiled a memorial tablet in St Andrew's church, Sharrow, dedicated to the young soldier's memory.

The years that followed his premature death proved difficult for his widow. Only allowed to draw the interest from the civic trust fund, she was compelled to take another job. At first the fund's trustees refused her request to draw on the capital. Eventually they relented, but the episode left a bitter taste. Years later, Arnold Loosemore insisted that his father's deeds had been quickly forgotten after his death. 'My father was just another hero down the drain,' he told one journalist. His campaign for official recognition was finally rewarded in 1983 when the city council named a street, Loosemore Drive, in his father's honour. Today a weather-worn stone cross marks the last resting place of Sheffield's most highly decorated soldier of the First World War. Its simple inscription reads: 'Awaiting Reveille.'

F.G. ROOM
Near Frezenberg, 16 August 1917

An attempt to make good the setbacks across the Gheluvelt plateau ended in almost total failure on 10 August. Not for the first time, and tragically nor for the last, early success was squandered by depleted units being unable to hold their gains. In places, scarcely a yard had been gained. Yet Gough was determined to launch another attack, along a broader front, with the intention of advancing almost twice the distance his men had proved incapable of covering on 10 August. What now seems an act of supreme folly was compounded by wretched weather and the near exhaustion of many of the men upon whom the main burden would fall.

The 16th (Southern Irish) and 36th (Ulster) Divisions were faced with crossing a mile of waterlogged ground north of the Ypres–Roulers railway. Neither division was in a fit state to attempt so daunting a mission. Worn down by constant shelling, sickness and twelve days of toiling in the worst conditions imaginable, the strength of the two divisions had been reduced by a third by the time the attack was launched at 4.45 am on 16 August. The 16th Division's two brigades, the 48th and 49th, hit trouble almost immediately. Machine-guns at Potsdam, Vampir and Borry Farms tore holes in the leading units of the 48th Brigade, although a few men toiled up the bare slope to within 100yd of the final objective. The 49th Brigade, consisting of the 8th Inniskillings, the 7/8th Royal Irish Fusiliers and the 7th Inniskillings, was held at Borry Farm, but units on the left overran Iberian and Delva Farms only to be checked 400yd from the summit of Hill 37.

When the attack was launched, the men of D, C and A Companies, the 2nd Royal Irish Regiment, moved forward to occupy the start line north of Frezenberg. Two platoons of C Company, sent to occupy the captured strongpoint at Beck House, suffered heavy casualties. Prospects of consolidating even the limited gains were soon ruined. Around 9 am, after a crushing bombardment, waves of enemy infantry poured across the crest of the Zonnebeke–St Julien spur. The frailty of the Irish units was exposed as the attack swept over them. Amid much confusion, the withdrawal quickly became a rout.

Around 10 am word reached the small group of the 2nd Royal Irish Regiment holding Beck House ordering them to pull back. By 10.15 am, the battle, so far as the 16th Division was concerned, was effectively over. For no appreciable gain, its two brigades had lost more than 2,000 men. The 2nd Royal Irish Regiment, which had hardly been engaged, suffered 116 casualties, most of them among C Company. The losses would doubtless have been greater but for the selfless courage of medical officers and stretcher-bearers who risked their lives to scour the battlefield for wounded men.

Courage in the midst of failure is rarely rewarded, but the case of Acting L/Cpl Fred Room was exceptional. He was in command of his company's stretcher-bearers and on that morning he brought succour to his wounded comrades regardless of enemy fire. Details of his unselfish heroism are sketchy. The unit history makes only fleeting reference to his actions and, unsatisfactory though it is, the only significant record remains the citation for his VC announced on 17 October:

> For most conspicuous bravery when in charge of his company stretcher-bearers. During the day the company had many casualties, principally from enemy machine-guns and snipers. The company was holding a line of shell-holes and short trenches. Lance-Corporal Room worked continuously under intense fire, dressing the wounded and helping to evacuate them. Throughout this period, with complete disregard for his own life, he showed unremitting devotion to his duties.
>
> By his courage and fearlessness he was the means of saving many of his comrades' lives.

The only stretcher-bearer to win the VC during the campaign, Frederick George Room was born at 24 Congleton Road, St Georges, Bristol, on 31 May 1895. Educated at Whitehall Council School, he was employed at the Mardon, Son & Hall's wagon works and the Western Engineering Company. He was a member of the St Ambrose Company of the 1st Bristol Cadet Battalion, Church Lads' Brigade, which had affiliations with the KRRC. Freddie Room was noted as being 'always smart, steady and regular'. One of four lads from Congleton in the same company, he was the only one to survive the war. Two brothers also served in the Army, although one was invalided out.

Room apparently tried to enlist in the Royal Engineers at Colston Hall in August 1914, but for some unknown reason he was rejected. Instead, he joined the Royal Irish and was posted to The Curragh. He proceeded to France as a private (No. 8614) in July 1915 and saw action on the Somme, where he was wounded. After three weeks in hospital, he returned to the trenches, taking part in the attack on Messines Ridge in June 1917, where he distinguished himself.

He was on ten days leave with his family in Bristol when his VC was announced. Described as a 'silent man', he refused any press interviews. According to one report in the *Western Daily Press*, he was 'absolutely determined to avoid fuss'. It did not, however, prevent him being fêted at a civic reception. On 8 November, his leave having been extended, he was one of two Victoria Cross winners among a long list of servicemen who received their awards from King George V at an open-air investiture staged at Durdham Downs, Bristol. His appearance on the royal platform was the signal for 'a great burst of cheering'.

A slight, fair-haired youth of 22, Room came through the rest of the war and was one of five Bristol VC recipients to receive inscribed gold watches and illuminated addresses in a ceremony at Colston Hall on 15 February 1919. He married and settled back in Bristol, working at the Thrissell Engineering Company. By his early 30s, however, his health, weakened by the war, had begun to fail. Severe lung trouble forced him to quit work.

In 1929 he attended the gathering of VC recipients at the House of Lords, but the following year he was admitted to hospital with pneumonia. His wife, Ellen, refused to leave his bedside. When news of his plight filtered out, offers of help poured in, but she declined them all. 'It is kind of people,' she told one journalist, 'but I will nurse him myself. I cannot possibly answer all the letters I received. Please let them know I am extremely grateful.' She took a job and continued to care for him at their home in Gorse Hill, Fishponds, but his health deteriorated and shortly after Armistice Day, 1931, he entered Ham Green Hospital with another bout of pneumonia which proved fatal.

Freddie Room died in hospital on 19 January 1932, aged 36. Six days later, crowds lined the roads from Gorse Hill to Greenbank cemetery and an estimated two thousand people congregated at the graveside. A few months later, a new headquarters of the Bristol CLB was opened, with pride of place given to a portrait of their hero. Further recognition followed in May 1933 when ex-service organisations gathered in Greenbank cemetery for the unveiling of a memorial headstone and marble block with a

Victoria Cross carved on its face. The inscription read: 'His name liveth for evermore ... Thy purpose Lord, we cannot see, But all is well that's done by Thee.'

At Room's funeral, the Archdeacon of Bristol had urged citizens not to forget his widow. A public appeal was launched, but it had little effect. There were reports that Ellen Room might be forced to sell her husband's medals. In a letter to the author, a relative, Joyce Lockier (née Room), recalled: 'In spite of all the furore at the time, nothing much was done to help her, and she eventually earned her living making ladies' corsets.' She died in 1964 and two years later Freddie Room's VC group was presented to the National Army Museum. Ellen was buried in the same grave as her 'beloved husband' and to the other inscriptions was added the simplest one of all: 'Reunited at last.'

W. EDWARDS AND E. COOPER

Near Langemarck, 16 August 1917

By the second week of August, the village of Langemarck had all but ceased to exist. A single devastating bombardment had reduced it to a smudge of brickdust on the muddy crest of Pilckem Ridge. Virtually the only structures visible from the line of shell-holes strung along the east bank of the Steenbeek were the sinister-looking concrete blockhouses which appeared to defy destruction. The pattern of pillboxes presented a formidable barrier which the men of the 20th (Light) Division would have to overcome on 16 August if they were to carry the line beyond Langemarck. It was a difficult operation made infinitely worse by the state of the ground. In the autumn of 1914, the fields around about the village had been the scene of 'Die Kindermord von Ypren', the fearful slaughter of young volunteer German soldiers who advanced singing to their deaths. Almost three years on, this dreadful killing ground had become a wasteland.

The task of taking Langemarck fell to the 61st Brigade. The assault battalions, the 7th King's Own Yorkshire Light Infantry and the 7th Somerset Light Infantry, had taken up positions in the shell-holes that gashed the forward slopes of Pilckem ridge. The whole area was little more than a bog. On the left the leading companies of the 7th KOYLI found themselves separated by a miniature lake 30yd wide.

Despite the conditions, the attack went in as planned at 4.45 am. Maj. J.T. Janson, acting CO, wrote: 'The barrage was splendid, and the men moved forward in excellent order, though apparently rather thin on the right.' The first objective, to be taken by C and D Companies, lay short of the village. There they were to wait before advancing towards the second objective, through the grounds of a ruined château, to consolidate a line 300yd east of Langemarck with the 7th Duke of Cornwall's Light Infantry leap-frogging to the final objective. Initially, all went well, but as the 7th KOYLI neared their first objective along a slight rise, they were bracketed by fire from three large strongpoints at Reitres Farm, the devastated railway station, and Au Bon Gîte, scene of Ivor Rees' VC action the previous month.

Advancing behind the leading waves, Major Janson found the centre of the attack bogged down in front of Reitres Farm. Moments later, the adjutant was mortally wounded. Small parties were trying to get forward, particularly on the left, but he observed that 'men were dropping all round'. By then, the 7th DCLI had closed up on the Yorkshiremen, but could do nothing except take shelter in congested shell-holes. They were still 100yd short of the first objective, yet already the 7th KOYLI had lost almost half its strength, including all its leading company officers save one. Then, after a delay of about 15 minutes, the firing from Reitres Farm suddenly ceased and Janson saw a large crowd milling round the pillbox. Prisoners were being marshalled and one of them, an officer, could not stop talking about the remarkable courage of a lone British soldier who had single-handedly forced the surrender of his position. If such a man had been German, he claimed, he would have been given an immediate Iron Cross.

The soldier concerned was Pte Wilfrid Edwards, a 24-year-old Leeds collier, and in the fullness of time his action would indeed be rewarded, thus fulfilling a promise he made to his wife that he would bring back a medal. Edwards had gone into action as company runner and orderly to 2/Lt A.C.H. Robinson. His company advanced with two platoons, a third acting as a mopper-up, but the ground and enemy fire resulted in Robinson's command splintering. Early on, Edwards saw his young subaltern wounded. He later recorded:

When that occurred I carried on on my own, as I did not know where my company was. Two or three of my colleagues were with me and we came to the concrete forts. We did not expect any opposition, but we got heavy machine-gun fire from them. We had then lost all our officers, and the attacking party were about to dig themselves in as it was thought impossible to take the forts at the time. I wanted to go forward, and I heard someone say that it meant certain death to go by myself. However, I went forward, and when I got to the fort a German officer fired point blank at me and missed me. I threw three bombs into the fort, and the German officer asked me to climb into it through the loophole. I declined the offer, and after more bombing the German officer surrendered with all his men – 30 in number – except the man that was firing the machine-gun. The German officer ordered the soldier to cease firing, and when he refused to do so I brought him out with the aid of my rifle. The German officer handed over his revolver to me, and subsequently I brought the machine-gun out of the fort. After they had surrendered there was a great deal of talk in the German language, which I do not understand, but something was said by the German officer about the Iron Cross ... Before I set out to the forts the officers of the Duke of Cornwall's Light Infantry said that it was impossible to take them, but I remembered that the 'Koylis' had never lost a trench yet or failed to take their objective, so I went forward ... I had no business to be there at all.

I should have been in the rear, being an officer's servant. When my officer got wounded I should have gone back with him to the dressing station, but he would not let me. He sent me forward, saying that men were needed ...

Pte W. Edwards

Edwards insisted that he was inspired to act by seeing so many of his officers and men killed or wounded. 'I went forth determined to do all I could to get my own back,' he declared. It was an exploit snatched from the pages of *Boys' Own* magazine. After bombing the pillbox he 'sprang on the top of the wall of the fort'. Shortly afterwards, the garrison surrendered, and Edwards recalled: 'I then shouted to my comrades, "Come on, Koylies, we've got them".' It was a feat confirmed by Maj. Janson and many others who recalled seeing him wave the line forward.

Edwards, however, was mistaken on one point. 2/Lt Robinson had not gone back to the dressing station. When Janson reached Reitres Farm, Robinson was still in action and, as the only surviving officer, was ordered to take charge of the forward troops. Robinson was later awarded a DSO for what Janson called his 'splendid example'. At considerable cost – B Company was reduced to twenty-six men in taking the first objective – the 7th KOYLI accomplished its mission, capturing around seventy prisoners, twelve machine-guns, including four from Reitres Farm, and three 4.2in howitzers, abandoned with a dugout full of ammunition.

Private Edwards' spectacular day's work, however, was not over. During the consolidation, he had a narrow escape while entering one of the German dugouts. He recalled: 'I heard someone say, "There is a German in there," and then he fired. He nearly gave me a wooden cross instead of the one that I have got ...' Edwards spent the rest of the day dodging shells, delivering messages to Brigade HQ and guiding reinforcements forward. When his battalion was eventually relieved, it was he, appropriately, who led them safely out of the line.

The experiences of the 60th Brigade units on the right bore a marked similarity to those of the 61st. Their job was to clear enemy strongpoints on the south-eastern fringes of Langemarck, with the 6th Ox. and Bucks. Light Infantry leading and 6th King's Shropshire Light Infantry and 12th King's Royal Rifle Corps following through to seize the final objectives. The first objective near Alouette Farm was reached with little difficulty, but then occurred the familiar log-jam as pillboxes checked the advance. Among those pinned down was 21-year-old Ned Cooper, of No. 1 Platoon, A Company, 12th KRRC.

Three years earlier, he had lied about his age to enlist. Now he was a sergeant of a few months under the command of a young subaltern straight from university and facing his first battle. Cooper had sought to assist as far as possible, advising what dispositions to make on the start line to avoid the enemy's counter-barrage. His suggestions paid off handsomely, enabling his platoon to reach the first objective with few casualties. But then the attack ground to a halt. Cooper recorded:

> We found that the battalion supposed to make good our positions had failed to advance far enough to clear these pillboxes that were standing in our way ... They were held up and we were held up on top of them. There were men all over the place. No cover. If anybody moved they provoked fire from the Germans.

Almost immediately, the 12th KRRC began to lose men. The CO, Acting Lt-Col R.H. Prioleau MC, was hit. Cooper's subaltern was killed together with another officer. Many others were wounded. Word went back for the adjutant, Temporary Capt. T. Lycett, to take command.

The main enemy position was a concrete blockhouse about 250yd away, set in a ruined farmhouse. Its two machine-guns appeared to cover the whole area but Cooper was not convinced. Picking up his officer's revolver and maps, he gathered a small party and set about putting his own plan into effect. More than fifty years later, he recounted:

> I could see that he was firing at an angle; that if I were at a certain point he couldn't fire at me, and instead of going straight at him I went across his flank and got out of the range of the machine-gun. I then found myself on a road. I had set off with four men, but I finished up on my own ... [a lance-corporal who had followed him was wounded as they reached the blockhouse and I was making good progress. I ran forward and got behind the blockhouse and instead of doing what I should have done, put a couple of bombs in and then ask them to surrender, I called them to surrender first, and I was patiently waiting for the first man to come out ...

But Cooper had failed to notice there were two entrances, and while he covered one with a revolver he had never used before, the first German emerged from the other, behind him:

When I turned round and saw this German I was that terrified ... I pointed it [the revolver] at him and the damned thing went off ... The Germans rushed back into the blockhouse and I had to start all over. So I decided that I would put the revolver in my belt and rely on my rifle and bayonet. I called on them again to surrender and eventually the next man [came] out. I was just standing near the opening and as he passed I just cuffed him across the ears and kicked him up the pants. I didn't realise what I was doing at that time. But then all the others came out and, to my surprise, there was [sic] forty-five prisoners and seven machine-guns ... Instead of taking them out of the front of the blockhouse, I kept them at the back where the Germans could see what was happening. That was a fatal mistake. I lined them up and waved my men forward ... and before we could get them moving again the Germans had opened up on us and killed several of their own men and wounded two or three of my own men.

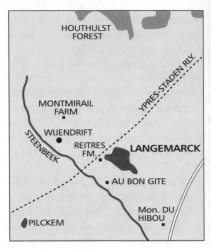

The Langemarck battlefield, 16 August

Cooper got his men under cover and ordered the prisoners to pick up the wounded and carry them to the rear. He was preparing to resume his advance when Capt. Lycett arrived on the scene:

I had just moved away from the blockhouse and I was ... in my wrong line of advance. I should have been going half right and I was going half left because this blockhouse was out of my territory ... We had lost connection with the barrage and the adjutant was giving me a ticking-off on the battlefield in front of my own men who were having a real joke about it. They were laughing their heads off ... In retaliation, I said 'Well, I've just captured this blockhouse. There's seven machine-guns there and forty-five prisoners.' He said, 'What?' I repeated it, and he said, 'Where are the prisoners?' And I said, 'There they are, just marching down.' He never said a word. He went off after the prisoners to see if there were any officers among them who could give them any information ... and he put me on my right line of advance and off we went.

His platoon by then reduced to fifteen to twenty men, Cooper pushed on to the next enemy position, where two prisoners were taken and he was almost knocked out by one of his own men's grenades. They eventually reached the final objective and dug in. Later, a German counter-attack recaptured a nearby trench, but Cooper's party appeared to escape detection. They clung on until some signallers reached them with orders to support a renewed attack by the 12th Rifle Brigade to retake the lost trench. In the ensuing struggle, Cooper was almost killed when a shell from the covering barrage landed nearby. Although half-buried, he managed to extricate himself and one other man, but a third was suffocated.

Some days after coming out of the line, the units of the 60th Brigade were paraded for a presentation of medals by the divisional commander. After the investiture, Cooper was called to the front. The general complimented him on his bravery, and then told him he had received a complaint about his behaviour.

> I didn't know what to expect ... He said, 'The German officer who you captured at this blockhouse complains that he was cuffed across the ears and kicked up the pants by a British sergeant, and he objected as an officer of the Kaiser's army at such treatment' ... I told the general what had happened. He said, 'Pity. He should have been the first man out, shouldn't he, Cooper? He'd have been dead now.'

Cooper knew nothing of his VC recommendation until he arrived at King's Cross station on his way home on leave. 'I accidentally knocked a newspaper on to the floor,' he recalled. 'It opened out and there was an account about nine new VCs and I was surprised to see my name among them.' The list also included the award to Wilfrid Edwards. Both men, in remarkably similar situations, had rescued the advance at critical junctures. More unusually, both had survived to experience contrasting reactions from their vanquished enemies.

Hailed as Leeds' fifth VC winner of the war, Wilfrid Edwards was born on 16 February 1893. Some accounts suggest he was born in Norwich, although research has failed to find any evidence to support this. Certainly he spent most of his childhood in Leeds and his parents both died before he won his VC. Educated at Park Lane Council School, he left at the age of 13 to learn the trade of tailoring. But in the summer of 1914, following a slump in business, he took a job at the Waterloo Main Colliery.

Together with ten colleagues, he enlisted as a private (No. 13303) in the King's Own Yorkshire Light Infantry on 4 September 1914. On 20 February

1915 he married Belinda Timlin, and the following August proceeded to France. Wounded in October 1915, he was evacuated to England and spent several weeks in Hoddleston Military Hospital before returning to the front in February 1916. Five months later, he was wounded again and sent to a hospital in Colchester. He eventually rejoined his unit in January 1917 and continued to serve with them until his VC action at Langemarck on 16 August. According to one account, he had been recommended for a decoration for his bravery on the Somme before being wounded a second time.

Following his exploit at Reitres Farm, he received a card from his commanding officer congratulating him on his 'fine behaviour' in capturing three officers and thirty men. But frustration grew as the days passed without news of any medal. On 5 September he wrote to his wife:

Men in my battalion keep getting honours, but I have not heard a word about mine. The officer tells me that I shall have to wait for my honour, as it will have to pass through a lot of hands before it is settled. The officers have congratulated me upon my work, and one has presented me with a watch. Other officers have promised me something, so I look like being well off when I come home.

Nine days later his Victoria Cross was announced. At 27 Harry Crescent, South Accommodation Road, Edwards' wife, a munitions worker, was besieged by reporters, but insisted she knew no details of the action. 'You see,' she said, 'my husband is a quiet, homely fellow, and in his letters to me he has had very little to say about his deed.'

Shortly after, Edwards returned to England, and his wife joined him for his Victoria Cross investiture at Buckingham Palace on 26 September. Two days later, Victoria Square in Leeds was packed with people hoping to greet him. Civic leaders took it in turn to hail his achievement and the celebrations rolled on into the early hours with Edwards being driven home through flag-bedecked streets. The rest of his leave was a whirl of engagements. On 10 October he was handed a cheque for £200 raised by public subscription, together with a framed photograph and a day later he received a rousing reception at his old school where he collected an inscribed silver watch.

Before the year was out, Edwards was back in Leeds, prior to undergoing officers' training. In December, together with Pte W. Boynton Butler, a West Yorkshire Regiment VC, he was entertained at the town tall. The following July, the former tailor was commissioned as a second lieutenant in the 4th KOYLI.

Demobilised in June 1919, he settled back into the relative anonymity of civilian life in Leeds and little is recorded of his later years. He enlisted in the Army again at the outbreak of the Second World War and rose to the rank of major, although he did not serve overseas. In 1950 he was made a Freeman of the City of Leeds and, throughout his life, he continued to take great pride in his former regiment. The last surviving KOYLI holder of the Victoria Cross, Wilfrid Edwards died on 4 January 1972, aged 78, and was buried with military honours in Oldfield Lane cemetery, Wortley, Leeds. A bugler from the 2nd Battalion, Light Infantry, sounded the Last Post. His medals were bequeathed to the Castle Museum, York, and they are now on loan to the KOYLI Museum in Doncaster.

Edward Cooper was born at Portrack, Stockton-on-Tees, on 4 May 1896, the sixth of nine children to William Edward Cooper, a steelworker, and his wife Anne (née Mackay). He attended Bailey Street Board School, leaving at 13 to work as an errand boy for his uncle who ran a butcher's shop. At 14, he joined the local Co-operative Society as an assistant on a cart selling fruit around the town. Two years later, he took charge of his own cart.

At the outbreak of war, the Army having commandeered most of the Co-Op's horses, Cooper, who was by then 18, found himself without a job. On 7 September 1914 he enlisted in the Army. Although initially rejected as being too young, he returned, 'advanced' his age by a year and was accepted into the King's Royal Rifle Corps, having been attracted by their green uniform and black buttons. Posted to the 12th Battalion, he was sent to a tented camp near Bisley, and for the first six months underwent training without the uniform he coveted.

He went to France in July 1915, and fought at Loos, the Somme and in the Ypres salient. Prior to being awarded the VC, he had had only one spell of home leave, and that was on compassionate grounds to attend the funeral of one of his sisters. Described as a 'conscientious, good-living lad, who loves his home', Cooper was also remarkably self-effacing. Although he had sent his parents the congratulatory card he received from Maj. Gen. W. Douglas Smith after the Battle of Langemarck, he made no mention of his action. 'He would never do that,' his mother later explained. 'He would be too much afraid anyone would make a fuss about it.'

When he arrived at Stockton station, he was mobbed by friends, relatives and crowds of well-wishers. The Mayor of Stockton led the civic welcome, and Cooper was granted an additional five days' leave in order to receive his medal from King George V at Buckingham Palace on 26 September.

Cooper was later awarded the Médaille Militaire by the French Government (*London Gazette*, June 1918), apparently for rescuing wounded men under shell-fire. Cooper, however, was less certain. He once confessed: 'Everyone makes a song and dance about the French decoration. I have no idea why it was awarded to me. Perhaps it was for the same action, but I honestly do not know.'

He rejoined his unit in time to take part in the fighting at Cambrai in November 1917, but was later posted back to England for officers' training. Commissioned second lieutenant on 25 June 1918, he rejoined the battalion on 4 September and served with them to the end of the war. Demobilised on 27 January 1919, he married Iris Kate Morris whom he had courted by letter since 1917, and returned to work for the Stockton Co-operative Society. In 1926 he moved to Sunderland as warehouse manager, returning to Stockton in 1938 as fruit department manager, a position he held until retirement in 1961. He served in the Home Guard during the Second World War, being promoted to major in command of the Thornaby G Company.

Sgt E. Cooper

During his long life, he took on many civic and private duties. He served for twenty years as a justice of the peace, but his chief interests were helping church, youth and ex-service organisations. An active president of the Thornaby branch of the Royal British Legion, he was also secretary of the Soldiers', Sailors' and Airmen's Families Association and attended every Armistice Day ceremony from 1918 until his death except one, which he missed owing to ill health.

A deeply committed Christian, he served as a Sunday school teacher, superintendent, deacon and elder of the United Reformed Church over a period of forty-five years. Ned Cooper never missed a reunion of VC holders, and took great pride in his honour, despite being, at times, somewhat bemused by all the adulation. Even in his 80s, with his sight failing, people would still approach him in the street and salute him. 'I become very embarrassed,' he admitted. 'I return the compliment, but I don't know who they are.'

He lived long enough to see his valour permanently recognised by the people of Stockton. On the sixtieth anniversary of his VC action, he attended the unveiling of a bronze commemorative plaque in the town's library. Eight years later, on 24 July 1985, he was made a Freeman of the Borough of Stockton-on-Tees. Only a fortnight later, this true 'Queen's man' and a gentleman of unfailing courtesy suffered a heart attack. He was taken to the North Tees Hospital, where he died on 19 August. He was 89, and at that time was the senior holder of the Victoria Cross in Britain.

His medals were presented on permanent loan to the Green Dragon Museum in Stockton on the seventy-fifth anniversary of his investiture at Buckingham Palace. Today the Cooper Room in Stockton's Masonic Hall and a Royal British Legion sheltered housing development at Seaton Carew near Hartlepool honour the memory of the last survivor of the sixty-one men who won their Crosses during the Passchendaele campaign.

W.H. GRIMBALDESTON
AND J.K. SKINNER
Near Wijdendrift, 16 August 1917

At 4.35 am on 16 August flares streaked through the mist blanketing the shell-pitted swamp east of the Steenbeek. If the weary German defenders manning the blockhouses and shell-holes north of the Ypres–Staden railway were showing signs of nervousness, they had good reason. Ten minutes later the jittery pyrotechnical display was swallowed in the storm of fire that heralded the British barrage.

The 29th Division's advance marked the northern limits of the British assault over ground described as 'the worst patch of the battlefield'. Their objective was to roll back the enemy between the Steenbeek and the Broembeek, a leap of about a mile. It involved overcoming a defensive system built around a screen of pillboxes, the most significant of which lay along the Wijdendrift–Langemarck road and around Montmirail Farm.

The assault waves had been waiting on the start line east of the Steenbeek for two days in appalling conditions. The 1st King's Own Scottish Borderers had suffered seventy-six casualties, mostly from the effects of mustard gas. Now the survivors, tired, cold and wet through, set off over the 'quaking morass', as one observer called it, towards the enemy blockhouses. The 1st KOSB, right leading unit of the 87th Brigade, attacked on a 400yd front with D Company on the left and B Company on the right, charged with securing the first objective beyond the ruins of Wijdendrift and Denain Farm. Close behind followed A Company on the left and C on the right with orders to take the second objective.

Protected by the barrage, the KOSBs made ground easily early on. Then came the first check. A pillbox on B Company's left was holding out resolutely. With the way forward raked by fire, it seemed as though only a direct shell hit on the pillbox could prevent the attack stalling. Acting CQMS William Grimbaldeston, a 27-year-old Lancastrian, was less pessimistic. He felt certain the strongpoint could be stormed and despite a slight wound urged his officer to let him try. Permission was granted, but his appeal for volunteers fell on deaf ears. Undaunted, Grimbaldeston, armed only with a rifle and a grenade, set off in the hope others might follow, but only one man crawled after him. With a shower of rifle grenades providing a desultory diversion, he pressed on. Approaching the pillbox from the flank, he crept round the back to the unguarded entrance where his presence, grenade held aloft, was sufficient to undermine the garrison's resolution. The firing ceased and, one by one, the enemy marched out. There were thirty-six in all and they left behind six machine-guns and a trench mortar. No one, it appeared, was more surprised than the gallant Grimbaldeston, who admitted: 'I never knew there were so many men in the place.' Colossal bluff or not, it was only as a result of his 'extraordinary courage and boldness' that the Borderers were able to continue their advance to the first objective.

A 20-minute pause followed while the barrage ranged on the enemy positions, and then A and C Companies headed off. Almost immediately, A Company was enfiladed by machine-guns. This was the signal for the day's second single-handed feat of daring carried out by another outstanding NCO, Acting CSM Jock Skinner DCM. A battle-hardened regular bearing the scars of more than seventeen years' soldiering, stretching back to the Boer War, Skinner was already a legendary figure in the 1st KOSBs. A veteran of the retreat from Mons, he had survived Gallipoli and the Somme, acquiring a fighting reputation second to none.

In an account of the fight around Montmirail Farm, Skinner's company commander, Captain Currie, wrote:

We met with strong opposition during our attack, three blockhouses especially giving a great deal of trouble, and holding us up on the left flank. The French having failed to move, my company's left flank was 'in the air'. At this time I had only one officer besides myself [one officer, 2/Lt Murray, and most of the NCOs having been either killed or wounded]. The three blockhouses were spitting out a terrific fire, and we were obliged to take cover and move gradually forward by squads in quick rushes. At this period Company Sergeant-Major Skinner and I crawled as near to the blockhouses as possible, and succeeded in disabling two of their guns by rifle fire. Company Sergeant-Major Skinner, after we had got within 70 yards of the blockhouses, crawled forward on his own initiative, while I covered his advance with my rifle. After 10 minutes he succeeded in reaching that on the extreme left, and going round the back of it bombed the team of gunners with Mills bombs and compelled the garrison to surrender. The second blockhouse he put out of action by inserting bombs in the loopholes where the guns were mounted. By this time I had passed orders for the company to advance, and we succeeded in reaching the third blockhouse, though only after suffering heavy casualties. Company Sergeant-Major Skinner's haul was six machine-guns, about sixty prisoners, and a few [two] trench mortars. This feat he performed practically single-handed, and it was at his own special request that I allowed him to attempt what appeared to be a hopeless task.

At no time did Skinner's supporting party amount to more than half a dozen men. More remarkable was the fact that the attack was carried out after he had been wounded in the head – the eighth of his career. Largely as a result of his sustained heroism, A Company reached their objective despite heavy losses. By 9.10 am the 1st KOSBs reported the second line secured, allowing the 1st Borders to complete the 87th Brigade's advance into the Broembeek swamp. On the right the 88th Brigade's attack met with similar success and the day ended with the 29th Division in firm control of a muddy swath of the Steenbeek Valley.

In a letter written to the KOSBs' CO, Sir Beauvoir de Lisle, GOC 29th Division, described the attack as 'the most successful we ever had'. He continued: 'The regiment did very good work, and I have recommended two for VCs – Grimbaldeston and Skinner. But for the fine spirit shown by your fellows, the SWB would not have been able to get on. No doubt you heard we got up to the whole of our line in scheduled time and held it – the only division that did so in both armies.' Less than a month later, the *London Gazette* of 14 September announced the awards of Victoria Crosses to CSM Skinner and Acting CQMS Grimbaldeston. The French also gave each of them the Croix de Guerre.

One of the greatest front-line soldiers of the war, John Kendrick Skinner was born at 76 Henderson Street, Glasgow, on 5 February 1883, the third son of Walter Skinner and his wife Mary (née Kendrick). His father, a tailor, originally came from Inver, in Ross-shire. He had four children by his first marriage and three sons and three daughters by his second to Barbara Grieve. The family moved to the suburb of Langside, but tragedy struck in 1889 when Skinner's mother died of consumption. Three years later, they moved to Pollokshields, a fashionable area of Glasgow, and his father commuted to his tailoring business.

Educated at Queen's Park School, Melville Street School and Allan Glen's Secondary School, Skinner gained a reputation as a tearaway, with frequent brushes with authority. A noted footballer, he worked for a short time with G.&J. Weir Ltd, pump and valve makers, but his heart was not in factory work. At least once, and possibly twice, he ran away from home and joined the Hamilton Militia, giving a false age. The first time his father bought him out, but when, aged 16, he enlisted in the King's Own Scottish Borderers on Boxing Day 1899, his father accepted defeat.

After training at Berwick, he was posted to the 1st Battalion. Skinner served through the remainder of the Boer War, receiving three wound stripes. When the unit returned home in December 1902, he was drafted to the 2nd Battalion, joining them in Allahabad where he was promoted lance-corporal the following February. The next twelve years were spent in a variety of imperial outposts, including three years in Aden, followed by spells in Glasgow and Dublin. Promotion was slow. He was made corporal in November 1905, but it was almost ten years before he gained his third stripe.

A/CSM J. Skinner

The 2nd KOSBs went overseas in August 1914 and Skinner, a member of D Company, fought at Mons and in the subsequent retreat. He gave early evidence of his courage. Near Missy, on the Aisne, in September, he and an officer stole a motor launch and two rowing boats from under the Germans' noses. The following month he was again in the thick of things. On 12 October, near Cuinchy, he led a daring reconnaissance of enemy positions which resulted in the award of a DCM. The citation noted his 'conspicuous gallantry and ability'. He was wounded two days later and evacuated to England. After a spell with the 3rd (Reserve) Battalion at Portland, he rejoined the 2nd Battalion on 16 March 1915, and was wounded for the second time during the fighting on Mauser Ridge near Ypres on 28 April. Evacuated again, he received his DCM from King George V at an open-air investiture on Glasgow Green three weeks later.

Shortly afterwards he joined a draft bound for the 1st Battalion, serving as part of the 29th Division at Gallipoli. The party sailed on 30 June and that same day Skinner was made acting sergeant. Five days after his arrival, his substantive promotion came through. When the peninsula was evacuated, the 1st KOSBs spent two months in Egypt, being shipped to France in time for the Somme offensive. On the opening day of the attack, he was wounded yet again after what his unit historian described as 'magnificent work, cheering on the RIF [Royal Inniskilling Fusiliers] from the parapet'.

There seemed no limit to his gallantry. By October 1916 he was back at the front with the 1st KOSBs, and the following June he was made acting CSM of A Company. After recovering from the wound received at Wijdendrift, he was sent home on leave to be fêted. Even his old school, where the staff had once despaired of him, hailed him as 'their hero'. On 26 September he was one of eight VC winners, six of whom had won their Crosses during the Ypres campaign, who received their awards from

King George V on the forecourt of Buckingham Palace. Three days later, Skinner married Annie Lee, a clerk, in Glasgow, giving as his address his father's home, 263 Maxwell Road. Jock Skinner was idolised by his family. A bright, cheery character, he was cynical of the way the authorities sought to lionise him and preferred to spend his time at home. A nephew, John Ireland, stated: 'From all accounts, he was glad to get away from all the fuss. He used to have races with the children in the family, and the local kids and dogs would all join in. He was quite an athlete and even with a staggered start, he would go charging past them.' His fame, however, did not prevent him once, while out of uniform, being handed a white feather.

Skinner was not particularly religious, but his family would remember that during his last leave he took an unusually keen interest in a framed print of Christ which seemed to have disappeared. He appeared unusually morose and given to spells of introversion. There was a suggestion that he might have had some premonition of his fate. More likely, it was born of frustration at being denied the chance to rejoin his comrades.

He had been wounded five times since the outbreak of war, and there were clearly those who felt he had done enough. Instead of returning to France, he was posted to the 3rd KOSB, a regimental training battalion, stationed in Duddington Park near Edinburgh. It proved a short attachment. In November, apparently without orders, he decided to return to France under his own steam. He got as far as Folkestone, where he was stopped and sent to Bevan Military Hospital to await further instructions. From there, on 23 November, he wrote to his friend, Sgt Adam Drylie:

There are enough loafers here without me. I am having a fine time but I am not contented and if something does not happen soon I won't be responsible. Give me the old crowd and that will suit me fine, where there are no swankers and everyone is on the same footing – Old Fritz included. I did not enjoy it when I was on leave. In fact I did not belong to myself but to the public, so if you come in for decoration have your own leave at the Red Blind. You will get more peace.

Eventually, he was issued with a travel warrant for Edinburgh, but he had had enough. He still had a return leave form in his pocket and used it to board a ship bound for France. Shortly afterwards a surprised GOC of the 29th Division stumbled across him during an inspection. Having explained how he 'chanced his arm', Skinner concluded: 'Besides, sir, I have a bit of a bet on with Sergeant Ross, who has been wounded eight times, as to who might get the ninth wound.'

A few weeks later, the 1st KOSBs returned to the salient. On 16 March 1918 they were manning the firing line on Bellevue spur, barely 5 miles from the scene of Skinner's VC action. Some time that day, Skinner himself crawled out to recover personal belongings and identification discs from three bodies. 'Their folks will like to hear they got a decent burial,' he said. The following day, a wounded man, lost during a night patrol, was heard calling out from no-man's-land. Once again, Skinner went out. Moments later, a shot rang out and Jock Skinner VC, DCM, Croix de Guerre, fell. A gallant stretcher-bearer who went out after him was also killed. Some of his friends brought his body in and, ignoring rules that specified the dead were to be buried near the trenches, carried him 17 miles to the rest area at Vlamertinghe. There, in pouring rain, one of the most remarkable funerals ever witnessed on the Western Front took place with six VC holders from the 29th Division – including James Ockendon, William Grimbaldeston, Joseph Lister and John Molyneux – acting as pallbearers.

Writing of Jock Skinner twenty-one years later, Sir Beauvoir de Lisle described him as 'the bravest man I met in a war won by brave men'.

Blackburn's first Victoria Cross winner of the war, William Henry Grimbaldeston was born in Hickory Street on 19 September 1889, the eldest son of Thomas and Isabella Grimbaldeston. One of ten children, he was educated at St Alban's School until the age of 13 when he left to start work as a weaver at the Ciceley Street Mill. During the next twelve years he was employed in a number of mills, including Cherry Tree Mill and Messrs Greenwood Bros Ltd's Rockford Mill, where he was working when war broke out.

A noted boxer, who appeared in amateur contests at the Palace Theatre, Grimbaldeston also won trophies as a weightlifter and athlete. Prior to the war he regularly attended the YMCA gymnasium, and served for a time as a gunner in the 1st East Lancashire Brigade, Royal Field Artillery (TF). He was a fine marksman and was appointed an officer's orderly. Grimbaldeston enlisted as a private (No. 13531) in the King's Own Scottish Borderers on 3 September 1914. Perhaps as a result of his military experience, he was rapidly promoted. By July 1915, when he sailed for France with the 7th (Service) Battalion, KOSB, he was already a sergeant.

Wounded at Loos, on 25 September Grimbaldeston nevertheless led his section into the enemy's trenches after all his officers had become casualties. At one point he noticed that a comrade's clothing had ignited and he beat out the flames with his bare hands. It was during this action that one of the battalion's pipers, Daniel Laidlaw, won a famous VC for playing the men over the top. The 7th KOSBs had performed heroically in their first major action, but at heavy cost. Grimbaldeston was one of 675 casualties. Evacuated to England, he spent six months in hospital, where the injuries to his left hand necessitated the amputation of a finger. Recovering from his wound, he returned to Blackburn and married Sarah Ellen Woodcock at Chapel Street congregational church.

Transferred to the 1st KOSBs, he joined his new unit in France in September 1916. Promoted acting CQMS, Grimbaldeston went through the 1917 fighting unscathed until Wijdendrift. Having survived his near-suicidal assault on the enemy pillbox, he was put out of action the following day during a gas bombardment. Evacuated to England, he was being treated in Warrington's White Cross Hospital when his VC was announced. To his mother, he wrote:

> It has often struck me what a lot of things have happened about September. It must be my lucky month. I enlisted in September, came home in September, went out again in September, and am in hospital again in September. Next September the war will be finished, mark my words. This winter will put the hat on Fritz. He was all out last winter.

Although time would prove this prediction wrong, his good fortune continued. Allowed out of hospital to receive his VC from King George V on 20 October, Grimbaldeston and his wife were caught up in a Zeppelin raid on London on the eve of his investiture. Grimbaldeston returned home on 11 January 1918 to be showered with gifts. Accorded a civic reception twelve days later, he received a cheque for £200 raised from public subscription and an illuminated address decorated with the town's coat of arms and his regimental crest.

Demobilised on 19 January 1919, he took a job as a clerk with the Blackburn Employment Exchange. A few months later, he became Keeper of the New Public Halls in Northgate, a job involving the ceremonial role as the town's mace bearer for which his tall, commanding bearing was well suited. In 1937 he resigned and became a porter at the Trustees Savings Bank in Lord Street West. By the late 1940s, he had begun to suffer poor health, attributed to the gas poisoning in the aftermath of the fighting near the Steenbeek. He retired in 1949 at the age of 60. A shy, retiring man, he had close ties with ex-service organisations, becoming chairman of the 15th (Scottish) Division Old Comrades Association (South of the Border Branch). He was also a leading Freemason, holding the rank of Provincial Grand Sword Bearer.

William Grimbaldeston collapsed and died at his home in Bold Street, Blackburn, on 13 August 1959. He had just taken a glass of water to his semi-invalid wife and had gone downstairs to fetch some milk. His funeral service at Pleasington crematorium resounded with echoes of his military service. A piper played the lament *Flowers of the Forest* and his old regimental march was played as mourners left the chapel.

A little over a year later, on the forty-third anniversary of the attack at Wijdendrift, Grimbaldeston's son presented his medals to the King's Own Scottish Borderers for display in the unit's Berwick museum. Today he is remembered in Blackburn alongside the town's three other VC winners – James Pitts, Percy T. Dean and John Schofield – on a memorial plaque in the town tall unveiled on Armistice Day 1956, the centenary year of the Victoria Cross.

J. CARMICHAEL

Imperial Avenue, near Hill 60,
8 September 1917

The transfer of command from Gough to Sir Herbert Plumer, the Second Army commander, at the end of August marked a sea-change in the conduct of operations. Grand ambitions born of wild optimism and an inflated opinion of British strength gave way to a more pragmatic approach. Plumer, the architect of the Messines Ridge success, planned an altogether more cautious advance. It would consist of four separate attacks, to be carried out at roughly six-day intervals, each limited step intended to push the British lines forward approximately 1,500yd until the whole of the Gheluvelt plateau was captured.

The key element was to be one of the heaviest concentrations of artillery enjoyed by any attacking force throughout the war. Under Plumer's direction, the guns would dictate almost every aspect of the fighting, controlling the rate of progress by means of a complex system of creeping barrages designed as much to shield the infantry as to subdue strongpoints, and limiting the extent of the advance to the range at which the field artillery could break up enemy counter-attacks. The plan placed heavy logistical demands on the engineers. During early September the ground approaching the front line came to resemble a vast construction site. Thousands of men were set to work, repairing roads, bridging streams and digging assembly trenches and gun pits. Generally fine weather and a drying wind proved useful allies. None the less, it was a wearisome and costly business, carried out mostly under cover of darkness and frequently under fire. During the first two weeks of September, more than 10,000 casualties were suffered, the overwhelming majority of them among units toiling near the front.

One such unit was the 9th North Staffordshires, pioneer battalion of the 37th Division. As part of the preparations for the new offensive, A Company was excavating a new communication trench, grandly known as Imperial Avenue, near the notorious Hill 60, scene of much bitter fighting two years earlier. Now, the struggle had moved eastwards, leaving its battered, man-made slopes 3,000yd behind the lines. It was in this unlikely setting that an act of sublime gallantry would result in one of the most unusual Victoria Cross actions of the war.

On 8 September work was continuing under the supervision of Sgt John Carmichael, a Scot from Airdrie whose civilian occupation as a quarryman made him peculiarly well suited to the job in hand. The arduous task the men faced that day was two-fold: to revet the walls of the freshly dug section of trench with wooden boards, sheets of corrugated iron and specially designed frames, and to carry on extending the line. Years later, while being interviewed for Lyn Macdonald's ground-breaking study of the campaign, *They Called It Passchendaele,* he recalled:

We had men working in the trench and men working outside of it as well. One of the chaps was deepening the trench when his spade struck an unexploded grenade, just lodged there in the side of the trench, and it started to fizz. I was an instructor in bombing so, knowing a bit about explosives, I knew that there would be seven seconds before it went off unless I did something. I couldn't throw it out, because there were men working outside the trench as well as the blokes in it. So I shouted at them to get clear and I had some idea of smothering it, to get the thing covered, keep it down until they were out of range. All I had was my steel helmet. So I took it off my head, put it over the grenade as it was fizzing away, and I stood on it. It was the only way to do it. There was no thought of bravery or anything like that. I was there with the men to do the job, and that's what mattered.

Instinctive or not, it was an act of extraordinary gallantry which should, by rights, have resulted in certain death. Instead, he survived, although grievously injured. Carmichael had no memory of what followed the explosion: 'They tell me it blew me right out of the trench, but I don't remember that. The next thing I remember is being carried away.'

According to the terse entry in the 9th North Staffordshires' war diary, Carmichael's injuries were dismissed as a 'fractured ankle and wounds'. In fact, both his legs had been shattered and his right arm slightly injured. He was unconscious most of the way back to No. 53 Casualty Clearing Station at Bailleul, 9 miles away, and he had little recollection of the first few days there. But if Carmichael's mind was understandably fuzzy about what happened, his comrades were in no doubt. That only one other man from A Company was wounded in Imperial Avenue was due entirely to Carmichael's quickness of thought and action.

'This splendid act of resource and self-sacrifice', as the VC recommendation would describe it, struck a chord with private soldier and general alike. The steady flow of visitors to Carmichael's bedside was led by his divisional commander, Maj.-Gen. H. Bruce Williams. Carmichael later recounted:

> They'd put me in clean pyjamas, and he patted me on the shoulder and called me 'my boy' and then he told me about the medal. I suppose I was pleased, but I've never been more surprised. And I was more pleased yet when my platoon came – the whole lot of them. I don't know how they did it, managing to come together, but they came into the ward and they lined up at the foot of the bed and every one of them saluted me. Oh, I was embarrassed, but it was a great feeling. It was good of them. They said I'd saved their lives, but I was there and I was in charge of them. I didn't think I was doing anything extraordinary.

The Victoria Cross to No. 34795 Sgt John Carmichael was gazetted on 17 October 1917.

John Carmichael was born in Glenmavis, a small village near Airdrie, in Lanarkshire, on 1 April 1893. His father, a quarryman, had moved from near Oban in the western Highlands, and when John left school he found work with his father in the local quarry.

When war broke out, he volunteered to join a locally raised unit of Royal Engineers. Months of training followed and, seeing little prospect of action, he applied to join an infantry unit. Posted to the 8th Sherwood Foresters, his wish for action was quickly granted. With his new unit, he took part in the fighting around Loos during the autumn of 1915, and on Vimy Ridge and the Somme the following year. In early 1917 he was transferred to the 9th North Staffordshires, a pioneer battalion, presumably on account of his civilian experience.

As a result of the terrible injuries he suffered in winning his VC, Carmichael saw no further active service. He spent two years in a Liverpool hospital before returning to Airdrie and a hero's welcome. The proud citizens raised £1,000 in recognition of his bravery. He invested the money in a small chicken farm in nearby New Monkland before branching out into public transport. This proved a successful venture. From one bus, his Highland bus company grew into a fleet of forty, operating between Airdrie and Helensburgh on the Clyde and northwards to Kilsyth in Stirlingshire. Throughout, he managed not only to maintain his agricultural interests but also to expand them, taking on two farms.

It was mark both of the man and his remarkable recovery that when Britain was threatened with invasion in 1940, he enlisted once again, serving as a lieutenant in the Lanarkshire Home Guard.

Despite work pressures, he played an active role in local ex-servicemen's organisations. He was president of the Coatbridge branch of the Royal British Legion and regularly attended functions of his old regiment until advancing years made travelling too difficult. His last regimental gathering was in 1969, when a memorial plaque was dedicated in Burslem to Sgt John Baskeyfield, who won a posthumous VC at Arnhem in 1944. Two years earlier, Carmichael had sold his bus company and retired.

Incredibly, for a man whose chances of survival had appeared infinitesimal sixty years earlier, he lived to the grand old age of 84. John Carmichael, the last surviving North Staffordshire Regiment VC, died at his New Monkland home on Boxing Day 1977. He was buried near New Monkland parish church with full military honours, a piper from the 1st Royal Highland Fusiliers leading mourners from the church, through the village to the graveside where a firing party and bugler from the 1st Staffordshire Regiment paid a last tribute.

Six weeks later, his widow, Margaret Lockhart Aitken, collapsed and died. The couple had been married for forty-seven years. Carmichael's medals were bequeathed to his former regiment, being handed over by his sister in May 1978, in a simple ceremony held in the Drill Hall at Airdrie. Writing of him, a regimental colleague recorded:

John Carmichael was a man of great strength of character and absolute integrity, who well deserved the success in life which he achieved after his return home from his war service. A lesser man might never have completely overcome the after effects of the severe injuries he had received ... Of a kindly disposition, modest and unassuming, he deservedly earned the respect of all who knew him.

J. MOYNEY AND
T. WOODCOCK

Ney Copse, 13–16 September 1917

By September the Broembeek resembled more a sluit than a stream. Shell-holes straddled its marshy banks and the waist-deep water was thick with clinging mud and a clutter of barbed wire. The fighting had washed over the narrow waterway leaving a trail of devastation in its wake. A land of woods, copses, farms, mills and tree-fringed roads all bore mute testimony to the ferocity of the conflict. The Broembeek cut through the northern sector of the Ypres front, between Wijdendrift and the southern edge of Houthulst Forest. For the most part it scribbled a gently curving line through no-man's-land, but in places it traced an unfortunate course between a scattering of advanced posts and the main British line. Such was the case on the extreme left, where the British and French lines fused. A cluster of isolated posts formed a fragile toehold on the east bank between Ney Copse and Ney Wood within 100yd of the enemy.

Its weakness was obvious. To Maj. R.H. Ferguson, CO of the 2nd Irish Guards, whose unit took over the position on 12 September, it was not merely 'tactically wrong' but courted disaster: 'This position on the east of the Broembeek could easily be cut off by the enemy as the line of the stream gives a definite barrage line, and if any rain set in the strong wooden bridge [would] be the only means of crossing ...' Yet despite his misgivings, he complied with his orders and six platoons, consisting of the whole of No. 2 Company and two from No. 3 Company, moved out. They had to negotiate a 30yd stretch of swamp on the west bank before crossing the bridge and picking their way along duckboards at the western corner of Ney Copse to reach the ragged line of unprotected craters.

The platoons, some divided among neighbouring posts, were distributed roughly according to their companies, with the men of No. 2 Company, under Lt B.O.D. Manning, occupying the right as far as Ney Wood, and the two platoons of No. 3 Company, led by Lt Smith, taking the positions in Ney Copse. Within Ney Copse, two advanced posts were occupied by a platoon led by L/Sgt Jack Moyney, a 22-year-old from Queen's County, Ireland, with orders 'not to withdraw unless completely surrounded, and not to eat their iron rations'.

Their unmolested stay east of the Broembeek lasted barely 3 hours. At 2.45 am on 13 September the sky was scorched red by a ferocious bombardment directed at them. About 25 minutes later, the barrage lifted and came down on the opposite bank, rolling westwards to engulf the main front line. In that instant, a force of Württemberg Sturmtruppen, clad in body armour and estimated at company strength, attempted to rush the guardsmen who were still reeling from the barrage. The heaviest blow fell on the right, against the divided platoons of No. 2 Company. The unit war diary recorded:

> Lt Manning, on the southern edge of Ney Wood, was surrounded and it is presumed either taken prisoner or killed. The barrage had blown the posts to pieces and the raiding party endeavoured to account for the survivors. All our posts south of Ney Copse were either blown up or bombed.

When the barrage fell, Capt. W.A. Redmond, OC No. 2 Company, was visiting his posts. Taking shelter in the nearest one, No. 6 post, he withdrew when that was hit, eventually forming a block near Ney Copse where he resisted all attacks. Two hours after the initial bombardment, the embattled east bank erupted again as enemy artillery covered the Württembergers' withdrawal. The Irish Guards had lost more than eighty men either dead, wounded or made prisoners, while the fate of others in Ney Copse was unclear. It was a reverse made yet more galling by having been foreseen. But the sorry saga did not end there. After sanctioning the abandonment of the remaining posts and a withdrawal of the main line to a new position, a patrol was sent across the Broembeek with orders to bring in casualties, cover the withdrawal of posts still holding out in Ney Copse and reconnoitre the enemy positions. All did not go well. The unit's historian noted: 'By a series of errors and misapprehensions Ney Copse was not thoroughly searched and one platoon of No. 3 Company was left behind.' This was L/Sgt Moyney's platoon. They had not been seen since the early hours of 13 September.

By the time the mistake was realised it was too light to risk another patrol. The missing platoon's plight appeared hopeless. Heavy shelling bracketed the whole sector, to be followed by a retaliatory bombardment directed against what were 'delicately called our "discarded posts"'. That night another patrol was despatched to assess the enemy's strength. It reported them in firm control of both river crossings and the duckboard path running into Ney Copse.

On 15 September the exhausted men of the battalion learned they were to be relieved the following day. But at about 4.30 am on 16 September, a bombardment shook the front line. Somewhere around Montmirail Farm, an SOS rocket was seen. Minutes later, Battalion HQ was rocked by a direct hit. As more SOS rockets shot into the sky, the rattle of machine-guns started. A wire arrived from Brigade HQ warning of an impending attack. Hardly had the news been digested than the enemy fire slackened, only to be replaced by British shelling.

The guns were still roaring when, at 6.30 am, Battalion HQ was startled by the appearance of L/Sgt Moyney, together with the remnants of his 'lost' platoon, who marched in 'tired, very hungry, but otherwise in perfect order'. The story of their stubborn defiance and daring escape was to become a regimental legend.

Moyney's platoon had been divided between two posts on the southern edge of Ney Copse. He took charge of one with fifteen men. The other post was commanded by Cpl Fitzgerald. According to the war diary:

Early on the morning of the 13th they were cut off by the big raid of the Sturm-Truppen, who established a machine-gun post between them and the Broembeek. Although his men had only 48 hours' rations and one water bottle each, Sgt Moyney kept them in their post for 96 hours, not even allowing them to touch their iron rations.

Thoughts of surrender did not enter Moyney's head:

I was trained not to withdraw, so I didn't. We were in that corner for four days ... being shelled by both the British and the Germans, and we had nothing to eat or drink, but we wouldn't get back. The Germans attacked on the fifth [sic] morning. They knew we were there, but they didn't know what strength we were in, because every time they'd send over a plane we'd fire at it, and they were afraid to come down too low. If they'd known how weak we were, they could have taken us in no time.

The 2nd Irish Guards' war diary assessed the strength of the German raiding force at about 250 men; they were opposed by fewer than thirty guardsmen:

Cpl Fitzgerald kept his men in their shell-hole and [he] has not since been seen, but Sgt Moyney, after allowing the enemy to approach within 25yd, ordered his party to jump out and attack him. The Lewis gun came into action on the flank and fired three whole drums before it was put out of action, while the remainder of the party emptied four boxes of bombs into the enemy at close quarters. Sgt Moyney then gave the order to charge through the Germans to the Broembeek.

Moyney added more details of the fight:

> We had two Lewis guns and twelve dozen hand grenades and I warned the lads not to shoot until I gave the order. When they attacked, we saw them coming ... and we gave them a shower of bombs. We must have killed about 150. They attacked a second time and we gave them the same. Now all our ammunition was running short. Our Lewis guns had been knocked out by German grenades, so I gave the lads the order to retreat to the bank of the river.
>
> Just as we got there, the Germans were closing in on us from both sides. I had two bombs, one in each hand, and I threw one right and one left, and that baulked them. Then the British artillery opened up. They put a barrage down and it saved our lives. But by the holy, that shellfire was coming down.

Reaching the stream, Moyney, assisted by Pte Tom Woodcock, covered the withdrawal with rifle and Lewis gun. The small party was pelted with machine-gun fire and grenades as they waded waist-deep through slime and a tangle of barbed wire. Moyney and Woodcock hung on until the enemy were almost on them, and then made a dash for it. Woodcock was halfway up the mushy west bank when he heard cries for help behind him. The war diary recorded:

> He at once turned round, ran down to the stream, and, in spite of a shower of bombs and machine-gun bullets, waded into the water and lifted out Pte Hilley, whose thigh was broken. He then carried him up the slope and deposited him in safety close to Craonne Farm.

The sound of the platoon's fight and its sudden appearance was initially misinterpreted as an enemy attack, hence the SOS rocket. But what might have proved a tragic error proved fortunate as the signal drew a curtain of artillery fire on the east bank, enabling Moyney's platoon to emerge virtually unscathed.

That night the battalion marched out of the line. Before reaching camp, they suffered two more casualties, bringing their losses for the five-day tour to three officers and 166 men dead, wounded or missing. It had been a wretched few days relieved only by the splendid courage of Moyney and Woodcock. As soon as they were out of the line, Moyney and his men toasted their good fortune with a round of beer.

A month later there was cause for further celebration when the *London Gazette* of 17 October announced the rare award of two Victoria Crosses to men from the same platoon for the same action – No. 7708 L/Sgt John

Moyney and No. 8387 Pte Thomas Woodcock. Moyney was astonished by the honour: 'I would sooner [have] thought I was going to Australia than winning the VC.' He explained:

> I don't really think I deserved to win the VC – I just did what I was trained to do. We never even thought of dying while we were trapped. After all, we were trained soldiers and we knew what we were involved in.

His company commander disagreed. Capt. D.W. Gunston, who had 'strongly recommended' Moyney for the highest award, stated: 'He was a very brave platoon sergeant and I think he was one of the best VCs of the war.'

Thomas Woodcock was born in Belvoir Street, Wigan, on 19 March 1888, the eldest son of Henry Woodcock, a colliery worker at the Arley mine. One of a large family, Woodcock, whose mother died some years before the war, was educated at St Patrick's Roman Catholic School. He followed his father into the mines, taking a job as a pit-boy at the John Scowcroft Colliery, Hindley Green, where he was later joined by his brothers Henry and Joseph.

By 1914 he was living at 2 Teck Street, Wigan. The nature of his work meant he was exempt from military service, but, together with some friends from the Hardybutts district, he enlisted in the Irish Guards on 26 May 1915. After five months' training, he proceeded to France with the 2nd Battalion.

A married man with three children, he was fêted as the first man from the Wigan Borough to be awarded the VC. His homecoming on 27 February 1918, was the signal for widespread celebrations. The modest hero, by then a lance-corporal, was showered with gifts at a special reception in the Wigan Pavilion. They included a marble clock, an illuminated address and more than £200 raised by public subscription.

On 9 March, together with his platoon sergeant Jack Moyney, Tom Woodcock went to Buckingham Palace to receive his VC from King George V. It was the proudest moment of a life that had almost run its course. His leave ended on 17 March with a special reception staged by the parishioners of St Patrick's church, Wigan, where he declared: 'I am going back tonight, to do a little bit more for the King.' He rejoined his unit in time for his 30th birthday, shortly before the Germans launched their Spring Offensive. In the days that followed, the Guards Division suffered heavy losses, struggling to stem the enemy advance. But no death would be more greatly mourned than that of L/Cpl Tom Woodcock VC, who was killed near Bullecourt on 30 March.

First reports of his death were greeted with disbelief. Eventually, official confirmation arrived, together with a pathetic parcel for his widow. It contained a blood-stained newspaper and a photograph of her husband, surrounded by his family and civic dignitaries. The picture was less than a month old. Woodcock was buried in Douchy-les-Ayette British cemetery, France. His headstone, erroneously giving his age as 29, carries the proud epitaph: 'First My God, Then My Country.'

John Moyney was born at Rathdowney, Queen's County, Ireland, on 8 January 1895, the son of James and Bridget Moyney (née Butler). His childhood was a hard one. His family was large and extremely poor. Moyney left school without qualifications to seek work on a local farm.

When he walked into the Army recruiting office at Maryborough to enlist in the Irish Guards on 6 April 1915, he gave his employment as labourer. He was 20, single and living with his father at Ballycolid, Rathdowney. Why he enlisted is debatable. Years later, he stated: 'I joined up to see a bit of life. There were posters all over showing a father shaking hands with his two sons saying, "Goodbye lads. I wish I was young enough to go with you." That poster put the idea in my mind.' But a report filed with his army papers gives a different reason. Dated 19 July 1915, it was written by an officer of the Royal Irish Constabulary, in reply to Moyney's application to be considered as a police candidate after completing his army service. It declared:

> I do not consider the above-named a suitable candidate for the Royal Irish Constabulary. He joined the Irish Guards because he had seduced a young girl named Bowe of Moore Street, Rathdowney. Apart from this his people are of such a low class that the prestige of the Constabulary would be very much lowered in the eyes of the public, especially the local Constabulary. His brother is married to the Barrack servant at Rathdowney.

Nevertheless Moyney, who was only 5ft 7in tall, proved a sound if unexceptional recruit. His record showed him to be 'good' on parade, 'average' at gymnastics, and 'fair' at field works and musketry. But it was as a front-line soldier that he made his mark. Posted to No. 5 Company, 2nd Irish Guards, he arrived in France in October 1915. He was appointed lance-corporal (unpaid) the following February and made corporal, unpaid lance-sergeant, on 18 September 1916. Moyney was not alone in preferring trench life to the dull round of working parties which characterised so many spells out of the line.

L/Sgt J. Moyney and Pte T. Woodcock

The regular loss of friends was approached fatalistically. 'There was nothing you could do,' he once said. 'You'd expect to go next any way. It was all in a day's work.' But Moyney seemed to bear a charmed life. Once, during a heavy bombardment on the Somme, he had a narrow escape after being buried alive. 'It's an awful sensation,' he recalled, 'like you're going down a draw well. It's a devil on the nerves. And oh the smell of the cordite. Oh, it was shocking …'

By the late summer of 1917 Moyney was a lance-sergeant in No. 3 Company, under the command of Capt. Gunston, who regarded him as one of his most dependable NCOs. It was a view borne out by Moyney's performance at Ney Copse and on 27 November 1917, almost six weeks after the announcement of his VC, he was made sergeant.

The following February he went home on leave, during which he received his award. The high point of his young life, however, was to be tarnished by an episode that would result in his dramatic fall from grace. Together with Tom Woodcock VC, Moyney was due back with his unit on 20 March. But he never arrived. He was missing for almost six weeks, during which time Woodcock was killed. When he turned up, he was charged with having been absent without leave while on active service from 20 March until 2 May 1918. Convicted by a Field General Court Martial on 13 June 1918, he was sentenced to be reduced to the ranks, a punishment confirmed by the GOC, 4th Guards Brigade. The barest outline of his misconduct was noted on his record. But no reason was given. His papers contain no details of the court martial and he made no reference to the episode in any of his subsequent interviews. It seems reasonable, however, to assume his actions were linked to his marriage on 17 March to Bridget Carroll, at Roscrea.

Moyney served the rest of the war as a guardsman. But his misdemeanour did not prevent him receiving a second gallantry award, the French Médaille Militaire (*London Gazette*, 10 October 1918).

After a short spell with the British Army of Occupation in Cologne, Guardsman Jack Moyney VC was demobbed and transferred to the Army Reserve on 4 June 1919. He returned to Roscrea and an uncertain future. He had no job, his wife had given birth to his first child the previous January and the country was ravaged by civil war. Like many ex-servicemen he felt betrayed by a government which failed to deliver a land fit for heroes. Several comrades swelled the ranks of the IRA, but he refused. 'Sure it was they who trained the IRA,' he later stated. 'And why wouldn't you feel bitter: after fighting for the British, they send over the Black and Tans and start killing your people.'

In 1920 he joined the Great Southern Railway as a porter at Roscrea. As his family grew to six children, he was plagued by money worries. In October 1921 he appealed to his old regiment to support his case for a pension, complaining that his treatment had been 'very unfair'. He spoke of being 'troubled by pains' which prevented him working constantly. His claims to have suffered a severe bout of trench fever were investigated and resulted in the award of a 20 per cent disability pension. His financial problems, however, worsened. His service file is littered with a succession of pathetic appeals. Support came from the Irish Guards' Regimental Charitable Fund, but it was not enough. By 1927 the Rosecrea branch of the British Legion reported: 'He now requires clothing and boots and applies to your charitable fund.' Thomas Shaw MP was angered by his shabby treatment, writing in 1929:

> His job is an all-weather one and it only requires a bad cold to put him out of action owing to his gas troubles. This man cannot actually be described as a necessitous case, but I consider that it is an example of the circumstances of many of our VC heroes.

Moyney's affairs were in a parlous state. The British Legion of Ireland declared: 'He owes a large sum of money for groceries, etc, to various traders whose accounts he is unable to meet in view of his small income and his large family.' The VC Remembrance Fund, via Capt. Alfred Pollard VC, MC, DCM, sought to help, but Moyney's old regiment was growing wary of bailing him out. The officer responsible for administering aid noted:

> Moyney has already had more than his share from my funds. I can provide nothing, as my funds are so low, but if you will put up a concrete suggestion as regards the payment of Moyney's debts I will endeavour

to help to a small extent, provided Moyney is made to understand clearly that it must be an absolutely final award as far as my funds are concerned.

Pollard complied. But his suggestion that help might be given to find Moyney a better paid job which would allow him to settle his debts with assistance from his old regiment was not to the liking of the officer in charge of the Irish Guards' fund, who replied in exasperation:

> I am very much afraid that Moyney is a hopeless case. He has had every chance. I have already assisted him to the extent of £20 and cannot make any further grant. Moyney, or rather his wife, does not want to come to this country. Knowing, as I do, what an improvident person Moyney is, I should be very sorry to recommend him for a job.

Despite everything, Moyney maintained a close association with his old regiment. During the Second World War, his only son was among many southern Irishmen who enlisted in the Irish Guards. He served in North Africa and was taken prisoner in Italy.

Jack Moyney retired as head porter at Roscrea station in 1960 after forty years on the railways. A lifelong member of the British Legion, he attended the Garden Party staged at Buckingham Palace for members of the VC and GC Association in 1962 and was a frequent visitor to his regiment's St Patrick's Day parades. He was also a devout Catholic who raised thousands of pounds to help poor boys study for the priesthood. Described in old age as a 'fit, bright-eyed man', he was a familiar figure in Roscrea, cycling each week to the local post office to collect his pension well into his 80s. The last surviving Irish VC winner of the First World War, he passed away on 10 November 1980, aged 85. His most valuable possessions, his hard-won row of medals, were bequeathed to the Irish Guards.

Shortly before his death, in a typically candid interview, he recounted his harrowing experiences on the Western Front. His abiding memory was of Passchendaele – 'an awful joint altogether'.

F. BIRKS AND R.R. INWOOD

Glencourse and Polygon Woods,
20–21 September 1917

Dawn on 20 September was wreathed in mist. At 5.36 am, as the first streaks of red glowed dimly through the murk, flares curved up from the enemy lines opposite the centre of the 1st Anzac Corps. A minute later came the unmistakable sound of German field guns ranging against the northern flank. The bombardment rumbled on until 5.40 am, when it was swallowed by the deafening roar which heralded the opening of what would become known as the Battle of the Menin Road, the first stage of Plumer's stepping-stone offensive.

Nine divisions had been given the task of capturing the strongpoints and woods on the Gheluvelt plateau which had defied Gough's Fifth Army throughout August. The tangled remains of Nonne Boschen, Glencourse Wood, Inverness Copse, Polygon Wood and Tower Hamlets were studded with pillboxes and fortified farms occupied by men from six divisions. The main thrust was directed either side of the Menin Road, with the British 23rd and 41st Divisions to the south and the Australian 1st and 2nd Divisions to the north. All were fresh to the fighting. Overnight downpours had turned the dusty ground to slippery mud in places, but the mist and swirling smoke thrown up by the bombardment helped the assaulting waves take many enemy outposts by surprise.

At Glencourse Wood the 6th Battalion, lead unit of the 2nd Brigade (1st Australian Division), used grenades and phosphorous bombs to great effect, hastening many surrenders. Senior officers had expected the debris in the wood to hamper the advance. But it wasn't so, although the Australians did not have things all their own way. Out of the mist, darts of fire shot from pillboxes near the wood's southern edge. One machine-gun sent the men of the 6th Battalion scurrying for cover. Confusion ensued as the attack spluttered and stalled.

Sizing up the situation, 2/Lt Fred Birks, the 23-year-old commander of No. 16 Platoon, D Company, sprinted towards the blockhouse, pursued by Cpl W. Johnston. Dodging the stabbing fire, they neared the concrete walls to be met by a shower of bombs. Johnston fell, badly wounded, but

Birks, an officer for less than five months who had won a Military Medal as a stretcher-bearer, reached the rear of the pillbox. According to Charles Bean, the official Australian historian, 'the garrison, seeing the rest of the line advancing, surrendered' to him. But the citation accompanying his award of the Victoria Cross stated that Birks 'killed the remainder of the enemy occupying the position and captured a machine gun'. Whatever the uncertainties, it is beyond dispute that he eliminated the strongpoint. He then gathered a small party and led them against another pillbox. For a second time that day his courageous tactics triumphed. From a garrison of twenty-five men, sixteen were captured and the remainder killed or wounded.

Despite the delays, the first objective, east of Glencourse, was reached on time at around 6 am. During consolidation, Birks busied himself reorganising men who had lost touch with their units. The confusion can be surmised from a message he sent at 7 am. In it he noted that '5, 7 and 8th Bn are retiring in disorder' and that the newly captured position was being shelled by 'our artillery'. His strength was estimated at thirty-nine men. Although in contact with No. 15 Platoon from A Company on the right, there was no sign of anyone on the left. Throughout this difficult period, Birks was a tower of strength. In the words of his corps commander, Lt-Gen. William Birdwood, 'his splendid bravery and coolness inspired his men with confidence'.

Skirting the northern edge of Glencourse Wood, the 10th Battalion (3rd Brigade), had had a more difficult time from German shelling. Nevertheless, the attack went in on time. The South Australians, many of them from Adelaide and Broken Hill, had been specially prepared for the operation. Two companies of hand-picked men led the advance with a mopping-up company and a carrying company following. As the third wave, their task was to take the final objective, cutting through Polygon Wood. Their first encounter with enemy pillboxes came in a sunken road bordering Glencourse Wood. After reaching the Red Line, there was a 45-minute pause before a renewal of the bombardment signalled the next stage of the attack. According to the Australian official historian, the 12th Battalion leading, and the 10th Battalion following, encountered little resistance. Most pillboxes surrendered without a fight. The old enemy trench line had all but vanished and Polygon Wood, stretching before them, was reduced to a stubble of sapling stacks scarcely breast high.

It was during this phase, in one of the few contested pillbox captures, that Pte Roy Inwood embarked on a series of astonishing actions, culminating in the award of his VC. Impatient to get to grips with the enemy, he moved forward alone through the barrage to an enemy strongpoint and captured it, together with nine prisoners, leaving several enemy dead.

With the Blue Line captured, the 10th waited 2 hours to resume the advance. Despite being hampered by pillboxes in front of the start line and numerous 'shorts' from the supporting barrage, the attack carried all before it. By 11.25 am the Australians were in control of the Green Line and preparing for counter-attacks. Throughout the afternoon parties of Germans were seen dribbling forward from higher ground in Polygon Wood known as the Butte, but any threatened movement was effectively answered by artillery fire. The night that followed was 'extraordinarily quiet' and while the enemy groped through the darkness to establish a new front the Australians probed deep into the wood. Among the brave individuals who left the Green Line to probe enemy positions was Pte Inwood, one of the 10th's leading scouts. He spent much of the night patrolling the disputed territory. Dodging enemy posts, he ventured 600yd into the wood and brought back details of the German dispositions in the vicinity of the Butte.

The next day dawned to the drumbeat of a fresh British barrage. This provoked a retaliatory bombardment which fell on the rear positions as far back as the Red Line which were being consolidated. Among many fatalities was Lt Birks. The 6th Battalion war diary tersely recorded:

From 04.30 (Stand To) until 05.39 our artillery put a stationary barrage in front of our forward lines in case the enemy were preparing for a counter-attack. The enemy replied vigorously to our artillery and shelled all our sector heavily. One shell-bursting in a post of D Company killed Lt Birks and four other ranks, and wounded two others.

It later transpired that Birks was killed while leading a desperate effort to rescue men buried by a shell-blast. Eyewitnesses stated that he had been 'standing exposed' to the shelling – a fact referred to by Gen. Birdwood, and stated in the recommendation, but strangely omitted from the VC citation. The barrage largely missed the Green Line occupied by the 10th Battalion. Some signs of enemy activity were, however, detected and a battery of Stokes mortars cleared a company of Germans out of shell-holes in front of the Australians. As a further precautionary measure, the 10th pushed out to establish new posts in front of the main line in Polygon Wood. It was during these early morning operations that Pte Inwood came once more to the fore. Together with an unidentified soldier from the 7th Battalion, he located a German machine-gun which was causing a number of casualties. Creeping behind the position, they bombed it, killing all but one of the team; they ordered the survivor to carry the gun back to their lines.

Seven days later, Inwood was promoted lance-corporal, a rank he had lost almost a year earlier for going absent without leave. The following month he was made corporal and then, on 26 November, came the announcement of his Victoria Cross for 'most conspicuous courage and devotion to duty'. Eighteen days earlier, the *London Gazette* had announced a posthumous award of the VC to 2/Lt Fred Birks. His repeated acts of gallantry during his first action as an infantry officer had made a deep impression on his comrades. A fellow officer wrote to his mother: 'I feel bound to him by reason of the glorious work he did and the magnificent courage he displayed under my eyes.'

Frederick Birks was born on 31 August 1894 at Buckley, in Flintshire, Wales, the third of seven children to Samuel and Mary Birks (née Williams). His father, who worked as a groom before becoming a collier, died in a mining accident in 1899 when Fred was 5. Educated at the St Matthew's Church School, he became a drummer in the Buckley Company of the Church Lads' Brigade. Years later, a boyhood friend, Edward Lloyd, remembered him as a 'naughty little devil, always full of beans'. They both worked as apprentices at the annealing plant in John Summers Steelworks, Shotton, where Fred was employed as a labourer and steel-roller man.

Despite being a committed Christian, Fred had a reputation as a high-spirited teenager. Lloyd recalled how they once called at a pub on their way home. Such was their youthful appearance, their order for beers was met with a row of lemonades. Fred reacted by pouring the drink over the land-lord before dashing out amid peals of laughter.

His decision to emigrate to Australia in 1913 was further evidence of his adventurous spirit. Together with two friends, Emrys Jones and Bill Gray, he left Buckley to make his fortune. His quest took him to Tasmania, South Australia and Victoria. He was working as a waiter in Melbourne when war broke out. Birks enlisted in the AIF on 18 August 1914, giving a false age, and was posted to the 2nd Field Ambulance, Australian Army Medical Corps. In fact, he was thirteen days short of his 20th birthday. He landed with his unit at Gallipoli on 25 April 1915, and was slightly wounded by shrapnel on 26 June while working as a stretcher-bearer. He returned to his unit the following day and remained at Anzac until 9 September.

He served in Egypt until March 1916 when the 1st Australian Division left for France. On 21 April Fred was promoted lance-corporal. He served through-out the Battle of the Somme and his bravery was marked by an immediate award of the Military Medal, promulgated on 14 September:

At Pozières, France, on the 26th July 1916, L/Cpl Birks continually led his squad of stretcher-bearers through Pozières Wood and village from

Pte R.R. Inwood

the front line, many of the Regimental stretcher-bearers being out of action. He was exposed to heavy shell fire the whole time.

Ten days later Fred was made temporary waggon orderly corporal, a promotion confirmed on 10 August. Later that year he returned to Buckley on leave. The following February he was selected for officer training. On 26 April 1917, he was appointed second lieutenant with the 6th Australian Infantry Battalion and joined his new unit on 12 May.

Birks, who was unmarried, was buried in Perth (Zillebeke) cemetery (plot 1, row G, grave 45). Among the personal items sent home to his mother was a Bible presented to him by fellow church-goers at Buckley. His elder brother Samuel, a sergeant in the Royal Field Artillery, returned from Italy to receive the VC from King George V at a Buckingham Palace investiture on 19 December 1917.

Fred Birks is remembered in both Wales and Australia. A stone obelisk in his honour stands in front of St Matthew's church. Originally sited in his old schoolyard, it was moved when the school was torn down. His name is also recorded on his parents' tombstone and on memorials inside the church. Meanwhile, a posthumously painted portrait hangs in the Australian War Memorial, in Canberra, and his Victoria Cross is displayed in the Hall of Valour. A fellow officer wrote of Birks:

> Freddie was a great chap, and so popular in the mess, and especially in the way of sport. I had the last Celebration of the Holy Communion with him a week before going into the line. He and I, whenever there was a Celebration, went together. He was a great Churchman, his faith so strong.

Reginald Roy Inwood, one of two brothers who distinguished themselves in the ranks of the 'Fighting 10th', was born in Adelaide, South Australia, on 14 July 1890, the eldest son of Edward and Mary Ann Inwood (née Minney). He was educated at North Adelaide Public School and Broken Hill Model School and was working as a miner when he enlisted at Railway Town, Broken Hill, on 24 August 1914. He was one of three brothers to serve in the AIF. Robert, a sergeant in the same battalion, was noted for his bravery at Rouge-de-Bout near Armentières on 6 June 1916, and was killed in action at Pozières on 24 July 1916, after taking part in a daring reconnaissance with Lt Arthur Blackburn, one of the actions for which the latter was awarded the Victoria Cross. Harold also served on the Western Front. He was wounded and returned to Australia in November 1917.

Roy Inwood was sent for training with the Broken Hill quota of recruits. Drafted into the original H Company, he proceeded with his unit to Egypt on 20 October. He took part in the landings at Gallipoli on 25 April, during which members of his unit made the day's farthest advance. Appointed lance-corporal in August 1915, he left the peninsula in September suffering from rheumatism and by April 1916 was serving with his battalion in France. Promoted temporary corporal in August, he was reduced to private two months later for absenting himself from a parade.

Having regained his corporal's stripes in the aftermath of his VC exploits, he was further promoted to sergeant. He remained with his battalion until 30 May 1918. Three months later he embarked for Australia. Returning to Broken Hill, he was given a hero's welcome. Flags flew from the station and civic buildings, and a party of returned soldiers formed a guard of honour. It was a reception far removed from the scenes which marred his departure in August 1914 when, according to one report, the new recruits were 'hooted by socialists and red-raggers'. Inwood could not resist remarking on the contrast when 'those mongrels were the first ... to shake me by the hand. If the boys stick together like they did in France there will be no Bolshevikism in this town ... I would like to be at one end of the street with a machine-gun and have them at the other end'.

His intemperate words provoked a heated debate in the House of Representatives, during which Inwood was accused of attempting to 'incite trouble between returned soldiers and the working classes'. Inwood left Broken Hill soon afterwards and moved to Adelaide. Demobilised on 12 December, he married a widow, Mabel Alice Collins (née Weber), on New

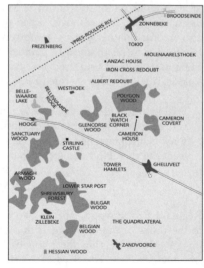

Southern sector of Menin Road battle, 20 September

Year's Eve. The transition to peace and civilian life proved difficult. He struggled to find work and his personal life was beset by trouble. In 1919 he was fined for assault and two years later his first marriage ended in divorce. Unable to settle, he moved to Queenstown, Tasmania, where he worked in a mine, and was then employed in a eucalyptus distillery on Kangaroo Island before returning to Adelaide, where he married Evelyn Owens in 1927. The following year he became an attendant with the city council, a job he held until his retirement in 1955.

During the Second World War, Inwood volunteered again, serving as a warrant officer in the Australian Military Forces. Tragedy struck with the death of his second wife, and in 1942 he married for a third time, to Louise Elizabeth Gates.

Described as 'a rugged independent, well-built man with the rough corners still on him', Inwood was a restless man who found peace in his later years. Perhaps as a result of his unhappy experiences in Broken Hill, he always maintained that 'his VC had not done him much good'. But his forceful opinions on the subject did not prevent him attending the celebrations in London in 1956, marking the centenary of the award's institution.

Roy Inwood died, aged 81, at Tara Private Hospital, St Peters, on 23 October 1971. His third wife had predeceased him. He was given a military funeral and buried in the AIF cemetery, West Terrace, Adelaide. His gravestone carried his unit colours and his army rank and number in recognition of the most outstanding period of his life. 'Lest We Forget' was the short but appropriate inscription.

Almost a year after his death, Inwood's VC was presented to the City of Adelaide by the 10th Battalion Club. Displayed in the Council Chamber until 1989, it was replaced by a replica amid concerns about security. But in 2005, following calls to pass the medal to the Australian War Memorial for display in its VC Gallery, it was decided to honour Inwood's dying wishes to keep his award in South Australia. Extra funds were provided to increase security and the Victoria Cross was returned to pride of place in the Chamber.

H. REYNOLDS AND
W.H. HEWITT

Near Frezenberg, 20 September 1917

The defences ranged against the 9th (Scottish) Division north of the Menin road were among the most formidable on the front. Twice in twenty-three days, the 15th Division had struggled in vain to capture and secure the miniature fortresses scattered across the open slopes to the east of the muddy waters of the Hanebeek and Steenbeek. The mutually supporting pillboxes and ruined farms, bristling with machine-guns, were sited in depth, and most had survived the storm of high-explosive rained on them. Opposite the South African Brigade lay the fortifications of Beck House, Borry Farm and Vampir Farm, and beyond them the defences of the Langemarck–Gheluvelt Line buttressed by the Bremen Redoubt and the strongholds of Zevenkote and Waterend Farm.

The 27th (Lowland) Brigade faced obstacles every bit as strong, from the machine-gun-infested Hanebeek Wood to the Ypres–Roulers railway line riddled with blockhouses. The position along the railway, slicing through the centre, was arguably the strongest defensive system of all. A row of five pillboxes formed a concrete chain straddling the earth banks which once carried the railway above the plain. Four pillboxes, numbered R1 to R4, were grouped on the southern side, with the nearest, R1, about 200yd from the front line. A fifth pillbox, R5, was sited on the northern side, 100yd beyond the first post. It in turn was flanked by a further blockhouse known as A1. Around 220yd beyond stood the fortified farm known as Potsdam to the British and Lindenhof to the Germans. The elaborate defences, sited to give flanking fire for the Bremen and Zonnebeke Redoubts, were linked by bunkers burrowed through the embankment.

The task of clearing the strongpoints fell to the 12th Royal Scots. They were under no illusions about the problems they faced. The last attempt to storm the position by their sister unit, the 13th Royal Scots, had collapsed in a welter of casualties without a single yard gained. In an effort to counter the danger posed by the pillboxes, new tactics were adopted. High-explosive and smoke shells would replace shrapnel in the creeping barrage and the attackers would divide into section columns with some enveloping individual block-houses while others pressed on. C Company, on the right, was to clear the line of blockhouses from R1 to R5. The task of seizing A1 and Potsdam fell to A Company, commanded by Capt. Harry Reynolds, a 34-year-old former member of the Northamptonshire Yeomanry who had been awarded the Military Cross a few months earlier.

By 3 am on 20 September the two companies were formed up ready to move off at 5.40 am. Steady rain had fallen overnight, and Lt-Col J.A.S. Ritson, the 12th Royal Scots' CO, grimly noted that the ground was 'frightfully cut up, very wet and the going very bad'. The attack suffered its first setback in front of R1, where the garrison made a tenacious defence, spraying C Company with fire as they struggled forward south of the railway. Ritson countered by sending up two platoons from D Company. Taking advantage of the distraction, the remnants of C Company leapt forward and captured the pillbox. Stubborn resistance from R2 was overcome and the capture of R5 effectively ended C Company's involvement. Of their remaining objectives, R3 had been pulverised by shells and R4 was 'full of water' and deserted.

Reynolds, leading the northern prong of the attack, was less fortunate. Both A1 and Potsdam were manned by garrisons determined to stand and fight. Moving forward in two lines of section columns, A Company followed close behind the creeping barrage. According to Col Ritson, their first target, the A1 blockhouse, 'was passed over'. Suddenly, in Ritson's words, 'it came to life again', causing a number of casualties and forcing the survivors into cover. With the attack stalled and his men reluctant to go on, Reynolds quickly gathered six men to cover him and attacked alone, darting from shell-hole to shell-hole under a galling fire.

Cpl Souter later recorded:

It was really a case of dodging death all the way. The enemy peppered him all the time ... Just when he was near enough, he threw a bomb, but it missed the entrance and the enemy then opened a furious fusilade on our brave officer. Captain Reynolds took cover in a shell-hole for a few minutes, but if the Germans thought they had done with him they were mistaken for he started crawling along towards the pillbox. The Huns put all their snipers on the job, and we could see the bullets striking against the stones ... Captain Reynolds wriggled and wormed his way towards the pillbox. Suddenly he rose to his feet. We saw his arm go up in the air. We also saw the enemy potting him and then we saw a great bright glare come from the pillbox. He had thrown in a 'devil's fire bomb' and set the place alight. Yells of rage came from the enemy in the fiery furnace ... and a party of them came rushing out. Captain Reynolds stood waiting to receive them with his revolver in his hand and one by one they surrendered.

Reynolds' own account, written on 25 September, was more succinct:

> In a 'Pillbox' immediately in front of POTSDAM, the garrison of eleven men was very stubborn. I got up to it and put five Mills and one smoke grenade through the loophole, setting the place on fire. This killed four men and the remainder surrendered. Two machine-guns were captured.

Col Ritson filled in some of the gaps. Noting that the loophole was cut in the side of the pillbox, he recorded that Reynolds' first attempt to capture the post was thwarted in unusual circumstances: '... when the Company Commander attempted to throw in a Mills grenade the enemy put a pack against the loophole, still keeping the gun going. Finding a hand grenade was no use, a smoke rifle grenade was pushed in.'

Incredibly, Reynolds was untouched. Brig. William Croft DSO declared: 'I saw his kit afterwards; every part of him was punctured with bullet holes – his clothes I mean, for the Almighty was merciful to Reynolds that day.' Reynolds wrote to his wife:

> My waist-belt on my equipment has got two bullet holes in it where the bullet passed along inside the belt and out again, another bullet has cut a brass buckle (cut one half of it right off and wedged it into the waist-belt). I am going to send you the pack, socks, sponge-bag and the buckle off my belt for a souvenir.

After the fall of A1, Reynolds turned his attention to Potsdam. While assessing the best method of attack, he was reinforced 'by nearly half a platoon of South African Infantry [who] came across to me saying they had lost their officer and would I take charge of them'. He agreed and shortly afterwards 'a SA Infy captain came along, wearing no equipment and appearing quite dazed'. Reynolds drafted the men into his force and issued orders for the attack. He planned to encircle the position before launching a frontal attack with one strengthened platoon. They moved to within 80yd of Potsdam when the barrage ceased. But just as they prepared to rush it, the shelling started again, forcing them to delay the assault. 'This appeared to give the defenders encouragement,' wrote Col Ritson, 'and they got their machine-guns going. There were two guns, both mounted outside, one just north of the pillboxes and one between the two northern ones.'

Despite heavy fire, 2/Lt E.H. Kerr, commanding No. 4 Platoon, reported that 'our grenadiers worked forward and fired rifle grenades at the garrison in

POTSDAM, who were throwing stick grenades in large quantities over the top of the pillboxes, so that we could not get near them'. The impasse lasted only until the shelling stopped. At that moment, Reynolds and his men charged and the fight was quickly over. 'The gunners were shot and the place rushed. The garrison then surrendered easily,' wrote Ritson. Approximately seventy men were killed, wounded or taken prisoner, together with two more machine-guns. A South African version of events, however, credited a mixed force, made up of men from the 3rd and 1st SA Infantry, led by Capt. Leslie Sprenger MC, with assisting in the capture of Potsdam, for which Sprenger later received a DSO.

While the battle raged around Potsdam, the South Africans on the left had forged ahead. Borry Farm and Beck House quickly fell and at 7 am, the supporting battalions, the 1st and 2nd South African Infantry, made their way forward to the second and third objectives. The 1st found the going easy, but the 2nd, on the extreme left of the 9th Division front, was forced to fight all the way under a terrific fire from machine-guns sited outside the divisional boundary. Among the men trying to keep pace with the barrage that morning was L/Cpl Billy Hewitt, a 33-year-old Suffolk-born farmer. His section had the job of capturing two pillboxes. The first was a small one, from which five Germans emerged to dash past Hewitt with their hands in the air. The second looked altogether different. In an account written thirty-five years later, Hewitt described the struggle:

We go a bit farther and then something seems to have happened as nobody is advancing any more; everyone seems to have got into shell-holes, so we do likewise, but before I've fairly got down, the platoon commander's runner says I'm wanted. I duck over and he says, 'That pillbox has got us in enfilade and is holding up the Australians [sic] on your left ... and we can't move this side. Go and take it.' I say 'Thanks for nothing,' or words to that effect, and duck back to my section – only to find disaster. A blasted shell had scored a direct hit and as far as I can see only Ziess is in one piece.

Well, there's no time to do anything for them so I make for the pillbox which has a sort of doorway low down on the right hand side. I heave a grenade down it and shout, 'Come out you so-and-so's'. They do, two of them and fire with rifles at me at about 10yd range, and miss. Then some stinkpot throws a jampot on a stick bomb which hits me on the chest and explodes. But the mutt who made it forgot to fill it with the odd bolts and nuts, so apart from blowing off my gasmask and half my clothes, knocking out four teeth, breaking my nose, giving me a couple of black eyes, with a lot of little cuts here and there and knocking me backwards into a convenient shell-hole, it didn't really do any damage – only made me damn mad.

You see I had become engaged to be married before I came out this time, and when I felt my teeth and face I thought that's spoilt my beauty. She won't fall for me any more … so rather gingerly I got up, picked up my rifle and made a dash for the back of the pillbox which was a real haven of refuge, as the barrage was away ahead and all was peace. I peered round the other side, and there was a jolly loophole with a machine-gun firing nineteen to the dozen.

I thought, this is where the old bomb comes in. I still had two, so as it looked easy, I lobbed one at the loophole; but it wasn't so easy as it looked and I missed and had to duck back behind the pillbox while it exploded. As I had only one bomb left I decided to make sure, so I crept right underneath, pulled out the pin, let the lever fly up, counted two and pushed it through the loophole. Some stinker shot me through the hand, but not too badly, and I heard the bomb explode and ran around to the door as I thought there would be some fun and games in that direction – there was.

You went down three steps inside that doorway, and as I was running in with rifle and bayonet at the ready a Hun was running out with his hands up. It was my first effort with a bayonet, and though I'd been told a hundred times 'if you can't pull your bayonet out, fire a round, that will do the trick', I forgot all about it and with my foot on the poor bloke, I was trying to pull it out when somebody grabbed me by the throat.

I got in a nice kick where I thought it would hurt him most … but then honestly I don't remember anything more till I was standing outside … looking at three Huns with their hands up and a sergeant coming out of the pillbox saying, 'There's fifteen in there, and they've all had it.'

Hewitt's injured hand was bandaged, then he retrieved his helmet from amid the shambles and set off in search of his company. He found them on the objective, but was ordered back to have his wounds treated. On the way, he was given a mug of rum. 'The effect on me was stupendous,' he wrote, 'and I was torn between going back and taking on the German army single-handed, and a desire for sleep.' His last recollection of the day's events was jolting away from the battlefield in an ambulance: 'I … went to sleep on the floor, and didn't wake until I felt somebody pulling at my ankle and heard a voice saying, "Lend a hand here Joe, here's another stiff one".'

In the days after the battle, Capt. Reynolds, aware that he had been recom-mended for the Victoria Cross, agonised over the award. On 30 September he wrote to his wife: 'I am anxious to know if it will be the VC or DSO that they will give me, don't mention it to a soul will you dear until I write and let you know which it is.' He did not have long to wait. On 8 November the *London Gazette* announced the award of the VC to Capt. Henry Reynolds 'for most conspicuous bravery'. Eighteen days later, a far-from-dead L/Cpl William Henry Hewitt learned that he had won the same honour.

Henry Reynolds was born at Whilton, near Daventry, in Northamptonshire, on 16 August 1883, the son of Thomas Henry Reynolds and Tryphena (née Godsden). Educated at Daventry Grammar School, Harry followed his father and grandfather into the family business as corn and coal merchants. He married Gwendolen Jones, of East Haddon, on 3 October 1905, and the couple had three children, Thomas Henry William, Gwendolen Tryphena and Velia Rosemary.

When war broke out, Harry was helping run the family business, which included a coal wharf at Long Buckby. He joined the Northamptonshire Yeomanry and was commissioned, being gazetted second lieutenant in the Royal Scots on 5 October 1914. During fighting around the chemical works north of Roeux, near Arras, he distinguished himself in the disastrous attack on Greenland Hill. The 12th Royal Scots lost more than 250 officers and men killed, wounded or missing, and Reynolds was awarded the Military Cross. The citation, gazetted in June 1917, read: 'For a series of actions on 12 April 1917, which meant being under artillery, machine-gun and rifle fire for a considerable time.'

Harry Reynolds was promoted lieutenant on 4 May and captain on 2 July. Following his VC action, he was honoured in Scotland and Northamptonshire. Granted the Freedom of Edinburgh, the Royal Scots' home base, and Northampton, he was also presented with a gold watch by General Lord Horne on behalf of the people of East Haddon, where his wife was brought up. Capt. Harry Reynolds was presented with his Victoria Cross by King George V at Buckingham Palace in June 1918.

After the war he served in the Loyal North Lancashire Regiment, having been recommended for a regular commission by Lt-Col Ritson, who wrote of him:

He is one of the most capable and conscientious officers that I have ever had under my command; he is attentive to every detail in connection with his company; has a sound knowledge of training and interior economy, and his company was always clean, smart, well-turned-out, thoroughly trained and efficient, and always willing and ready to take part in any action. Captain Reynolds is physically a powerful man, capable of standing any amount of strain, and his unusual sense of duty was so pronounced that in action he was invaluable.

Harry Reynolds served as Superintendent and Steward of the Sir Frederick Milner Homes, in Beckenham, Kent, from 1930 until his death, at Carshalton, Surrey, on 26 March 1948. He was buried in St Giles' churchyard, Ashtead, Surrey.

William Henry Hewitt was born at Copdock, near Ipswich in Suffolk, on 19 June 1884. Educated at Framlingham College (1894–1900), a private school which numbered Gordon Flowerdew VC and Augustus Agar VC, DSO, among its distinguished pupils, he immigrated to South Africa in 1905. He served for a year as a member of the South African Constabulary, a quasi-military organisation founded by Baden-Powell, and then transferred to the Natal Police. His three years' service included the period of the Zulu Rebellion.

A farmer in Natal at the outbreak of war, Billy Hewitt enlisted in the South African forces on 24 November 1915. Despite being a noted horseman (his uncle had won the Grand National), he entered an infantry unit, the 2nd SA Regiment, part of the 1st SA Brigade. He arrived in France in July 1916, and, a few days later received his baptism of fire at Delville Wood.

On 24 October, during the fighting around La Butte de Warlencourt, Hewitt, by then a Lewis gunner in No. 2 Platoon, B Company, was wounded in the leg and evacuated to England. While undergoing treatment at Tooting Hospital, he met his future wife, Lily Olett. Hewitt returned to his unit in April 1917. Shortly afterwards, as No. 1 in a Lewis gun section, he was promoted lance-corporal. Having recovered from the injuries sustained in capturing the pillbox during the battle north of the Menin Road, Hewitt was presented with his Victoria Cross by King George V at Buckingham Palace on 16 January 1918. Later commissioned, he ended the war as a second lieutenant.

L/Cpl W.H. Hewitt

In October 1918 he married his fiancée and after demobilisation the couple settled on his farm in Natal. They had four daughters, one of whom died in infancy. In 1925 the Hewitts moved to East Africa where they ran a coffee farm, called Aintree Farm in memory of his uncle's success. According to his daughter, Pam Colvin, the Kenyan venture was blighted by 'droughts, disease, locusts …

together with the depressingly low prices fetched for coffee crops'. Cheerful in the face of adversity, Billy Hewitt was running his own farm and managing others round about when the Second World War broke out. Enlisting again, he served as a military liaison officer and then as Assistant Provost Marshal in Mombasa, rising to the rank of major.

After the war, his health began to fail. In 1950 he retired to Hermanus, on the Cape coast, and five years later became a registered South African citizen. The following year, he attended the Victoria Cross centenary celebrations in London. By the end of the 1950s Hewitt could scarcely speak. When surgeons were eventually compelled to remove his larynx, they discovered pieces of shrapnel still embedded there. Not long afterwards, Hewitt was found to have contracted Parkinson's Disease. In 1961 his wife took him to Britain in search of an operation that might cure him. It proved a vain hope. Throughout his long periods of illness, Billy Hewitt showed great fortitude. Ian S. Uys, author of the standard work on South Africa's Victoria Cross holders, recorded:

A specialist once said to doctors at Hewitt's bedside, 'This brave man won the VC in World War I. If he can fight cheerfully the chronic stages of this terrible crippling disease, he'll deserve a Bar to that VC – and I know he will, won't you sir?' And he did. Although crippled, voiceless and finally completely helpless, Hewitt fought it without complaint.

His suffering ended on 7 December 1966, at Cheltenham. Some time afterwards, his widow presented his Victoria Cross to Framlingham College. Thousands of miles away, near their former seaside cottage at Hermanus, a bench was dedicated in his memory. A plaque on it states: 'In proud memory of Maj. W.H. Hewitt VC, 2nd South African Infantry 1884–1966 (he loved sitting here).'

As a young soldier, Billy Hewitt had been noted for his bluntness and bluff good humour. Such character traits were clearly evident in the short war memoir he compiled for his family. Recalling that momentous day near Frezenberg in September 1917, he wrote dismissively: 'On reading this through it seems a lot of tripe, and when one thinks of what thousands of others did, certainly not deserving of a VC.'

A.J. KNIGHT

Near Hubner Farm, 20 September 1917

The improved September weather had done little to improve the rain-saturated ground east of the Steenbeek. Trenches scarcely existed. Near Keerselare, a necklace of waterlogged shell-holes, linked here and there by shallow scrapings, formed the front line. To reach these posts meant a long trek over duckboard trails, mostly at night, frequently under shell-fire and always with the risk of men stumbling, sometimes fatally, into the deep morass. Progress was invariably slow and on 19–20 September it was even slower than usual as the men of the 2/8th London Regiment (2nd Post Office Rifles) slipped and slithered along boards made treacherous by rain. The tortuous journey involved negotiating a derelict tank, an ammunition train and scrambling over gaps cut by recent shelling. It was little wonder they reached their assembly positions 90 minutes late.

Ahead of them lay the western edge of the Gravenstafel spur, jutting out from the main Ypres ridge, studded with strongpoints and camouflaged machine-gun posts. The men of the 174th Brigade (58th Division), fully aware of the position's immense strength, had christened it Blunt Salient. Two recent raids had merely confirmed at considerable cost the thoroughness of the enemy planning in which pillboxes, fortified farms, shell-hole machine-gun nests and barbed wire had been welded into a veritable fortress barring the way. These operations, however, had one beneficial result. They convinced the staff that a direct attack could not succeed. Instead, the bold plan adopted involved a feint frontal assault with the main thrust being made on the flank, with three battalions advancing one behind the other south-eastwards up the spur before swinging right to take the fortifications in reverse. Leading the way would be twelve officers and 431 men of the 2nd Post Office Rifles. They were well prepared, having spent days thoroughly rehearsing the operation over a model of the ground. Each of four assault companies was assigned specific strongpoints to capture. Even individual platoons had clearly defined objectives.

The three officers and ninety-four men of B Company had the job of punching through Hubner Trench on their way to clearing two clusters of pillboxes around Hubner Farm. It was a daunting prospect. As zero hour approached, Sgt Alfred Knight was probably not alone in questioning his chances of survival. Years later, the powerfully built Nottingham postal worker recalled: 'I was thinking what could happen the next day – curious about the emotions of a condemned man the night before he takes the last walk.'

The attack went in at 5.40 am. Progress was initially slow owing to the 'very broken' state of the ground. Hubner Trench proved something of a misnomer, being merely a 'mass of shell holes, some half covered over with timber and camouflage'. In places, however, these posts, manned by handfuls of men with light machine-guns, offered stubborn resistance and had to be attacked individually. It was during these brutal contests that Sgt Knight showed his mettle. A report of B Company's assault recorded:

> In every instance they were dealt with either by shooting the gunners or rushing them with the bayonet. It was found, however, necessary to get up to 10yd of the barrage in order to rush these posts. In two instances a sergeant rushed through our barrage and bayoneted the gunners who were causing casualties with their fire. One particular instance is worthy of mention when this sergeant [Knight] rushed through our barrage to a post of 12 of the enemy, shot one, bayoneted two and scattered the rest, capturing the MG, all unaided.

Elsewhere, A Company, on the right, captured all of their objectives within 45 minutes, but not without heavy casualties. One platoon was reduced to five men within 50yd of the start line. C Company battled on towards Genoa Farm, having lost all their officers, while on the left D Company mopped up part of the Hubner Trench defences before pushing on to Hubner Farm. B Company, having detached a Lewis gun section and a few men to provide covering fire for C Company's attack on Genoa Farm, made for the pillboxes which represented their second objective. By then, as a result of casualties to officers, Knight had taken command of No. 6 Platoon and the remnants of another. Their advance was briefly interrupted by some Argylls from the neighbouring 51st Highland Division who strayed across the left flank, forcing Knight to pull back one party before leading a successful attack on the right-hand group of pillboxes.

Then, reinforced by some men from company headquarters and the battalion reserve, they struck at the blockhouses on the left with the same results, adding two officers and a number of machine-guns to their tally of captures. At one point, Knight had become bogged down in mud up to his waist but, exposed as he was to all kinds of fire, he still managed to shoot six of the enemy.

Over on the left, the assault on Hubner Farm itself was developing. The battalion's final objective proved a difficult nut to crack. A report of the struggle recorded:

> Strenuous resistance was met ... from the enemy who were not only in the farm but in the shell-holes in the rear and on the flanks. No. 15 Platoon was detailed to capture this farm. [It] arrived ... with one Lewis Gun Corporal (with his gun) and 4 men, who immediately took up a position and engaged the entrances to the farm. In the meantime B Company on the right had detached a LG to engage the parties of enemy in shell-holes and a party of 9th Royal Scots (4 in number) moved to the left flank and fired while 5 men of the 2/5th LRB (London Rifle Brigade) crept up to the left flank and got in rear of the farm. The farm was then rushed and the defence cracked up, between 70 and 100 prisoners throwing down their arms and surrendering. They were unwounded men; in addition a great number were killed and there were 30 wounded enemy in the farm and 2 medical officers and 8 stretcher-bearers.

Once again Knight featured prominently. Realising that the men of D Company were having trouble subduing Hubner Farm, he collected a few men and advanced towards the flank from where he 'brought a heavy fire to bear'. His intervention helped tip the balance, enabling D Company to mount a decisive charge. Astonishingly, in view of the numerous occasions in which he appeared to court certain death, Knight survived the battle unharmed. There had, however, been many near misses. Years later, he recalled being fascinated 'by the pattern made all the way round me in the mud by the German bullets'. He referred to his survival as a 'miracle', and added:

> All my kit was shot away almost as soon as we were in it. Everything went, in fact. Bullets rattled on my steel helmet – there were several significant dents and one hole in it I found later – and part of a book was shot away in my pocket. A photograph-case and a cigarette-case probably saved my life from one bullet, which must have passed just under my arm-pit – quite close enough to be comfortable!

Knight recounted that one of the men he took prisoner, a youngster, had been fast asleep in his shell-hole while all kind of 'terrors of the air' were flying. He was handed over along with a party of sixty to seventy unwounded men, presumably those captured at Hubner Farm, who, Knight claimed, were 'waiting for something to turn up at an enemy dressing station'.

By 6.30 am, the 2/8th Post Office Rifles' part in the fighting was over and consolidation began. The estimated number of prisoners exceeded 185 and the booty included eight heavy and seven light machine-guns. Their casualties amounted to sixty-five officers and men killed, 144 wounded and thirty-eight missing – more than 50 per cent of their attacking strength. B Company came out with one officer and forty-three men. Much of their success was due to sound planning, although the Rifles' CO laid as much store in the gallantry displayed by his men, leading him to conclude 'the important weapon is the rifle and bayonet'. Perhaps thinking of Sgt Knight's feats of daring, he added: 'Any one or two determined men rushing on a fortified shell-hole can clear it with the bayonet.'

The close-quarter nature of the fighting had indeed been exceptional. The Rifles' CO cited the 'large number of men and officers [who] carried on after being wounded'. There were numerous individual acts of bravery which were reflected in the long list of awards. They included a DSO, eight MCs, two DCMs and twenty-eight MMs. There could, however, be only one award for Sgt Knight and it came as little surprise when, on 8 November, the *London Gazette* announced the award of the Victoria Cross to No. 370995 Sgt Alfred Joseph Knight. The citation rightly proclaimed his key role in one of the battalion's most outstanding exploits:

> His several single-handed actions showed exceptional bravery, and saved a great number of casualties in the company. They were performed under heavy machine-gun and rifle fire, and without regard to personal risk, and were the direct cause of the objective being captured.

Alfred Joseph Knight was born at Ladywood, Birmingham, on 24 August 1888, the eldest of three children to Joseph and Annie Maria Knight (née Rowbotham). His father, a former glasscutter, ran a confectioner's shop in Islington Row. Educated at St Philip's Grammar School, Edgbaston, he started work with the city's post office as a clerical assistant. A keen sportsman, he was secretary of the football and cricket teams connected to the Little Oratory Roman Catholic church. In 1912, he left Birmingham for Nottingham when the PO engineering department was relocated and was working at the Carrington Street depot when war broke out.

He enlisted in the 2/8th London Regiment (2nd Post Office Rifles) on 26 October 1914, but it was not until January 1917 that the unit moved to France. Initially, the battalion had furnished drafts to the 1/8th Battalion, and it was only towards the end of 1915 that serious training as an active service unit began. The 2/8th moved to Sutton Veny in July 1916, where it became part of the 58th Division. Its first major action was in the Second Battle of Bullecourt in May 1917. Knight, then a lance-sergeant, distinguished himself on 14 May by bringing in wounded men under heavy fire, earning a special certificate from his divisional commander 'for gallant conduct'. As further recognition, he was promoted sergeant.

Knight, who had married Mabel Saunderson on 8 May 1915, spent a brief leave with his wife and baby daughter at his Balfour Road home in June 1917. The announcement of his Victoria Cross turned him into a minor celebrity. When he returned to Nottingham in December 1917, he became a magnet for journalists, although of his exploit he insisted 'I hardly know myself how it all happened'.

In the space of a few days, he was presented with his VC by King George V at Buckingham Palace and was accorded civic receptions in both his native and adopted cities. At Nottingham, civic leaders presented him with an ornate silver tea service and a £100 war bond while postal workers clubbed together to buy him an inscribed marble clock. The people of Birmingham gave him an illuminated address and another clock. Knight jokingly dismissed press accounts of his VC action which, he claimed, made him out to be 'a man from whom the bullets bounced'. The press were much taken by his sense of humour. One Birmingham newspaper dubbed him 'the Jolly VC'.

Having been well and truly fêted, he returned to France and served as a training instructor. He soldiered on until after the Armistice and was commissioned a second lieutenant in the Sherwood Foresters on 17 March 1919.

Following demobilisation, Knight resumed his civilian career, transferring from the post office to the Ministry of Labour in May 1920. In 1931, he moved to York to take over as manager of the city's Labour Exchange, settling in Severus Avenue with his wife and three children (Marjorie, b. 1916, Geoffrey, b. 1924 and Valerie, b. 1927). His work was recognised by further promotion to the Trade Board Section in Leeds in 1937. That same year, with the threat of a second world war looming ever larger on the horizon, he volunteered for the Observer Corps. Granted the rank of captain, he served with the corps throughout the war, combining air-raid duties with his Civil Service work. Another promotion brought him back to Birmingham in 1941 and he eventually retired from his post as senior wages inspector for the Midlands section of the Ministry of Labour, following a stroke, in 1951. In the same year's Birthday Honours List, he was appointed a Member of the Order of the British Empire (Civil) for his services.

The only member of the Post Office Rifles to win the Victoria Cross, Alfred Knight died, aged 72, at his home in Elvetham Road, Birmingham, following a third and fatal stroke, on 4 December 1960. He was buried in Oscott cemetery. More than half a century later, his solo charge on the Gravenstafel spur is commemorated in a variety of places and a variety of ways. His medals are displayed at The British Postal Museum, a painting of his VC action by the celebrated artist Terence Cuneo hangs in the British Forces post office at RAF Northolt and a road in Edgbaston – Alfred Knight Way – honours his memory close to where he lived and worked for so many years.

Remembered as a modest man who only brought his medals out on formal occasions, Knight always insisted they belonged not simply to him but to all his comrades. 'He was a very straight, firm dealing kind of man who came at things head-on,' recalled his granddaughter, Anne Walsh. 'He wasn't the sort to dwell on things, or get moody. I think that's what his men appreciated about him. They knew they'd get a square deal from him and, by all accounts, they thought the world of him.'

M.S.S. MOORE

Tower Hamlets, 20–22 September 1917

The excitement of battle had not yet been dulled by exhaustion when 2/Lt Monty Moore attempted to describe the most extraordinary drama of his life. Scarcely 48 hours had passed since the 15th Hampshires had trudged out of the line, and his account betrayed a confusion of emotions. The only one of his circle of friends to survive unscathed the terrible struggle west of Gheluvelt, he made little attempt to conceal the horrors as he scribbled his hurried letter to his mother: 'Dad was right when he said I was coming back to hell. Well I have been through a hell I hope never to face again.'

Four days earlier, the 15th Hampshires had spearheaded the 122nd Brigade's attack south of the Menin Road. Part of the 41st Division, on the right of the main thrust, their objectives lay either side of the Bassevillebeek. Once captured, they were to be consolidated while the 11th Royal West Kents and 12th East Surreys pushed on up sharply rising ground to take Tower Trench on a flat-topped spur speckled with pillboxes and concrete dugouts which someone had christened Tower Hamlets.

Launched at 5.40 am, the attack soon ran into trouble. Pillboxes missed by the barrage around Java Avenue resisted fiercely, taking a heavy toll of the Hampshires. Many officers, including all four company commanders, became casualties, but the survivors pressed on to capture all of their objectives. Other units, however, had not fared as well. Withering fire from machine-guns sited in three ruined cottages turned the neighbouring 124th Brigade attack into a shambles. No ground was taken at all on the right and the East Surreys were forced to guard the open flank. In the confusion, the West Kents lost their way and were mown down trying to reach Tower Trench. Those few who made it up the exposed slopes were soon forced to retreat, leaving the brigade's final objective in German hands.

Around 5 pm an order reached Lt-Col Cecil Cary-Barnard DSO commanding officer of the 15th Hampshires, to renew the assault in an hour's time, using what remained of his battalion and the West Kents with another brigade in support. Not for the first time and certainly not the last, the order bore no relation to reality. As Cary-Barnard later recorded: 'There were no West Kents in our area ... and the only thing to do was to take what men I could spare for the attack.' Hurrying back to the front line, he hastily mustered as many men as he could find – some 120 men and about half a dozen officers – and placed 2/Lt Monty Moore, who he accurately described as 'a boy of perhaps 20 years of age', in command.

In his letter describing the day's events, Moore said it was at 6 pm when the CO 'sent for me and said he had been asked to try and capture the next objective which should have been taken by another Batt; would I do it?' He had been back with the battalion less than a fortnight after being wounded at Messines three and a half months earlier. And having survived the morning's grim fighting he now faced the prospect of another costly attack across 400yd of open ground, exposed to the fire that had already routed one attack. Yet he didn't hesitate:

> To cut a long story short I got over under a heavy rifle fire and machine-gun fire through TOWER HAMLETS and in his line with 4 men and 1 sergt captured 8 prisoners, 2 machine guns and 1 light field gun. Well, I stayed there until the rest of my men came up, dug in and held off the Boche. That night he bombed us but we drove him off. The next morning our guns put a most deadly barrage on us thinking we were all gone. It was a most awful time. Finally, I was left with 10 men. In the afternoon, he counter-attacked, but I spotted it and got the SOS up. Once again the guns opened and fairly pasted our dugout. All that night 21–22 Sept, first a Boche barrage and then ours. My hat, it was awful. Well, in the early morning mist I cleared out with my men, being absolutely usless [sic] staying there any longer, got back greatly to the astonishment of the General and the CO, they had given me up as dead long ago, and fairly fell on my neck. Well, I got a hat for you, a most beautiful pair of glasses worth £15, 2 watches and several other odds and sods.

It was a remarkable story of survival against the odds. Moore's party had been effectively cut off since 10 am on 21 September. Later that same day, Lt-Col Cary-Barnard had seen German troops massing for an attack on his subaltern's position, but had been powerless to intervene. He later wrote:

> I could not warn Moore nor our own Brigade as all signal lines and methods had gone except runners. So, although it was abnormally quiet, I sent up an SOS hoping to bring down the barrage in front of my own men, and in any case warning them. Our artillery fired three or four shells and stopped, explaining afterwards that as everything was so quiet they could not believe an attack was pending. At four it came.

The usual intense barrage and then, after an hour, silence. I sent out an officers' patrol and another under a trusted and gallant Company-Sergeant-Major. They both reported ... that all trace of Lieut Moore and his men had vanished. I then agreed with the Brigade Headquarters that the counter-attack must have been successful and the whole of the Corps barrage was rolled over the area two or three times.

Given all of that it was little wonder that Moore's appearance out of the mist around 7 am on 22 September was greeted with such amazement. According to Cary-Barnard, most of the 120 or so men who took part in the second attack were killed or wounded. All told, he claimed that of the 375 men who went into action on 20 September, only 129 came out. These figures are at variance with the regimental history which records six officers and eighty-three men killed or missing and seven officers and 251 men wounded, but either way the Hampshires' losses were grievous. In fact, the casualties in the 41st Division were the heaviest of any division in the Second or Fifth Army. The high number of casualties resulted in a rapid rise for the young hero of the hour. In the days that followed what Cary-Barnard called 'a most extraordinary' action, Monty Moore was elevated to company commander with the rank of temporary lieutenant, acting captain.

Writing home, he enlarged on his initial account, his tone seesawing from boyish bravado to weary lament. In one letter, he told his father with evident pride that he had 'shot 3 Boche with my revolver at 10yds range' and in another to his sister he admitted to not feeling 'too bright ... after the last show'. His letters also revealed a growing resentment at what he felt were misleading accounts of the fighting. Writing on 25 September, he urged his father to 'tell the papers it was the Hampshires who did all the work and not the DLI, who left me in the lurch with 10 men and no rifles'.

For the most part, the brutality of the fighting was blurred by a veneer of youthful jollity, as though he were a schoolboy describing a particularly demanding game of rugger. To his father, he wrote on 29 September: 'I lost all my pals [nearly] on this last push ... In fact I was the only one who came out without a scratch. Damn fine piece of luck too, don't you think?', and two days later, he related: 'I captured 8 prisoners and shot 3 with my revolver. That was a day, Sept 20th, shall never forget it. All with their hands up, "Shoot" I yelled and over they went like nine pins. No quarter given to that little lot. The prisoners were taken later on from a dugout, the one I was in through our barrage.'

The shooting of prisoners was by no means unusual. From his description, it would appear to have taken place during the early fighting, probably in the struggle to subdue the blockhouses around Java Avenue. Much evidence exists to show that British troops, having suffered heavily at the hands of pillbox garrisons, were reluctant to accept the surrender of men who only moments before had been slaughtering their comrades. More details of Moore's desperate fight in Tower Trench emerged in a letter to his sister written on 7 October:

> Did I tell you about clearing the dugout? Got up there and found a large concrete dugout full of Boche. In went one bomb. No result. 1 more. That was a dud. Another one. That was a dud too, and then in went the 4th that bust my hat. There was a yell from inside, 'Kamerad, merci, etc'. Out they came, 8 of the beauties, hands full of souvenirs, which I carefully collected and afterwards lost. I was standing at that time next to an officer when, crack and down he went with a bullet through the head, evidently meant for me, then we spent 36 hours in our own barrage. Very good for the nerves I can assure you.

A day later, in response to his father's prodding, he wrote a fuller account of the action which had become the talk of his battalion:

> I took 120 men and 2 officers with me. 4 men, 1 sergt and myself alone reached our objective, the remainder hung back in shell-holes until brought up half hour later, both officers were knocked out and only about 25 men reached that line. During that period of half hour, my sergt and myself cleared the dugout as already described and then we crept into shell-holes and waited for what might turn up. The prisoners were sent back. The only wounded that ever got back were those who could look after themselves and a few who were found that night. Reinforcements came up making my party up to 70-odd. I left on the morning of Sept 22nd with 9 men and 1 wounded corporal, who we assisted back. The guns had to be left behind, we all being too exhausted to carry any surplus kit or arms at all. The great point was that being there on Sept 21st the Boche failed to get through and so his whole advance was held up, mainly because he knew we were there but was uncertain as to our strength and had not got guts enough to risk it. According to the Div General, this saved the whole Div. If they had advanced our barrage would have just missed them and the whole line would have been lost. It is something to know that I was of some use to them. It was just luck …

His opinion that 'anybody else would have done the same in my position' was not shared by his commanding officer. In recording his courageous action, Lt-Col Cary-Barnard noted: 'It is impossible to speak too highly of the gallantry and leadership displayed by this officer.' Others agreed. Moore's fellow subaltern, 2/Lt George Barker, one of two officers sent forward with a reinforcing party, felt 'ever so proud of him': '… a more gallant action I've never seen. To see Monty going up with a handful of men as coolly as if it were only a practice attack was a sight I shall never forget.'

By 22 October the first list of awards for the unit's part in the battle had been published: three Military Crosses, including one to each of the officers who brought up reinforcements to Moore's small party, three Distinguished Conduct Medals, 28 Military Medals and one Bar to the MM. 'I am told I am in for something good,' Moore wrote. 'Only a rumour I expect, but live in hopes … My sergt [Sgt Gannon] got the DCM and the 10 men a MM each. Quite a record isn't it?' But as the days passed without any news, Moore grew increasingly testy, telling his sister on 7 November:

> Now don't go shouting all over the place about VCs etc, because it's most unlikely. It's strange that the whole batch got something except their leader, but it's just bad luck as usual. After all I didn't come out here for those things. My only thought is to get some leave which they might have given me at least …

The waiting, however, was almost at an end. A day later, the *London Gazette* announced the award of the Victoria Cross to 2/Lt Montague Moore. The citation told how at one point during the defence of Tower Trench Moore's force was compelled to use captured enemy weapons to hold off the enemy counter-attacks. It concluded: 'As an example of dashing gallantry and cool determination this young officer's exploit would be difficult to surpass.' It was the signal for celebrations to begin. Writing to his sister, he declared: 'It has happened. You were quite right. It's the VC. Well, I shall be home very shortly to buy up Bournemouth and we will go bust. Don't worry about money I have plenty to blue [sic]. Tell dad to bring out all that fizz he has got stored up.'

Montague Shadworth Seymour Moore was born in Bournemouth, Hampshire, on 9 October 1896, the eldest of two children, to Frederick William Moore and his wife Gertrude Ann Seymour (née Guscote). His father had served in the Army and he had a general for a grandfather and a vice-admiral for an uncle. The family lived at Goathland, Tower Road, Branksome Park, and he was educated at Bedford Grammar School. His academic career was undistinguished and, years later, as a celebrated war hero Moore could not resist taking a 'dig' at one of his old teachers who had written him off 'as a dud'. Following Bedford, he received a year's private tuition in Bournemouth (one of his teachers also taught Leefe Robinson VC) and attended classes at the town's municipal college.

He passed into the Royal Military College, Sandhurst, in March 1915, at the age of 18. Commissioned into the Hampshire Regiment on 16 August 1916, he proceeded to France the following month. Posted to the 15th Battalion, a Kitchener unit raised in Portsmouth, he revelled in his new existence. Writing to his father on 5 November 1916, he wrote of trenches infested with rats and cats playing 'with the wind vanes on top of the parapet'. 'It is a most extraordinary life,' he noted. 'All is peace and quietness most of the day as far as the Bosche go, only 40 to 150yds away.' He described sniping the enemy positions as 'jolly good fun but very tiring, especially as the whole place is under wet deep mud'.

A brief attachment to Brigade HQ was followed, in January 1917, by a posting to the 1st Hampshires. He was back, however, with the 15th Battalion in time for the Messines operations on 7 June. During the advance he was wounded by shrapnel in the leg and evacuated. Although the injury was not severe, he was sent back to England for treatment, where he remained until September.

After the battle for Tower Hamlets, Moore's unit was pulled out of the line and, much to his displeasure, he found himself training drafts from a yeomanry unit who were to make good their losses. Promoted acting captain, he served briefly as a bombing instructor at the divisional reinforcement camp before being appointed an ADC to Lt-Gen. Sir John DuCane, GOC XV Corps.

On 16 November the French awarded him the Croix de Guerre. The citation stated that he 'has shown the most brilliant military qualities and rendered exceptionally good services during the battles delivered in Flanders in Sept and Oct 1917 by the Franco-British troops'. It was presented in the field, and Moore posted the medal home to his father, commenting: 'Not much to look at is it?' Five days after the announcement of his second honour, the youngster received his VC from King George V at Buckingham Palace.

His next posting was to the Fifth Army Infantry School, but when the Germans launched their Spring Offensive on 21 March 1918, his was one of many training units pitched into battle in a desperate attempt to stem the tide. The nature of the fighting was revealed in a letter written on 2 April: 'Had a very nasty four days holding up Huns. Got buried once by a damn shell. Fairly put the breeze up me but am still alive and living in hope of leave some time.' Two days later, he noted 'most of our unit is scattered all over France'. His luck, however, held good and he was apparently still serving as an instructor when the war ended. His fighting days, however, were not over. In May 1919 he was serving with the 2nd Hampshires, part of the 238th Special Brigade of the North Russia Relief Force, despatched to Archangel ostensibly to assist the withdrawal of Allied troops threatened by Bolsheviks. It was a force peppered with distinguished soldiers. Both his battalion commander, Lt-Col John Sherwood Kelly, and his brigadier, George Grogan, were VC holders. Moore endured many hardships and survived a number of small-scale operations to emerge unscathed from this inglorious episode.

During one engagement on the Dvina River front, his battalion was ordered to carry out a deep incursion into enemy territory to attack Bolshevik positions from the rear. In a letter home to his 'dear old mum' dated 25 June 1919, he described what he referred to as 'a tough time' that cost the life of a friend, Capt. D. T. Gorman MC:

> We started off at 4 am on 19th, marched through the Russian forest for 18 miles, through swamps up to your knees, in some places over. [It was a] blazing hot day and the flies were pretty bad. We halted at about 11 pm. At 2 am the next morning we moved off to our attacking position (well behind the Bolos), at 4.30 we attacked, taking the Bolos by surprise. However, they were prepared for an offensive ... They gave us a very warm time but our better shooting told heavily. However we were nearly surrounded and cut off, so, fagged out as we all were, we had to retreat at 9.30 am in the blazing heat. No rest, little food. My platoon was the last to leave. The enemy had worked up to within 70 yards, covering us with very heavy fire the whole time. We got out and had to trek right back over our old trail. We got in to TOPSA at 12 midnight, done in completely, only to hear he [the Bolsheviks] was counter attacking, so off we went again and took up a position until morning. Being light the whole time, we could see what was going on, and nothing happened. Our casualties were all nil, a few wounded and 2 killed. Poor old Gorman (15th Bn with me) got one in the stomach and died some 16 hours later after having been brought back through that awful forest ...

Returning to England, he was transferred to the 1st Battalion, which was ordered to Constantinople to join the Army of the Black Sea. Then in March 1921 he was posted to the 2nd Battalion, King's African Rifles, in Tanganyika Territory, formerly German East Africa. 'I'm very excited about it as I hear it is a very fine part to start in, plenty of game etc,' he wrote. The posting proved a turning point in his life. By October he was enthusing about his new surroundings: 'This is a fine country and I like it immensely; game is very plentiful round here and have seen some fine sights already.' Most of his letters were filled with tales of hunting and safaris. He retired from the Army in 1926 and joined the Tanganyika game preservation department as a ranger, accompanying the Prince of Wales during a shooting trip two years later.

In 1933, during a leave in England, Moore married Audrey Penn Milton and they settled in the vast Serengeti reserve. Home was the remote game ranger's station where the nearest post office was more than a hundred miles away across five bridge-less rivers. Banagi camp, as it was known, consisted of a small white tin-roofed bungalow and an assortment of mud huts located on a slight rise cleared of thorn trees. From the top of a nearby hill, there was a hazy view of the Ngoro-Ngoro heights and between it and Banagi lay 'the most famous lion country in the world' – the Serengeti, with its river the Seronera and the great Serengeti Plain.

Audrey came to share her husband's fascination for wildlife and love of Africa. She later chronicled their life on the reserve in a best-selling book which was translated into French and enjoyed success in the United States. Influential in the conservation of threatened species, Monty and Audrey Moore helped lay the foundations for the Serengeti's world famous reputation as a stronghold for wildlife.

Moore, himself, became expert in the ways of the wild, but his bush skills were almost entirely self-taught. A man whose compassion towards animals belied his sometimes blunt and fearsome reputation, he was also a pragmatist. His son, Charles, recalled: 'He would do what he had to do as a game warden perfectly happily. If that meant shooting an animal, he would shoot it. But it would have to be done properly, in other words quickly and it had to be done without causing the animal any undo [sic] stress. Everything he did had to be spot on.' His ability and judgement marked him out for promotion and in 1944 he was appointed chief game warden, in charge of all of Tanganyika's reserves. It was a post he held until 1951, by which time his health – he had developed diabetes at the age of 42 – was beginning to deteriorate. But never for a moment did he consider moving back to England. According to his son, the prospect held as little appeal as peacetime soldiering in the 1920s. 'There was no chance at all of going to England,' he recalled. 'He'd have hated it. He wanted the freedom, the wilderness.' Instead, the couple retired to Kenya and it was there, at Kugenzo, that Monty Moore died of renal failure on 12 September 1966. As befitted a former game warden, his ashes were scattered in the Nairobi National Park.

Always a man to speak his mind, Monty Moore was an old-school colonialist who believed in the justice of the imperial cause. But he was also an authoritarian with a streak of the rebel about him. While serving as a junior staff officer, albeit one with a Victoria Cross, he ran into trouble for giving a general a piece of his mind. 'He didn't give a bugger for anybody,' said his son. 'There was no nonsense about him. Like so many other young subalterns, he'd been thrown in at the deep end and had a really rough time. But he wouldn't talk about it, certainly not his experiences in the trenches.

Sometimes he'd talk about North Russia ... but all he'd ever say about his VC was that it came up with the rations which we all knew was absolute rubbish. He was a man of his time; a stickler for what he considered correct and proper behaviour. In many ways, he continued to behave in the manner of an officer of the Hampshire regiment and that's something he upheld all his life.'

W.F. BURMAN AND E.A. EGERTON

Near Bulgar Wood, 20 September 1917

The failure of the 124th Brigade to subdue enemy machine-guns in the Bassevillebeek Valley proved expensive in lives on 20 September, not only for the 41st Division but for its neighbour, the 39th Division. The 16th Rifle Brigade and 17th King's Royal Rifle Corps, left-hand battalions of the 117th Brigade, were raked throughout the 800yd of their advance by machine-guns firing from hidden positions north of the divisional boundary.

Lt-Col the Hon. Edward Coke DSO, MC, commanding the 16th Rifle Brigade, reported that his men came under fire almost as soon as they left the start line near Shrewsbury Forest. In the face of heavy casualties, the riflemen succeeded in capturing the Lower Star Post strongpoint, together with another, known as Point 58, in a sunken road. Losses might have been worse but for one company employing the novel tactic of fixing their entrenching tools across their chests as makeshift armour.

Within 10 minutes of zero hour, the intermediate objective was reached, although it was not until 11 am that it was effectively consolidated. Long before then, and in keeping with the divisional timetable, A and C Companies, wearing identifying ribbons on their shoulder straps, pressed on to their final objective. Once again, the riflemen were enfiladed from the left. One post was dealt with by a party which crossed the divisional line, but no neighbouring units could be found. Consequently, Coke was compelled to form a curving line, with C Company on the final objective and A Company, having lost all its officers and 75 per cent of its men, echeloned back as a defensive flank.

Snipers made life uncomfortable as the riflemen tried to dig in. According to Coke, the enemy 'were using incendiary bullets'. Several wounded men had their clothing set on fire and had to be rolled over in the mud to douse the flames. Among those struggling to consolidate the position was Sgt William Burman, a 20-year-old Londoner, who had already featured prominently in C Company's advance. Four days after the battle, his company commander wrote home:

> I am so proud of my boys that I cannot say enough about them ... The only thing I am sad about is my losses for I have lost some of the very finest fellows you could wish to see, and our officer casualties are very heavy indeed. I had three officers with me at zero, and in a very few minutes two of them were killed, and one severely wounded, so when I reached my objective I found myself alone, with only my company sergeant-major and one sergeant [Burman] to help me supervise affairs.
>
> However, this was no time for grieving and we had to dig in for our lives because machine-guns and snipers were firing at us from pillboxes on the opposite rise in the ground. I and my servant were together in a shell-hole looking after one poor fellow wounded in the back, and Cox, faithful servant and good soldier that he was, was shot and fell back into my arms. He did not speak a word, but I could see I could do nothing for him, and he died in a few minutes from being hit.
>
> At this point, however, I could not stop to realise my loss for troops on my right flank [16th Sherwood Foresters] were being held up, and I had to find out the reason. Looking through my glasses I soon discovered a party of about forty Germans lying along a road [Forest Road, at approximately J.26.c.4.4] about 50yd away, shooting at us and enfilading these other troops in our brigade. My sergeant-major and Sergeant Burman, together with a lance-corporal, worked their way forward, got round the back of them, killed six, wounded two and captured two officers and 29 other ranks.
>
> This deed is one of the finest I have yet heard of, and I am recommending C-Sergeant-Major [H.W.] Bean for the DCM [awarded, *London Gazette*, 26 November 1917] and Sergeant Burman for the VC.
>
> Sergeant Burman is the finest fellow that ever lived, standing only 5ft 4in, but with the heart of a lion, knowing no fear. When we had gone half-way to our objective a machine-gun opened fire at us from 30yd range in a shell-hole position, and my poor fellows were falling down everywhere. Sgt Burman went on all alone in face of what appeared to be certain death, killed the three gunners and captured the gun, saving, by his gallant deed, the lives of his chums behind and allowing the company to continue to advance. He carried the gun all the way to the final objective, and turned it on the retiring enemy, and his courage and fortitude throughout were amazing to see.
>
> He is the hero of the battalion today, and he is my company, hence my pride, and I do sincerely hope he gets his VC. He thoroughly deserves it ten times over.

According to Lt-Col Coke, Burman's second exploit took place a little over 15 minutes after the final objective had been reached. In his official report, he said that Burman's party had advanced against the superior enemy force 'firing their rifles' until 'the enemy wavered and then came out into the open and surrendered'. They amounted to more than half of the fifty-eight men from the 6th and 395th Regiments captured by the battalion that day at a cost of two officers and twenty-seven men killed, eleven officers and 168 men wounded or missing.

On their right, the 16th and 17th Sherwood Foresters fared better, being shielded from the destructive enfilading fire as they advanced against the line of enemy posts in Bulgar Wood. The 16th (Chatsworth Rifles), following behind the 17th, moved forward with each man wearing a ribbon bearing the colour of his objective. Thick mist made direction-finding difficult and officers were forced to pick their way forward using compasses. A few casualties were caused by enemy artillery and there was some mixing of the two battalions as the 16th moved out of the line of fire. The mist both added to the confusion and helped reduce the number of casualties. It was at this juncture that Capt. P.E. Burrows MC, commanding Support Company, went forward and, having discovered machine-guns in action around a position known as Point 73, led a platoon in a daring attack through the barrage. Two guns and thirty prisoners were taken and the strongpoint became the 16th's Battalion HQ, from where Maj. J.R. Webster, who had only recently taken command of the unit, directed operations.

The advance on the second objective began at 7 am. Shells were falling short, causing a number of casualties, but the 16th pressed on through what their historian called the 'seeming confusion, chaos and pandemonium' to take many enemy strongpoints by surprise. One man, an officer's servant, actually passed through the barrage, entered a dugout near Chatsworth Castle and emerged with nine prisoners, including an officer who congratulated him on his bravery. Yet even as the tide of battle swept towards the fringes of Bulgar Wood, Maj. Webster's attention was drawn to a threat much closer to home. The mist having dispersed, it was realised that the attacking troops had missed the strongpoint at Welbeck Grange. This position, bristling with snipers and a machine-gun, posed a clear threat to the leading waves, leaving Webster no option but to attack despite the obvious risks. He later wrote:

An attack ... was quickly organised, covered by the fire of one of the attached Vickers Guns from the 57th Brigade. A party was sent to take the dugouts from the northern side, which was led in a most gallant manner by Cpl Egerton of my Support Company. Several of the enemy were shot. 29 prisoners, including one officer and the machine gun were taken here.

Behind this terse narrative lay a story of astonishing heroism. It emerged that 19-year-old Ernest Egerton had dashed forward alone even before his comrades had had a chance to move. According to the official account, 'he shot in succession a rifleman, a bomber and a gunner'. By then, the rest of his bewildered party had caught up with him and the remainder of the garrison, no doubt stunned by Egerton's audacity, surrendered. What seemed a desperately hazardous enterprise had been accomplished by one man in less than 30 seconds! A few weeks later, the youngster supplied his own version:

> I was in a shell-hole in front of some concrete dugouts, and someone with a machine-gun was causing heavy casualties on our left flank ... I could see the damage which they were inflicting, so I took it into my head to go forward. I kept running from shell-hole to shell-hole until I got at the back of this particular concrete dugout, and having gone so far I could see three men with a machine-gun. I first shot the man who was firing the gun; then I shot the second, who was waiting with another belt of cartridges, and I also shot the third man who was a bomber. By that time I was supported by other men who had followed me up, and twenty-nine Germans, including an officer, came out of their dugouts holding up their hands and surrendered.

Maj. Webster, in a postscript to his battle report, called it 'the most reckless piece of gallantry I ever saw'. The motive for Egerton's remarkable exploit was contained in a letter received a few days before the attack, informing the young NCO that his elder brother William had been killed in action on 17 August. 'It was my object from the time I heard of his death to get revenge,' he later remarked. 'I was longing to get into action and pay back a debt.' Thus the assault on Welbeck Grange became a personal vendetta.

Later in the day, two attempts by the enemy to win back lost ground were forestalled by units of the 117th Brigade, supported by artillery. On one occasion an enemy force estimated at two battalions of roughly 2,000 men were plainly seen assembling to attack the remnants of C Company, 16th Rifle Brigade. William Burman's company commander recorded: 'The men had cylinders on their chests, containing burning oil apparatus, but they never lived to use them. Our artillery opened out with swarms of machine-guns and they simply melted away, and in half an hour all was quiet with not a sign of a German anywhere.'

The 16th Sherwood Foresters and 16th Rifle Brigade spent the following day dodging shells before being relieved. Despite heavy casualties – the 16th Sherwood Foresters alone had lost three officers and sixty men killed or missing and two officers and 126 men wounded – morale was high. Major Webster wrote: 'I shall never forget Sept 20th; it was the greatest day of my life. The dash of the men was simply amazing and nothing could stop them. They came out with their tails right up and every man had stories to tell of the Bosche they had killed.'

None more so than Ernest Egerton. 'I am sorry to hear about Will's death,' he wrote to his parents. 'I can tell you it upset me very much; I could not say anything all day. We have just been into action again. We took a large number of prisoners. I am pleased to say I have come through another battle quite safely … Well, I had a bit of revenge … I accounted for a few Germans, I can tell you.'

Both units were showered with honours, the 16th Sherwood Foresters receiving no fewer than thirty-two awards, including a DSO for Maj. Webster. The last honour to be announced was the Victoria Cross to No. 71130 Cpl Ernest Egerton on 26 November 1917. Published in the same *Gazette* was the award of the VC to No. P/649 Sgt William Burman 'for most conspicuous bravery'.

Ernest Alfred Egerton was born on 10 November 1897, at Mier Lane, Longton, Staffordshire, the third son of Thomas Henry Egerton. Educated at Queen's Street, Cooke Street and Blurton Church Schools, he entered Florence Colliery at the age of 16, working as a haulage hand. On his 18th birthday, he enlisted at Shelton recruiting office in the 3rd North Staffordshire Regiment. Two brothers also served in the Army: his eldest brother Thomas was discharged on medical grounds and his second brother William was killed. After undergoing training at Wallsend-on-Tyne, Ernest was posted to the 1st North Staffordshires in France, and transferred in October 1916 to the 16th Sherwood Foresters.

Promoted lance-corporal on 21 February 1917 and corporal on 23 August 1917, he came through the fighting on the Somme and at Ypres unscathed. He received his Victoria Cross from King George V at Buckingham Palace on 5 December and was given a tumultuous welcome in his home town. Among the many letters of congratulation was one from the Duke of Devonshire, who had taken special interest in the unit which took its name from his family's seat at Chatsworth. After pressure from Stoke's civic leaders, Egerton was granted extended leave to attend an official reception where directors, managers and workers at the Florence Colliery presented him with an inscribed silver cigarette case and war bonds worth £85.

Egerton was badly gassed during the enemy's Spring Offensive the following year. After a spell in hospital in France, he returned to his unit and was promoted sergeant on 11 May. He left the battalion on 20 August and returned to England for officer training. He joined a cadet school at Ripon, but evidently declined a commission, joining the 3rd Sherwood Foresters as a sergeant instructor.

On 30 August he was given a public reception at Longton town tall, where he received an illuminated testimonial. Two days later he married Elsie May Gimbert at Forsbrook parish church. The effects of his gas poisoning, however, were beginning to be felt. He entered Sunderland War Hospital suffering from tuberculosis and had a spell in a sanatorium, before being discharged from the Army on 25 April 1919 as permanently unfit for further military service. So serious was his plight that doctors considered he had only months to live.

But Egerton confounded them all. Ten years later, he attributed his 'miraculous recovery' to a twelve-month sojourn at Preston Hall, Aylesford, in Kent, where the Ministry of Pensions, and later the British Legion, staged training courses for injured ex-servicemen. Training as a gamekeeper, he obtained the full benefits of open-air life in the Kentish countryside. He returned to live in Leigh, near Creswell, North Staffordshire, acting as agent for a firm marketing ex-servicemen's handicrafts. The work was not a success, and Egerton's future appeared bleak until the intervention of his old school headmaster in 1924 secured him a job as a bus conductor with the Potteries Electric Traction Company. His health was further helped by being employed on mainly rural routes. Four years later, he was appointed an inspector. By 1929 Egerton, who was living at Blythe Bridge, was cycling into Stoke for work each day.

During the Second World War he served in the Home Guard and later became a security officer at Rootes Aircraft Works, Blythe Bridge, and then the Staffordshire Potteries in Meir. Despite his sometimes fragile health, Ernest Egerton survived into retirement, dying at his Blythe Bridge home on 14 February 1967, aged 68. He was buried with full military honours in Forsbrook cemetery, not far from the church where he was married, and in the years since his death his courage has not been forgotten. On the 80th anniversary of his VC action traffic in Blythe Bridge was brought to a standstill as a procession marched through the village during a ceremony to unveil a memorial plaque on his former home. Five years later, the local council named a new housing development in the village Egerton Close in honour of a brave 'Staffordshire lad'.

William Francis Burman was born at 5 Baker Street, Stepney East, London, on 30 August 1897, the son of George and Agnes Burman. Educated at Stepney Red Coat School, he became a member of D Company, 1st Cadet Battalion, the Queen's (later the North East London) Army Cadet Force affiliated to the Royal Green Jackets. Burman left school in 1911 and enlisted in the Rifle Brigade on 23 March 1915, aged 17. He proceeded to France with the 16th (Service) Battalion and his ability and keenness were quickly recognised. On 20 April 1916, still only 18, he was promoted sergeant.

Following his VC action, the Mayor of Stepney, where Burman's widowed mother and sisters were living, opened a public fund. In December Burman was given a hero's reception at his old school. The 'joy' day was hailed as the proudest moment in the school's history and, while Burman 'was too modest to speak of his exploits', the local newspaper recorded: 'The cheering of the boys was terrific, and ... might have been heard in the trenches.'

Sgt W.F. Burman

Burman was decorated by King George V at Buckingham Palace on 19 December 1917. The following August he was presented with an illuminated testimonial by the Mayor of Stepney. By then, the subscription fund had raised £220. Demobilised on 7 March 1919 he stood as a candidate in the Stepney Borough Council elections in November 1919 for Mile End south ward. He became a chauffeur for the managing director of the *Daily Mirror*, a job he held for thirty years.

In November 1929, when he attended the dinner for VCs at the House of Lords, Burman, by then married and with a two-year-old son, found himself seated on the right of the Prince of Wales following a ballot. The juxtaposition of the heir to the throne and the humble chauffeur (Viscount Gort VC, DSO, MC was on the Prince's left) held a special appeal for the press who milked him for gossip. He told one reporter:

> Naturally, I was excited but I soon found that I had no need to be embarrassed. The Prince soon put me at my ease and we had a long chat. In fact, it was like talking to your brother. When he heard that I was a chauffeur, we discussed cars and he asked me which I liked best ...

Burman even brought away his own unusual souvenir of the occasion – the stub of a cigarette the Prince had given him!

After leaving his job with the *Daily Mirror*, he started his own car hire business which operated from Temple Grove, Golders Green. Burman retired in 1964 and seven years later, by then a widower with two sons, moved into a Royal British Legion Home in Cromer on the north Norfolk coast. He died there on 23 October 1974, aged 77. The Rifle Brigade's last-surviving VC holder, Burman was cremated at St Faith's near Norwich. The service was attended by representatives of his old regiment and two buglers from the 3rd Royal Green Jackets. His medals, consisting of the Victoria Cross, 1914–15 Star, War and Victory Medals, 1937 Coronation Medal and 1953 Coronation Medal, were presented to the Imperial War Museum in 1995. William Burman remained unaffected by his signal honour and was not much given to discussing his exploits. Once when he did, he was almost apologetic as he confided: 'I couldn't help it. It was a case of going on or going back. I couldn't go back.'

H. COLVIN

Hessian Wood, 20 September 1917

The night of 19–20 September was excessively dark as the men of the 9th Cheshires, wet through from the relentless drizzle, slipped and slithered towards the assembly positions near the remains of Klein Zillebeke. Progress was slow, yet by 1.45 am the twenty officers and 556 men, forming the left assault battalion of the 58th Brigade (19th Division), were in position without mishap. Even so, the last few hours were a test of nerves. The unit diarist wrote: 'There was no cover or protection for the ... troops who had to lie out in the open, and unfortunately no rum was issued. However, silence was maintained and no movement made, the troops lying there confident and quiet.'

The calm was shattered at 5.40 am when the barrage erupted. The Cheshires, led by Lt-Col J.A. Southey, pushed off in two waves, their task to help secure the southernmost flank between Groenenburg Farm and the Comines canal. A smokescreen, designed to shroud enemy observation posts on Zandvoorde Hill, combined with the damp mist to mask their movement and early progress was swift. According to the unit diarist, enemy strongpoints at Jarrocks Farm, Pioneer House and the intermediate objective were 'easily carried'. Many Germans were reported killed or captured and, although the Cheshires' losses were light they included two company commanders wounded before the first objective was reached.

On the right, Maj. W.H. Jones' place as D Company commander was taken by 2/Lt Hugh Colvin. At 30, Colvin was older than the average subaltern. A pre-war cavalryman and superb gymnast, he had served in the ranks for more than eight years. Commissioned in the field, he was posted to the

Cheshires the previous spring, where he had gained a reputation as a daring patrol leader. Consolidation was disrupted by 'disconcerting enfilade fire' and by 6.44 am, when the Cheshires set off towards their final objective, resistance had stiffened. On the left, Potsdam Farm fell, but only after a furious struggle. 'On the right,' recorded the unit diarist, 'matters were more obscure and more difficult.'

Machine-guns in Hessian Wood had checked the 9th Welsh Regiment in the centre. The guns, hidden amid the mist-shrouded tangle of tree stumps, threatened the entire operation. If the Welsh failed, the Cheshires would have to surrender their gains. 2/Lt Colvin, whose company was nearest, peeled away to assist them. Detaching two platoons to reinforce C Company, who were held up by snipers, he led the remaining two in a flank attack through the north-east corner of Hessian Wood.

The ground was pitted with craters, any one of which might have served as a shelter for enemy guns. To reduce the risk to his men, Colvin approached the nearest dugout with only two men. Leaving them to cover him, he then entered alone to emerge with fourteen prisoners. Heartened by his success, Colvin, followed by his two bodyguards, pushed on to a second dugout, manned by machine-gunners, riflemen and bombers, which was instrumental in frustrating the Welsh advance. Creeping up to the post, he led a rush which resulted in the death or capture of the entire garrison. The fight was barely over when the trio were set upon by fifteen Germans who leapt out of a nearby dugout. In the opening fusilade, one of the Cheshires was killed and another fell wounded. Colvin snatched up a rifle – thought to have been a discarded German weapon – and shot five of his would-be assailants. A sixth he took prisoner and then, using him as a human shield, forced most of his comrades to surrender. The shoot-out, reminiscent of a wild-west gunfight, was followed by more capitulations as Colvin, often assisted by only one man, cleared the warren of dugouts. All told he took fifty prisoners and the way was thus opened for the Welsh to regain contact with the Cheshires, who had reached their final objective at 6.58 am.

Colvin rejoined the remnants of C and D Company, sheltering in boggy ground north of Hessian Wood. As the senior surviving officer, he took command of the composite force. At a cost of an officer and forty-three men killed or missing and 116 wounded, the 9th Cheshires had captured all their objectives. That they did so was in great measure due to the outstanding courage and leadership displayed by one of their most junior officers. On 8 November the *London Gazette* announced the award of the Victoria Cross to 2/Lt Hugh Colvin 'for most conspicuous bravery in attack'.

Hugh Colvin was born at Rosegrove, Burnley, on 1 February 1887, the eldest son of Mr and Mrs Hugh Colvin, who hailed from Aberdeenshire. He was 9 when the family moved to Romily, in Cheshire, where Hugh's father was employed as a gardener. Educated at Hatherlow Day School, he followed his father into the gardening trade in Lancaster. Later, he moved to live with his sister's family in Belfast and in September 1908 he enlisted as a private in the 8th (King's Royal Irish) Hussars. After a year's service in England he spent six years in India and was at Ambala when war broke out.

Little is recorded of his wartime service prior to winning his VC. According to press reports, he served with his unit in France and Belgium from 1915 without suffering 'even a scratch'. Promoted lance-sergeant, he was commissioned in the field for good service and gazetted to the Cheshire Regiment on 13 April 1917. Posted to the 9th Battalion, Colvin, a fine all-round athlete, soon displayed evidence of energetic leadership. On 15–16 June, near Messines, he led a patrol which resulted in a divisional commendation. Having searched enemy positions, Colvin's party mopped up a series of concrete dugouts hidden in a hedge, returning with valuable information about the location of enemy posts.

His coolness under fire was remarkable and made a deep impression on his fellow officers. Years later, while being interviewed for the Imperial War Museum Sound Archives, Lt John Mallalieu recalled an incident during the Third Ypres campaign that illustrated the point:

Colvin came into my concrete dugout and there were various odd shells round about while he was in there. A small shell hit the corner outside of the concrete which didn't do a great deal of damage. The place was lit by candles stuck in bottles and of course all the candles went out and there was a general air of fumes and so forth – that's all that really happened. But the place was pretty hot inside and the ceiling was covered with flies. When I lit the candles again Hugh Colvin was sitting in a chair opposite and he just looked up at the ceiling and said, 'You know, that didn't even shake the flies off the ceiling!' He was a very calm character with no nerves, no imagination at all. A marvellous bloke, marvellous, very capable and a very brave type too.

Colvin was staying with his parents in West Didsbury, Manchester, when his VC was announced. On 28 November he went to Buckingham Palace to receive his Cross from King George V. Five days later he was given a civic reception by the Mayor of Chester. Cheered by crowds and led by the depot band, he was driven to Chester Castle, where he inspected a parade in the midst of a hailstorm. Later, he joined civic leaders at the town tall, where he received a congratulatory address. Colvin replied by speaking of the brave men who had earned Victoria Crosses 'by the bucketful', only to be killed with their deeds unwitnessed. He concluded with the rousing cry that 'any Britisher was worth a dozen Boches'.

That night he was entertained in the officers' mess and 'by way of earning his rations [he] performed some wonderful gymnastic feats, including a long arm balance on a rickety armchair (government property)'. Four days later, Colvin returned to France. Promoted lieutenant on 13 October 1918, he was employed as chief instructor at the Army's Physical Training School with the rank of temporary major.

After the Armistice, Colvin soldiered on with the 2nd Cheshires. With his squashed nose, cauliflower ears and endearing sense of humour, he was a popular personality with officers and men as well as being a firm favourite at children's parties. Promoted captain in 1928, 'Father Colvin', as he was affectionately known, served with the 1st Battalion in India, where he narrowly escaped serious injury when a lorry overturned and fell 80ft down a hillside. He retired in 1935, universally admired for his modesty and unselfishness. A subaltern in his company later wrote of him:

> There was something in his style that appealed to both officers and men serving around him. Whether he was giving some unorthodox instruction on the firing point [his was the Colour Company], whether he was showing the art of dealing with mules (he made me sleep between them when with a column on the North-west Frontier to keep warm: he was very right), or whether he was walking on his hands at the age of 45 (he was a great gymnast and runner!) – it all went home with us. We loved and respected him.

From 1938 to 1947 Colvin served as Army Recruiting Officer in Preston and then Chester. Retiring a second time, he settled in Northern Ireland. The hero of Hessian Wood died at Bangor, County Down, on 16 September 1962 and was buried at Carmoney cemetery, near Belfast, with full military honours. Representatives of the 8th (Royal Irish) Hussars and the Cheshire Regiment attended, together with members of the British Legion and Belfast Old Contemptibles Association. The following year his Victoria Cross and other medals were presented to the Cheshire Regiment. In his regimental obituary, one of his former commanding officers recorded: 'There were very few like him, whether as a soldier or man.'

J.B. HAMILTON
North of the Menin Road, 25–26 September 1917

The German counter-attack system had proved a failure at almost every point on 20 September, but any hopes the British might have nurtured about the waning strength of Count Rupprecht's Fourth Army were quickly shattered. At 5.15 am on 25 September, the pitted ground from Polygon Wood south to the Menin Road quaked beneath the impact of one of the heaviest artillery concentrations ever mounted in support of a divisional assault. In 15 devastating minutes, the massed guns of forty-four field batteries and twenty heavy batteries poured a storm of high-explosive, shrapnel and gas shells on an 1,800yd strip of British front.

The attack was designed to disrupt the anticipated resumption of Plumer's offensive as well as recovering ground lost on 20 September; it could hardly have been worse timed for the men of the 33rd Division. The advance guard of the 98th and 100th Brigades had only just taken over the position, in readiness for covering the Australian attack across the Gheluvelt plateau planned for the next day. Weary and unfamiliar with their new surroundings, they were in poor shape to resist the savage attack which followed.

The experiences of the 1/9th Highland Light Infantry, the Glasgow Highlanders, commanded by Maj. E. McCosh MC, were typical. To reach their assembly positions south of the Reutelbeek, they had traversed 5 miles of broken country, much of it through a furious barrage which caused heavy losses among every platoon. With many guides killed or wounded, the survivors stumbled on blindly to reach their positions before dawn. Their plight was precarious. No one knew how many men had been lost. Communications had been destroyed and the front line they had inherited was scarcely a line at all but rather a scattering of craters and shallow trenches dotted with the pillboxes and concrete shelters which had once formed the Wilhelm Line. As headquarters and medical staffs took over the ruined fortifications, A and D Companies sank into the slimy shell-holes, leaving B and C Companies in support. They had hardly settled in when the bombardment, already heavy, reached a crescendo. About 500yd to the east, some 'shorts' fell among two regiments of the 50th Reserve (Prussian) Division, delaying by 15 minutes their assault, delivered out of the mist at 5.30 am. An unpublished history of the Glasgow Highlanders records:

> Lewis gun and rapid rifle fire was opened on them, but still they came on, breaking into our front line where there was desperate hand-to-hand fighting among the shell-holes. A and D Companies fought stubbornly, but in several places the enemy broke through; on the right the Highlanders were pressed back, leaving many killed and wounded behind them and some 20 prisoners. As far as the forward companies were concerned, it was a case of every man for himself ...

On the flanks, the struggle was more intense. To the south, the 1st Queen's were pushed back 200yd, while the 1st Middlesex, covering the 98th Brigade on the fringes of Polygon Wood, yielded 600yd. In the Glasgow Highlanders' sector, the struggle swayed back and forth. Parts of the support companies were thrown forward in a desperate effort to shore up the battered line. Among those pitched into the fray was Acting L/Cpl John 'Hammy' Hamilton, an energetic 21-year-old B Company runner from Cambuslang, who, in a rare moment of bravado, had been heard to remark that he would win a VC.

As the fighting lapped around the shell-hole line, the most desperate need was for more small-arms ammunition. The only source of supplies was in the support lines but to reach them meant a dash across cratered, bullet-swept ground in full view of the enemy only a few yards away. It was a risk bordering on the suicidal, yet 'Hammy' Hamilton, having already delivered messages across the open, volunteered to make the attempt. Thus began a one-man supply operation that would run into the following day. No one knows how many times he made the journey back and forth. Time after time he braved the fire, emerging from the pall of smoke and shell-bursts to dole out handfuls of bullets.

He worked out his own method for limiting the risks. It involved not so much dodging shells as following them. Operating on the premise that shells never landed in the same spot twice, he literally chased the explosions on his charmed path through the maelstrom. It was, of course, a flawed theory. After all, near misses could kill just as well as direct hits, but such thoughts, if considered, were evidently discounted. Even when stocks of ammunition ran low, he refused to break off his self-imposed duty. Instead, he turned to the dead for salvation. Flitting from shell-hole to shell-hole, he scoured the battlefield, filling his pack with bullets from the pouches of fallen men, before returning to the embattled front line. It is impossible to exaggerate the impact of his actions on the outcome of the struggle. Not only did his exploits bring great practical benefit, they served as an inspiration to the men clinging to their exposed posts.

By the end of the morning, the Scots had been forced back 400yd, and the salient occupied by 100th Brigade north of the Menin road flattened out. But the line still held. Heavy shelling continued through the night, and the following day a counter-attack, supported by the reorganised Highlanders, recovered almost all the lost ground. During two days' fighting, the 1/9th HLI had suffered horrendous losses, most of them on 25 September. Roll calls revealed the extent of the carnage: eight officers wounded and approximately 450 men killed, wounded or missing.

Two months later, the *London Gazette* provided the survivors with a measure of compensation with the award of the Victoria Cross to No. 331958 Pte (Acting L/Cpl) John Brown Hamilton. The award was greeted with great pride, particularly among the men of B Company. The commander, 2/Lt W.R. Glen, wrote to Hamilton:

Hearty Congratulations!

You richly deserve the high honour which has been conferred upon you.

I feel proud to have commanded the company of which you were such a shining light and to which you have brought such fame.

No one knows better than I how nobly you earned the distinction of being the first Glasgow Highlander VC.

Characteristically, Hamilton dismissed such praise. 'I always believed it was the battalion that won the VC, and I was the one picked to carry it,' he once remarked.

John Brown Hamilton, known as Jack, was born at Dumbarton on 26 August 1896, the youngest son of Thomas Hamilton and Agnes (née Brown). Hamilton's father, a foreman in Messrs Hardie & Gordon's Levenbank steel foundry, had moved from Cambuslang to Dumbarton, where his family, consisting of five sons and a daughter, lived at 190 High Street, and later Bon Hill. Educated at Bridgend School and the Dumbarton Academy, John was a keen footballer and an enthusiastic member of the

2nd Company, Bridgend UF Church Boys' Brigade. Leaving school in 1912, he worked as an apprentice electrical fitter in the Leven Shipyard. But when his family returned to Halfway, Cambuslang, he resumed his training at the Newton Steel Works, Hallside, remaining there until 1914 when he joined the Electrical Co., Pitt Street, Glasgow.

Shortly before enlisting with a group of friends in 1915, Hamilton, a member of the Cambuslang Glenburn Football Club, married Mary Maxwell, at Hallside church, where both were choristers. The wedding, in defiance of their parents who thought them too young, was one of a group staged on the church steps for men enlisting. According to regimental records, he joined the Glasgow Highlanders on 21 October 1915 at the Drill Hall, Greendyke Street, Glasgow. Promoted acting lance-corporal a few months later, he went to France in April 1916. A fellow volunteer, G.M.C. Robertson, later described him as 'a boisterous type, always on the go and always finding something to talk about. He was heard to say he would get a VC. He ... was a non-smoker, a teetotaller, a good fellow to know who always had good thoughts.'

Hamilton was wounded on the road up to High Wood, during the fighting on the Somme in July 1916. He rejoined his unit about September 1917, shortly before the action in which he won his Victoria Cross. Shortly after, he was ordered home to the 5th (Reserve) Battalion, HLI, on the grounds, as his CO, Lt-Col A.H. Menzies, put it, that 'the VC should be a living VC'.

Hamilton, who ended the war a sergeant instructor, was honoured in Dumbarton and Cambuslang, where the citizens made him a Freeman of the Burgh. Returning to his electrical job, he maintained his regimental connections, serving in the Territorial Army. Tragedy struck when he lost two sons to the influenza pandemic which swept the world after the war. He was left with a daughter, Jessie, born in October 1918, and a son, Ian, born six years later.

In 1939 Hamilton himself became seriously ill after a bout of influenza and, much to his chagrin, he was declared unfit to go overseas with his battalion. Forced to break his service, he re-enlisted and was commissioned into the Pioneer Corps in 1941. After serving at Prestatyn, he took command of a prisoner-of-war camp, guarding Italians captured in the Middle East. He threw himself into his new role with all his old energy. His daughter, Jessie, recorded:

I well remember him saying when he went to this camp the prisoners were wandering about with their hands in their pockets. This made him angry, and he ordered all trouser pockets to be sewn up. He always said, 'idle hands lead to trouble', so he set about getting them to work and found a lot of those young men were talented in many ways ... One young soldier was always trying to paint or draw, but had no decent materials to work with. My father, out of his own money, bought paints, etc. At the end of the war, when the prisoners were going home, my father was presented with a large painting at a farewell concert. I have that painting hanging in my home now.

Searching for a fresh challenge after the war, he applied to become the first probation officer for Lanarkshire. It was a job promising long hours and demanding enormous commitment, an attribute he possessed in abundance. Initially operating alone, he eventually retired in 1962 with a staff of twenty. A glutton for work, he derived immense satisfaction from seeing young offenders make good.

His wife died a year after his retirement, but Jack Hamilton retained his zest for life. His daughter remembers his visits to Dundee in a Wolsey car 'which he drove like Stirling Moss', but his greatest enthusiasm was reserved for his beloved Cambuslang Rangers FC. One of the team's most passionate supporters, Saturday afternoons were devoted to 'shouting and whistling at "The Boys" to get them going!' A member of the Cambuslang ex-servicemen's bowling club, he also became an ardent campaigner on behalf of pensioners' rights. Even during his last painful years when he was dying of cancer, he continued to petition political and union leaders for bigger pensions. His daughter recalled: 'It kept his spirits up writing to many MPs to get something done. He thought it was a disgrace. We never quite knew what we would read about in the papers if his mind was made up to take up the fight on behalf of a good cause.'

Jack Hamilton, a fighter to the end, died in Hairmyres Hospital, East Kilbride, on 18 July 1973, aged 76. Four days before his death, he was reputedly sitting up in his hospital bed, demanding to know the latest news of his favourite football team. His medals, originally held at the Glasgow Highlanders Regimental Club, were presented by his daughter to the Scottish United Services Museum, in Edinburgh Castle, following the demise of her father's old unit.

J.J. DWYER AND P.J. BUGDEN

Near Zonnebeke and Polygon Wood,
26–28 September 1917

The enemy's spoiling attack on 25 September had failed utterly to achieve its purpose. Plumer was not deflected. The second stage of his offensive continued on schedule with only minor amendments. By the early hours of 26 September the assault troops were in position. South-west of Zonnebeke an officer of the 4th Australian Machine-Gun Company noted in his diary: '5.45 am. All the fighters on the tape and ready to hop off. An ideal morning, misty. Can see just about 100 yard in front.'

Five minutes later the Battle of Polygon Wood began, with troops from seven divisions attacking along a 6-mile front. Once again the main effort was in the centre, where the 4th and 5th Australian Divisions advanced south of Zonnebeke. According to Charles Bean, the attack was supported by 'the most perfect barrage that had ever protected Australian troops'. To the machine-gun officer, it seemed like 'one continuous thunder'. So intense was the bombardment that the infantry could feel the warm air generated by the shells' friction. Bean recorded: 'The ground was dry and the shell-bursts raised a wall of dust and smoke which appeared almost to be solid ... Roaring, deafening, it rolled ahead of the troops like a Gippsland bush-fire ... Direction had to be kept by officers with compass in hand.'

The 4th Australian Machine-Gun Company's role was two-fold: to cover the 4th Brigade's advance towards the first objective and to offer close support to the leading waves. To this end, eight Vickers guns and their crews from Nos 2 and 3 Sections were attached to the infantry. Sgt Jack Dwyer, a 27-year-old Tasmanian recently returned to the unit after being wounded at Messines, was in charge of one gun team. Among the three battalions his unit was supporting was the 15th Battalion, with whom he had served at Gallipoli.

Such was the accuracy of the barrage that many of the German front-line posts fell without firing a shot. Sweeping across the depression at the source of the Steenbeek, the Australians reached their final objective on Tokio spur around 8 am. The fighting, however, was far from over. During the latter stages of the advance opposition had intensified, and as the Australians set about consolidating they found themselves coming under increasing fire from pockets of resistance which had evaded capture. One source of trouble was a machine-gun sited on the right, opposite Molenaarelsthoek, which had inflicted numerous casualties and brought the advance at this point to a standstill. Dwyer's contribution thus far had been unspectacular. He was in the process of moving his gun to a new site in advance of the captured line, ready to repel any counter-attack, when he spotted the enemy position. What followed was recorded by Capt. A. Mitchell, OC 4th Machine-Gun Company:

> Unhesitatingly he rushed his gun forward to within 30 yards of the enemy gun and fired point-blank at it, putting it out of action and killing the gun crew. He then seized the gun and, totally ignoring the snipers from the rear of the enemy position, carried it back across the shell-swept ground to our front line and established both it and his Vickers gun on the right flank of our Brigade.

By 11.30 am word had reached the 4th Machine-Gun Company's Advanced HQ that all its guns were in position: '4in or about the Blue Line and 2 near the Red Line. Only one man wounded.' Ammunition and rations were sent forward, but the next report was less encouraging. The war diary records: 'Message received that the Boche were collecting in certain vicinities in front of our positions apparently for a counter-attack.'

Around 3 pm, following an intense but inaccurate bombardment, the Germans attacked, only to be slaughtered in their hundreds. Dwyer, directing the fire of both his own and the captured machine-gun, was prominent in the defence. According to Capt. Mitchell, he 'commanded these guns with utter coolness and when the enemy counter-attacked ... he rendered great assistance in repulsing them'. Around 6 pm another barrage fell around the Australians, to be followed by a counter-bombardment which appeared to deter the enemy. The artillery duel, however, claimed its toll of machine-guns. Two were destroyed, with two men from the unit being killed and one officer fatally wounded. But as darkness fell, the Australians were still holding firm.

To the south two brigades of the 5th Australian Division attacked with the objective of clearing Polygon Wood. The 15th Brigade, on the right of the Anzac front, included the 31st (Queensland and Victoria) Battalion and the 29th (Victoria) Battalion from the 8th Brigade in place of two units which had suffered heavily during the enemy's counter-attack the previous day. The late change in personnel caused difficulties which became apparent in the early stages of the attack when differences in training caused the units to become hopelessly mixed.

The confused fighting was at its worst on the extreme right. As the leading two platoons of the 31st Battalion pushed on towards the second objective, they ran into heavy enfilading fire from positions across the divisional boundary missed by the barrage. Much of the fire was coming from a network of pillboxes about 300yd away on a slight spur running towards Jerk House. Lt R. Thompson detailed two Lewis gun sections to attack the pillboxes while the rest of the leading company swung quarter right and headed straight towards them. During the series of stubborn fights which ensued around the pillboxes a 20-year-old infantryman from Alstonville, New South Wales, played a leading role.

Paddy Bugden was a natural athlete. At 6ft tall and weighing over 14st, he was a towering presence in the B Company football team, where his exploits earned him the nickname 'the Tank'. But in the early morning of 26 September the young Lewis gunner with a passion for sport found himself at the forefront of a far more deadly contest. Twice, in the face of devastating fire, the burly Australian led small parties in successful attacks on the pillboxes. From one blockhouse seized by Thompson's Lewis gunners, no fewer than four machine-guns were captured. But the enemy defences proved too strong and, having suffered numerous officer casualties, the Australians were driven to ground. Bugden's part in the battle, however, had only just begun. With the attack at this point apparently stalled, enemy troops occupying Jerk House and Cameron Covert boldly counter-attacked, capturing two officers and twenty men at heavy cost. Right across the southern sector, where the Australians' right flank hung open for much of the morning, the fighting ebbed and flowed. As the struggle fragmented, a number of men found themselves cut off. In a letter home, Cpl Alf Thompson, of the 31st, recorded:

After we had advanced and gained our objectives, our boys on the right flank got the order to fall back owing to the English Division [33rd British Division] that was on our right not being able to come up. I was out in a shell-hole in front and did not get the order to retire so I did not know that I was left on my own. When Fritz counter-attacked us I got two of them with my rifle but I had to duck down in the shell-hole owing to a machine-gun firing on me. Just then, three Fritzs tumbled into the shell-hole on top of me giving me no chance to put up a scrap. They immediately disarmed me and the youngest Fritz, who was about 18 years of age, put his revolver at my head and was going to shoot. The eldest Fritz of the three started gibbering away in German and eventually made the young Fritz take his revolver away from my head (much to my relief!) A moment or so after ... the Fritz who had just saved me from being shot made a jump into the next shell-hole and got shot through the stomach. I looked up to see what was happening and saw a private named Paddy Bugden charging

Les Andrew leads the New Zealand contingent at the Coronation of King George VI in 1937

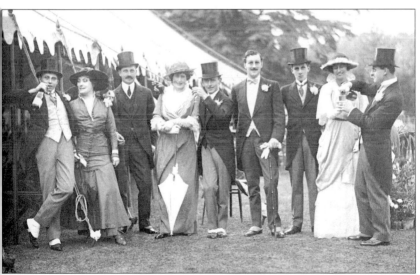

'Riv' Colyer-Fergusson, extreme left, in high spirits at a family wedding, Ightham Mote, 18 July 1914

Clifford Coffin leaving Buckingham Palace after his investiture

Artist's impression of Tom Mayson's VC action

George McIntosh receives his VC
from King George V at Ibrox Park,
September 1917

Ivor Rees talking to young soldiers at the Welsh Brigade Depot on the fiftieth
anniversary of the Battle of the Somme

Robert Bye winning his VC, portrayed by David Rowlands

Thomas Whitham VC with Burnley child celebrity known as 'Little Kitchener'

Artist's impression of Arnold Loosemore's VC action

Harold Ackroyd as a house
doctor at Guy's Hospital,
1902

Artist's impression of Wilfrid Edwards' VC action

Edward Cooper leading G Coy, 9th N Riding Bn, Home Guard

John Skinner with his bride Annie Lee, whom he married three days after receiving his VC

John Carmichael being congratulated on his VC award by the Revd E. Sherwood Gunson at his home in Glenmavis

John Moyney, wearing his VC group, meets the Queen at an Irish Guards reunion

Roy Inwood, wearing his VC, in a family group portrait shortly after returning to Australia. His brother, Robert, far right back row, was superimposed by the photographer. Robert had been killed in 1916

Alfred and Mabel Knight, centre, with regimental comrades gather for his
Buckingham Palace investiture

Billy Hewitt is
congratulated on the
award of his Victoria
Cross

John Hamilton returns to Hallside Steel Works, Newton, after his VC award

Artist's impression of Hugh Colvin's VC action

James Dwyer is carried shoulder high across South Bruny Jetty after his return to
Alonnah, Tasmania, in 1918

Clement Robertson, on the left at the back, in a family group, with his parents and
brothers, Fred, alongside him, and Charles, seated at front. The picture was taken at
Struan Hill, Delgany

Lewis Evan's wedding to Dorothea Pryse-Rice, October 1918. His uncle, Lt-Gen. Sir James Hills-Johnes, an Indian Mutiny VC winner, is in the centre of the back row

Thomas Sage in later life. He had lost his right eye as a result of his VC action

Arthur Hutt being fêted on his return to Coventry in January 1918

Brothers in arms: Fred, seated, and Harry Greaves. Harry earned the DSO, MC and two Bars all in the space of a year's fighting

James Ockendon returns home to Southsea in November 1917, with his wife, Caroline, at his side

John Molyneux shakes hands with the Prince of Wales, later King Edward VIII, at Victoria Park, St Helens. Behind him is another VC, John Thomas Davies, who won his award during the German spring offensive of 1918

Tommy Holmes, centre

Artist's impression of Fred Dancox's VC action

George Mullin being congratulated on his VC award by Capt. L. Drummond-Hay, who received an MC in the same action

Christopher O'Kelly

up with a few men to my rescue. The other two Fritzes made to get away and Bugden quickly finished them off and I was then able to get back to our lines safely. The whole ... episode took place under very heavy shell, rifle and machine-gun fire, so you can understand the debt I owe to Paddy Bugden for his bravery in rescuing me.

The fighting rumbled on into 27 September. Opposite Molenaarelsthoek, the 4th Brigade's positions were heavily shelled, compelling Sgt Dwyer to constantly change his gun positions. His commanding officer noted: 'On one occasion his Vickers gun was blown up by shell-fire and he conducted his gun team back to HQ through the enemy barrage, secured one of the reserve guns and rushed it back to our positions in the shortest possible time.'

At some point during that second day, the surviving gun teams were relieved and as Dwyer and his comrades made their way back to the transport lines each man was handed a cup of port-wine or coffee. It was richly deserved. They had helped to beat off every attack thrown at them at a cost of nine men killed (or died of wounds) and fourteen wounded. Remarkably, Dwyer was untouched. In his recommendation for Dwyer's VC, Capt. Mitchell concluded: 'During the whole of the attack, he displayed extreme coolness and his contempt of all danger and his cheerfulness and courage raised the spirits and admiration of all who were in his sector of the line.'

The same could have been said of Bugden. According to his citation, he was 'always foremost in volunteering for any dangerous missions'. He had already done enough during the fighting to earn the VC, yet he continued to risk his life. Five times he dashed out amid shell- and machine-gun fire to rescue wounded men lying in the open. It was apparently while engaged on another of these missions, on 28 September, that he was killed. The precise circumstances are unclear. The 31st were relieved on the night of 27–28 September and moved back to reserve trenches near Black Watch Corner. While there, parties were sent out, in the face of 'constant shell- and machine-gun fire', to recover the dead. It seems likely that Bugden was killed during this period. Cpl Thompson, the man whose life Bugden had saved earlier in the fighting, simply recorded that he was killed 'by a shell a couple of nights later'.

The Victoria Crosses awarded to Bugden and Dwyer were both gazetted on 26 November 1917. Bugden was buried close by where he fell. Later, his isolated grave, set among the ragged tree stumps on the southern edge of Nonne Boschen, was fenced off and an ornate wooden cross placed over it. Writing to Bugden's mother on 18 March 1918, Alan G. Corrie, a member of the 31st Battalion, included a rough sketch of the site and added:

The boys of the battalion have also paid for an artificial French cross made of china and glass which also rests on the spot at the foot of the large white wooden cross. On it is written in metal letters: 'In loving memory of our dear comrade' ... I shall ever think of Paddy with pride and reverence ... By the death of so gallant a soldier and a gentleman, the world is so much the poorer.

Patrick Joseph Bugden was born on 17 March 1897 at South Gundurimba, New South Wales, the eldest child of Thomas Bugden, a farmer, and his wife Annie (née Connolly). He was only 6 when his father died, leaving four children. His mother later married an hotelier in the Brunswick district, J.J. Kelly, and had a further four children. Bugden was educated at the Gundurimba Public School, the convent school at Tatham and later the local public school, where his powerful physique brought him success as a shot-putter, cricketer and footballer. Leaving school, he worked in the post office at Mullumbimby, but later resigned to join his stepfather as a barman at the family's New Brunswick Hotel in Billinudgel and then at the Federal Hotel, Alstonville.

He enlisted, aged 19, at Lismore on 25 May 1916, giving his occupation as hotel-keeper and his age as 21. His only previous military experience consisted of twelve months' training under the compulsory system of 'boys conscription'. As No. 3774 Pte P.J. Bugden, he underwent four months' training at Enoggera, in Queensland, embarking for England on 19 September with the 9th Reinforcements, 31st Infantry Battalion. Arriving at Plymouth on 9 December, he joined the 8th Training Battalion. During his spell on Salisbury Plain, he visited London and struggled to come to terms with the English climate. He developed mumps, but was recovered enough to join a detachment going over to France in January.

Posted to the 5th Base Depot at Etaples, he sought to come to terms with the possibility of death. A Catholic with strong religious convictions, he had spoken at length with the camp padre in England. Now, he wrote to his mother, '... if by chance anything happens to me rest ashured [sic] that I feel in my heart that I shall gain a place of happiness for I have never did [sic] a deed in my life that I am ashamed of'. On 19 March, two days after his 20th birthday, he was officially taken on the strength of the 31st Battalion near Bapaume. Optimism was running high. The Germans were pulling back to the Hindenburg Line, and the front was fluid. Bugden was attached to a Lewis gun section and, writing home on 9 April, he declared:

I am an old veteran now (or consider myself so) for I have seen a fair bit of scrapping. I don't think it will take us long to fix them now and I will be disappointed if I am not back for the New Year. There is one God since the weather is a lot warmer now. It was a holy terror a few months ago. I would sooner face Fritz any time than it ...

His letters were filled with the enthusiasm of youth and the excitement of new experiences; from learning French to representing his unit in drill and sporting competitions. As the weeks passed, however, the realisation dawned that his hopes of an early end to the war had been over-optimistic. In the aftermath of heavy fighting around Bullecourt, he noted: 'I have been innoculated again against fever and we want it too for the smell is high about our sector ... Fritzy got what is commonly called hell and we got nearly the same. I would not take twenty to one on his chance now although he will hold out a year yet.'

From June until September the 31st Battalion enjoyed a rest from the front line. Despite the fearful mauling at Bullecourt, Bugden's confidence was unshaken. While visiting Amiens on 23 June, he saw his first Americans:

In appearance they are a lot like us. If they are as good, lord help poor Fritz. I often wish there were about three million of us but I'll bet Fritz don't. The Russians are big squibs. The war would shure [sic] been over by October if they had had a kick in them. It means another winter now but we'll fix them. I tip October twelve months. Just see how far I'm out ...

Bugden spent much of August competing in inter-unit sports contests and

assisting French farmers with their harvest. It was a happy time, involving much good-humoured fraternisation. Bugden, who had featured in a propaganda film entitled *The Australians at Sport*, wrote excitedly to his sister: 'I am going strong with a French girl ... We can't understand one another. Only sit down and wink at one another. It all helps to pass the time. I keep an eye on the old man and when ever I see him approaching with a pitchfork I turn the steering wheel for the billet.'

By the third week of September, the 5th Division's holiday was over. Their move into Belgium en route to the Ypres Salient was complete and as the day of their entry into the battle drew nearer Bugden took pride in his growing reputation. To a

Pte P.J. Bugden

friend, he wrote on 24 September: 'I have a great name amongst the Batt Boys as a footballer. They call me the "Tank" and they think there is no one like me as a player.' The following day, he scribbled a brief note to his grandmother. There was no mention of the coming battle. 'News', he wrote, 'is scarce.' The only hint of menace was in a reference to his Lewis gun section guarding against aerial attack. Much of his time, he claimed, was spent in gathering in hops, although whether this was merely intended as a cover to protect them from the grim reality is not clear. It was the last letter his family would receive.

After the war, Paddy Bugden's remains were exhumed and reinterred in the Hooge Crater British war cemetery, Zillebeke. The people of Alstonville, New South Wales, remembered him by naming a street Bugden Avenue in his honour, and it was there, in 1948, that the local sub-branch of the Returned Services League raised the Paddy Bugden Memorial, a sandstone cross on a concrete base, as a focus for Anzac Day observances. His Victoria Cross has been displayed in Brisbane since 1980, after being presented to the Queensland Museum by Mrs Rose Elliott, his eldest surviving sister.

James Dwyer was born at Port Cygnet, Tasmania, on 9 March 1890, the eldest son of Charles Dwyer, a farmer, and his wife Mary (née Scanlon). Jack Dwyer lived with his parents at Alonnah, Bruny Island, and was educated at Mills Reef School until the age of 12. In 1910 he left Tasmania to become a cane-cutter in Queensland, returning three years later to work on the Mount Lyell Company's Lake Margaret hydro-electric power scheme.

He was employed as a labourer and a 'first-rate axeman' at Queenstown when he enlisted as a private (No. 2060) in the 15th Battalion at Claremont, Tasmania, on 4 February 1915. He was described as being 5ft 11in tall, weighing 12st 2lb and having very curly brown hair. Posted to the 5th Reinforcements, 15th Battalion, on 15 April, he joined the unit on Gallipoli in August. The following month, after a bout of influenza, he was attached to a military police unit at Anzac beach. Dwyer's spell with the 15th ended in March 1916 when he was transferred to the 4th Machine-Gun Company, with whom he saw much fighting. Promotion followed. He was made lance-corporal in December and the following April, as a result of losses during the Bullecourt fighting, he leapt two ranks to temporary sergeant in the space of 24 hours. Wounded in the left arm and shoulder at Messines on 9 June, he was evacuated to a Base Hospital at Le Havre where he relinquished his sergeant's rank. He rejoined his unit on 22 August and a week later his third stripe was restored.

Dwyer received his VC from King George V at Buckingham Palace on 23 January 1918. Appointed temporary regimental sergeant-major on

9 April, he was commissioned second lieutenant in the field on 20 May. Returning to Tasmania in August as a lieutenant, he was carried shoulder-high along the South Bruny jetty at Alonnah to the island's only car.

In December he left the Army and established an orchard under the soldier-settlement scheme. He married Myrtle Mary Dillon at St Brendan's Catholic church, Alonnah, on 24 September 1919, and they had six children. Such were the vagaries of the fruit farming trade that Dwyer was forced to take a job at his father-in-law's sawmill.

Around this time he took his first tentative steps into the political arena, serving as a Bruny Island councillor from 1924 to 1926. Two years later, he moved to New Norfolk where he established his own saw-

Sgt J.J. Dwyer (after being commissioned)

mill. In May 1931 he was elected to the Tasmanian House of Assembly as a Labour member for Franklin, a seat he held until his death. Largely self-taught, Jack Dwyer was not noted as an orator. But he did possess a colourful turn of phrase. One of his favourite expressions was: 'As Ned Kelly said to his girl, there's no time like the present.' As Speaker of the House from 1942 to 1948, he insisted on 'a fair go for all'. A former member of the House of Assembly remembered:

He had natural dignity and with his handsome looks and greying hair soon became known as 'Old Silver' to most members ... He was always enormously popular and returned servicemen especially regarded him as their own. But he also spent quite a bit of time in bowls and golf clubs. He was in every sense of the word a man's man.

Appointed Minister for Agriculture and Fisheries in 1948, he held the post for thirteen years until failing health forced him to stand down. He was particularly interested in fishing and his dedicated support of fishermen's rights made him one of the most effective ministers in Tasmania's history. From August 1958 until May 1959 he served as the island's Deputy-Premier, an outstanding achievement for a man who had left school with few qualifications.

Remembered affectionately as a true Labourite politician of the old school, he believed in maintaining close personal contact with his constituents, a source of strength that made him unassailable in ten elections. Although a regular visitor to RSL clubs, where he enjoyed a beer with his old comrades, he seldom discussed his war experiences. Once asked about his VC action, he claimed he 'was drunk at the time'. His daughter, Mollie Goggins, wrote of him:

> He was a very caring man, worked extremely hard to provide for his wife and children, and always gave praise when due but found it very hard to express his feelings into words. I can remember him always helping the poor and the needy ... many times sharing meals with the unfortunate, even up to his death. One of his many attributes was being known as a very caring man.

Jack Dwyer, known as 'JJ' to a generation of Tasmanians, died on Bruny Island on 17 January 1962. He had been hospitalised the previous year suffering from dermatitis, thought to have been a legacy of exposure to mustard gas on the Western Front. Accorded a state funeral, the 'father' and most popular member of the House of Assembly was buried in Cornelian Bay cemetery, with the Governor, the Premier, numerous civic dignitaries and three holders of the Victoria Cross among more than two thousand mourners.

Two decades later, his son, an AIF veteran of the Second World War, and other family members presented Dwyer's VC medal group to the Australian War Memorial in Canberra as a lasting tribute to a man of humble roots who became one of Tasmania's greatest sons.

P.E. BENT

Near Polygon Wood, 1 October 1917

As Plumer's piecemeal offensive edged across the Gheluvelt plateau, the Germans signalled their determination to hold the eastern end with a series of desperate counter-attacks, each one timed to take advantage of the thick ground mist shrouding the district in the early morning hours. On 30 September one such assault, led by parties of flame-throwers and bombers, was repulsed between the Reutelbeek and the Menin road, not far from where Jack Hamilton had won his VC. The next day, undeterred by their heavy losses, they attacked again, with twelve sections of specially trained assault groups leading the way.

Some of the hardest fighting took place in and around Polygon Wood where a scattering of shell-holes was manned by units of the depleted 110th (Leicestershire) Brigade. They had only just moved on to the newly won ground and conditions were appalling. David Kelly, an officer at Brigade HQ, described the grim setting as 'dreary and miserable'. The night was bitterly cold and the Leicesters were, in the words of one of their number, 'mud-wallowing in the open air'. The headquarters party of the 9th Leicestershires dug in as best they could near a German pillbox, where they contrived to make a shelter out of some abandoned planks of wood that were lying about. Patrols were sent out and dispositions made, but preparations for defence were still incomplete when the ground quaked beneath a devastating bombardment. It was the heaviest shelling Kelly had experienced in more than two years' front-line service. It smothered the British lines to a depth of 1,000yd and was rapidly followed by a well-timed assault by storm troops charging out of a curtain of smoke from the direction of Cameron Covert and Joist Farm.

The struggle which ensued would go down in regimental history as a minor epic distinguished by the outstanding courage of one of the Army's youngest battalion commanders, 26-year-old Lt-Col Philip Bent, a Canadian-born former Merchant Navy seaman whose substantive rank was that of a mere lieutenant. Such was the confusion and the high number of casualties that details of the action are sketchy, but it is clear that the initial storm burst heaviest on the positions occupied by A Company. An outline of the fierce battle that raged from early morning into the afternoon is provided by the battalion's war diary. The blow-by-blow account begins with the lightning bombardment:

5.25 am. Enemy put down heavy barrage on front Company and POLYGON WOOD and at the same time put up a smoke-screen all along Battalion front.

5.27 am. Enemy attacked through smoke-screen. SOS sent up. First wave of enemy driven off by A Coy by Lewis Gun and Rifle fire. Capt A.A.D. Lee MC, killed.

5.30 am. Enemy second wave driven off on our front, but enemy attack on Battalion of [sic] right flank successful. Right flank of A Coy (front line Coy) threatened.

5.40 am. 2 Platoons of D Coy (in reserve) under Lt-Col P.E. Bent DSO, and B Coy (in support) under Lt Burn immediately counter-attacked enemy. Counter-attack was entirely successful and drove enemy from our front. Lt-Col Bent killed whilst leading the charge.

5.45 am. Enemy continued to make headway on right flank ... and launched his third Wave against our front. Two platoons of C Coy sent up to counter-attack enemy on our right flank. Lt Burn killed.

6.00 am. C Coy counter-attack reported to have stopped enemy advance. 2 Platoons of C Coy sent up to reinforce and to get in touch with troops on right flank who had been driven back some distance.

Enemy attacking troops driven off but owing to heavy casualties in front Coy, a defensive line was organised approximately 100yd in rear of our front line, along E[astern] edge of POLYGON WOOD. Enemy shelling POLYGON WOOD extremely heavy, causing many casualties. 2/Lt Barratt killed. 2/Lts Faulkner, Scott and Hallam wounded. C Coy established defensive flank ... in front of CAMERON HOUSE ... Full report sent to Bde and reinforcements asked for. Enemy repeatedly attempted to advance but was driven back by our Lewis Gun and Rifle Fire, and the line was held against further attack.

Throughout, the 9th had maintained contact with the 8th Leicestershires on the left, but the right flank lay exposed. At 9.30 am, as shells bracketed the track running from the western edge of Polygon Wood and Glencourse Wood to Black Watch Corner, the first reinforcements began to arrive. Two platoons of the 7th Leicestershires were sent forward, but two more companies did not fare as well. Caught by the enemy barrage, they reached the position only seventy strong. While one party was sent to bolster the defensive flank, another dug a second line 100yd inside the wood's eastern fringes.

Low-level strafing attacks hampered the work, but a corporal exacted partial revenge by shooting down one aircraft. No further attack came and German stretcher-bearers were seen carrying away their wounded. The war diary noted: 'Enemy casualties appear to be very heavy.' At noon, the CO of the 7th Leicesters arrived to take charge, and the rest of the afternoon was spent preparing to meet a fresh attack, reportedly planned for dusk. But despite numerous alarms late into the evening the Leicesters were left alone. As 1 October 1917 faded into history, the night sky was aglow with 'thousands of Very lights' as a bombardment pounded the enemy lines. Next morning, pockets of Germans, cut off near the Leicesters' position, were seen running back. Few made it. What was left of Bent's command came out of the line in the early hours of 3 October, the survivors forming two companies to merge with the depleted 8th Battalion.

The Leicesters' stubborn defiance had thwarted enemy designs at heavy cost. The inspiration behind their brave defence had undoubtedly been Philip Bent. If the times in the unit war diary are accurate, his involvement in the fighting amounted to a bare 20 minutes from the moment his men recoiled from the initial shock of the enemy thrust to his death at the head of a scratch counter-attack force. Yet his short-lived intervention was a decisive factor in galvanising the defence at a critical moment when any delay or hesitation could have proved disastrous not just for his battalion but for Plumer's planned attack three days later. With SOS rockets shooting into the sky all along the front, the Leicesters' plight had seemed parlous. D.A. Bacon, a private soldier serving at 9th Battalion Headquarters, described how, as the 'threatening' situation developed, Bent had called Brigade Headquarters for immediate help only to discover that he could expect no support for some hours 'owing to the conditions of approach and the heavy and deep enemy barrage'. It was at that point, with A Company falling back and catastrophe looming, he took matters into his own hands. In a memoir published thirteen years later, fellow Leicestershire officer David Kelly gave a description of what followed, based on personal conversations with a company commander and the adjutant of the 9th:

Colonel Bent ... was in a 'pillbox' on the west side of the wood when a runner came in saying 'SOS gone up from (the reserve) company'. 'Then we'd better get on,' said the Colonel, and went forward with his headquarter personnel. Collecting the reserve company and everyone available, the Colonel led a counter-attack, and, struck down in the moment of victory, was last seen – for his body, doubtless blown to pieces, was not found – waving his pipe and calling, 'Go on, Tigers!'

That same stirring battle cry, or a version of it, would enter the annals of Leicestershire regimental history and even found a place in the citation for the posthumous Victoria Cross published in the *London Gazette* of 11 January 1918:

> For most conspicuous bravery, when during a heavy hostile attack the right of his own command and the battalion on his right were forced back. The situation was critical owing to the confusion caused by the attack and the intense artillery fire. Lieutenant Colonel Bent personally collected a platoon which was in reserve, and together with men from other companies and various regimental details, he organised and led them forward to the counter-attack, after issuing orders to other officers as to the further defence of the line. The counter-attack was successful, and the enemy were checked.
>
> The coolness and magnificent example shown to all ranks by Lieutenant Colonel Bent resulted in the securing of a portion of the line which was of essential importance for subsequent operations. This very gallant officer was killed whilst leading a charge which he inspired with the call of 'Come on, the Tigers.'

Philip Eric Bent, the first Canadian-born VC recipient of the campaign, was born on 3 January 1891 in Halifax, Nova Scotia, the youngest of three children to Frank and Sophia Bent. His Canadian father was a clerk and later superintendent in the railway mail service and Philip was brought to England at an early age by his mother.

Educated at Ashby-de-la-Zouch Grammar School in Leicestershire, he spent his holidays with relatives in Weymouth and , with a view to pursuing a career at sea, he joined HMS *Conway*, the Mersey-based Merchant Navy training ship, in 1909. His time there was brief but successful. He earned a silver medal for boxing and left Conway in December 1910 with an 'extra certificate' as Senior Cadet-Captain Port Main. His first sea-going appointment was as apprentice aboard the 2,233-ton four-masted barque Vimeria owned by John Hardie & Co. of Glasgow. He sailed with her for three years, gaining his Second Mate's ticket in early 1914.

Ashore when war broke out, Philip Bent enlisted in the Army at Prince's Street recruiting office, in Edinburgh on 3 October 1914. His attestation papers show him as having a distinctive frog tattoo on his left forearm and give his mother, then living in Oxford, as his next-of-kin. Quite why, as a Merchant Navy officer, he joined the Army rather than the Royal Navy remains unexplained. Whatever his reasons, he served as a private in A Company, 1st City of Edinburgh Battalion, Royal Scots until 29 November when he was granted a temporary commission in the Leicestershire Regiment. Five months later he was posted to the 7th Leicesters, a New Army battalion, based at Aldershot. Promoted lieutenant in June, he was transferred to the 9th Battalion and sailed for France with his unit in July. Soldiering was clearly to his liking and spells in the line in Flanders and the Arras sector were sufficient to convince him to re-think his career. With the support of his commanding officer, he applied for a permanent commission in the regular army, preferably with the Leicesters. Writing in support of him on 13 March 1916, Lt-Col C.H. Haig noted: 'He is a particularly efficient officer and a very good disciplinarian. He is at present Battalion Grenade officer and has done very good work in that appointment.' A medical board stated that he had impaired vision of the right eye, but thought that glasses could overcome the problem. Either way, it proved no handicap to his ambition and the following month the former Merchant Navy officer was granted a permanent commission as a second lieutenant in the Bedfordshire Regiment. He retained the temporary rank of captain, to which he had been promoted on 21 April, and remained with the 9th Leicesters. Thus far, he had experienced some discomfort but relatively little action, as was illustrated by a letter he wrote home that spring:

Life in the trenches this winter has not been very pleasant, owing to the excessive bad weather, which has made our trenches canals and our dugouts to fall in. However, the last week has been glorious, sunshine and good north-westerly winds: so we are all hoping the worst of the weather is over.

Everything is very quiet with us, a few hours' bombardment and an occasional bombing escapade make up our daily routine.

All of that was to change in July when the battalion was moved to the Somme sector. A costly attack on the Bazentin ridge was followed in September by a bloody assault on Gueudecourt. Philip Bent, who had been Mentioned in Despatches in June and promoted temporary major in mid-July, escaped both actions unhurt only to suffer gunshot wounds to the neck in October. Evacuated to hospital at Boulogne, he was back with the unit in less than ten days and his meteoric rise was made complete on 26 October when he was appointed acting lieutenant-colonel in command of the battalion. The rank was made temporary on 1 February 1917 and three months later he led his unit into action for the first time at Bullecourt. Losses were again heavy and little ground gained, but the young battalion commander's leadership was recognised by a second Mention in Despatches (gazetted 22 May) and the award of a Distinguished Service Order (gazetted 4 June). A second assault over much the same ground on 15 June proved equally unsuccessful and the following month the 9th Leicesters were withdrawn into divisional reserve. That same month, the Leicesters' temporary lieutenant-colonel was promoted lieutenant!

Details of his final action at Polygon Wood were slow in reaching his family. As late as January 1918 relatives were writing to the War Office asking for information about the circumstances of his death. There was also uncertainty as to whether his body had been buried and any grave marked. Two months later, his mother, who had been appointed sole executor of his will, travelled to Buckingham Palace to receive her son's Victoria Cross and Distinguished Service Order from the King. Five years later she, in turn, presented them to Philip's old school, where they remained until 1972 when they were passed to the Royal Leicestershire Regimental Museum on permanent loan.

Today, Philip Bent is remembered in England and Nova Scotia. War memorials at Hindhead in Surrey, where his mother lived for a time, and his old school honour his sacrifice. His sword was also hung in the church in Ashby-de-la-Zouch where he had his first communion. Across the Atlantic, the Army Museum in Halifax, Nova Scotia displays a portrait together with mementoes of his days aboard HMS *Conway*.

Despite thorough searches of the battlefield Philip's body was never found. His name is among more than 34,000 commemorated on the Tyne Cot Memorial, a few miles from where he fell, making his last gallant gesture.

W. PEELER AND L. McGEE

Levi Cottages and Hamburg Redoubt,
4 October 1917

The Australians of the 37th Battalion who crowded into the narrow assembly positions on the wet ground along the Gravenstafel Spur on the eve of battle were within 200yd of the enemy outposts. Behind them, across the wilderness of mud, three more battalions, each around 500 strong and laden with bombs, grenades, rifles, bayonets, sandbags, stretchers, picks and shovels, edged towards the lines of tapes which straddled the shell-holes. Looking back, Lt L.P. Little watched the 'awe-inspiring spectacle' of the 'slow-moving figures of men silhouetted against the sky' by the flashes of guns. Enemy flares illuminated the gloom but, according to Little, the men managed to form up 'right under the nose of the enemy without being seen or heard'.

These men from the 37th, 38th, 39th and 40th Battalions formed the 10th Brigade, 3rd Australian Division, one of the assault formations that would deliver the main attack in the third stage of Plumer's offensive, designed to clear the eastern end of Gheluvelt plateau and seize Broodseinde ridge. Their task was to take a 1,950yd strip of the Gravenstafel spur, chequered with pillboxes, from Levi Cottages to the vicinity of Dab Trench, north of Broodseinde. Each battalion was to leap-frog the other, with the 37th leading to the first objective 600yd ahead. Among the men in the first wave was a battle hardened, 30 year old lance-corporal from Castlemaine, Victoria. Wally Peeler was not a member of the 37th Battalion and nor, in all probability, had he ever been trained to operate as part of an assault force. He was simply one of twenty-four men from the 3rd Pioneers' Lewis gun section assigned to the 37th to provide defence against low-flying enemy aircraft.

Zero hour was at 6 am on 4 October, but half an hour earlier, with the troops clogging shell-holes and ditches, the tense quiet was shattered by an enemy barrage. For an anxious few moments, it appeared that the plan had been discovered. 'That half hour was nerve-racking,' admitted Lt Little, 'but instead of demoralising our assembled troops [it] tended only to develop and strengthen the fighting spirit requisite for an attack.' Only later, as the first enemy prisoners arrived, would the truth become clear: the Germans were planning their own attack, timed for 6.15 am.

Dead on time, the British guns thundered, drowning the sound of the enemy barrage. A curtain of smoke merged with the murky twilight and drizzly rain, limiting visibility. As the barrage crept forward, the Australians followed, their advance marked by the glow of hundreds of cigarettes. Little wrote:

> 'We're in it, boys,' shouted someone. Forward they went in attack formation; a few fell as the enemy shells and shrapnel burst about them. Machine-gun bullets filled the air with whistling noises but soon died down as the barrage caught the emplacements. 'Major Story's cracked', yelled someone. Two company commanders were now out of action ... Already the appealing cry of 'Kamerad' was heard and groups of frightened Huns with hands upraised hurried past back to our lines.

Within a few minutes, the Australians were among the pillboxes near Levi Cottages. Small groups of men sheared off from the main lines to deal with each blockhouse in turn. It was near here that Peeler, who had been lugging his Lewis gun over the broken ground, found his first target. Germans occupying a shell-hole were sniping at the front wave as they tried to make their way forward. Peeler darted out from cover, firing his gun from the hip, and wiped out the party of nine men, allowing the advance to go on. The fighting pioneer was evidently in his element. Twice in quick succession he repeated his earlier feat. Each time he added to his toll and each time he emerged unscathed.

The men of the 37th, encountering such defences for the first time, employed bomb and bayonet to deadly effect as they drove the Germans back across the spur. The bag of prisoners grew dramatically, but here and there small groups continued to resist. At one point, a machine-gun sited in the open barred the way ahead. However, Peeler, his blood well and truly up, was not deterred. Having had the enemy position pointed out to him, he immediately swung into action. With one burst, he disposed of the gunner, and that was sufficient for the remainder of the detachment, ten men in all, to scuttle for cover into a nearby concrete shelter. A well-aimed bomb quickly dislodged them, allowing Peeler to complete his work.

Four times in the space of an hour, Peeler had almost single-handedly destroyed enemy posts menacing the Australian advance. In so doing, he accounted for more than thirty men without receiving so much as a scratch. Fortune had, indeed, favoured the brave. Years later, he recalled:

> I never saw the faces of those I killed. They were just men in an enemy uniform. It was simply them or me. I don't think I was brave – not any more than the other Aussies who were with me. I simply had a job to do

and I did it ... Only afterwards did I realise how lucky I'd been not to get killed myself.

By 7.15 am the 37th had captured the first objective and were consolidating, having captured eight pillboxes, numerous concrete dugouts, twenty machine-guns and 420 prisoners, many of whom seemed only too relieved to be out of the fighting.

The fighting intensified with each bound as first the 38th, then the 39th and finally the 40th Tasmanians carried the advance over the Gravenstafel Switch towards Dab Trench, where the intimidating fortifications of the Flandern I Line marked the last objective. There was a good deal of confusion as the Tasmanians, in particular, found their progress hampered not only by increasingly heavy machine-gun fire but also by wire entanglements and large tracts of impassable swamp. The officers and NCOs of B Company, leading the 40th's thrust on the right, had much difficulty in maintaining order and direction throughout the long advance. Lt E. Boyes recorded:

On moving towards the second objective the men were inclined to ease off to the right, owing to the ground ... being very wet and difficult to pass over, but during the long halt of the barrage this was remedied to a certain extent. A number of our guns seemed to be firing short and several casualties occurred ... On passing the second objective fairly heavy machine-gun fire was experienced in gaining the third objective. The men were got away to the right of the sector again and were there extended into wave formation.

The Tasmanians now faced their toughest fight of all. They had lost the barrage and faced a withering fire from machine-guns on the left, sited along Bellevue Spur, and from the numerous strongpoints studding the crest 300yd in front. A thick belt of wire and another bog broke up the leading formations. B Company veered left and shortly afterwards the commander and another officer were lost, both severely wounded, leaving Lt Boyes as the only remaining officer. The men struggled to within 100yd of their final objective before a tornado of fire from Dab Trench and its screen of pillboxes at Hamburg Redoubt drove them into shell-holes. Further advance appeared impossible, until D Company's commander managed to work his men along a stretch of dead ground on the left of the redoubt, where he was able to subdue all but the pillboxes. This gave the remnants of B Company, pinned down in front, their chance to attack and none seized the opportunity with greater alacrity than Sgt Lewis McGee, of No. 6 Platoon. Armed only with a revolver, he dashed straight for the nearest pillbox, directly in front of the Hamburg blockhouse. The unit historian recorded:

This pillbox contained a number of the enemy, who had their machine-gun in a recess on the top of the fort, and were firing straight at B Company, the machine-gun bullets cutting the tops of the shell-holes where our men were taking cover. Sgt McGee rushed straight at the pillbox in the face of what looked like certain death, but he got across that 50yd of open ground and shot the crew with his revolver.

Shortly afterwards, he organised a small bombing party and captured another machine-gun post. McGee's success acted as a spur to others. A succession of miniature battles followed until the whole of the Hamburg Redoubt, together with

Sgt L. McGee

Dab Trench and Dagger Trench, was cleared. The main Hamburg strongpoint, a double pillbox, partly skirted by a moat, fell to a platoon from A Company gallantly led by Lt A.R. Grant and by 9.15 am the 40th were in complete control of the crest, with 300 enemy swelling the ranks of prisoners. Even so, it had been a hard-earned victory. During two days of fighting, the Tasmanians sustained nearly 250 casualties and their sacrifice was not over.

Eight days later the 40th resumed the offensive. Barely rested from their ordeal, they were plunged into a catastrophic attack in drenching rain across a quagmire of a battlefield dominated by enemy pillboxes. During the stumbling advance into Augustus Wood, a muddle of men from the 37th, 38th and 40th were caught in a torrent of machine-gun fire. Among the many who fell was the hero of Hamburg Redoubt, Lewis McGee. He had already been recommended for a Victoria Cross and a commission, and on that final morning of his life he was acting as CSM of B Company. His commander, Lt Leslie Garrard later wrote:

The attack began and as we sprang forward side by side he said to me, 'How glad I am to be here; I wouldn't have missed this for anything.' Turning to his men, he cried, 'Steady, lads; keep a good line.' A machine-gun opened on us from the front, and some fell. Then another machine-gun took us in the flank. The sergeant-major's face was shining and his jaw was set. More men fell, and some took cover in shell-holes. No cover for him, the gallant man; straight for the guns he rushed, and might have taken them; but it was not to be; a bullet pierced his head, and he fell dead.

Wally Peeler's luck ran out the same day, though he, at least, survived to be hospitalised with a bullet in his right arm. He was still recovering from his wound when the *London Gazette* of 26 November announced that both he and Lewis McGee had been awarded Victoria Crosses for their 'conspicuous bravery'.

Lewis McGee was born at 'Verwood', a country property about 12 miles west of Ross in central Tasmania, on 13 May 1888, the youngest of eleven children to John Dedman McGee, a farmer, and his wife Mary (née Green). Three sisters had died in infancy before he was born and tragedy struck again with the death of his mother from pleurisy when he was 7. Little is recorded of his early years and education. Some time after his wife's death, John McGee moved his surviving family to a new property, 'Snow Hill', near Avoca. It was around here that McGee spent most of his life prior to enlistment. Although some accounts state he was employed by the Tasmanian Department of Railways, it seems more likely he worked as an engine driver at local mines such as Storey Creek and Royal George. A powerful athlete, he was an accomplished cyclist, achieving considerable with the Avoca Cycling Club. On 15 November 1914 he married 17-year-old Eileen Rose Bailey at Avoca and they had a daughter a year later.

In the early months of 1916 a major recruiting drive was launched across Australia to establish the 3rd Infantry Division. Tasmania provided one battalion, designated the 40th. Among the first rush of recruits was Lewis McGee. He enlisted at Avoca on 1 March 1916 as a private (No. 456), giving his occupation as 'engine driver'. He was aged 27, 5ft 8¾in tall, dark haired and supremely fit. Three months' training followed at Claremont in the suburbs of Hobart. By the end of this period, McGee was a lance-corporal, being promoted on 22 May. The 40th sailed from Tasmania on 1 July, arriving in England late the following month to continue training at Larkhill.

The battalion proceeded to France on 24 November. While at Armentières on 4 December, McGee was promoted corporal and five days later the 40th went into the front line, manning the waterlogged trenches south of the Lys, near Houplines. McGee proved himself a natural soldier and on 12 January 1917, following casualties inflicted by an enemy raiding party, he was made sergeant in No. 6 Platoon, B Company.

After various small-scale operations, the 40th took part in the fighting at Messines Ridge in June, which was followed by a period of rest and recuperation. By the time of his death, Lewis McGee had clearly stamped his mark on the battalion. Lt Garrard, who was with him when he was killed, insisted that 'had he lived his commission would have been assured'. Maj. L.H. Payne, who was McGee's first company commander, referred to his 'sterling qualities as a leader' and noted: 'His ability in the carrying out of certain important tasks early in the year was most marked and ... there was in my opinion, and the opinion of many others, no more gallant and capable non-commissioned officer in the battalion.'

According to Lt Raymond Smith, McGee's courageous action had been 'the talk of the whole battalion'. In writing to his widow, he enclosed an Iron Cross that McGee had captured from a German officer during the fighting. To this was added the Victoria Cross, which Eileen McGee received from the Governor-General, Sir Ronald Munro Ferguson, at a ceremony in Launceston's York Park on 4 April 1918. McGee was buried in the Tyne Cot cemetery, within sight of a farm rebuilt on the location of the Hamburg Redoubt where he had earned his Victoria Cross. Barely 550yd further on up the ridge lies Augustus Wood, where he died. He is commemorated on the war centotaph in Ross, not far from where he was born, and his memory lives on in the form of the McGee Soldiers' Club at Anglesea Barracks, Hobart, which was opened in April 1956. Avoca also remembers Lewis McGee. During the town's 150th anniversary celebrations in March 1984, the Governor of Tasmania, Sir James Plimsoll, unveiled a memorial plaque on the Returned Servicemen's League Cenotaph in Boucher Park. Among hundreds who attended the ceremony was his widow, who had remarried in 1929, and their daughter, Nada.

Eight months later, the Tasmanian Government paid $36,000 to buy the McGee VC group at a Sydney auction. The medals were handed to the Queen Victoria Museum and Art Gallery in Launceston, where Tasmanians had gathered for the original presentation sixty-seven years earlier.

Walter Peeler, the only Australian pioneer to win the Victoria Cross in the First World War, was born at Barker's Creek near Castlemaine, Victoria, on 9 August 1887, the eighth surviving child of William Peeler, a farmer and miner from Tasmania, and his English-born wife Mary Ellen (née Scott). As a youngster, Peeler worked in his father's orchard and, prior to his enlistment, he was employed at Thompson's Foundry, Castlemaine. A popular figure in sporting circles, he was a leading member of Castlemaine Cricket Club and secretary of the Wesley Hill Football Club. He married Emma Hewitt on 10 July 1907 at the Congregational parsonage, Castlemaine.

When he enlisted as a private (No.114) in the Australian Imperial Force on 17 February 1916, he was living at 159 Cubitt Street, Richmond,

L/Cpl W. Peeler

with his wife and three daughters. Posted to the machine-gun section of the 3rd Pioneer Battalion, he embarked for England in June. The following month he had the first of a string of run-ins with authority when he forfeited a day's pay for going absent without leave for 6 hours during a stopover in Capetown. The minor misdemeanour did not prevent him being promoted lance-corporal in November, the same month his unit moved to France. Two months later, however, he was in trouble again, for conduct 'prejudicial to good order and military discipline'. He had broken censorship regulations by writing a letter, indicating his unit's position by means of a code. Found guilty by a court martial hearing he forfeited a further two months' pay. A further transgression on 28 March, when he failed to comply with standing orders by leaving a loaded revolver hanging in his billet, resulted in a severe reprimand. His lowest point, however, came on 8 May while carrying out a Lewis gun demonstration. In the course of showing a class how to clear a stoppage the gun accidentally went off, wounding one of the class. Accused of disobeying an order by using live ammunition, Peeler, who was a fully qualified instructor with a first class certificate, faced a Field General Court Martial. Despite claiming he was never informed of such an order, he was found guilty of 'careless and negligent' behaviour resulting in 'grievous bodily injury', but escaped with another telling off and the loss of his lance-corporal's stripe. The demotion, however, proved short-lived. Three days after receiving his punishment his rank was restored and a little more than a week later, on 7 June, he was leading his Lewis gun team into action on the first day of the Battle of Messines Ridge. Wounded in the eye and right cheek by shell splinters, he was back with his unit within three days. His next major action was the Battle of Broodseinde. Eight days later he was badly wounded in the right forearm and evacuated, first to Rouen and then to Northampton War Hospital which he reached on 16 October.

News of his VC award prompted a wave of celebrations in Castlemaine. Flags flew in his honour and one of his daughters found herself being cheered by fellow pupils at the Cremorne Street School. Peeler was still a convalescent when he received his Cross from King George V at Buckingham Palace on 8 January 1918 and he did not rejoin his unit until

17 May. Promoted temporary corporal two weeks later and sergeant on 30 July, he returned to Australia in October 1918, being discharged from the Army on 10 December.

He worked with the Victorian Department of Lands for six years as a member of the soldier-settler branch, and then took an orchard in the Castlemaine district. It was a short-lived venture. Moving to Melbourne, he joined the staff of the H.V. McKay Harvester Works at Sunshine, where the workforce included Laurence Dominic McCarthy VC. But when the city's Shrine of Remembrance was opened in 1934, Peeler became its first custodian. For most of the next thirty years the Shrine would be his second home.

The only interruption came during the Second World War when he enlisted in the 2nd AIF, understating his age by fourteen years. In May 1940 he was posted to the 2/2nd Pioneer Battalion. He was 52 – twelve years over the maximum age limit – although he always insisted he was not the 'oldest fellow in my unit'. He served overseas, taking part in the Syrian campaign as company quartermaster sergeant of D Company. During the fighting against the Vichy French in June 1941, he led a patrol to recover four wounded men. Early in 1942 his unit was part of a small Australian force, under the command of Brig. Arthur Blackburn VC, which was hastily diverted to Java in an attempt to stop the Japanese advance. It proved a futile gesture. Peeler's unit arrived in Java the day Singapore surrendered, and within a month all were prisoners. He thus became one of three First World War Australian VC holders swept up in the Japanese advance. (Brig. A.S. Blackburn and Sgt W.E. Brown were the others, although the latter is thought to have been killed attempting to evade capture.) Peeler was among a large contingent of Australians transported to work on the notorious Burma Railway. In later years, he played down his harrowing ordeal. 'I wasn't treated too badly, apart from nearly starving,' he said. 'But what the Japs did to the others on the railway was pretty horrifying.'

He returned to Australia in October 1945 to discover that his son, Donald, had been killed during the south-west Pacific campaign, on the island of Bougainville, while serving with the 15th Battalion. Peeler resumed duty at the Shrine of Remembrance, guiding parties of visitors around the building. His 'long and dedicated service' was recognised in the Queen's Birthday Honours List of 1961 with the award of the British Empire Medal (Civil Division). He retired three years later, aged 76, saying: 'It's time I had a rest.' Wally Peeler died at his home in Moore Street, South Caulfield, on 23 May 1968 and was buried in Brighton cemetery. He is commemorated in the Victoria Garden of Remembrance at Springvale and his impressive VC group, which includes a Meritorious Service Medal and decorations spanning service in two world wars, is displayed in the Hall of Valour at the

Australian War Memorial, Canberra. A soldiers' club in Casula, New South Wales, was named after him, but Peeler himself was always dismissive of his great honour. 'My wartime experiences are nothing to make a splash about,' he once said. 'I'm not a hero. I'm just an ex-soldier who did his job.'

C. ROBERTSON AND L.P. EVANS

Near Reutel and Joist Farm, 4 October 1917

Acting Captain Clement Robertson's preparations for the assault across the eastern edge of the Gheluvelt plateau were painstaking and perilous. Between 30 September and zero hour, 4 October, the 26-year-old Tanks Corps section commander laboured without rest, frequently under heavy shell-fire, to tape a route for his tanks to follow on their journey across the churned wilderness to the front line near Polygon Wood. His hazardous work started at Observatory Ridge, on the fringes of Sanctuary Wood, east of Zillebeke. Accompanied only by his orderly, Gunner Cyril Allen, he marked the way as far as Stirling Castle, a distance of some 1,000yd, over two nights. The next day he guided his four tank commanders over the ground they would have to traverse from Stirling Castle via Black Watch Corner and the remains of the Hooge–Reutel road to the front line. As darkness fell on 3 October he and Allen set off again to tape the last leg from Stirling Castle to their jumping-off point at Black Watch Corner. It was a desolate stretch of ground, only recently fought over. Even as they strove to complete their work, more shells added to the destruction, so that it was not until 9.30 pm that the final tapes were laid. Robertson then returned to bring up his tanks in readiness for the morning's attack. By around 2 am, after four gruelling days, No. 12 Section of No. 3 Company, A Battalion, the Tank Corps, comprising the four tanks A56, A58, A59 and A60, was in position.

Their task was a crucial one. They were to provide close support for the infantry of the 64th Brigade (21st Division) as they advanced against pill-boxes barring the way to Reutel and Juniper Cottages on the eastern end of Gheluvelt plateau. Success hinged on avoiding the treacherous bog, well over half a mile wide, formed by the Polygonbeek and Reutelbeek which, by the first week of October, had become 'belts of oozing mud of uncertain depth'. They had little room for manoeuvre. The only way forward was along a narrow strip of firm ground traced by the much-battered Hooge–Reutel road which ran eastwards between Cameron House and

Joist Farm, crossing a marshy brook by way of a bridge which had somehow survived the shelling. Robertson knew that to leave the track was to risk disaster. He therefore decided to lead on foot, accompanied initially by his orderly, in the full knowledge that the slow-moving column was certain to draw heavy enemy fire.

With everything prepared, Robertson and Allen spent the last few hours sheltering beside the foremost tank. 'We laid together,' wrote Allen, 'and talked of how well we had done, so far ...' Despite all they had been through and with the prospect of worse to come, Robertson appeared, in Allen's words, 'very

A/Capt. C. Robertson

calm and not in the least worried'. The waiting ended at 6 am, as the barrage came down. 'We had not many yards to go before we reached the enemy's lines,' wrote Allen. 'Here, we commenced to go forward, Capt Robertson and myself still leading, until we came face to face with the Boche [sic] ...' Shells were already falling close to the track and within 3 minutes of setting off Robertson's command had been reduced to three tanks as shell fragments tore through A60's armour plating, slightly wounding two crewmen and rupturing a petrol pipe. While 2/Lt F.S. Hunnikin's crew started to repair the damage, Robertson, conscious that a delay could jeopardise the infantry's chances, pressed on, followed, in order, by A58 (Lt V.H.G. Foxwell), A56 (Sgt D. Davies) and A59 (2/Lt J.A. Ehrhardt). Above the din of battle, he called to his orderly to check he was still all right. Then, they parted company, Robertson remaining at the head of the column, while Allen was sent back to guide the last tank forward. How far Robertson led them alone along that exposed stretch of track, riven by shells and pelted by bullets, is unclear. He certainly advanced beyond the first wave of infantry and on towards the small bridge. To have survived that far was a minor miracle. Bullets and shrapnel were rattling against the tanks' plating, sending shards of metal ricocheting around the cramped interiors. Yet, according to one account, Robertson was still on his feet and striding ahead of Lt Foxwell's lead tank when they reached and crossed the bridge. Foxwell later reported: 'Capt Robertson directed me along the track by the side of Polygon Wood, until I ... was easily able to distinguish the pavé road to Reutel.'

It seems that shortly after the tanks had negotiated the bridge and begun their crawl along the Reutel road Robertson's luck ran out. According to his company commander, Maj. M.L. Lakin DSO, the young section commander, 'was killed by machine-gun fire while leading his tanks with the first wave of infantry'. Apparently, he was shot through the head, although none among his crews reported seeing as much. Allen simply returned to find him 'missing'. By then, the enemy fire from machine-guns and riflemen was intense. 'I had to creep on my hands and knees,' he wrote, 'and not many yards away, I found Capt Robertson, laying in a shell hole, wounded ... I did my best for him ... I held him in my arms until he died. His last moments could have been of no pain ... as he was unconscious ... I thereupon let the Tanks successfully career on to their objectives ...' With Robertson dead, it was left to the individual tank commanders to exploit the opportunity handed them by their leader's dogged courage. All three enjoyed some success, although only one was still in action by the end of the day.

Soon after losing sight of Robertson, Lt Foxwell's A58 encountered enemy troops on the left. These were quickly dispersed with Lewis gun fire. Pushing on, over the ridge, Foxwell's crew dealt with 'several strongpoints on both sides'. Although all but one of the crew were wounded by splinters, A58 struggled on to its objective, near Reutel cemetery, knocking out more machine-gun posts. Later, while returning from the front line, A58 was hit by a shell which blew in the bottom of the right sponson. Fortunately, the only casualties were two carrier pigeons. The tank limped on until its gears failed, forcing the crew to complete their journey on foot.

As A56 progressed to within about 250yd of Reutel cemetery, Sgt Davies and his crew found no shortage of targets. Initially, the enemy either ran or surrendered, but resistance later stiffened. Nevertheless, A56 silenced a number of machine-gun nests sited in shell-holes near Judge Cottage. 'We circled in and out for some time trying to find pockets of enemy,' recorded Davies. Finding no more, he too headed back, dropping off four boxes of ammunition to the infantry, before making a safe return to Gunners Lodge.

2/Lt Ehrhardt's experiences in A59 were yet more eventful. Having endured a hail of machine-gun fire while negotiating the pavé road, Ehrhardt brought his tank to a halt at the crossroads near Reutel. Finding the advance checked by machine-guns near Juniper Cottages, he decided to attack the enemy positions even though it meant venturing on to 'treacherous' ground. The gunners succeeded in silencing the machine-guns, but A59 'ditched' while attacking another strongpoint. Forced eventually to evacuate the tank – although not before they had knocked out the enemy post – Ehrhardt's crew spent 2 hours fighting alongside the infantry before retiring, having lost one man missing.

Despite the losses among the tanks, they had achieved their purpose. As a result of their assistance, the three battalions of the King's Own Yorkshire Light Infantry succeeded in gaining most of their objectives along the ridge's eastern rim. The attack by No. 12 Section had shown that, given favourable conditions, intelligent handling and bold leadership, tanks were capable of making a major contribution to the fighting. In his report of the action, Maj. Lakin attributed the operation's success 'entirely to Capt Robertson'. He concluded: 'There is not the slightest doubt that Capt Robertson deliberately sacrificed himself to make certain that his tanks would get to their objectives.' Tank Corps historian Maj. Clough William-Ellis described it as 'one of the most patiently courageous actions of the war'. But not even so splendid an achievement could assuage the sadness at his loss.

Allen returned to camp that night 'absolutely done up, more with sorrow than anything else'. Unable to retrieve his officer's body, he had gathered his maps and personal effects, before reporting back to company headquarters. 'It was a great pity that he did not live to see the success his work had led his Section on to … I am told that at noon on the 4th inst, when the news of his death reached camp, everybody became miserable, and not even the report of the unique success his Section had attained could cheer anyone up.'

The attack to the north of the 64th Brigade's line of advance was carried out by units of the 62nd Brigade (21st Division), spearheaded by the 3/4th Queen's. In reserve for the operation, with orders to 'act according to circumstances', were the 1st Lincolnshires. Their commanding officer was a man with an unusual history. Acting Lt-Col Lewis Evans DSO was descended from a noble Welsh family. He had fought as a subaltern in the Boer War, where he had worn the dark green tartan kilt of the Black Watch, and had started this conflict as an observer in the Royal Flying Corps. Two years earlier, he had won his DSO near Hooge, barely 3 miles from his battalion's assembly point on the eastern edge of Polygon Wood.

The Lincolns moved in single file along the duckboard trail, taking more than 2 hours to cover the 4 miles from Zillebeke Lake to their jumping-off position, which Evans conceded was 'unlikely to be a pleasant spot'. Around midnight, they dug in to await developments, but at 5 am there was a late change of plan. Evans returned from reconnoitring the forward assembly positions with news that the battalion was to take over the role of the 10th Yorkshires, assigned the task of capturing the second objective. According to the 1st Lincolns' war diary, the 'whole battalion was delighted' with this decision, although no explanation was given for the extraordinary alteration to the order of battle. Incredibly, the battalion was in position with 5 minutes to spare.

At 6 am, the 1st Lincolns moved forward en masse. Machine-guns and a few 'shorts' from the creeping barrage inflicted some casualties and, as they reached the first enemy strongpoint, Evans, noticing that gaps were appearing in the front line of the attack, ordered C and D Companies to push on after the barrage. Assisted by Evans' rapid deployment, the 3/4th Queen's took the first objective at around 6.40 am. About 200yd further on, a pillbox sited just in front of Juniper Trench and about 300yd north-east of Joist Farm, burst into life. It was a critical moment, but Evans, who had already shown masterly judgement in his handling of the attack, proved equal to it. The unit war diary stated:

> [The] pillbox at J.10.d.5.6 ... was burning and the leading waves passed without encountering resistance, but one compartment on the North side escaped observation. A machine-gun opened fire from this place, inflicting casualties until Col Evans silenced it by firing his revolver through the loophole. Germans then came out with their hands up but were not taken back as prisoners. Men showed a decided preference to use the rifle rather than the bayonet.

The reference to the garrison 'not' being taken back as prisoners and the cryptic comment about the men's preference for the rifle in the context of the pillbox's capture is puzzling and conflicts with both Col Evans' VC citation and the Lincolns' regimental history. Both of these simply refer to the surrender of the garrison, while the inference from the accounts in the war diary and the citation that Evans made his attack alone is flatly contradicted by the unit history which appeared after the war. In it, the regimental historian stated that the commanding officer was 'assisted by an officer of the Machine-Gun Corps and several men of the Lincolnshire Regiment' who approached the pillbox from two directions while Evans administered the coup de grace. Whatever the truth, it is clear that an action many witnesses considered daring in the extreme seemed to Evans of no consequence whatsoever and hardly meriting of special distinction.

In a letter written to his future wife on 31 October, Evans, angered by rumours that he was to be awarded a Victoria Cross, declared:

> I don't expect to get it for I did nothing deserving of it so the less said about it the better. I am sure I don't know what they can have said I did, certainly nothing I consider deserving of it, in fact I am the reverse of proud of myself for having come away with the wounds I had. In fact the feeling I had about the whole business was that every dog has its day but this one had certainly not been mine ...
>
> Our job was the second objective. We had however got considerably mixed up in the fighting for the first objective and much scattered and disorganised. We had an hour's halt on the first objective during which

we had a good number of casualties from snipers, long distance machine-gun fire and shelling.

When it came to the time for us to go on there were no officers with two of the three front line companies and the enemy was holding out in a pillbox and a trench between us and the barrage, and things were not moving; the men were ready enough to go on, but really did not know what was expected of them having been hurled into the fight at the last moment.

I organised and pushed of[f] an attack on the pillbox which I did not lead; the men took it on their own, but just before this I got my first wound. I got this tied and was moving on to join them when I encountered the trench with anything from 20 to 40 Bosches in it, holding up the right company. I was just on their flank, looking down along their line and they did not notice me.

However one rather frightened looking rabbit did, and I made a sign to him to come over, which he did, seeing which they all seemed to think they had had enough and followed suit which cleared our troubles, and enabled us to get ahead. Unfortunately at this moment I was bowled over by the second bullet, after which my infernally cautious nature got the upper hand and instead of going on with them, as I ought to have done, I came back, sent the reserve company up to help them along and left the battlefield.

I did not at the time realise that I had as much strength left in me as I had, but I am not the least bit proud of the performance and what they may have said that I have done I cannot tell you, nor in all probability shall I ever know as I don't expect to get a VC, in fact don't feel that I deserve one.

No more tonight dearest, your would be husband is no hero and you had better know the truth.

Far from clarifying the matter, Evans' indignant letter merely poses more questions. Not only does it present an altogether different version of the pillbox fight to those accounts in the unit war diary and the subsequently published citation and regimental history, it also gives a different timing for his first wound and makes reference to an incident worthy of note that is wholly ignored in all the other accounts, namely the capture of a trench more or less single handed! Most published reports of the battle would seem to imply, apparently wrongly, that Evans sustained his initial injury, a bullet wound in the shoulder, after the pillbox struggle and before the advance on the second objective, in other words some time during the hour and 40 minutes spent waiting to move on. However, on a rare occasion almost twenty years later when he was persuaded by his brothers to relate the story of that memorable day his version of events was somewhat different, although it did serve to add further detail of some of the incidents touched on in his letter that went unreported in other accounts. Subsequently written up by one of his brothers and deposited among family papers, it has Evans 'drawing his pistol' and stalking the pillbox with his leading company pinned down 40yd away. Evidently, he approached the machine-gunners, sheltering by the concrete bastion, from their blind side. Standing up, he then signalled his leading platoon forward and they joined him unseen:

> The six Germans were busily firing away on the other side. Fortunately he was seen by a party of the right Battalion who were on a line with the pillbox and they, by working their way round behind the machine-gun, were able to shoot down the party working it.

From there, according to this account, he led the battalion on to the first objective, 'a line of unoccupied German trenches' where they were heavily shelled. It was while checking to ensure his men were deployed for the advance to the next objective that he, accompanied by his orderly, 'inadvertently' walked up to a trench some 100yd in front of his position and found it occupied by 'a German company':

> He said to his orderly, who was behind him, 'Shoot', but from the orderly's horizontal position on the ground, which he had at once adopted, this was out of the question, and thinking of nothing better, he shouted out 'Throw down your rifles!' This order, fortunately, was immediately obeyed by the nearest German and this movement gradually spread down the line until the remaining 40 Germans had grounded arms. He waved his arms towards his own line and the whole party of Germans sprinted across. For a moment his men thought it was a German counter attack and opened fire. Luckily for him the Germans were too far from their rifles to turn back and the last he saw of them was a scattered line of grey figures dashing wildly through his deployed battalion into the shelled zone to take cover in some old trenches behind.

Assisted by a barrage, the assault on the second objective got under way from near Judge Trench with A Company sandwiched between C and D Companies and B Company in reserve. According to the citation for his Victoria Cross, Col Evans was by then seriously wounded but had refused medical attention in order to lead his battalion towards their goal. To his brothers, however, he told a different story:

> By this time, he was back with the Reserve Company and moving forward. He was first hit by a bullet that grazed his ribs and then knocked down by a bullet that, luckily for him, was deflected by his shoulder blade. He carried on for a few minutes as a reaction to his orderly's remark 'Now,

Sir, that finishes this war for you!' However, the second objective was still 1000 yards away and he began to feel that if ever he did get there he would not get back, so having put the Reserve Company into the attack to ensure sufficient drive, he got slowly back to a Dressing Station, where his wounds were attended to. He was offered a stretcher but after a strong dose of whisky, he said he felt like going on and went to the nearest Battalion Headquarters to report. With the stimulus of a second whisky he then had every intention of returning to the line, but found himself physically unable to do so. He ended in the inevitable ambulance and a bed in a hospital.

Once again, Evans' own account conflicted with the official record. According to his citation, he 'continued to command until the second objective was won' and it was only 'after consolidation' that he 'collapsed' from loss of blood. What is irrefutable is that the battalion, under Evans' bold direction, had attained its goals. Of the twenty-two officers and 570 men he led into battle that day only four officers and 160 men made it as far as their final objective. Total casualties were recorded as twenty-four killed, 167 wounded and thirty-six missing, leading the battalion diarist to observe: 'These figures were considered light in the face of the fact that the German artillery fire in this battle was considered to be the heaviest and most concentrated of the whole war.'

Col Evans was in England, recovering from his wounds, when the *London Gazette* of 26 November 1917 announced the award of his Victoria Cross. In the words of his citation, his cool bravery had 'stimulated in all ranks the highest valour and determination to win'. His own comment on the official record was predictably dismissive. 'It certainly reads very nicely,' he wrote to his fiancee. 'I don't know that I quite recognise myself.' Indeed, in later years, he came to believe that his decision to go forward without his headquarters and take personal charge of the attack was, 'on reflection, a mistake'. Family legend also has it that when a telegram arrived congratulating him on the honour, he was all for refusing to accept it, complaining that his exploit had been exaggerated and was, in any case, a collective triumph. Shortly afterwards, a second cable reached him, reputedly stating: 'We are sorry to hear your wounds are rather worse than we thought!'

Three weeks later, it was announced that 2/Lt (Acting Captain) Clement Robertson had been similarly honoured 'for outstanding valour'. It was no less than he deserved. In a letter written shortly afterwards to Robertson's mother, Gunner Allen struggled to find adequate words to describe the sense of loss felt at the death of 'so brave and sporting a leader'. 'Capt Robertson,' he added, 'will never be forgotten in this Company.' Allen also remembered his captain's last words to him: 'Stick to me.' He had done just that and earned a richly merited Distinguished Conduct Medal in the process. His good fortune, however, was almost exhausted. A little more than seven weeks later, he too was dead, a victim of the first day's fighting in the great tank attack at Cambrai.

The first member of the Tank Corps to earn the Victoria Cross, Clement Robertson was born at Pietermaritzburg, Natal, in South Africa on 15 December 1890, the second youngest of five brothers, to Major John Albert Robertson and his wife Francis Octavia Caroline (née Wynne). His father was at that time serving in the Royal Horse Artillery, but shortly afterwards the family returned to Southern Ireland. They lived in a number of rented houses in Delgany, County Wicklow, before buying Struan Hill which became the family home in 1898. With his younger brother Charles, Clement Robertson went to prep school at Hill House in St Leonard's-on-Sea before progressing to Haileybury College (1904–06) and Trinity College, Dublin, where he graduated in engineering in 1909. A fine all-round sportsman, he was a keen tennis player and a gifted golfer. The five Robertson brothers were all founder members of Delgany Golf Club and Clement was the inaugural winner of the Captain's Prize in 1908. Following his graduation, he took a post with the Egyptian Public Works Department and was involved as an engineer in Nile irrigation projects.

When war broke out he immediately abandoned his career and hurried home to enlist as a private soldier in the 19th (2nd Public Schools) Battalion, the Royal Fusiliers (service number 826) on 8 October 1914. He applied to become an officer on 30 December and was duly commissioned second lieutenant in the 3rd (Reserve) Battalion, Royal West Surrey Regiment on 16 January 1915. His eldest brother, Willie, was already serving in the Royal Garrison Artillery, and would the end the war with a Distinguished Service Order, and his second eldest brother, Albert, was serving as an officer with the 2nd Cruiser Squadron in the Grand Fleet. Details of Clement Robertson's service career are sparse. In 1916, he was employed with the Royal Engineers, but towards the end of the year he transferred to the 1st Battalion, Heavy Branch, Machine-Gun Corps, embryo unit of the Tank Corps, as one of the original officers.

Robertson served initially as a tank commander, and by June 1917 he was a member of No. 12 Section, of No. 3 Company, A Battalion. During the Battle of Messines on 7 June Robertson had a narrow escape while cooperating with 47th Division. His 'female' tank, A56, was hit by a 5.9 shell. He wrote: 'The explosion broke one of the side doors off and blew in the plate under the left sponson. My crew NCO was killed and two men were wounded (one severely) and, as I considered the tank and crew unfit to fight, I returned to Elton Point.' Despite the severe damage, Robertson managed to bring A56 and his wounded crewmen back to base. Not long after, he was made acting captain and given command of No. 12 Section and its complement of four tanks.

Clement Robertson was a dedicated and greatly admired officer. A colleague described him as 'one of the best of fellows' and went on: 'He was very popular, both with his brother-officers and with the NCOs and men under his command, for his unfailing cheerfulness and camaraderie won for him a place in the hearts of all those with whom he was associated.' His mother was presented with the Victoria Cross by Brig.-Gen. C. Williams CB at a ceremony in the Royal Barracks, Dublin on 27 March 1918. A plaque was later dedicated to his memory in Christ Church, Delgany, where his proud descendants still live.

One of the most notable of all the Tank Corps pioneers, Robertson was buried in Oxford Road cemetery, a short drive from the Tank Memorial at Poelkapelle which was unveiled in 2009 in a ceremony attended by members of his own and his gallant orderly's families. The brainchild of ex-Tank Regiment soldier Chris Lock, the memorial is dedicated to the 243 tank crewmen who were killed in Belgium during the First World War.

Lewis Pugh Evans was born at Lovesgrove, Abermadd, near Aberystwyth, in Cardiganshire, on 3 January 1881, one of three sons to Sir Griffith Pugh Evans KCIE, DL, JP, a barrister, and his wife Lady Emelia Savi Evans (née Hills). The Evans family (motto: God Feeds the Ravens), part of the Welsh gentry, could trace their line back to the 'Second Royal Tribe of Wales'. Evans' father was a member of the Indian Legislative Council and four of his uncles were distinguished army officers, two of whom, Lt-Gen. Sir James Hills-Johnes and Col William Cubitt, had won Victoria Crosses during the Indian Mutiny.

He was educated at Eton (1895–98), where an early report described him as 'interested, industrious, lively and well-mannered.' A small boy of slight physique, he proved himself a gifted scholar and his army class tutor remarked: 'He has plenty of spirit and will do well when he gets a bit bigger.' In fact, he grew no taller than 5ft 7in. From Eton he went to the Royal Military College, Sandhurst. He passed out in December 1899, shortly after the outbreak of the Boer War, with a commission in the Black Watch, having been invited to join the regiment following heavy losses at the Battle of Magersfontein.

'Curly' Evans, as he was affectionately known, joined the 2nd Battalion in South Africa in February 1900, and was soon in the thick of the fighting. He took part in the operations in the Orange Free State from February to May, including the actions at Poplar Grove, Drietfontein and Vet River, and later in the Orange River Colony. He was also engaged in the struggle in the Transvaal. Evans was promoted lieutenant on 1 May 1901 and took part in anti-guerrilla operations around Ladybrand as a member of a mobile column. Much of their time was spent in fruitless sweeps designed to trap the Boer commandos and their cattle. In one engagement, frustration turned to indignity when the young subaltern found himself among sixty officers and men taken prisoner after being cornered on a kopje. Evans called it 'a most unlucky business'. Although his spell in captivity was brief, his later service in South Africa was dogged by illness as first diptheria and then rheumatism kept him in hospital for two months.

After the war, he served with his battalion in India; at Peshawar in 1905 he was placed on the 'dangerously ill' list, suffering from enteric fever. Fears for his survival were such that his mother took the unusual step of travelling out to help nurse him. Evans made a full recovery and the following year was made captain. In 1913 Evans trained as an observer with the fledgling Royal Flying Corps. Shortly afterwards he attended the Staff College at Camberley and passed out in the summer of 1914, being appointed a junior staff officer (GSO3) at the War Office. Germany had just launched its attack on Luxembourg and Belgium and Evans felt that Britain's entry into the conflict was inevitable. But in a note to his future wife, Dorothea Pryse-Rice, he admitted: 'I confess I have no thirst for war in itself, only a desire to be there if it must take place ... Though I do think all the powers on the continent seem to have taken leave of their senses.'

To his annoyance, Evans found himself posted to the RFC at Netheravon where he helped prepare new squadrons for combat service. Efforts to gain a transfer to a Kitchener battalion were dismissed, and he eventually found his way to France in September as an observer in No. 3 Squadron, whose ground crews included a certain James B. McCudden. From then until December he was engaged in reconnaissance work. Most of the dangers during those early days were posed by mechanical defects and the weather. While flying over the front with Sgt Reggie Carr on 19 October, Evans had a lucky escape. He wrote to Dorothea:

> We were just coming home after being out 2½ hours, coming up to the German lines, when the engine stopped. Fortunately, we were 5,000ft up and had the wind behind us and we fetched up just inside the French lines. I was not certain whether we had done it or no, though I knew we were clear of the German trenches, and we made for a wood. I was just off to question a ploughman when up came some French infantry, which was a great relief ... The Frenchmen very kindly insisted on pulling the machine under cover for they said we were within sight of the German guns ... Sgt Carr got his engine right in no time and we got off home.

His spell with the RFC ended in December when an application to return to his regiment was accepted. Posted as a company commander to the 1st Black Watch, he was in the trenches by January. 'It is a rough life for one is in a constant state of filth and seldom dry,' he observed. 'Very little sleep ... plenty to eat but the trouble is to keep it clean.'

A/Lt-Col L.P. Evans

Five months later, he was appointed brigade major to the 7th Infantry Brigade, 3rd Division. While serving in this capacity at the Battle of Hooge on 16 June, he won a DSO (*London Gazette*, 24 July 1915) for 'conspicuous bravery' in helping reorganise troops who had become mixed up during the fighting. Evans was unconvinced by the operation's limited success. Writing to Dorothea on 19 June he stated: 'These attacks I suppose have to go on if we are to wear these Germans out, but looking at each one of them alone, one always feels that the few hundred yards gained and the few hundred prisoners captured have been paid for over heavily.'

Promoted major on 1 September, his next step came the following March when he was promoted GSO2 with the 6th Division. By then he was engaged to Dorothea, thoughts of whom provided him with some relief from what he called 'this rather wearisome war'. After a year on the staff, he was given command of the 1st Lincolnshires on 23 March 1917, with the rank of acting lieutenant-colonel. His appointment was interrupted by the wounds sustained during the action in which he won his VC.

After a spell in hospital, he returned home on 28 November. His award had been announced two days earlier and a reception committee was waiting for him at Aberystwyth. A deeply embarrassed Evans told the gathering: 'I did no more than my fellow countrymen ... It really makes me feel unworthy of the honour I have got that I should have it more than anybody else.' He asked that plans to award him the Freedom of the Borough be delayed until the end of the war 'when, probably, there would be others whose services the council wished to recognise'.

He rejoined the 1st Lincolnshires in January 1918, only to be given command of the 1st Black Watch a fortnight later. He led them during the German Spring Offensive and, for his courageous leadership over a three-day period at Givenchy in April he was awarded a Bar to his DSO (*London Gazette*, 16 September). According to his citation, he had been largely responsible for checking the enemy advance and driving them back. His star was in the ascendant. On 10 June he was promoted temporary brigadier-general in command of 14th Infantry Brigade, 32nd Division, a post he held to the end of the war. Lewis Evans married Dorothea on 6 October 1918, at Holy Trinity church, Sloane Square in London. They had one son, but tragically Dorothea died in a railway accident three years later.

Evans relinquished command of the 14th Brigade in February 1919, becoming Base Commandant of the Rhine Army at Rotterdam. He was created a CMG in May. In the shrinking post-war army, he lost his temporary general rank. Various appointments followed before he was given command of his old unit, the 2nd Black Watch, in 1926. Seven years later, he regained the brigadier's rank he had held at the end of the war when he took charge of the 159th (Welsh Border) Brigade. He retired on 3 January 1938 and six months later, in recogition of his distinguished service, he was appointed a Companion of the Order of the Bath. Re-employed during the Second World War, he served as Military Liaison Officer, Wales Region HQ, from 1939 to 1941.

Lewis Evans, landowner and farmer, retired to the Lovesgrove estate and took an active part in the public life of Cardiganshire. A deputy lieutenant since 1937, he was president and later patron of the Aberystwyth branch of the Royal British Legion, honorary colonel of the county's cadet force, county commissioner of the St John Ambulance Brigade a magistrate and a president of the West Wales Jersey Society. A charming man of great personal gallantry, he took great pride in his old regiment, frequently making the long journey to Perth to attend reunions. His modesty, particularly in relation to his Victoria Cross award, was no act. As his grandson, Christopher Evans, explained: 'He felt there had been many others more deserving of the award who had not got it.'

On 30 November 1962 Lewis Evans set off from Aberystwyth to attend his grandson's confirmation. At Paddington station, the doughty warrior suffered a fatal heart attack. 'I cannot tell you how I miss "Curly",' wrote his old comrade, Gen. Sir Henry Jackson. 'He was the most faithful of friends. His judgement was so sure and his admonishment so sound.' He is remembered in Aberystwyth, where the town museum displays a scroll and sword presented to him by civic leaders at the end of the war. A portrait by S. Morse Brown, one of a series of twenty-four depicting distinguished Welshmen, is held by the National Museum of Wales. Brig. Lewis Evans VC, CB, CMG, DSO and Bar, holder of the French Croix de Guerre, the Belgian Order of Leopold and seven times Mentioned in Despatches, was buried in the family plot at Llanbadarn church, where he was a warden. In keeping with his character, the grave is modest and unprepossessing. The simple slate headstone bears no mention of rank or honours. An anonymous obituarist wrote of him: 'His mind was clear of cant or sentimentality. He lived his life according to his own high-set principles.'

T.H. SAGE

Tower Hamlets Spur, 4 October 1917

The German defenders on Tower Hamlets Spur overlooking the Bassevillebeek Valley had defied repeated attempts to capture the position. The mass of concrete pillboxes and shelters flanked by the machine-gun-infested Quadrilateral had destroyed two assaults made by the 41st Division on 20–21 September. It was the only significant setback of Plumer's first attack, and although they fell to the 39th Division on 26 September a determined German counter-attack had regained the Quadrilateral, leaving the British 200yd short of the western face. Undeterred by the failures, orders were given to the 63rd Brigade (37th Division) to make a further attempt as part of the Broodseinde offensive on 4 October.

The attack was launched at 6 am by the 8th Somerset Light Infantry and 8th Lincolnshires. Things did not go well. After taking their first objective, the leading companies of the 8th SLI lost the barrage. Their goal lay on the crest of Tower Hamlets Spur. But it was clear that the Germans were resolutely manning a series of strongpoints on the same level just beyond their objective. The unit war diary recorded:

Immediately the Coys appeared on the crest line they were received by machine-gun and rifle fire. They reached their objective by sectional rushes and attempted to consolidate under intense machine-gun fire from J.27.a.05.05 [a strongpoint to their front] and three machine guns 450yd away on the right flank ... It was hoped a flank barrage would keep them quiet; this, however, was not the case.

No sooner had the depleted companies reached their objective than the Germans counter-attacked with specially trained bombers, who, unhindered by any other equipment, advanced throwing two stick grenades simultaneously: 'Our posts did not withdraw but were almost wiped out by bombs and machine-gun fire, a large gap occurring between the 8th Lincoln Regt and ourselves.' Increasingly desperate fighting ensued with the 8th SLI making two vain attempts to capture the strongpoint marking their main objective. Each attempt was met by a withering fire, the survivors scattering into shell-holes. From one of these attacks only four men returned, having been showered with grenades most of the day.

On the left the 8th Lincolns buckled under pressure from Joist Trench and Berry Cottage and fell back. The casualties among both battalions were heavy. From an SLI reinforcement party sent to bolster the assault companies only one wounded officer and three unwounded men regained their old position. Throughout the day and night, survivors continued to straggle back. They included one man, covered in blood and horribly disfigured, who told an extraordinary story. Pte Thomas Sage, a barrel-chested west countryman, had been trapped in a shell-hole following an unsuccessful attempt to capture an enemy strongpoint holding up the advance. He later recorded:

> Five of us took shelter [and] we were joined presently by a sergeant and two men, making eight in all. In front of us was a German with a machine-gun in a pillbox. This pillbox man shot me through the head.

Bleeding heavily and blinded in the right eye, Sage lay in terrible pain, propped against the side of the crater. Any movement back was out of the question as the pillbox had the whole area covered. So they stayed there, a captain, sergeant and six men. At some point a decision, born of desperation, was made to try to break out. According to Sage:

> The sergeant thought he could do something with a bomb. Just as he released the five seconds spring, he was shot dead and the bomb dropped with him. It doesn't do to take any chances when there's a live bomb about with a five-seconds time limit. There was one thing I could do. I threw myself on the bomb. What happened? Well, the bomb exploded. My left thigh was torn to pieces ...

He was hurled across the shell-hole. Yet, despite being peppered with at least seventeen separate pieces of shrapnel, he did not lose consciousness. How many lives he saved is unclear. One contemporary newspaper account states that a captain and five men survived the blast as well as Sage. His VC citation merely refers to 'several' men being spared.

Having miraculously survived, it hardly seems credible that Sage could live long enough to reach safety. When the rest of the party decided to make a break for their lines, the captain handed him his water bottle and revolver with the advice not to let himself be taken alive. Abandoned to his fate, Sage decided to make one last superhuman effort to escape. Incredibly he succeeded, crawling unaided back to the Somersets' start line. Only when he reached an advanced dressing station did he finally lapse into unconsciousness. He had lost his right eye but his eyelid, which had been shot away, was restored by surgeons who also removed a piece of shrapnel from his thigh. Several smaller pieces, however, remained embedded in his body for the rest of his life.

Later, while undergoing treatment, Sage wrote to his wife. He explained how he had thrown his overcoat on the grenade before sitting on it to smother the blast. He also said he had been recommended for the highest award for bravery but urged her to 'keep quiet and not let everybody know, for you know what it is with the papers!' She wrote back: 'You don't seem to have given a thought about yourself', to which his response was: 'Well, they were all married men in my company, and I thought one life was better than the lives of them all. I don't know what gave me the presence of mind to do it.'

Sage was recovering in the Horton War Hospital in Epsom when the *London Gazette* of 18 December announced his award of the Victoria Cross 'for most conspicuous bravery'. Six days later, in reply to a congratulatory letter from his regimental depot, he remarked: 'I am sure that there is no one more Prouder than I am to be able to bring such a big Honour to there [sic] Regiment.'

Thomas Henry Sage was born in Ham Lane, Tiverton, on 8 December 1882, the son of Thomas and Jessie Sage. His father, who was born in New York, worked as a stone mason with the Tiverton Town Council. His mother, who was born and bred in Devon, was a lace winder. Educated at Chilcott's School, during which time he was a member of the Church Lads' Brigade, young Thomas went on to work for several years as a blacksmith for Mr Pethwick in Newport Street. Later, however, he joined Messrs Starkey, Knight & Ford's brewery in the town, where he was described as 'a steady, hard-working, unassuming man ... of good physique, vigorous and robust'.

Thomas Sage was one of thirty-seven workers from his brewery who volunteered for the Army. He enlisted in the Devonshire Regiment in December 1914 and was subsequently transferred to the 8th Somerset Light Infantry, with whom he served until May 1918 when he was officially discharged on account of his injuries. Married to Evelyn Maud Langworthy before the war, he already had four children when he performed his outstanding feat of valour during the struggle for Tower Hamlets Spur.

His recovery was long and painful, but he was well enough to make the journey from Horton Hospital to the capital on 2 February 1918 for a ceremony staged in his honour by London Tivertonians. To the strains of 'See the Conquering Hero come', he was congratulated on his 'hair's-breadth escape' before being presented with an illuminated address 'in recognition of his self-sacrificing and heroic conduct'. On 8 March Sage, now fitted with an artificial right eye, received a hero's welcome in his home town where thousands of people waited to cheer him. Following behind a grand procession, Sage was hauled through the streets in an open carriage by workmen from his brewery. The *Tiverton Gazette and East Devon Herald* recorded:

> The route was gay with flags and bunting; and on either side were dense throngs of cheering people, old and young, many of them eagerly pressing forward to shake Pte Sage by the hand as the carriage slowly went by. From many who had known him in pre-war times came friendly greetings – 'Good old Tom', and the like.

More than 500 townspeople had subscribed to a fund. As well as another illuminated address, Sage received £100 in war bonds and a case of Treasury notes. After the war, he returned to his old job at the brewery but difficult times followed. His wife gave birth to their fifth child, but then died in 1932. A year later Sage was forced to quit work due to ill health. He never fully recovered and died on 20 July 1945, aged 62, after what a local newspaper described as a 'long illness'. Sage, who had been living at 44 Council Gardens, Tiverton, left three sons, the youngest of whom was serving in Burma at the time, two daughters, and four grandchildren. When news of his death reached the local authorities, the flag over the town tall was lowered to half-mast.

He was buried in Tiverton cemetery alongside his wife in a ceremony attended by civic dignitaries and old comrades. A little over forty-one years later the grave was marked by a memorial headstone provided by the Somerset Light Infantry Association. It was dedicated on 6 December 1986, in a service which ended with buglers from the 6th Battalion, the Light Infantry, sounding Last Post and Reveille. His Victoria Cross was presented to the Somerset Light Infantry in Taunton, while Tiverton Museum has the illuminated address presented to him by the London Tivertonian Association amid much pomp and ceremony almost eighty years ago.

A. HUTT

Near Terrier Farm, 4 October 1917

South of the swollen Lekkerboterbeek, the Warwickshire battalions of the 143rd Brigade (48th Division) found it hard going across sodden ground pitted with shell-holes and dotted with fortified farms. The 1/7th Battalion, on the left, attacked towards Tweed House with two companies and almost immediately ran into trouble. C Company's commander was killed and the men sustained heavy casualties from machine-gun fire. Only after a struggle lasting half an hour was the opposition overcome. D Company made quicker progress until they too were halted by a machine-gun in Tweed House. Eventually, having silenced the gun and captured the garrison, they pushed on to their objective.

The advance was then taken up by A and B Companies who had avoided becoming embroiled in the fighting thus far. B Company, on the right, succeeded in exploiting on the far side of a position known as the Cemetery but, with their flanks in the air, they were forced to pull back to gain touch with the 1/6th. A Company, however, pressed on behind the barrage and had an early success at Terrier Farm, before meeting heavy machine-gun fire from a well-camouflaged strongpoint. No. 2 Platoon was hardest hit, losing all its officers and NCOs. There seemed little prospect of further advance until Pte Arthur Hutt, a pre-war Territorial, took charge. An officer in his battalion subsequently wrote:

The men were leaderless, and like all leaderless men were in consequence at a disadvantage. Quick as a flash Hutt realised what was needed and, calling to the men to follow, he worked his way round the post, bombing it as he went, and then firing at the Germans nearest him; he killed an officer and three men. The rest of the Huns were glad to surrender.

Hutt took command of the captured post and held it for some time in spite of repeated enemy attempts to rush it with strong forces, and in spite, too, of the fact that he held as prisoners in the post more Germans than there were men under his command. Later in the day matters were going nicely on that part of the front, and Hutt realised that he could not hold on longer. He decided to withdraw the party, and after moving out the prisoners, he remained behind to cover the withdrawal, bombing the enemy vigorously, and thus defeating their repeated efforts to recapture the prisoners, who numbered forty-six. When the withdrawal was effected Hutt started back on his own, and when some distance from the post he came on a wounded man. He dressed the man's wounds under fire, and helped him back to safety.

Then he set to work consolidating the position occupied by his men, and preparing to resist the attacks which the enemy were making. The enemy soon after that sent round strong patrols to pick up our wounded, who were lying about. Hutt went out alone with a rifle and a few bombs and made his way to where some of these men were. He brought in four of them in succession, each journey being made under heavy machine-gun and rifle fire. During one of the journeys Hutt was fired at by enemy snipers and bombers [sic], who pressed to within a few yards of him, but he came through unscathed.

Through it all he behaved with a coolness and a daring that I have never seen equalled. The officers and men who saw him declare that they never imagined any man could be so cool under such circumstances ...

Hutt and the remnants of his platoon took up a position near County Crossroads, linking up with the 9th Lancashire Fusiliers from the 34th Brigade. According to the 1/7th Battalion's war diary, three enemy attacks launched from Beek House were 'dispersed' along with two others from another enemy position. Eventually, two Vickers guns were set up in Tweed House to cover the battalion front. The battalion held their ground for the three days, amid drenching rain and shelling. They marched out on the night of 7–8 October having lost twenty-five officers and men killed, 143 wounded and fourteen missing. Their success had provided another striking example of how the actions of a single soldier could influence the outcome of an operation. One of Hutt's officers wrote: 'But for the courage and resource of this soldier ... it would have gone hard not only with the Warwicks, but with the whole of the troops operating in that region.' The same officer claimed that Hutt's actions had even won the admiration of the Germans, who were stung into making special efforts to stop him:

One of the German officers who saw Hutt's handling of the men said that he was a born leader, and ought to have been an officer ... Another prisoner we caught said that when Hutt was first noticed from the German lines their officer offered a reward to the German soldier who brought him down, and all through the subsequent operations he was the subject of all the enemy operations. They sniped at him from all parts, but never hit him once. He was also treated to machine-gun fire, and at times had to move through streams of bullets. While he was carrying in one man the Germans had no less than forty snipers after him, and though they kept blazing away all the time they never got the brave chap even once ... He certainly ought to be an officer.

Hutt had to make do with a corporal's stripes, but his outstanding contribution to his battalion's success was duly rewarded on 26 November 1917, when the *London Gazette* carried the announcement of his Victoria Cross.

Arthur Hutt was born at Earlsden, Coventry, on 12 February 1889, the son of Samuel Hutt. Educated at Holy Trinity School, he worked for Courtaulds and, when their factory at Foleshill formed a company in the Warwickshire Territorials in 1909, he was among those to enlist.

When war broke out, Hutt, who was married and living in Caludon Road, was at annual camp in North Wales with his battalion, the 7th Warwickshires. He proceeded to France in 1915 and served on the Somme and in the Ypres Salient before his division was transferred to Italy. At the time of his award, he was described as 'quiet, unassuming, trustworthy and independently minded'.

Returning to Coventry on 12 January 1918 he was given a grand reception. His home street was decked out in flags and bunting and a banner straddled the centre of the street proclaiming: 'Welcome Home to Our VC.' Neighbours and friends presented him with a silver cigarette case, while at a civic reception in the Council House he received an illuminated address. After acknowledging the crowds gathered outside, Hutt was the guest of honour at the Drill Hall, where he was presented with £250-worth of war bonds by the mayor on behalf of his old employers and learned that a mayoral fund opened on his behalf had already raised nearly £500. A chorus of 'For he's a jolly good fellow' echoed around the room as Hutt addressed the packed hall:

All I did was my duty to my king and my country. I saw that the officers and NCOs had been knocked out. The duty had got to be done by someone. It was the duty of the senior soldier to take command, and so I took command of the platoon. I saw what was in front and I thought: 'If someone does not do it, we shall be in Germany very soon', and of course I carried on and did my duty.

Arthur Hutt was demobilised in 1919 and returned to his home city. In the years between the wars, he had a variety of different jobs and suffered a bout of unemployment around the start of the Second World War. His last job was in the packing department of the Standard Motor Company. A keen supporter of ex-service organisations, he was a member of both the Old Comrades' Association of the 7th Battalion, the Royal Warwickshire Regiment, and the Regimental Association. In November 1938 he volunteered for the Auxiliary Fire Service, and was serving with them when war broke out, although some reports state that he later joined the Home Guard.

Arthur Hutt died after a long illness at his brother's house in Sewell Highway, Coventry, on 14 April 1954. He was 65. By a strange quirk of fate, a younger brother died just 24 hours later. More than 350 people attended Hutt's funeral service at Canley crematorium, including two Warwickshire-based VC winners, William Beesley and Henry Tandey. The following year a Cornish-granite memorial dedicated to the only Coventry-born holder of the Victoria Cross was unveiled in the city's War Memorial Park. The ceremony was attended by Hutt's widow and other relatives, and was followed by a military parade half a mile long. Two months later, at an Old Comrades' Day, the Royal Warwickshire Regiment's most distinguished former officer, FM Viscount Montgomery, presented Mrs Hutt with a case containing miniatures of her late husband's VC and six service medals, which included the Territorial Efficiency Medal.

Arthur Hutt is still remembered in his native city. Each Armistice Day a former member of the 7th Battalion, the Royal Warwickshire Regiment, lays a wreath of poppies at the foot of his memorial as a poignant salute to one of the most gallant individual actions of the Passchendaele campaign.

C.H. COVERDALE AND F. GREAVES

Near Poelcappelle, 4 October 1917

Harry Coverdale could scarcely believe the news. A few months earlier, he had been awarded the Military Medal. Now he was being hailed a hero all over again. To his widowed mother he wrote: 'I have won another honour for attacking a strong enemy position and bringing in two guns. I hear I have been recommended for the VC but I think it is too good to be true.' Too good or not, it was certainly true. The letter was written in the aftermath of the 11th Division's assault on Poelcappelle, an operation that yielded two Victoria Crosses, including one to Sgt Charles Harry Coverdale of the 11th Manchesters.

The most significant of the Fifth Army's contributions to the third stage of Plumer's autumn offensive, the move was designed to clear the enemy outposts, including numerous strongpoints, as far as the western edge of Poelcappelle and then, depending on the strength of the opposition, to exploit eastwards towards the Flanders line, running due north of Gravenstafel. Launched at 6 am, behind a hurricane bombardment, the attack achieved almost all its objectives at relatively small cost. Much credit for the victory was given to the tanks from D Battalion, 1st Tank Brigade. Despite the rain, the going had proved good enough for them to play a leading role in the advance along Poelcappelle Spur, through the ruined streets and beyond. Even so, the infantry did not have it easy. They had to overcome a number of machine-guns, many of them scattered in shell-holes.

The 11th Manchesters and the 9th Lancashire Fusiliers led the 34th Brigade effort. Following close behind the barrage, they captured the Red Line which was found to be strewn with enemy dead. Resistance had been generally feeble, although snipers had threatened to slow the advance until Sgt Coverdale intervened. Dashing forward, he killed an enemy officer and took two men prisoners. Shortly afterwards, two machine-guns opened up on his platoon. Once again his response was immediate. Ignoring the hail of fire, he rushed straight at them, killing or wounding every member of the gun crews. With the position captured, and the enemy guns facing their former owners, the enterprising Coverdale was given a new task. The unit war diary recorded:

> Patrols went out, under protective barrage, to clear the ground of enemy. One platoon under Sergeant COVERDALE attempted to get through to capture Munier House [sic], but after having several casualties [nine men] from our own guns was obliged to return.

It was not quite the end of the matter. Coverdale decided to have another go at the enemy strongpoint east of Poelcappelle. With consolidation continuing and supports arriving, he led out a second patrol at 1.30 pm. His luck, however, was out. The small party ran into 'severe rifle-fire from the front of the hillock, and having become heavily engaged with an attempted enemy counter-attack, were compelled to withdraw'. The enemy were beaten back, but orders to push on were cancelled and the Manchesters contented themselves by breaking up parties of enemy infantry concentrating near Meunier House and in shell-holes along the ridge north-east of Beek Houses.

On the left, the 33rd Brigade made similar progress. Attacking with the 9th Sherwood Foresters and the 7th South Staffordshires, the brigade reached its first objective with little opposition. B Company, 9th Sherwood Foresters, cleared two machine-gun nests, the survivors fleeing with the gun locks. A Company, advancing in two waves of two platoons each, faced greater difficulties. 2/Lt J. Adamson MC, the acting company sergeant major, and two platoon sergeants were hit early on, and casualties from machine-guns increased as the men crested the rise. The battalion war diary noted:

> Men could not see the barrage owing to the wet ground and a number tried to get near HE bursting on the ground; this caused some casualties. Three machine-guns were met in shell-holes; in two cases the enemy picked up the gun and ran back with it. After the first quarter of an hour rifles began to jam with mud and wet, otherwise more of the retiring enemy would have been killed. The enemy seemed disinclined to surrender but ran back before the advancing troops got within 20yds, in nearly all cases leaving their rifles behind them ... The company noticed that the enemy had a trick of lying quiet while the troops passed over, after which they would get up and surrender to the stretcher-bearers.

At one point, however, the enemy stood and fought. A large concrete emplacement which marked the company's objective offered stiff resistance. It was the signal for the first of a series of gallant deeds performed that day by Acting Cpl Fred Greaves, a pre-war Derbyshire miner. According to the unit diary, the pillbox was:

> found to be occupied with two machine-guns on top and two on the flank outside. Corporal GREAVES, accompanied by Sergeant TERRY, seeing that there was no time to deal with it in any other way, rushed forward and threw a bomb inside. Five men inside surrendered but in the rush 20 others ran back. Four machine-guns were in this emplacement.

A more complete account of the action, based on an interview with a wounded NCO, later appeared in the *Nottingham Guardian*. It spoke of the 'exceedingly critical position' facing the company before Greaves took charge:

> Our force ran into one of the enemy blockhouses ... and we were also caught between the fire of two groups of machine-gun posts. The officers and non-coms went down with the exception of Greaves. The men suffered most severely, and, left without a leader, they were wavering. Greaves saw what was required. Shouting to the men not to mind, he went forward with some bombs in his hand. Another non-commissioned officer who was only slightly wounded went after him. Both were fired on by the enemy and had hair's-breadth escapes. They seemed to be running through showers of bullets. Greaves got round the pillbox, after dodging death from the snipers many times. He hurled in a couple of bombs and the fire from the pillbox ceased. He made his way inside and brought out four machine-guns in succession. That saved the day for us. Our men were no longer galled. They were able to consolidate the position ...

Despite a number of casualties, the Sherwood Foresters pushed on to capture Ferdan House. The final objective taken, patrols were sent out but danger threatened again shortly after 1 pm when the enemy counter-attacked. A neighbouring unit was pushed back 400yd, leaving the Foresters' flank exposed. But once more Greaves proved equal to the task. An eyewitness recorded:

> Calling to his men to hold on, he went forward into the thick of it, posting men here, moving a machine-gun there, and generally making it clear to both our chaps and the enemy that there was a chap on the job who knew enough of the business to make it impossible for the enemy to get the best of us. The enemy attacked in masses. Greaves went about among the men, encouraging them and spurring them on by his example of cheerfulness and courage. Again and again the enemy attacked. Each time they

were flung back ... The example of Greaves and his band of Sherwoods was infectious. Our men gradually recovered the ground given up, and the enemy was sent rolling back in disorder once more. That this result was achieved was due entirely to the brilliant leadership and fine courage of Greaves.

Sporadic shelling developed into a continuous barrage later in the day, but no further counter-attacks were attempted and the fighting petered out with the Foresters holding their new line. Greaves was credited with having saved the day. 'How he kept going, I do not know,' remarked a fellow NCO. 'He was everywhere and seemed to know just what to do at the proper time.' Greaves was more reticent. Commenting on the battle half a century later, he merely stated: 'It was a very hot place, but I expect I was one of the lucky ones.'

Eight weeks later, the *London Gazette* of 26 November 1917, announced the award of the Victoria Cross to No. 23715 Acting Corporal Fred Greaves. Sgt Harry Coverdale had to wait twenty-two days longer for confirmation of his honour. Shortly after the action, in his modest note to his mother, he had declared: 'I know that I am in for something for that last big push, although I only took a strong enemy point and captured two guns. I keep smiling and just do my duty quietly, and look after my platoon.'

Charles Harry Coverdale was born on 22 April 1888 at 12 Albert Terrace, Stretford, Manchester, the second of three sons to John Coverdale and his wife Emily (née Goddard). His father was an upholsterer and the large family included four sisters. Harry went to Bangor Street Board School in nearby Hulme, where he was noted for his sporting ability. A keen cricketer and footballer, he kept wicket and played in goal for local teams in the Old Trafford district of Manchester.

When war broke out Harry was unmarried and working as an engineer's fitter at Galloway's Boiler Works, in Knott Mill, while living with his parents at 7 Skirton Road, Old Trafford. He volunteered at Chorlton-on-Medlock on 7 September 1914, in answer to Kitchener's call to arms. Writing at the end of the war, he recalled: 'I enlisted in the [Royal] Engineers ... was told that I would have to wait; I didn't wish to wait, so asked to be put in the infantry, and was put in the Manchester Regiment.'

He was posted to the 4th (Reserve) Battalion at Riby, near Grimsby, for training. Appointed lance-corporal (unpaid) on 1 January 1915, he was confirmed in the rank three months later but blotted his copybook in August when he was severely reprimanded for 'neglect of duty' while in charge of a blockhouse. On 20 September, he embarked for Gallipoli to join the 11th (Service) Battalion which had landed at Suvla Bay the previous month. Having endured the harsh conditions on the peninsula, Harry took part in the evacuation and, after a spell in Egypt, transferred with his unit to France where it became embroiled in the Somme offensive. Promoted corporal on 27 October 1916 and then sergeant a little over six weeks later, he enjoyed a brief spell of home leave the following summer before returning to the thick of the action in the Third Battle of Ypres. During an attack on 16 August he was commended for 'carrying on and holding the objective after his officer and other NCOs had been killed or wounded'. His brave leadership, which involved him taking temporary command of his platoon, was recognised by the award of a Military Medal. The medal was announced in corps routine orders on 12 September (gazetted on 2 November) and was presented only after he had been mistakenly wearing the ribbon of the Distinguished Conduct Medal for fourteen days.

Recommended for officer training in the wake of his Victoria Cross action, Harry returned to England on 14 January 1918 to join No. 16 Officer Cadet Battalion at Kinmel Park, Rhyl. A training injury, which resulted in him being hospitalised for two months, delayed his commission until 9 October 1918. Posted to the 3rd (Reserve) Battalion, he visited Buckingham Palace to receive his VC at the end of the month and saw out the last days of the war at Cleethorpes as part of the Humber garrison. According to one of his sisters, he was offered a regular commission, but not having a private income decided against it, a claim that has not been substantiated by any records.

Demobilised in March 1919, Harry returned to his pre war employment and on 29 October he married Clara Florence Travis (née Baron), a local war widow whose husband had died in the last month of the conflict. That same year he received a silver rose ball from Stretford Council in recognition of his outstanding war record. Four years later, he was selected to lay a wreath on behalf of ex-servicemen at the unveiling of the Stretford war memorial. In the years between the wars, Harry, who was living in Radcliffe, near Manchester, attended a number of events associated with the Victoria Cross, including the 1920 Royal Garden Party and the Gala Dinner at the House of Lords on 9 November 1929. At some time after that, Stretford's local hero, by then a family man with two sons, moved across the border into Yorkshire to Huddersfield, where he worked as chief engineer of four mills owned by Joseph Lumb & Sons. He remained in Yorkshire for the rest of his life, becoming a staunch member of the Almondbury branch of the Royal British Legion and serving as an officer in a local battalion of the Home Guard affiliated to the Duke of Wellington's Regiment during the Second World War. A guest at the Victory Parade in 1946, Harry's military associations continued into the

1950s with service in the country's Cold War Home Guard. His final promotion to captain in the re-designated 25th West Riding Battalion came at the age of 67 on 13 May 1955, just six months before his death.

Charles Harry Coverdale died, following a ruptured aneurysm, on 20 November 1955 in Huddersfield Royal Infirmary. He was buried with military honours in Edgerton cemetery, alongside his wife who had died in 1940, his name and distinctions being added to her headstone. A modest man, he had proved a natural soldier, possessing considerable powers of leadership. A sister later recalled: 'He was always proud he had held every rank [up to] captain.'

Fred Greaves was born at Killamarsh, Derbyshire, on 16 May 1890, the eldest of twelve children to Jude and Edith Greaves (née Rogers). Originally of farming stock, his father had turned to mining as a means of supporting his growing family. Fred was educated at the Bond's Main Council School and was remembered as a 'quiet lad' with no sign of 'youthful devilment'. On leaving school aged 13, he followed his father down the pit, working at Bond's Main Colliery. Later, when his family moved to Barlborough, he was employed at Barlborough No. 2 Pit.

His early working life was plagued by injuries suffered in a succession of mining accidents. The most serious one occurred in his late teens when he was struck by a coal truck. He suffered two broken legs and a crushed pelvis that put him in hospital for two years. Prolonged treatment followed, but with money short Fred was forced to make the weekly 8-mile trek home from hospital on crutches! The injuries left him with a deformed leg and a protruding bone that required constant strapping to relieve the pain, but he refused to give in. At the suggestion of a doctor, he took up cycling on a bike bought for him by his father. Intended as a means of rebuilding his wasted muscles, cycling became a favourite sport at which he excelled. As a member of the Sheffield Road Cycling Club, he won a clutch of awards over long and short distances. They included a gold medal for completing 190 miles in 12 hours and a trophy for winning the club's 25-mile championship in May 1914. The same year, Fred, who thought nothing of cycling 140 miles for a day trip to Skegness and back, was crowned 50-mile and 100-mile champion of Derbyshire.

Yet for all his strength and stamina, the county's supreme cyclist was deemed unfit for military service when he tried to enlist in September 1914. Rejected on account of his leg injuries, he persisted with his efforts to join the Army and, eventually, on 26 February 1915, he was accepted into the 9th Sherwood Foresters, a Kitchener battalion.

His baptism of fire came at Suvla Bay on the Gallipoli peninsula. The battalion suffered heavily, but he came through unscathed save for a bout of dysentery. In his weakened state, he briefly broke with his teetotal convictions to consume a quantity of rum which he later credited with saving his life. Evacuated along with his battalion in December, he served briefly in Egypt before being shipped to France where he arrived with his unit shortly after the Somme offensive began. The heavy fighting that continued into the autumn took a heavy toll. In September, Fred's closest friend, George Farby, who also came from Barlborough, was killed in an assault on Thiepval, and a few weeks later he was wounded in the upper thigh during an attack on Beaumont Hamel. After a spell in hospital, he rejoined his unit and on 21 May 1917 Fred, by then a member of a Lewis gun section, was made acting corporal.

Little detail remains of his war service, beyond the action which earned him his Victoria Cross. He left no record and rarely spoke of his experiences. 'They used to ask him down the pit, "how'd you win your VC, Fred?"' recalled his daughter, Hazel Greaves. 'He'd simply say, "You don't want to know, laddie".' In later years, however, he did occasionally recall incidents from his time in the trenches. One episode in particular stood out. It involved a night patrol in no-man's-land. 'Apparently, he was very good at carrying out reconnaissances,' said Hazel. 'He was sent out to report on the German positions and he reckoned he approached so close he could have touched them. They were smoking and laughing. He crawled away, but halfway back he ran into a couple of Germans who taunted him, tearing at his uniform with their bayonets until he heard his officer call out, "Hold still, Greaves", before shooting them both. He thought he'd had it.'

Though regarded 'as one of the most modest chaps in the battalion', Fred's courage had not gone unnoticed. He had been recommended for a Military Medal for rescuing wounded men under heavy fire. The award was not granted, but it was clearly not an isolated incident, as a fellow NCO observed:

Before the acts that won him the Cross, he had already come under the notice of his superiors for his coolness and dash. On one occasion ... he rushed a machine-gun post single-handed and on another occasion he risked his life to bring a comrade out of action.

Such daring appears to have been a family trait. His younger brother Harry also volunteered for the Sherwood Foresters, was commissioned, attached to the 1st Battalion and, as a junior subaltern, earned a Distinguished Service Order and a Military Cross with two bars in less than a year.

Promoted acting sergeant on 30 November 1917, Fred was granted leave to receive his Victoria Cross in January 1918. Wearing civilian clothes en route to Buckingham Palace, he was given a white feather by a woman travelling on the same train. According to his daughter, he merely smiled at her and said nothing. Returning to his unit, he was made full sergeant and soldiered on until the Armistice, before being demobilised on 28 January 1919 with an 'exemplary' record. According to one account, he was offered a permanent commission, but turned it down. Instead, he returned home, married and had a family. Tragedy struck in 1927 when his wife, Harriet, died, leaving him with a son and daughter below the age of 3 to care for. Typically, Fred rose to the challenge and three years later, he married Gladys Jepson, a war widow, at All Hallows church, Harthill.

After leaving the Army, Barlborough's local hero resumed his career as a miner. Working at Markham Colliery, he became a colliery deputy and for many years served as a pit safety officer as well as being a member of the local St John Ambulance Division. His daughter recalled, 'If ever there was an accident down the pit, they used to say, "Send for Fred Greaves, he'll know what to do".' Such a call came in 1938 when an explosion tore through Markham pit, trapping 150 men underground. Hazel Greaves remembered:

I heard the pit sirens and I knew that something was wrong. My father ran past me in the street and was heading towards the pit. We did not see him again for about a week as he worked tirelessly, digging people out and helping the injured.

In all, seventy-nine men lost their lives in the Markham Pit disaster, but the death toll could have been higher still but for men like Fred Greaves. His selfless devotion then and on countless other occasions resulted in him being honoured by the St John Ambulance with the Order of Jerusalem.

Variously described as 'quiet and reserved' and a man of 'unblemished character', he was, in his daughter's words, a 'good, clean living man who was full of fun and definitely not a stuffed shirt'. A man of strong religious principles, he was a prominent member of the Barlborough Primitive Methodist church and a leader of the Band of Hope whose commitment was reflected in his donations to chapel funds throughout his First World War service. His mild-mannered appearance masked a rare inner strength. 'He was a very special man,' his daughter recalled. 'He was a very strong character and a man who was greatly admired.'

Fred Greaves retired in 1955, following Second World War service in the local Home Guard and a belated reminder of his First World War service. While climbing into a coal wagon down the pit, he felt a twinge from his old war wound. Fellow miners thought he was joking, but shortly afterwards surgeons removed the German bullet that had been embedded in his left thigh for thirty-six years!

A staunch supporter of ex-service organisations, he was chairman of both the Barlborough and Brimington branches of the Royal British Legion. He also joined the Sherwood Foresters' Old Comrades Association, but declined invitations to hold office. A fellow member recalled: 'He didn't want any fuss made of him. Fishing and gardening were his main interests. He was good-humoured, but very quiet. He never spoke about his war career.'

The last surviving Sherwood Forester VC died at his home, Whitelands, in Ringwood Road, Brimington, on 8 June 1973. He was 83. A few days later his coffin was borne to Chesterfield crematorium by staff sergeants from the Worcestershire and Sherwood Foresters Regiment. In accordance with his wishes, his son presented his medals, consisting of the Victoria Cross, 1914–15 Star, British War Medal, Victory Medal, Defence Medal, Coronation Medals (1937 and 1953) and St John Ambulance awards, to the trustees of the Sherwood Foresters' Regimental Museum.

His heroism has not been forgotten. A plaque on his old home in Barlborough, an inscription on the village war memorial and a bench near Chesterfield war memorial all pay tribute to his valour. And there have been other more unusual acts of remembrance, including a pie baked in his memory and, most ironic of all, a beer named after him. The Fred Greaves VC Extra Special Bitter was brewed in honour of Derbyshire's teetotaller VC in 2009 in support of the annual RBL Poppy Day appeal.

As for the hero himself, he preferred to forget the horrors of the war to end all wars in which he had served with such distinction. In a letter written eight years before his death, he related that he had never revisited the old battlefields, nor had he wished to do so. 'Perhaps it is better that all those places are forgot [sic],' he wrote. 'And we thank God that we got away safe and are able to pray for those, our Friends and Mates, who never returned.'

J. OCKENDON

't Goed ter Vesten Farm, 4 October 1917

On the eve of battle the 1st Royal Dublin Fusiliers received an historic visit from the GOC 29th Division, General Sir Beauvoir de Lisle. It was in the form of a farewell gesture. After serving with the division since its formation, the 'Old Dubs' were being transferred to the 16th (Irish) Division. The attack planned for the following day was to be their parting shot. The general's address was a rousing affair. Approaching the last platoon, he asked: 'Now, who is going to win a VC tomorrow?' Whether in jest or not, one man reputedly answered: 'I am sir, or I will leave my skin in dirty old Belgium.' His name was Acting CSM James Ockendon, a 26-year-old English-born pre-war regular who only two months earlier had won a Military Medal.

During the night Y and Z Companies, who would lead the assault, filed into Eagle Trench. Covering posts crept into no-man's-land and within an hour of zero, all was ready. The barrage came down 'in great accuracy' and the Dublins set off on what would prove an almost textbook operation. Whereas the 4th Division on their right suffered a series of setbacks, the 29th Division's sole assault unit carried all before them on 4 October. 'We went through them like the way the Divil went through Athlone – in standing jumps,' wrote one man. It was not, however, plain sailing everywhere.

Y Company, on the right, lost all its officers and company sergeant-major, yet still managed to attain its objectives, linking up with the leading unit of the hapless 4th Division. On the left, men of Z Company captured Chinese House and cleared a number of shell-holes, before running into heavy fire from across the Broembeek, roughly 500yd beyond the 't Goed ter Vesten Farm strongpoint which marked their final goal.

It was during this advance that James Ockendon embarked on a series of exploits which earned him the third of six Victoria Crosses to be awarded to members of the 29th Division during the campaign. General de Lisle described the first of these actions as 'a very sensational act' and there was no question that it left an indelible impression on all who witnessed it. According to one account, it began when a machine-gun opened up, causing casualties among a leading platoon and pinning down the survivors. General de Lisle wrote:

> Seeing a platoon officer hit and the advance stopped by a machine-gun, he charged it from a flank, killing all the detachment but one, who ran away. He chased this man across the whole front of the Battalion and bayoneted him, and in spite of the bullets the whole Battalion rose up and cheered him.

Oddly, Ockendon's own version made no mention of a dash across no-man's-land to account for a third machine-gunner, although he did refer to a second incident omitted by both de Lisle and the citation for his VC. Interviewed about the action when events were still fresh in his mind, he declared:

> When going into action my platoon officer got wounded, and another officer was killed, and the company were left to me. On going to the front wave I found the company held up by machine-gun fire. I asked the corporal to cover me off, in case anything happened to me, and then I rushed the gun, and killed the crew, all but one. I turned the enemy machine gun round and fired it. While firing the gun I got sniped by an enemy gunner. I then made for that gun, and I got that, too, killing the crew.

Having silenced this post, Ockendon collected the remnants of his company and pushed on to 't Goed ter Vesten Farm. Once more they were met by heavy rifle and machine-gun fire. But Ockendon proved equal to the test. Dodging a hail of fire, he dashed forward, shouting to the Germans to give themselves up. 'The garrison would not surrender,' he later stated, 'but continued to fire. I killed four of them and the remainder surrendered, and I took them prisoner.'

It was a masterpiece of understatement. Yet again, the tide of battle had been turned by one man's exceptional daring. Aside from the four men disposed of by Ockendon, a further sixteen capitulated in the face of his irresistible assault. In all, Z Company had taken more than fifty prisoners and captured two machine-guns in their advance to the banks of the Broembeek, at a cost, said by Ockendon to consist of two officers and fifteen men.

On 8 November the *London Gazette* carried news of the award of the Victoria Cross to the gallant non-commissioned officer for his repeated attacks on enemy machine-gun posts 'regardless of his personal safety'. James Ockendon had proved as good as his word.

James Ockendon, the first Portsmouth-born recipient of the Victoria Cross in the First World War, was born at 56 Albert Street, Landport, on 10 December 1890, one of nine children to Alfred Ockendon and Mary Anne (née Verrall). He was educated at St Agatha's School, and worked at Messrs Chalcraft's drapers in Russell Street, Portsmouth, prior to joining the Army as a private in the 1st Battalion, the Royal Dublin Fusiliers on 22 May 1909 at the age of 18. He underwent basic training in Dublin, and not long after, his unit, which had been stationed at Victoria Barracks, Portsmouth, was posted to India, where it continued to serve until the outbreak of war.

Ockendon took part in the landings at Cape Helles, on the Gallipoli peninsula on 25 April 1915. During the first two days his unit suffered more than 550 casualties. Ockendon went through some of the heaviest fighting of the campaign, surviving a bullet wound in the face, splinters from which remained embedded in his forehead for the rest of his life. Promotion followed swiftly. Having spent six years as a private, he rose to sergeant in less than a year. Following evacuation of the peninsula, he served in Egypt before moving to France and the Somme offensive.

Described as a 'clean-cut soldier hardened by active service', Ockendon was an unassuming man for whom actions spoke louder than words. He was recommended for bravery on numerous occasions, being awarded a Military Medal on 6 August 1917 (*London Gazette*, 28 September). It resulted from an incident while his battalion was relieving another unit in the front line. A heavy enemy barrage caused a number of casualties and led to considerable confusion as men became separated. Ockendon, however, rallied the survivors and led them forward.

Shortly afterwards, he returned to Portsmouth on leave and on 28 August married Caroline Anne Green, at St Luke's church, Southsea.When he rejoined his unit he took with him one of his wife's white wedding slippers and it was later reported that this had stopped a German bullet, thus saving his life. Ockendon was given leave prior to his VC investiture at Buckingham Palace on 5 December 1917. Arriving in Southsea on 27 November, he found his home street decorated and local residents waiting to cheer him. The *Hampshire Telegraph and Post* noted:

> Wearing his full military pack, with his steel helmet strapped to his kit and rifle slung over his back, the sergeant greeted the neighbours with an unassuming smile, and was eager to get indoors. Press photographers were there betimes, however, and Sergeant Ockendon and his wife

obligingly waited on the pavement while, surrounded by an admiring crowd, they were 'snapped' for the picture papers.

Civic honours followed. Ockendon received an illuminated address from Portsmouth Corporation and a silver casket from his local newspaper. His courage was further recognised in January 1918 by the award of the Belgian Croix de Guerre. It was officially gazetted on 12 July, by which time Ockendon had left the Army and was living in Sophia Place, Portsmouth.

He was officially discharged from the Royal Dublin Fusiliers on 30 April 1918 as 'being no longer physically fit for war service', though his record gives no indication as to what had occurred in the intervening period. It seems likely, however, that he had been badly gassed. Ten years later, he was assessed as 100 per cent disabled by the Ministry of Pensions on account of 'tubercle of the lungs' and the effects of the wound to his forehead sustained at Gallipoli. He was granted a life pension, and his son recalled him in later years 'picking out pieces of shrapnel' which worked their way to the surface.

Ockendon settled down to family life. He and his wife had four children – Eileen (b. 1918), Irene (b. 1920), James (b. 1922), who later served in the Royal Navy, and Betty (b. 1924). He worked as a crane driver in Portsmouth Dockyard until his retirement at the age of 60. Later, he took a job as a cleaner at No. 3 Training Battalion, Royal Army Ordnance Corps, in Hilsea. During the Second World War, he served in the Hampshire Home Guard and was selected to have his portrait painted by Eric Kennington.

He remained a keen supporter of ex-service organisations. A life member of the Portsmouth British Legion Club, he also belonged to the 29th Division Association until its demise in 1965. In June 1920 he attended the Buckingham Palace Garden Party for VC recipients. It was the first of many functions he took part in associated with his award. They included the 1929 Dinner at the House of Lords, the VC Centenary Review in 1956 and a host of VC and GC Association gatherings. Aside from such events, Ockendon made little of his honour. His son recalled: 'He talked very little about what he did to win it, to me or anybody else. Hardly anybody knew he had the VC apart from one or two neighbours. He didn't advertise the fact. He only ever brought it out for British Legion parades and VC reunions.'

James Ockendon died at his home at 5 Yorke Street, Southsea, on 29 August 1966. He was 75. Four years earlier, Portsmouth City Council named a new street Ockendon Close in his honour. His body was cremated at Portchester crematorium on 1 September 1966, and his ashes scattered in the Garden of Remembrance.

W. CLAMP

Near the Brewery, Poelcappelle, 9 October 1917

In the aftermath of the Broodseinde success, Haig was convinced that the Germans were on the brink of collapse. The next stage of the offensive was thus brought forward by 24 hours to 5.20 am on 9 October. This time the objective was to drive the enemy from the commanding positions along Passchendaele Ridge. Even allowing for the curtailment of the more ambitious aspects of the original plan, the operation took little account of worsening conditions. For five days it had rained almost unceasingly and by 8 October the steady downpour had become a torrent. The battlefield had taken on the appearance of a vast swamp. One senior engineer described the upper valley of the Steenbeek and its tributaries as 'a porridge of mud' in which duckboards drifted away, guns disappeared and movement became a tortuous ordeal of life-threatening proportions. In these conditions, the men's endurance was stretched to breaking point. The official historian observed:

> ... in all that vast wilderness of slime hardly a tree, hedge, wall or building could be seen ... no landmarks existed, nor any scap of natural cover other than the mud-filled shell-holes. That the attacks ordered were so gallantly made in such conditions stands to the immortal credit of the battalions concerned.

Never was human courage to be squandered to so little effect.

The experiences of the 6th Green Howards were typical. Part of the 32nd Brigade, 11th Division, they were to carry the advance 1,200yd across the Poelcappelle Spur towards Westroosebeke. After a 6-hour slog through drenching rain, they arrived near Pheasant Farm cemetery in the early hours of 8 October, having been bedevilled with difficulties. Runners had gone astray, guiding tapes vanished and not until 1 am on the morning of the attack did detailed instructions reach the assault companies in the front line.

Throughout the night, the men were forced to endure heavy shelling. In contrast, the 6th Green Howards' diarist noted that the British barrage 'was very ill-defined and the HE and heavy batteries fired very short'. It did not augur well for an operation already robbed of tank support due to the wretched weather. The attack went in as planned, the leading troops advancing into Poelcappelle with deceptive ease. The 6th Green Howards took around 150 to 200 prisoners, but progress slowed as they approached strong enemy positions near the site of a brewery which the tanks had been intended to subdue. In the ensuing struggle, several pillboxes fell to small parties braving a storm of fire from strongpoints at Meunier House and String Houses. Among the bravest of these gallant bands was Cpl William Clamp, a 25-year-old Scottish Territorial.

Picking out the largest pillbox he set off for it with two men. Their initial charge was beaten back, both of Clamp's comrades being 'knocked out'. Undeterred, Clamp merely collected another supply of grenades, gathered two more men and set off again. Moving first to the blockhouse, he hurled in his bombs before disappearing inside; he emerged with a machine-gun and a posse of prisoners whose number varied in different accounts from twenty to thirty-five. Capt. Clive L. Bayliss, who recommended Clamp for the Victoria Cross, described the action as 'one of the bravest examples of pluck and initiative that has ever been seen in this regiment'. In a letter to Clamp's mother, he added: 'He rushed a German pillbox, threw a bomb in the door, killing a few, and bringing out 35 prisoners and a machine-gun, which he brought back to his company officer.'

Despite such bravery, the Green Howards continued to take losses from machine guns dotted along the spur, rendering further advance impossible. By 8 am a line of sorts was established in the face of heavy close-range fire. Three hours later they were reinforced by a company of the 8th West Ridings. 'The remainder of the day', wrote the unit diarist, 'was quiet except for sniping and some machine-gun fire.' It was during the consolidation that William Clamp became engaged in another series of actions which culminated in his death. Having captured the pillbox, Clamp was prominent among a band of men who sought to counter-act the menace posed by enemy snipers hidden in a number of ruined buildings close to the Green Howards' positions. Operating with much the same degree of dash which characterised his earlier actions, he hunted out the enemy riflemen, 'rushing' one position after another until his luck ran out. Captain Bayliss wrote:

Later in the day, he was shot by a sniper whilst endeavouring to find the whereabouts of another machine-gun. The whole battalion mourn his death and we are all very proud to have been in the same regiment as he.

Tragically, it was all to no avail. At around 5 pm the enemy began filtering back into their old positions. One party reoccupied the dugouts that had been so bravely captured north-west of the brewery, compelling a partial withdrawal. Little had been accomplished at considerable cost. The Green Howards' casualty list ran to forty dead, 161 wounded and thirty-one missing. Further south it was much the same story as the main attack foundered in the mud.

Nine weeks later, the *London Gazette* announced the posthumous award of the Victoria Cross to No. 42537 Cpl William Clamp. The citation gave little hint of the day's failed endeavours. It concluded: 'His magnificent courage and self-sacrifice was of the greatest value and relieved what was undoubtedly a very critical situation.'

William Clamp was born in Bridge Street, Motherwell, on 28 October 1891, the son of Charles Clamp, an iron and steel factory worker, and his wife Christina. One of nine brothers, with nine sisters, he attended Craigneuk Public School and the local Salvation Army's Sabbath School. Later, he became a member of the Good Templar Lodge and played in the cornet section of the Motherwell Corps Band. When his parents moved to Reid's Terrace, Shields Road, Flemington, he found work at Messrs Hurst, Nelson, building wagons. While living there he enlisted on 22 January 1914 in the 6th Scottish Rifles (Cameronians), his local Territorial unit.

Called up immediately on the outbreak of war, he saw action with the battalion at Festubert in 1915. During service with the 6th Scottish Rifles he was seriously wounded twice and after coming out of hospital the second time he was transferred to the 6th Green Howards on 10 January 1917. He made a quick impression, his new company commander, Capt. Bayliss, describing him as a 'very efficient lad'.

As well as being a fine soldier, Clamp was also a man of strong Christian principles. An account published in the *Motherwell Times* stated:

A fine type of young man, quiet and steady, his exemplary life and deep-rooted beliefs had a marked influence on those with whom he came into contact, and it has been said by one who knew him well that 'if ever there was a lad who lived the Christian life in the workshop and in the trenches it was William Clamp'.

News of his exploits, based on Capt. Bayliss' account, were reported in the local press on 26 October 1917. Nine days later, an impressive memorial service was held at the local Salvation Army Citadel. Absentees included two of his brothers who were on active service. Clamp's posthumous honour was presented to his parents by King George V at Buckingham Palace on 2 March 1918, and is now held by the Green Howards Museum in Richmond.

William Clamp's memory has been perpetuated in his home town in a variety of ways. The publication of a local brochure, *One of the Old 6th Scottish*, raised sufficient funds to pay for a gold medal to be awarded annually in his honour at Craigneuk Public School. Almost sixty-five years later, the council named a road after him and not long afterwards his sister presented a framed portrait together with his medal ribbon and citation for display. It was a fitting tribute to a brave Scottish soldier, of whom his mother once remarked: 'Aye, he was a good lad. He never at any time caused the least worry or bother. His letters were always cheery and bright. In the last letter I received from him, he said: "Don't worry about me, mother, for whatever happens, my soul is right with God".'

J. LISTER, J. MOLYNEUX
AND F.G. DANCOX

Olga House, Conde House, Namur Crossing,
9 October 1917

As Lt-Col A.H.S. Hart Synnot DSO struggled towards the jumping-off positions 800yd north-east of Langemarck on the night of 8–9 October, he was
filled with a growing sense of unease about the morning's attack. The CO
of the 1st Lancashire Fusiliers had issued his orders and was anxious to
make certain preparations were complete. But events seemed to be conspiring
against him. He wrote:

> A good deal of rain had fallen and the ground was very wet, muddy and
> slippery. There was no moon and the night was very dark. I expected great
> difficulty in getting into position, particularly in moving the two compa-
> nies ... which were to form my support lines ... I had some difficulty in
> finding my way. The whole of the country between Langemarke [sic] and
> the jumping-off line was kept under steady shell fire during the night.

His plan was uncomplicated. A Company (Capt. R. Downes MC) and
B Company (Lt C.L. Rougier) were allotted the first objective, labelled the
'Green Dotted Line', an advance of 500yd across ground occupied by a
number of enemy strongpoints, of which the most significant lay around
Olga House. Once gained, C and D Companies were to pass through and
seize the second objective, the 'Blue Dotted Line', almost 500yd further on.

But Hart Synnot's preparations were hampered by a series of problems,
an awkward angle of attack, a shortage of tape to mark forming up positions and, finally at 2 am, the realisation that two of B Company's platoons
had gone astray. Hurried plans were made to replace B Company with
D Company, only for the missing platoons to reappear.

At 4.30 am Hart Synnot issued new orders reverting to his original plan.
'By 5.10 am,' he wrote, 'everything was ready'. Zero hour was just 10 minutes away.

The 1st Lancashire Fusiliers were spearheading the 86th Brigade's advance astride the Staden railway. Behind came the 2nd Royal Fusiliers with orders to push on towards the final objective. On their left, the 4th Worcestershires led the 88th Brigade's advance north of the railway embankment, with the Royal Newfoundlanders in support. The orders were to press on at all costs. Hart Synnot recorded:

> At 5.20 am the barrage fell and the whole Battalion moved forward. The night was fine. There was some moonlight and dawn was just beginning to break. As the barrage advanced my support Companies shook out ... The advance went exactly according to programme. About 5.27 am the German artillery shelling appeared to thicken up, but I could not locate any distinct hostile barrage. The shells seemed to be falling indiscriminately in every direction ...

If the counter-barrage was ragged, the enemy's machine-gun fire most certainly was not. Two pillboxes, one to the south and the other to the east of Olga House, offered particularly fierce resistance to A Company and produced the first hold-up. Sgt W. Brain DCM, MM, a veteran of Gallipoli and France, won a Bar to his DCM for silencing both of them, wiping out one garrison with bomb and bayonet and taking twenty-five prisoners from the other. Capt. Downes, the company commander, led parties against other posts until a serious wound put him out of action. Two platoon commanders were also hit.

Lt S.H. Winterbottom, later awarded a Military Cross for his leadership that day, took command of A Company and led them on. They had not gone far, however, when a hail of fire from Olga House stopped them in their tracks. This position, the main obstacle standing between the Fusiliers and their first objective, was a strong one. At its heart lay a pillbox, shielded by a machine-gun post sited in a shell-hole and flanked by riflemen in the waterlogged craters scarring the sodden battlefield. The dilemma facing Winterbottom was an invidious one: either to make a frontal attack, almost certainly resulting in heavy loss of life, or accept a potentially disastrous delay. Before he could make any decision, however, the need to do so was removed in decisive fashion.

Recognising the dangers of a lengthy hold-up, Sgt Joseph Lister, who had been noted for bravery on at least one other occasion, made up his mind to act. Leaping up, he dashed towards the enemy position. There is some discrepancy about what followed. According to his VC citation, he shot two men operating the machine-gun in front of the pillbox and then headed for the building itself. But the regimental record contended that the gallant NCO 'disregarded' the shell-hole post, going straight for the pillbox.

There is, however, no disagreement about what happened next. The unit historian stated:

> ... he shouted to the occupants to surrender. Only one man refused and him Lister shot dead; the rest came out, whereupon more Germans, to the number of about a hundred, emerged from shell-holes behind and gave themselves up.

It was one of the greatest single-handed captures of the war, and almost certainly the most spectacular individual haul of the Passchendaele campaign. Most important of all, however, was its bearing on the operation. The unit historian wrote:

> The effect of Lister's prompt initiative was to enable the advance to continue with a barely perceptible check and the troops to keep up with the barrage, at a moment when serious delay night easily have occurred. If the line had been held up here and the barrage lost, it is very probable that the first objective would not have been reached over a wide area, with incalculable consequences to the operations.

Lister was more modest. In a letter to his wife, he merely noted: 'I have some good new to tell you. I went over the top again and came out all right. You will hear before long, and you will be surprised. I am recommended for the VC, so you see I have done my bit and will do it again.' Of the risks he had undertaken, he later reasoned: 'It only needs a bit of dash and it is better for one man to take the risk than that 200 should be cut up.'

By 5.58 am, the men of A Company were in position on the 'Green Dotted Line' and in touch with B Company on the left and the 2nd Lancashire Fusiliers (4th Division) on the right near Millers Farm. Shortly after, Lt-Col Hart Synnot reported 'prisoners in large numbers' arriving at headquarters. They were Hessians from the 441st and 477th Regiments and within half an hour their number had swollen to 150, the majority presumably from Olga House.

While A and B Companies dug in, C and D Companies took up the advance, together with parties of the 2nd Royal Fusiliers who had mingled with them when, according to the reserve unit's diarist, 'the line was held up for about 15 minutes' around Olga House. On the left, X Company of the 2nd Royal Fusiliers followed by W Company, under the command of Capt. Pearson, pressed forward. There was a measure of confusion, due in part to the mixing of units and the delay which the Royal Fusiliers claimed resulted in their losing the barrage. The 2nd RF's war diary stated:

After the 15 minutes' wait the LFs in front advanced about 100yd when they again halted apparently on first objective. Officers commanding W and X Companies were together preliminary to the advance on second objective. They noticed the thickening of the barrage and advanced by the watch. They passed through a line of LFs in shell-holes and thought another line was in front, but could neither see or get in touch with them ...

Despite the uncertainties, lack of communications and apparent absence of any troops on the right, a decision was made, in keeping with 29th Division orders, to go on. They went forward, only to be held up by shells falling short near Conde House. The position bore some similarity to that at Olga House. The shell of the ruined house masked a concrete pillbox close to which ran a trench from where a machine-gun kept up a persistent fire. Once again, however, the struggle was largely decided by the inspiration of one man. Sgt John Molyneux, of W Company, a 6ft 5in tall Lancastrian miner from St Helens, had taken command of his platoon when his officer was hit. He later recalled:

We were nearly up to our waists in mud, and were getting mixed up owing to the check in front. I realised there was some strongpoint holding out, so my pal, Sgt Day, and myself tried to work round the spot from where the damage was coming in the shape of machine-gun bullets and things. While we were going across, Sgt Day got two nasty wounds, and as soon as I saw this it seemed to get my temper up, and I was determined to get at those Germans with the machine-gun. We could not get at them from the front, for they were strongly posted in a house and pillbox with machine-guns and rifles, so we had to work round the flank again. At the corner we came across a small trench with six or seven Germans, and, getting our men together, I gave the order to bomb them out and we did so. We soon got the better of that lot. There was still the house in front of us from which a stream of machine-gun bullets were coming, so I told the boys to follow me, and we rushed in the direction of the broken down house. It was full of snipers and after a hot time of it we managed to get them out of it ... When we had taken the house we found there was a small pillbox at the back of it, and the men followed again, and we got the man and gun. The German was killed in the place.

After that, we went back to our positions, and the attacking troops carried on the advance. It turned out to be a very strong point, and the general advance was held up by it until we had cleaned it up. I escaped without a scratch, but some of the boys were wounded.

According to his VC citation, Molyneux was first into the house: 'By the time the men arrived, he was in the thick of a hand-to-hand fight; this only lasted a short time, and the enemy surrendered, and, in addition to the dead and wounded, between 20 and 30 prisoners were taken.'

Despite the great gallantry displayed, the 2nd Royal Fusiliers failed to reach their final objective. The remains of Molyneux's company 'found that there was nobody in front and the second objective had not been taken'. A line, therefore, was established near Tranquille House. The unit historian recorded:

> It was literally a filthy advance; it was costly; it was unsatisfactory. The battalion had advanced according to plan, but apparently no one else had. There was no obvious landmark to stake out the day's work and round off the ordeal. But it was not so much a misfortune of the battalion's as a general characteristic of the operations in this phase of the battle.

To the north of the Staden railway embankment, the advance of the 88th Brigade had been no less hard-fought. Indeed, so difficult did their task appear to the CO of the 1st Lancashire Fusiliers that he felt his own operation would be jeopardised. 'I was very anxious about my left flank,' confessed Lt-Col Hart Synnot, 'because I feared that the heavy rain of the night before would have made the Broembeek and the marshes on its banks extremely difficult for the Worcesters and the Guards on my left to cross. Any delay in their advance would, I saw, expose my left flank to enfilade fire from Namur Crossing and Pascalls Farm, where all information received pointed to the presence of German machine-guns.'

While his concerns proved largely unfounded, the intelligence assessments were entirely accurate. To reach their first objective at Namur Crossing, where the remains of a road ran beneath the Staden railway, the 4th Worcestershires, led by Lt-Col C.S. Linton DSO, MC, had to overcome a network of pillboxes sited along the embankment. The plan took account of the swampy ground. Anticipating progress to be slow, the advance was to proceed in three bounds, with lengthy pauses to allow lagging troops time to catch up. Each halt was to be covered by a barrage laid in front of the objectives, while to help with the crossing of the Broembeek, a cumbersome artificial bridge was prepared.

In the event, it was not needed. When the leading companies reached the stream, they found the enemy's foot-bridges still intact. Large numbers of Germans were killed or captured amid the shell-hole positions lapping the Broembeek and by 5.50 am the 4th Worcestershires, intermingled with leading elements of the Newfoundlanders, were on their first objective at Namur Crossing, having silenced a string of pillboxes.

Losses were comparatively few and they began to dig in. The protective barrage, designed to screen them from the enemy, threw up a curtain of smoke, but it failed to shield them from one pillbox, roughly midway between the railway and the stream, which from a range of 200yd poured a stream of fire at the toiling troops. The Worcesters' historian wrote:

> Officers and men were shot down or were driven to shelter in the shell-holes. Musketry was useless against the concrete walls, and messages were sent back for trench-mortars to deal with the blockhouse. But before the mortars could be brought up the fire of the machine-gun suddenly stopped. A minute later every man within sight was on his feet cheering and laughing, for stumbling through the mud towards the British line came a little crowd of the enemy with hands raised in surrender, and behind them came a solitary British soldier, labouring along under the weight of the machine-gun – *the* machine-gun. The cheering grew as he was recognised: 'Dancox!' the troops shouted, 'Good old Dancox!'

It was a rare moment of elation, and one characterised by a considerable amount of caustic humour. For there was little doubt that in Pte Fred Dancox, a 38-year-old family man with four children, the 4th Worcesters had discovered an unlikely hero. Described as 'a stolid old soldier', he was, like Sgt Molyneux of the Royal Fusiliers, a veteran of battles in Gallipoli and France. However, there had been no evidence of the kind of initiative and daring he displayed to such spectacular effect at Namur Crossing.

Prior to going into action, he had been employed in the less than glamorous role of battalion headquarters sanitary orderly. Legend has it that his imagination had been fired by talk of combating the enemy pillboxes, and had asked to rejoin his company for the coming attack. Permission granted, he was assigned to a ten-man 'mopping up' party, with instructions to deal with those pillboxes skirted by the leading waves. At some point during the advance, he had become separated from his comrades and appears to have reached the first objective on his own when the pillbox burst into life. One regimental account records:

> Nothing daunted, he proceeded to attack the blockhouse single-handed. No attempt could have been more hazardous, for the ground in front and on each side of the blockhouse was swept by the German machine-guns, while close behind and around the blockhouse our own shells were bursting; but with cool courage Pte Dancox made his way unobserved from shell-hole to shell-hole round to the back of the blockhouse. Running the gauntlet of our own bursting shells, he reached the back wall of the concrete fort. Then with a bomb ready in his hand he walked inside, into the midst of the enemy. Surprised and terrified, the machine-gunners put up their hands. Pte Dancox slowly backed out of the doorway, menacing them with his bomb and beckoning them to follow. When all were outside he ordered

Pte F.G. Dancox

them off to our lines, and they went in haste, glad enough at their respite from almost certain death. Then he thought of the machine-gun, went again into the blockhouse, dismounted the weapon and brought it back in triumph ...

According to one account, the prisoners numbered about forty and Dancox, who treated the captured gun as his personal possession, used it against the enemy 'throughout the rest of the day, in great good humour and amid the laughing congratulations of all around.'

Despite failures elsewhere, the 29th Division had achieved almost all its objectives by 8 am, a feat celebrated by the notable distinction of three Victoria Crosses and a flood of lesser awards. The 1st Lancashire Fusiliers alone received no fewer than fifty-three medals for bravery, headed by the Victoria Cross to No. 8133 Sgt Joseph Lister. The *London Gazette* of 26 November also carried the announcement of the same award to No. 1817 Sgt John Molyneux and No. 21654 Pte Frederick Dancox. It was an honour one of that gallant triumvirate would not live long to enjoy.

Frederick George Dancox was born in St Stephen's parish of Barbourne, Worcester, in 1878, the middle child of three sons to William Danocks, a labourer, and his wife Louisa (née Chance). The discrepancy over his surname appears to have been the result of an error on his enlistment papers which resulted in the name of Dancox being perpetuated for the rest of his life, although the same erroneous spelling can be found in his entry in St Stephen's church baptismal register for 23 November 1878. No christian name was given for the child and it has been suggested that this was an indication that Fred was a sickly baby and his baptism hurriedly arranged.

Whatever the truth, it is clear his early years were difficult. His father died, aged 39, before his second birthday when his mother was pregnant with her third son, Henry George, who was born in January 1881. Three years after her husband's death, Louisa married labourer William Whittle and the censuses of 1891 and 1901 show Fred Dancox living in a growing family with his mother, stepfather, two brothers, two stepbrothers, from Whittle's previous marriage, and several younger half-siblings at 55 St George's Lane and later 59 Hylton Road, Worcester. Along with his brothers, William and Henry, it is thought Fred was educated at St Stephen's School. After leaving school, he worked as a hay-trusser, living in Dolday, one of the poorest districts of Worcester, until he volunteered for the Army in 1915. Shortly after enlisting in the 4th Worcestershires and while based in Norton Barracks, he married his long-time partner, Ellen Pritchard, at a ceremony in Pershore on 8 March 1915. By then the couple were already the parents of four children – Frederic (b. 1902), Florence (b. 1906), Harry (b. 1909) and Ellen (b. 1913). A fifth child, George, was born in July 1915 but died shortly after his 1st birthday.

A tall, heavily built man with a reputation for speaking his mind, 'Dando', as he was known, was a popular figure in and around the farms about Worcester. He was reportedly 'as strong as an ox' and a spirited man of 'forcible action', though records give little indication as to his soldierly ability. Despite service in Gallipoli, Egypt and on the Somme, there is no evidence of him having been promoted, wounded or noted for any acts of bravery prior to his extraordinary exploit at Namur Crossing. In letters home, he made no mention of his action and prior to the announcement of his Victoria Cross the only information his wife had received about his act of valour was taken from a comrade's correspondence which had been passed on to her.

Hailed as Worcester's first winner of the VC – incorrectly, for that honour actually belonged to George Wyatt, who won his Cross in August 1914 – Dancox was promised a welcome home party. Indeed, as soon as his award was announced, flags and bunting were strung across his narrow street. He was due to go on leave on 30 November, four days after his VC had been gazetted. His family was informed and civic leaders in Worcester planned an official reception. According to one account, a welcoming committee even went to Shrub Hill station. But Dancox never arrived. A few days later his family's worst fears were realised. A press report published on 19 December stated:

News was received in Worcester yesterday that Pte F.G. Dancox ... has been killed in action. He had been given fourteen days leave to come home to receive the honour but was delayed by a counter-attack. He fell within a few yards of a shelter after assisting to drive back the Germans.

Dancox had been among the troops moved south to Cambrai for the new offensive. At first the attack, spearheaded by 370 tanks, had gone well, but opposition hardened and the exhausted British formations were sent reeling by a counter-stroke launched on 30 November. The 29th Division fought a brave but costly defensive action around Marcoing and Masnières, and it was near the latter place that Dancox was apparently struck in the head by a piece of shrapnel and killed. His death was one in a line of tragedies to strike his family. A year earlier, his brother William, a veteran of the Boer War, had died while serving with the Worcesters, and in the months that followed his stepbrothers Thomas and John Whittle were both killed in action. Fred Dancox has no known grave. His name is recorded on the Cambrai Memorial at Louverval.

On 31 July 1918 Ellen Dancox received her husband's VC from King George V at Buckingham Palace. To assist the family and in recognition of Dancox's distinction, Worcester City Council had opened a fund with an initial donation of £50. After a slow start – a council minute in February 1918 noted that 'subscriptions were not coming in very satisfactorily' – the fund eventually reached £451 and was administered by trustees appointed by the council. Even so, the family struggled to make ends meet. According to a newspaper report, Dancox's widow pawned his VC before eventually selling it to the city council. In 1923 it was placed on display in the Guildhall, before being presented on permanent loan to the Worcestershire Regimental Museum.

Almost a century after his death, the valour of a humble sanitary orderly continues to be remembered. In the centre of Worcester a sheltered housing complex bears his name and on the battlefield where he earned the country's highest honour a memorial plaque now stands as mute testimony to his solo charge. It was unveiled at Namur Crossing in September 2006 by the hero's grandson and namesake in a ceremony organised by the Worcestershire and Herefordshire Branch of the Western Front Association and attended by three generations of the Dancox family.

Joseph Lister, Stockport's first VC recipient, was born in Fenney Street, Higher Broughton, Salford, on 19 October 1886, the son of Joseph Lister and Nancy (née Gee). His father had his own book-keeping business and in 1896 the family moved to Longsight and then Harpurhey, Manchester. Joseph went to Houldsworth School until the age of 13 and was a member of St Elisabeth's Boys' Brigade. He married in 1910, and was working as a labourer at Lowes Chemical Works in Reddish when war broke out. With a number of other men from the factory, Lister, who was then living in Prenton View, Reddish, enlisted in the Lancashire Fusiliers on 7 September 1914, in answer to Lord Kitchener's call for volunteers.

His leadership qualities were soon recognised and he became an NCO in 1915. After training at Salisbury, Bournemouth and Aldershot, he was posted in 1916 to the 1st Battalion, then serving on the Somme. According to newspaper reports published at the time of his Victoria Cross award, Lister saw considerable action before being evacuated sixteen months later with 'trench fever'. After spending ten weeks recuperating, he returned to his unit. In all, he was wounded on four separate occasions, once in the mouth and later in the shoulder and leg, but none was of such severity for him to be evacuated to England. Prior to his gallantry at Olga House, Lister had been recommended for the Distinguished Conduct Medal, although the circumstances are not known.

Sgt J. Lister

He returned home in December and after receiving gifts of money from his workmates, he travelled to Buckingham Palace with his wife, Harriet, to receive his VC from King George V. Despite a mix-up during their return journey, a large crowd that included the Reddish Prize Band were on the platform at Edgeley to greet him. A torchlight procession followed to the town tall, where Lister, his wife and two children, received a huge ovation.

The following May, Lister, who had by then received the Belgian Médaille Militaire for the same action, was given another civic reception, during which he was given £150-worth of war bonds, the result of a public subscription. He also received a gold medal from the Church Lads' Brigade of St Elisabeth's, Reddish. Lister had just been discharged from the Temple Road Military Hospital in Birkenhead, where he was recovering from being badly gassed. Responding to the crowds who turned out once again to greet him, he declared: 'If it is my luck to go out again, I shall do the same thing again if it ever comes my chance.'

Demobilised in 1919, he returned to Reddish and took a job as a postman. He was among 320 VC holders who attended the Prince of Wales' banquet at the House of Lords in 1929. During 1940 Lister, who had been working as a watchman at Craven's works, rejoined the Lancashire Fusiliers. He later received the Defence Medal in respect of his service.

In later life Lister, who was a life member of the Houldsworth Working Men's Club, became a familiar figure in Reddish as a school-crossing warden, shepherding children across the road. He died in hospital on 19 January 1963, a little over a month after his wife's death. After a service at St Elisabeth's church, Reddish, he was buried with military honours in Willow Grove cemetery, with seven NCOs of the 5th Lancashire Fusiliers acting as pallbearers and a bugler from his old regiment sounding the Last Post and Reveille at his grave side.

Sgt J. Molyneux

His Victoria Cross now forms part of the Lord Ashcroft Victoria Cross Collection displayed at the Imperial War Museum.

John Molyneux was born on 22 November 1890 at 3 Marshall's Cross Road, Peasley Cross, St Helens, in Lancashire, the son of Joseph and Minnie Jane Molyneux. His father, who worked as a miner at Sherdley Colliery, was well known in the district as an amateur concertina player, while one of his grandfathers had served twenty-one years in the Royal Marines. The only boy of seven children, Jack, as he was known, was educated at the Holy Trinity Church of England Schools, in St Helens. As a youngster, he was a keen nature lover, especially enjoying bird watching, sometimes at the expense of attending classes. He left school at the age of 12, and went to work for the Sutton Heath and Lea Green Colliery Company, owners of the pit where his father worked.

Described as 'a fine muscular man of great strength', Jack Molyneux enjoyed boxing as a youth, and when war broke out he was among the first rush of volunteers, enlisting in the Royal Fusiliers on 7 September 1914. At that time, he was still living with his parents at 81 Sherdley Road. After training at Dover, he was posted to the 2nd Battalion, and sailed with them to the Dardanelles, where they took part in the Gallipoli landings on 25 April 1915. Slightly wounded during the fighting at Suvla Bay, he was evacuated to Malta suffering from frost-bite in the aftermath of the blizzard which struck the peninsula in late November 1915.

He rejoined his unit in Egypt. By then, the Gallipoli campaign was over and he sailed with the rest of the 29th Division to France in March 1916. He took part in some of the worst fighting on the Somme, being wounded a second time and evacuated to hospital in England where he spent Christmas 1916. Posted back to his battalion, Molyneux saw further action in the Ypres Salient, culminating in his courageous exploit at Conde House. A few years later, he recalled the Battle of Poelcappelle as 'one of the worst I ever experienced, owing to the bad conditions of the ground, and also many blockhouses which we had to clear. I got through this battle without any wounds and none the worse after my experiences.'

Among many letters of congratulation which followed his award was one he came to treasure. It was written by a nurse who had treated him during his spell in hospital the previous December. She wrote:

I am glad to know that you have won such a coveted honour as the VC. Well done, 'Bed 34'. I feel quite a little reflected glory to think we had you here, and in our small way helped you back to health and strength, to go out and win your spurs. It is a grand thing you have done, sergeant. Deeds live on after we are gone, and inspire those who come after.

He returned to England to receive his Victoria Cross from King George V on 12 December 1917, and on New Year's Day 1918, St Helens was en fête to honour the local hero. Amid 'remarkable scenes of enthusiasm', Jack Molyneux was transported from his home in an open carriage through streets lined with cheering people to the town hall where he received gifts of war loans, an illuminated address and rapturous acclaim. Although outgoing enough to play his concertina in public, he was by nature a quiet, rather retiring man and he found the celebrations something of an ordeal. His sister, Fanny, recalled one example of his shyness: 'When picked up from home by the Mayor and Mayoress of St Helens in their open carriage, he sat with head bowed until a jolly, stout woman, a well-known character and neighbour of the family, shouted, "lift thee 'ead up, Johnny!"'

Molyneux was modest of his award. He told the gathering:

The Victoria Cross has not made me a proud man; not at all. I have seen thousands of men earn it, but they have not got it. I got mine because it was rather a high position, and I was seen by four or five others and I got four recommendations. I know the boys who were with me were all worthy of the VC. I am sorry to say most of them got wounded ... The position we rushed was where the bullets were coming from that wounded our men. I set my teeth, and you know what it is when a British bulldog sets its teeth; it goes red-hot into it.

The reception concluded with Molyneux, at the mayor's request, giving a rendition of *The Blue Bells of Scotland* on his concertina, a performance repeated on the town hall steps in front of a crowd several thousand strong. During his hectic stay in St Helens, the young VC winner was showered with presents. They included a gold watch and £50-worth of war bonds from his workmates at the Sherdley Colliery, a silver cigarette case from the management of a local theatre and a new concertina from the Peasley Cross Concertina Club, where he was a member and his father was the band leader.

In February 1918 he was awarded the Belgian Croix de Guerre, almost certainly in respect of the same action that earned him his VC. He served with his unit to the end of the war and was demobilised at Cologne on 5 January 1919. He went back to work at the colliery and got married, his wife being Mary Agnes Molyneux, and they had a son and daughter. In 1925 he left the pit and joined the glassmaking firm, Pilkington Brothers, where he worked first as a 'teazer' and then, for the last thirty years of his career, as a gas producer in the sheet works.

During the Second World War he served as a warrant officer in the Lancashire Home Guard. A close friend of fellow VC winner John Thomas Davies, who grew up in the same area of Peasley Cross, he attended a number of functions for holders of the Victoria Cross, but he rarely spoke in any detail about the events surrounding his award, preferring to concentrate on his gardening and musical appearances in the clubs and on the radio with his concertina. He once told a journalist: 'I don't like talking about it. I just keep my medals in a special wallet and take them out on big occasions like Remembrance Day. I have been offered £600 for my VC, but the Bank of England hasn't enough to buy it.'

He died on 25 March 1972, aged 81, at the Ashtons Green Hostel for the elderly in Parr, his home for the last six years of his life. He collapsed while running an errand for one of his pals and passed away 2 hours later. 'He was one of the old brigade,' declared a member of staff. 'A brave old man who never complained even when he started to go blind.' His body was cremated and his ashes scattered in the Garden of Remembrance at St Helens crematorium. Almost a year later, Jack Molyneux's decorations appeared at a Sotheby's auction and were acquired at a cost of £2,100 by his former regiment for display in the Tower of London.

J.H. RHODES

Near the Houthulst Forest, 9 October 1917

On the northern flank elaborate plans for overcoming the Broembeek were rendered unnecessary as the Guards Division achieved one of the few outstanding successes on 9 October. The two assault brigades carried more than 400 portable bridges and specially-designed mats for straddling the swampy watercourse. But in the event, few were used, the majority of men preferring to wade through the mud under the cover of a well-orchestrated barrage. The 2nd Guards Brigade, with the 1st Scots Guards and 2nd Irish Guards leading, reached their first objective on time, the supporting companies passing through to complete the capture of the second goal by 8.15 am. Ahead, the southern fringe of Houthulst Forest, a heavily defended locality dotted with pillboxes and machine-gun nests, marked the final objective. It fell to the 3rd Grenadier Guards and 1st Coldstream Guards to make the last bound. Deliberately held back on the southern banks of the Broembeek until the first objective had fallen, they did not cross the stream until 7.30 am, thus avoiding the early fighting. Approaching the second objective, the 3rd Grenadiers deployed into their assault formation: No. 3 Company on the right and No. 4 Company on the left with Nos 1 and 2 Companies supporting.

Moving through consolidating units, the Coldstreamers and Grenadiers faced an advance across open ground raked by fire. According to the Grenadiers' historian, 'there seemed every prospect of desperate fighting'. And so might have been the case, but for the courageous enterprise of a single non-commissioned officer. While the Coldstreamers adopted the by now customary out-flanking tactics to overcome a blockhouse barring their way, L/Sgt John Rhodes, already the holder of a Distinguished

Conduct Medal and Bar, favoured the direct approach against a pill-box in the line of the Grenadiers' advance. Having already 'accounted for several enemy', Rhodes, who was commanding a Lewis gun section, sprinted forward, oblivious of enemy machine-gun fire and shell-bursts from the supporting barrage. Noticing three men leave the pillbox, he made straight for the entrance, reaching it unscathed. Scarcely pausing, he darted inside, where his threatening presence was apparently sufficient to induce a rapid surrender.

According to the Grenadiers' account, Rhodes took eight prisoners, although his VC citation claimed nine and at least one witness counted ten, including a forward artillery observation officer linked to his battery by telephone. Whatever the true tally, it was a startling success and may, in part, have been due to the garrison's mistaken impression that Rhodes was merely the vanguard of a much larger force. Supporting the recommendation for Rhodes' VC, a fellow NCO stated:

> I certify that I saw Sgt J.H. Rhodes capture a pillbox and ten prisoners, including an officer from whom valuable documents were taken. This was done under enemy machine-gun fire and fire from snipers, and at great danger of being caught in our own barrage. The pillbox was a hundred yards in front of our final objective.

Rhodes was aware of the efforts to honour his courage. He told his wife about being recommended and enclosed with his letter trophies taken from the captured pillbox, including a photograph of the German officer wearing an Iron Cross. His award was eventually confirmed on 26 November, the same day that Elizabeth Rhodes received another letter from her husband stating that he still did not know if he would 'definitely' receive the VC. The following day, while his family and the citizens of Tunstall, North Staffordshire, celebrated his honour, John Rhodes went into action again near Fontaine, France. The British offensive around Cambrai was in its last weary stages and on that mist-shrouded battlefield Rhodes' luck finally ran out. Carroll Carstairs, an officer in the 3rd Grenadiers, saw him being carried back, mortally wounded. He recorded:

> He was a fine big man, but lying deep in the stretcher and covered with a blanket, seems immeasurably to have shrunk. Only his head, immense and white, like an indomitable will, appears to keep life in him. But soon he will be a corpse, all his great strength and courage are ebbing fast.

Eight days later, his CO, Lt-Col Andrew Thorne DSO, wrote to his widow:

I am afraid he never knew that he had got his VC. He was wounded on the morning of 27th Nov. and died as he reached the Casualty Clearing Station. We called there to tell him but it was too late.

John Harold Rhodes, the most highly decorated non-commissioned officer in the history of the Grenadier Guards, was born in Mellor Street, Packmoor, on the edge of the Potteries, on 17 May 1891, the eldest of ten children to Ernest Rhodes and Sarah (née Hanford). His father was a miner who had served with the Royal Scots Fusiliers and his mother came of a line of staunch Wesleyan Methodists. Educated at the Church School, New Chapel, he was a noted sportsman with a reputation for being a daredevil. His cousin, Anne Risley, recalled:

Packmoor was a poor little village, and one night the three older boys, John, Jabez and Bill, got up in the middle of the night, climbed through the back bedroom window, slid down the tiles, went across the street to the farmyard. There, they caught two horses. With two on one and one on the other, the galloped off. There were only three streets, and they galloped as hard as they could down one street, then the other and then came back to the farmyard, returned the horses and got back to their beds without being missed. The next day everyone was talking about horses running through the streets! It was typical of John. He was so high-spirited and adventurous. That's why he joined the Army.

After working in the mines, Rhodes enlisted in the Grenadier Guards at Stoke on 16 February 1911. He served with the 3rd Battalion for three years before being transferred to the reserve in early 1914. At the outbreak of war, he was employed at the Chatterley Whitfield Collieries, Tunstall. Recalled to the colours, he was posted to the 2nd Grenadiers and proceeded to France on 12 August 1914. Eleven days later, he took part in the BEF's first major engagement at Mons. During the battle his unit was sent forward to reinforce the firing line. He later wrote:

When we got to the base at a bank we were met with a deadly Maxim and rifle fire. It was lucky for us we were underneath the bank or else I don't think many of us would have lived to do much fighting. It was our first taste of war, all we could do was to lie low as to advance would have been suicide.

He came unscathed through the subsequent retreat, including the fights at Landrecies and Villers Cotterets, and took part in the Allied counter-offensive. During one action before the Aisne in September 1914, he had 'a narrow squeak' when 'a chap behind stepped into my place [and] got shot in the heart'. He described the struggle at the Aisne as 'like hell upon earth'. At Ypres, his unit was decimated. Once again, he was lucky: 'One day I was helping to make a dugout and was chopping a tree down when a piece of shell cut the tree in half about a yard above my head … it seems marvellous how any of us came out alive.'

On Christmas Eve, while manning a waterlogged stretch of the front line, Rhodes was caught in a barrage. One shell-burst just in front of his position. He informed his parents: 'I saw stars and landed up to the neck in mud and water, but they had me out in no time.' Promoted lance-corporal in January 1915, he soon acquired a reputation as a daring patrol leader. During the fighting near Rue du Bois on 18 May, he carried out a successful reconnaissance, bringing back valuable information. Later, he braved heavy fire on two occasions to bring in wounded men. Each time, men with him were hit, but once again his luck held. His conspicuous bravery was marked by the award of a Distinguished Conduct Medal. Writing to relatives on 1 July, he declared:

I suppose by now you know all about the DCM. For myself, I am tired of writing about it … I received it last Sunday, or rather received the ribbon, as the medal is kept back at Buckingham Gate until the end of the war or else the end of me. Let us hope I see the end of the war and that it won't be long, which I am rather doubtful of.

He returned home to a rousing reception. A procession wound through the surrounding mining villages, and Rhodes was presented with a 'purse of gold and a marble time-piece'. He drew large crowds wherever he went.

As the war rolled on, he remained in the thick of things. On 6 August, while the Grenadiers were holding the line near Givenchy, he performed a second act of heroism, resulting in him being awarded a Bar to his DCM. Enemy shelling had blown in the advanced saps, burying a number of men. Despite heavy fire, Acting Cpl Rhodes and Guardsman Barton, who also received a DCM, ran forward and dug out several men, including their officer, Capt. H.F.C. Crookshank. In the course of their rescue mission both were wounded, Rhodes being hit in the right shoulder.

The gallant Grenadier spent four months in England recovering before being promoted lance-sergeant and posted as an instructor to the 5th (Reserve) Battalion, Grenadier Guards. On 11 December 1915 he married Elizabeth Meir. Rhodes spent sixteen months in England and, having made a complete recovery from his wound, joined the 3rd Battalion in France on 19 January 1917. During the next eleven months, he took part in numerous actions, surviving unscathed with his faith in eventual victory apparently unshaken. Writing home on 20 March, he declared:

> We must put up with all hardships and get this over, the sooner the better, and I believe that in a month or two's time we shall tighten old Fritz up a bit and the outlook of the war will be a great deal different. We have been doing well of late and the Germans must look out when the weather cheers up.

His son John was born on 13 May, and following his exploits at Houthulst Forest he had hoped to go on leave. He had not seen his son and, tragically, he never would. The hero of so many fights succumbed at No. 48 Casualty Clearing Station, and was later buried in Rockuigny-Equancourt Road British cemetery (plot 111, row E, grave 1). The news came as a terrible blow to his family and the people of Tunstall and Packmoor, who were still celebrating his VC and Croix de Guerre, awarded for the same action. Letters of condolence poured in, including one from the directors of Stoke City FC. A memorial service was held at the Primitive Methodist church, Packmoor, on 23 December. Due to 'domestic difficulties', Mrs Rhodes was unable to attend a Buckingham Palace investiture and her husband's medal was presented to her at her home on 15 July 1918.

Lizzie Rhodes never remarried. She died at Cheadle Hospital on 1 March 1988, aged 97. That year, her husband's VC group was acquired by the Grenadier Guards. A painting by the artist Sean Bolan, commissioned by the sergeants' mess of the 1st Battalion, Grenadier Guards and unveiled at Elizabeth Barracks, Pirbright, in 1999, presents a vivid depiction of John Rhodes' valour. He is also honoured on a memorial plaque, originally located in the Chatterley-Whitfield Mining Museum and now displayed in Packmoor School. But perhaps the most poignant tribute to John Rhodes VC, DCM and Bar is one contained in faded letter written to his widow on 8 December 1917 by the chaplain of the 3rd Grenadier Guards:

> The other day I passed by the grave of your husband on the side of a hill facing the sun. And as we passed by we thought of you, of the tremendous loss we have suffered. It is one of the cruellest things of this war that just at the moment of great things the best are taken away. Your husband had won the greatest honour any soldier could have and had won it over and over again; yet he was always the same, quiet in his manner, never boastful, always doing his duty, a pattern to soldiers and a pattern to us all.

C.S. JEFFRIES
Hillside Farm, 12 October 1917

An icy wind blew squalls of rain across the desolate Flanders bog as the Australians of the 34th Battalion, the advance guard of the 9th Brigade, struggled towards their assembly positions below Passchendaele Ridge on the night of 11–12 October. At the entrance to Broodseinde railway cutting the leading company commanders, Capt. Clarence Jeffries and Capt. T.G. Gilder, halted. Many of the direction tapes had been destroyed or swallowed in the mud and there were fears that they might blunder into enemy positions in the darkness. To avoid such mishaps, the two officers pushed on alone as far as Keerselaarhoek cemetery to find the tapes marking the start line. Thus, by 3 am the men of the 34th (Maitland's Own) were formed up.

Despite the depressing conditions, confidence was high. One unit had a flag to plant in the ruins of Passchendaele and there was even talk of cabling Australia with news of its fall. 'Some keen spirits,' wrote Charles Bean, 'looked on the operation simply as a dash for Passchendaele.' Rarely was optimism more misplaced. Of all the battles fought during the campaign, none was more ill-conceived than First Passchendaele. It was merely a repetition of the failed attacks of 9 October, but with deeper objectives, shorter preparations, inadequate artillery support and a pace of advance not attempted even in the dry conditions of September. It was a doomed operation born of Haig's grand delusion. While he talked of 'only flesh and blood … not blockhouses' separating his army from a victory with which he sought to vindicate his ill-judged continuation of the campaign, the 3rd Australian and New Zealand Divisions were preparing to advance across ground peppered with pillboxes that were not only untouched by past bombardments, but protected, in many cases, by a forest of barbed wire. Bean described the opening scenes of the tragedy:

> At 4.20 the rain ceased and at 5.25, when the British barrage descended, a whitish streak on the eastern horizon was lighting the low, dun-coloured, fleeting scud overhead and the dull, green and brown moorland below. Despite its imposing sound, the barrage, as on October 9, afforded no screen and only light protection; all day it was possible to see clearly through it.

One officer of the 34th thought the bombardment so 'very weak' it was 'difficult to determine which was our barrage and which was fire from the enemy. This made it difficult for the men to keep up with the barrage'. The 34th's war diarist observed:

> There were many men who were lost altogether in the Bog. The pace of the advance was slowed up, owing to the assistance it was necessary to give men who had sunk into shell-holes, and could not extricate themselves without assistance.

Inevitably, men bunched on the firmer ground, to be flayed by fire from blockhouses Haig had assured them no longer existed. The fire came from all directions: from a ruined house on the right near Defy Crossing to machine-gun posts on the left in Augustus Wood. In the centre, serious resistance was encountered at Hillside Farm, a strongpoint to the east of Augustus Wood on the highest part of the ridge. The position consisted of two pillboxes, supported by a 50yd trench occupied by about thirty men with four machine-guns. Withering fire forced the 34th, already hopelessly mixed with men of the 35th Battalion, to seek cover on the exposed crest and threatened to halt the entire operation.

But Captain Jeffries, the 22-year-old commander of B Company, refused to accept defeat. Quickly organising a bombing party of two NCOs and a dozen men, he set about outflanking the pillboxes. Accompanying him was Sgt James Bruce, a 37-year-old Scottish-born miner from the Hunter Valley district of New South Wales. According to popular legend, Bruce, who had worked for Jeffries' father in the Abermain Collieries, had promised to look out for his boss' son. Whatever the truth of this, Bruce remained at Jeffries' side as the youngster put his daring gamble to the test. In the event, it worked perfectly. Working round the position, they took it in the rear, capturing thirty-five prisoners and four machine-guns. The advance revived, a party of the 35th Battalion rushed the trench behind.

The first objective was reached but heavy losses left gaping holes in the line. Consolidation was further hampered by machine-guns on the right. Nevertheless, at 8.25 am parties from the two battalions headed out along the south-eastern edge of the ridge towards the outskirts of Passchendaele. Almost immediately, they came under fire from a pillbox close by a railway embankment. Maj. J.B. Buchanan, the senior brigade officer with the advance party, fell dead, leaving Capt. Jeffries to assume control. In what was almost a carbon-copy of the assault on Hillside Farm, he led an eleven-strong party into the attack. Edging across the open ground, it seemed at first as though they might succeed. Each yard took Jeffries closer to the spitting gun. Bean recorded:

> It was shooting in short bursts, and he was able to work up fairly close. Seizing a moment when it was firing to the north, he and his men rushed at it from the west. It was switched round, killing him, and sending his men to ground. But when its fire eased they worked round it, rushed the position, and seized 25 Germans and two machine-guns.

According to Lt A. Gibson Farley, the 34th Battalion adjutant, Jeffries was 'mortally wounded' in the stomach. Details of the captures made by his men vary. The unit war diary claimed forty prisoners while Lt-Col Ernest Martin put the figure at thirty in his recommendations for Jeffries' VC and Bruce's Distinguished Conduct Medal. Such details scarcely mattered to the men of the 34th as their hard-won success dissolved into bloody fiasco.

With the second objective only partially captured, the remnants of the 9th Brigade, battered by artillery and enfiladed by machine-guns, were forced to relinquish their fragile grip. By 3.30 pm they were back to where they started. Not a yard had been gained. When night fell, all that remained of the 9th Brigade on Passchendaele ridge were the dead and wounded and those poor wretches trapped in the bog. Among the dead was Clarence Jeffries, whose body had been left behind. In time, he would be counted among the thousands of men with 'no known graves'. But it was not the end of his story.

On 18 December 1917 the *London Gazette* announced his posthumous award of the Victoria Cross. In Col Martin's words he had 'displayed the greatest fearlessness and gallantry' and 'it was entirely due to his bravery, dash and initiative that the centre of the attack was not held up for a lengthy period'. Writing to Jeffries' father, Martin added:

> Our artillery barrage was thin owing to the soft nature of the ground and the gun trails sinking, consequently many enemy strong points were left entirely for the infantry to deal with.

The behaviour of your son was gallant in the extreme; from strong point to strong point he led his men, and was successful in putting several enemy machine guns out of action and capturing many prisoners.

Sadly, of course, it was all to no avail. The 34th Battalion diarist blamed the state of the ground, which he likened to a marsh, and the paucity of artillery support for the failure. Echoing his commanding officer's words, he complained bitterly: 'Many strongpoints were left, able to take active participation in the fight, which should have been blown out.' but the real blame for the tragedy lay elsewhere.

The last Australian VC winner of the campaign, Clarence Smith Jeffries was born at Wallsend, New South Wales, on 26 October 1894, the only child of Joshua Jeffries and his wife Barbara (née Steel). He attended Dudley Primary School and the Newcastle Collegiate and High Schools before being apprenticed as a mining surveyor at the Abermain Collieries, where his father was general manager. Noted as a cricketer, 'Jeff' Jeffries was also a keen horseman who took a particular interest in breeding thoroughbreds.

He joined the 14th (Hunter River) Infantry Regiment, a militia unit, as a private in July 1912, rising to lieutenant three years later. At the time he was instructing volunteers for the Australian Imperial Force at Newcastle and Liverpool. On 1 February 1916 he was appointed second lieutenant in the 34th Battalion and sailed from Australia in May. Promoted lieutenant three months later, he arrived in France in November 1916. After early service in the Armentières sector, he was wounded in the thigh on 9 June 1917 while leading a reconnaissance patrol during the Battle of Messines Ridge, his first major action.

Evacuated to the 3rd General Hospital in London, he was promoted captain on 26 June and after making a full recovery he rejoined his unit in September. Barely five weeks later he was dead. For his family, the tragedy was made worse by the unknown fate of his body. Haunted by his son's 'disappearance', Joshua Jeffries set out in the summer of 1920 to find his son's 'lost grave'. He returned disappointed, only to learn, in January 1921, that his son's body had been exhumed from a battlefield grave on 14 September 1920 and re-buried in Tyne Cot cemetery. The grave was located 150yd north-west of Heine House and 750yd north-west of the point where the Ypres–Roulers railway crossed the Zonnebeke–Passchendaele road. The body had been identified by a set of captain's stars, Australia numerals and the pencilled initials 'C.S.J.' found on the ground sheet in which it was wrapped.

Three years later, Mr Jeffries returned to Belgium to pay his last respects to his gallant son. By then, an inscription had been carved on his headstone:

On Fame's eternal camping ground
Their silent tents are spread.

In the aftermath of the war, Joshua Jeffries also repaid a debt of gratitude to the family of the late Lt James Bruce MC, DCM, who as a sergeant had tried in vain to safeguard his son's life. Bruce had been killed on 17 July 1918 and, as a mark of respect, his two eldest sons were appointed trainee mining surveyors.

'Jeff' Jeffries' brave legacy endures in a memorial park named after him in Abermain, a carved chair in Holy Trinity Anglian church and the library at Dudley Primary School which bears his name together with that of fellow VC recipient William Currey. His Victoria Cross, which had been presented to his father at a ceremony in Sydney on 4 April 1918, was bequeathed by his mother to Newcastle's Christ Church Cathedral in 1950. Barbara Jeffries also left £200 to St Luke's church in Wallsend for a memorial dedicated to deceased servicemen of the district and the resulting lead glass window remains a magnificent tribute to sacrifice. Half a century later, the unveiling of the Currey-Jeffries VC Memorial Wall in Sandgate cemetery serves to further perpetuate the memory of a gallant Australian.

Speaking at the unveiling of a full-size portrait of the young hero in June 1919, Lt-Col Edward Nash, who was Jeffries' first commanding officer, paid glowing tribute to his 'straight, upright and manly' qualities:

A better or more promising officer I did not know. He was highly respected by those serving under him and by his superiors. One can well imagine Captain Jeffries, on finding the enemy in position doing considerable damage to his comrades, calling for volunteers to follow him, and with his small band going forward and destroying that stronghold, unfortunately sacrificing his own life in doing so to save his comrades. Actions such as this won the war, and helped in no small way to build that fearless determination 'to do or die', always so prominent in the traditions of the Australian army and so characteristic of the Australian soldier when he gets his back to the wall.

A. HALTON

Near Poelcappelle, 12 October 1917

Fifth Army's contribution to the First Battle of Passchendaele was, once again, a subsidiary one. Units from five divisions were employed in covering the northern flank of the main assault. Their fortunes varied markedly. South of Poelcappelle, the 9th Scottish Division's effort bogged down in the mud while units from the 18th Division were slaughtered by machine-guns untouched by a barrage as desultory as that which failed the Anzacs. Only on the extreme edges were results significantly different to those experienced by Second Army.

North of the ruins of Poelcappelle, the 4th Division advanced at 5.25 am with the 12th Brigade, a composite force spearheaded by the 1st Warwickshires and the Household Battalion with the 1st King's Own Royal Lancaster Regiment in support. Their commander was one of the youngest brigadier-generals in the British Army, the enigmatic Belgian-born Adrian Carton de Wiart who, in the space of three years, had won a VC and a DSO and lost a hand and an eye in the process. In his memoirs he described the ground over which his brigade 'of odd battalions' attacked as 'a vast sea of malignant mud and water'. It ran bare and exposed towards some fortified farms. But the main source of trouble came from the ruins of Poelcappelle where the machine-guns that had stopped the 18th Division wrought heavy losses among the Household Battalion. Small parties struggled to Requete Farm, but the failure on the right posed a danger which compelled Carton de Wiart to form a defensive flank with a company of the King's Own and a company from his reserve unit, the 1st Rifle Brigade.

It was during the fighting that followed this manoeuvre that a soldier from the King's Own became the last British serviceman to win a Victoria Cross in the campaign. Details of 24-year-old Pte Albert Halton's act of supreme bravery are sparse. His unit's war diary made no mention. Even the citation published in the *London Gazette* was unusually terse:

> After the objective had been reached Pte Halton rushed forward about 300yd under very heavy rifle and shell-fire, and captured a machine-gun

and its crew, which was causing many losses to our men. He then went out again and brought in about twelve prisoners, showing the greatest disregard of his own safety and setting a very high example to those around him.

Quite what inspired Halton to act in this way is unclear, although years later Carton de Wiart did draw attention to one unusual feature of the incident when he wrote:

> In the middle of the battle one of my men charged a machine-gun which was holding us up, and upon reaching it killed every man who was serving it. Having recommended him for a VC which he was awarded, and richly deserved, I asked him about his action. To my amazement I found that he remembered nothing whatsoever about it.

An enemy counter-attack pushed the 12th Brigade back from Requete Farm. The fighting petered out in the evening and a line curving back from the first objective gains made by the Warwicks to the defensive flank formed on the right was held. The battle cost the King's Own forty-six officers and men killed, 159 wounded and eighteen missing. Owing to the state of the ground and the darkness, the improvised brigade could not be relieved until the following evening. They tramped away in pouring rain to be congratulated by the Fifth Army commander for their gallantry in appalling conditions.

Albert Halton was born at Warton, Carnforth, a small railway town near Lancaster, on 1 May 1893, the third of four sons to Jonathan and Sarah Halton. His father worked as a blast furnaceman at Carnforth Ironworks. Educated at Carnforth National School, Halton left at the age of 13 and worked as a farm labourer and on the London & North Western Railway before joining John Rigg & Son builders and contractors in Carnforth. He was working there as a labourer when war broke out. He was one of twelve men from the company to enlist, joining the 5th King's Own Royal Lancaster Regiment on 15 August 1915.

Halton took part in the fighting on the Somme and was wounded on 22 October 1916. Evacuated to Britain, he was hospitalised in Aberdeen and after convalescence was posted to the 1st Battalion, with whom he won his VC (*London Gazette*, 26 November 1917). The people of Carnforth gave him a great reception, forming a long procession to escort him home.

Shortly after the Armistice in 1918 he married Emily Tatman from Gargrave, near Skipton, and they had two daughters. Discharged in May

1919, he worked at Carnforth Ironworks until its closure, after which he found employment at Lansil Works, Lancaster, remaining there until his retirement in 1961. During the Second World War, he served in the Lancaster Home Guard.

A quiet, unassuming man, Albert Halton conducted his life with dignity. 'He quickly observed a problem whenever one arose and promptly suggested a practical solution,' recorded his son-in-law, Frank Bromley. His war experiences, however, remained a taboo subject and although the conflict would influence the rest of his life he never discussed it with his family. A staunch supporter of the Regimental Association, he laid a wreath at the shrine in the King's Own Memorial Chapel, Lancaster priory church, on most Armistice Sundays until his death.

The most tangible wartime legacy, however, was his home. From 1939 until his death, on 24 July 1971, Albert Halton VC was the most distinguished resident of Westfield War Memorial Village, Lancaster, a development originally designed to provide sheltered homes for wounded servicemen and their families.

Halton was accorded military honours at his funeral service at Lancaster and Morecambe crematorium. His medals were presented to the Regimental Museum, Lancaster, by his family twenty-two years later. Today, Albert Halton's memory lives on in Westfield, where a memorial plaque displayed on his former home pays tribute to the British Army's last VC winner of the Passchendaele campaign.

T.W. HOLMES, R. SHANKLAND
AND C.P.J. O'KELLY

Wolf Copse and Bellevue Spur, 26 October 1917

By mid-October the brooding spectre of Bellevue Spur with its seemingly impregnable fortifications hung like a dark, menacing cloud over Haig's diminishing ambitions. A cordon of pillboxes, varying in shape and size and protected by thickets of barbed wire, straddled the slight rise, less than 1,500yd from the outskirts of Passchendaele. Twice in the space of three days these grim defences, forming part of the enemy's Flanders I barrier, had dealt crushing blows to British hopes. Following the repulse of the New Zealand Division and the consequent defeat of the Australians on 12 October, Haig's misguided optimism had finally given way to realism. In turning to the Canadian Corps to salvage something from the wreckage of his plans, he lowered his sights. The talk was no longer of breakthroughs but of securing a defensible winter position and diverting attention away from new plans for an armoured strike at Cambrai. Thus was a campaign born of extravagant designs subverted into little more than a costly distraction.

The Canadians arrived from the Lens sector to find an army wallowing in mud. Almost half the area in front of Passchendaele was either under water or reduced to swamp. The Ravebeek valley, cutting through the British line below Bellevue, was all but impenetrable. But at least Gen. Sir Arthur Currie, GOC Canadian Corps, was given time to prepare. As planked roads stretched across the wasteland, the artillery ranged with far greater accuracy on the notorious barbed-wire entanglements strung across the spur. By 25 October clearer weather revealed gaps torn in the wire but as the infantrymen filed towards their jumping-off position, observers noted bleakly that the pillboxes lining the crest were still largely intact.

The Canadian plan was reminiscent of Plumer's original approach. Currie intended to carry Passchendaele in three bounds, each attack separated by at least three days. In the first, the Canadian 4th Division was to advance south of the flooded Ravebeek valley with the 3rd Division employing two brigades against Bellevue and Wallemollen spurs.

Once again the weather proved an implacable foe. The attack was launched at 5.40 am on 26 October in driving rain. The northern assault was led by the 4th Canadian Mounted Rifles of the 8th Brigade, the 43rd Battalion (Cameron Highlanders of Canada) and the 58th Battalion, both of the 9th Brigade. At first all appeared to go well. Despite losing a number of men to enemy shells on the start line, the Canadians made ground quickly over the broken wire. The 43rd's war diarist recorded: 'When dawn broke sufficiently our men could be clearly seen moving slowly over the skyline and round the two formidable-looking pillboxes on the crest of the ridge overlooking Bn HQ.'

The 4th CMR, advancing on the left, enjoyed similar success. With C and D Companies leading and A and B Companies in close support, the Canadians soon overcame the first belt of blockhouses. Their objectives were Woodland Copse and Source Farm, but having battled with bomb and bayonet through the concentrated fire sweeping across the lower slopes they suffered a serious check north-east of Wolf Copse. Fire from two machine-guns either side of a pillbox thinned their ranks, forcing them to seek cover. A Company had overtaken D Company, and mixed parties attempted to rush the position, although none got closer than 50yd. Suddenly, 19-year-old Pte Tommy Holmes, described as a 'frail, delicate youth with a contagious smile', leapt from a shell hole and headed for the pillbox. The unit historian recorded:

Before those around him realised what he was about to do [he] rushed forward and tossed a bomb so accurately into the trench of the machine-gun crew that they and their guns were put out of action. He then returned to his companions for more bombs, which by this time were getting scarce, but he succeeded in getting one from Pte Dunphy. Again he dashed forward, this time going directly up to the pillbox, and threw his bomb into the entrance where it exploded; those who were not killed or wounded came out and surrendered.

Nineteen prisoners were taken and an officer who observed the action sent a runner forward to identify the youngster so that he could recommend him for a bravery award. Before the runner returned the officer was killed, but fortunately there were other witnesses to ensure that Holmes' courage did not go unrecognised. His daring had relieved a critical situation but, even as the Canadian riflemen pressed on, a greater disaster threatened to overwhelm 9th Brigade's operation.

By 7 am early optimism had evaporated. Through the rain and drifting smoke officers at 43rd Battalion HQ at Waterloo Farm could see that the 58th Battalion's attack had stalled on the right. Wounded began

Lt R. Shankland

drifting back followed by the remainder of the battalion, fleeing in some disorder back to the original start line. For a while chaos reigned across the 9th Brigade front. Of most concern was the fate of the Canadian Highlanders. Since dawn, when groups of men were seen pushing on towards the crest, little definite news had been received. It was known that all of the officers in B and C Companies, leading the attack, were out of action, but no one knew the whereabouts of D Company or its two senior officers Capt. D.A. Galt and Lt Bob Shankland DCM. As close supports, it was their job to capture and consolidate the final objective, for which purpose they had the assistance of a small party of the 9th Canadian Machine-Gun Company. Equally uncertain was the location of A Company, tasked with holding the support line.

Each assault battalion had a company of the 52nd Battalion in reserve, and it was decided to push them forward while runners searched for the 'missing' companies. A Company was soon found on the left, held up by an enemy trench 250yd beyond two pillboxes. But by 9.30 am there was still no word of D Company. At that moment, another panic, this time among the 52nd's companies, saw large numbers of Canadians streaming back. Some rallied near the start line, but others did not stop until they reached 43rd Battalion HQ across the Ravebeek. Worse news followed. Due to the precipitate retirement, the 4th CMR had been forced to pull back.

It was at this bleak moment, around 10 am, that Lt Shankland, who had been virtually given up as dead, made a startling appearance at Battalion HQ. His coat was torn with bullets and spattered with mud. No stage entrance could have been more dramatic. And the news he brought with him was no less electrifying. The 43rd diarist noted:

Lt Shankland reported ... that he was holding the ridge about 40yd forward of the two pillboxes with about forty men including men of the 9th MG Coy with two of their guns which were in action. He stated that provided his ammunition held out he could hold his position against any attack as he had already dispersed one counter-attack which was forming up in the low ground 500yd forward on his front. He did not know where Capt Galt, his Company Commander, was as he had last seen him during the attack attempting with 5 ORs to capture a strongpoint on the right of the position he now held, suffering considerable annoyance from snipers half left on his frontage and also from the direction of the strongpoint Capt Galt had tried to capture. His men were, however, using their rifles with great effect upon isolated Germans who were seen going back and also along with the Brigade guns against the enemy assembling.

What he neglected to say was that he had been the leading figure in the brave stand. After silencing two pillboxes and capturing two half-completed strongpoints, only twenty men and one machine-gun had made it on to the crest. It was Shankland, joining them shortly afterwards, who inspired them to cling on. Gradually more men trickled forward in support, including another machine-gun detachment which helped them beat off a flank attack. One machine-gun was knocked out, but every enemy attack was driven off. Their defiance was typified by the machine-gun subaltern whom Shankland left in command while he made his perilous dash to HQ to plead for reinforcements. According to Shankland, Lt Ellis 'though wounded ... refused to go out while his guns remained in action'.

News of the resolute defence by a few men on Bellevue spur marked the turning point in Canadian fortunes, revitalising the attack just as it seemed that a repetition of the previous reverses was inevitable. Fresh orders were issued. A makeshift company, including many men who had fled back to Battalion HQ, was led back up the slope to form a defensive flank on the right of Shankland's isolated party. At the same time, another company of the 52nd Battalion was pushed forward to fill the gap between the Canadian Highlanders and the 4th CMRs. This was A Company, commanded by Acting Capt. Christopher O'Kelly MC, and with his arrival the battle entered its final decisive phase.

O'Kelly's company had begun the day in brigade reserve at Abraham Heights. At 8.30 am, amid alarming reports of the 'reverse' suffered by the 43rd and 58th Battalions, A and B Companies of the 52nd Battalion, had been warned to 'hold themselves in readiness to move at a moment's notice'. That order arrived an hour later, O'Kelly's men advancing to Waterloo Farm to await further instructions. They were still there when Shankland burst in.

By 11.30 am O'Kelly's company was moving up the bare, northern slopes, through an enemy barrage pounding the spur. They advanced without artillery support and without knowing what opposition faced them. All they knew was that Shankland's party was pinned down in front of enemy blockhouses and totally exposed on both flanks. In fact, the slopes were freckled with pillboxes. Some were loop-holed while others were simply concrete shells with platforms built over the doorways, enabling machine-gunners to fire over the top. O'Kelly lost a few men to these and to the shelling, but the majority swept over the brow to find an enemy attack threatening the Highlanders' left flank. Scarcely pausing, O'Kelly led his company in a charge which drove the enemy off with heavy loss. But any elation was short-lived as they quickly became the target for a hail of fire from the pillboxes confronting Shankland's party.

The struggle resolved itself into a series of small-scale actions as O'Kelly led his men against one pillbox after another. These posts housed anything up to five machine-guns and thirty or more men, supported by riflemen and bombers. O'Kelly's method of attack was simple and effective. It involved edging to within rifle-grenade range, creating a diversion by firing off a shower of grenades and peppering it with machine-gun fire while a small party, often only three or four strong, made a dash for the blind side from where they tossed in bombs as a signal for the place to be rushed. O'Kelly had already cleared two pillboxes by noon when B Company, led by Lt H.M. Grant MC, arrived to join the attack. By then Shankland himself, although slightly wounded in the face and neck, had rejoined his men. Two battalion scouts who accompanied him later returned with three prisoners, including a German officer who spoke good English. He explained that he had expected to find his company on the ridge and had simply blundered into the Canadian position. An incongruous interlude in the midst of battle ended with him nonchalantly pulling out a silver case and lighting a cigarette.

Across the front, the impetus of the 52nd proved irresistible. The two companies 'took out' nine pillboxes and the fortified Bellevue Farm in succession, capturing almost 200 officers and men in the process. O'Kelly's men's share was six pillboxes, 100 prisoners and ten machine-guns. One unexpected result of the advance was the sudden re-emergence of Capt. Galt, Shankland's company commander, who had been missing since early in the day. It transpired he had led a party into an enemy strongpoint only to find their path blocked by a tangle of wire shielding a sniper's nest. As they attempted to return whence they came, heavy machine-gun fire killed two men and forced the remainder to shelter in a shell-hole until liberated by the 52nd's attack. His return, at around 1.25 pm, enabled the exhausted Shankland to retire and have his wounds dressed.

The main battle was over but sporadic fighting continued. During the afternoon O'Kelly's men were instrumental in defeating an enemy counter-attack, described as 'heavy' in his VC citation and 'faint' by the 52nd's war diarist. As darkness fell, the offensively minded O'Kelly led his men in another foray, during which he captured an enemy raiding party consisting of an officer, ten men and a machine-gun, thus swelling the number of prisoners taken by the 52nd to 275, together with twenty-one machine-guns. By 7.25 pm, despite shelling and minor clashes across the ridge, it was clear that the Canadians were there to stay. Capt. Galt reported: 'The situation looks OK as far as I can judge. The 52nd are 100yd in front of us and in fair strength. It has to be regretted we did not get further but it was not possible ... conditions considered we are OK.'

The 3rd Division had advanced an average of 500yd, driving the enemy from the Flanders I Line between the Ravebeek and Wolf Copse. But the price of establishing a foothold on the main Passchendaele ridge had been dear. By the end of 26 October the 4th CMR had only four officers out of twenty-one unhurt. In all, the unit lost 321 officers and men killed, wounded, missing or evacuated suffering from exposure. The 43rd, meanwhile, sustained 339 casualties, and their wounded were still being recovered from the battlefield two days later.

Perhaps in atonement for this, as well as in recognition of the great courage displayed, honours were distributed with a degree of largesse unusual among Commonwealth forces. The 43rd received no fewer than thirty-two gallantry awards while the 4th CMR's list of twenty-one honours included ten Distinguished Conduct Medals, surely something of a record for a single action. The decorations were headed by three Victoria Crosses. Bob Shankland's was the first to be announced, on 18 December. It prompted a wave of congratulatory letters, including one from a chaplain who had been present during the fighting. George Taylor informed Shankland's father: 'Everyone who knows agrees that the man who was the means of saving the day and bringing in a brilliant victory was your son ... We all agree that the VC should be given him.'

Three weeks later the *London Gazette* of 11 January announced the awards to No. 838301 Pte Thomas Holmes and Lt (Acting Captain) Christopher O'Kelly 'for most conspicuous bravery'.

A college student at the outbreak of war, Christopher Patrick John O'Kelly was only 21 when he won his Victoria Cross. It was the high point of a life which promised much yet ended in tragedy three days short of his 27th birthday.

Born in Winnipeg, Manitoba, on 18 November 1895, he was the son of Christopher and Cecilia O'Kelly, who lived in Yale Avenue. Educated at public schools in Winnipeg, Chris O'Kelly was an undergraduate at St John's College when he decided break his studies to enlist on 22 February 1916. He joined the 144th Battalion (Winnipeg Rifles), known as the Little Black Devils, and proceeded overseas as a lieutenant with his unit on 18 September 1916. Shortly after arriving in England, he was transferred from the 144th, then being used as a reinforcement unit, to the

52nd Battalion. He reached the trenches in March 1917, and soon made a name for himself as a daring leader.

In the aftermath of the Vimy operations, O'Kelly, who was commanding No. 9 Platoon in C Company, played a distinguished part in a minor action in the Avion-Mericourt sector. In the early hours of 28 June, the 52nd launched an attack on Avion Trench. Dashing across no-man's-land, they were confronted by uncut wire and a machine-gun post. Covered by a Lewis gunner, the men scrambled into the trench, with O'Kelly leading a bombing section against the gun. Capt. E.R.C. Wilcox, C Company commander, recorded:

> As [O'Kelly] climbed the eastern side of TORONTO ROAD he threw a bomb. One of the gun crew threw a stick bomb at practically the same moment ... Lt O'Kelly's bomb exploding [sic] killed the machine-gun crew. He at once shouldered the gun and brought it in and superintended placing the block.

The enemy grenade fatally wounded one of O'Kelly's men, but he escaped unharmed to receive the Military Cross (*London Gazette*, 26 September 1917). Promoted acting captain on 28 August and given command of A Company, O'Kelly seemed destined for glory, provided he lived long enough. Fortune continued to smile on him and he came through his greatest test on Bellevue Spur without injury. But the fighting had left some scars: Capt. Theodore Roberts of the Canadian War Records Department, who met him shortly after the 52nd came out of the line, subsequently edited a volume on his country's VC winners, in which he noted: 'He was very young. His manner was quiet and somewhat grim, as if he had looked too closely into a hundred faces of death.' Unaware that he had been put up for the VC, O'Kelly applied for leave to return home on account of his mother falling seriously ill. This was granted, but not before he had been offered and had declined a staff appointment.

One of ten Winnipeggers to win the VC in the First World War, he was the first to make it home, his return on 9 April 1918 sparking huge celebrations. Civic and military dignitaries met him at the Canadian Pacific Railway depot and thousands lined the streets to cheer him as a procession of automobiles and bands made for the Fort Garry Hotel and a private reception. Five days later O'Kelly, described as a 'rather retiring, modest youth', was fêted at the Columbus Hall in a gathering organised by the city's Catholic Club.

Returning to England in the summer, he headed back to France in August and rejoined the 52nd Battalion on 8 September in the midst of the Allies' war-winning offensive. Barely three weeks later, on 28 September, he was badly wounded leading A Company in an attack towards the heavily fortified Canal du Nord, near Cambrai. Hit in the left groin by machine-gun fire, he was unable to move and, while 'lying out', was injured again by shrapnel in the left leg. Initially treated at 30 Casualty Clearing Station, he was transferred to 20 General Hospital before being evacuated to the Prince of Wales' Hospital in Marylebone Road, London. His wounds healed quickly and he moved to a convalescence hospital in Matlock Bath three days before the end of the war. Transferred to the 18th (Reserve) Battalion on 19 November, his recovery was almost complete when he suffered a setback. While out riding on Boxing Day, his horse slipped and fell on an icy road, crushing his right foot and necessitating further medical treatment. It was not until 17 March 1919 that he was fit enough to embark on the SS *Olympic* bound for Canada and demobilisation.

In 1921 O'Kelly rejoined the Winnipeg Rifles, a militia unit, as a major. The following autumn, together with a business partner, he ventured to Lac Seul in northern Ontario to prospect some gold-mining sites. They were last seen alive on 15 November 1922, taking their motor-powered canoe across the lake. That day a storm blew up and when it was over, material from the boat was washed ashore. Nothing more of the two men was seen until the spring thaw released the body of O'Kelly's companion. There was no sign of the ill-starred war hero.

A wooden cross was raised on Goose Island, close to where he disappeared. Submerged when a dam was built at Lower Ear Falls, it was eventually recovered ten years later and presented to the local branch of the Royal Canadian Legion. To mark the forty-third anniversary of his death, a provincial plaque was unveiled at the Legion Hall in Red Lake, Ontario, in honour of Chris O'Kelly VC, MC.

At the time of his award Thomas William Holmes was the youngest winner of the Victoria Cross in the Canadian forces. He was born in Montreal, Quebec, on 17 August 1898, the second son of John and Edith Scarfe Holmes, who originally came from Owen Sound, Ontario. In 1903, after six years in Montreal, the Holmes family returned to Owen Sound. Tommy Holmes was then aged 4 and he went on to attend several schools, the last years of his education being spent at Ryerson School, where he was remembered for his high-spirited daring.

He was working as a poulterer on a farm at Annan when he decided to enlist in the 147th Battalion, a Grey County unit, on 12 December 1915. Holmes was only 17, and looked even younger, but he advanced his age by a year and was accepted. His elder brother, Roy, was serving with the 58th Battalion at the time. The 147th, known as the 1st Grey Battalion, trained at Niagara and Camp Borden. A diptheria outbreak delayed their passage overseas and they eventually arrived in England on 20 November 1916. Transferred initially to the 8th Reserve Battalion, Holmes was sent as part of a draft to the 4th Canadian Mounted Rifles. Two months after arriving in France, he went into action with his machine-gun section at Vimy Ridge. Two days later, on 11 April 1917, he was wounded in the left arm. Evacuated to England, he met his brother who had been blinded in one eye at Sanctuary Wood the previous June and was working at Hastings Hospital.

After a spell with the 8th Reserve Battalion at Shorncliffe, Holmes rejoined his unit in October, shortly before the Canadian Corps' introduction to the Passchendaele campaign. In letters home Holmes made no mention of his gallantry. His only reference came in a note to his parents in December when he said some of his comrades had told him he had been recommended for 'a decoration'.

Holmes was the second Owen Sounder to be awarded the Victoria Cross, the first being the legendary Canadian air ace, Billy Bishop. Discharged at the end of the war as a sergeant, he arrived home to a hero's welcome in the spring of 1919. Crowds turned out to greet him and a round of parades, receptions and speeches followed. Not long afterwards, he left Owen Sound for Toronto, where for the next fourteen years he worked as a chauffeur for the Harbour Commission. The good fortune that marked his war career appeared to desert him in peacetime. In 1935 a burglar ransacked his Toronto home and stole his prized VC. It was never recovered and a replacement was sent to him. The theft was not his only problem. The months spent in the trenches had undermined his health. It emerged that the teenage hero, whose boyish grin had provided Canadians with one of their abiding images of the conflict, had contracted tuberculosis. Only after a fight with several federal government departments, however, was he granted a pension. Holmes overcame his bout of TB only to be stricken by cancer. Ill health had already forced him to quit his job, and for the last ten years of his life he fought a losing battle against the disease. He died in Toronto on 4 January 1950 and was buried in Greenwood cemetery, Owen Sound, the inscription on his headstone simply reading 'Rest in Peace'.

Nine years later his sister, Annie King, unveiled a commemorative plaque in Queen's Park, Owen Sound. However, the chequered history of Holmes' VC continued even after his death. In August 1978 the replacement Cross which had been presented to the Owen Sound Branch of the Royal Canadian Legion by his daughter was stolen. This theft, however, at least had a happy ending as Tommy Holmes' second VC, minus a piece of its ribbon, was recovered and restored to its proud owners.

Robert Shankland was born at 68 Church Street, Ayr, Scotland, on 10 October 1887, the only son of William Shankland, a railway guard who had spent forty years working for the Glasgow & South Western Railway Company. Educated at Smith's Institution and Russell Street School, Ayr, he enjoyed a distinguished academic record, winning a string of medals. A member of the 2nd Ayr (Parish Church) Company, of the Boys' Brigade, he spent two years in John T. Scott's accountant's office in Newmarket Street before following his father into the G&SW Railway Company, working as a clerk in the stationmaster's office at Ayr. At the time, he was living with his parents, but, like many adventurous young Scots in the early years of the century, he sought wider horizons. In 1911 he decided to quit his job and seek his fortune in Canada.

He settled in Winnipeg, joined the Crescent Creamery Company, and rapidly worked his way up to assistant cashier. A popular figure, Bob Shankland was a keen sportsman, playing baseball for the works' team and serving as secretary for the provincial soccer champions. When war broke out, he was living at 733 Pine Street, where his fellow residents included two more future winners of the Victoria Cross, Frederick William Hall and Leo Clarke.

Shankland enlisted as a private (No. 420933) in the 43rd Battalion (Cameron Highlanders of Canada) on 18 December 1914. Initially, his skills as a book-keeper and organiser marked him down for deskbound duties and he was made orderly sergeant while the unit was quartered at the city's Minto Street barracks. The 43rd sailed for England in June 1915 but it was not until the following February that Shankland, still a sergeant, arrived at the front. Promotion followed swiftly. He was made company sergeant-major and was serving as acting regimental sergeant-major at Sanctuary Wood in June 1916 when he earned the Distinguished Conduct Medal (*London Gazette*, 19 August 1916). The citation read: 'For conspicuous gallantry in volunteering to lead a party of stretcher-bearers, under very heavy shell fire, and bringing in some wounded and partially buried men. His courage and devotion were most marked.'

He went through the bitter fighting on the Somme and during the autumn was commissioned a second lieutenant in the 43rd. The following year he saw service at Vimy Ridge. Although slightly wounded during his unit's epic struggle on Bellevue spur during which he won his VC, Shankland enjoyed numerous narrow escapes. On one occasion a bullet struck a tin box of fudge in his breast pocket before emerging through the bottom without touching him.

He was on leave, staying with his parents in Ayr, when his VC was announced. Naturally quiet and retiring, he had neither written nor spoken of his actions. The only hint his parents had of his bravery was from the

Canadian chaplain, George Taylor. When confronted with the chaplain's comments, however, he dismissed them, saying 'Ministers can write anything'. A journalist who visited Shankland's parents received much the same response. His mother recalled how his 'ire had been roused' when his photograph appeared in the press following his award of the DCM. 'There's to be no more advertisement, he says,' declared Mrs Shankland, 'and if he was here just now you would get nothing out of him.'

Reluctant hero or not, Ayr's first VC winner, remembered by his former workmates at the railway station as 'a game yin', could not entirely escape the attentions of the local citizenry. On 31 December, in front of a packed town hall chamber bedecked with flags, the 'Auld Toun' conferred on him the honour of becoming the youngest Freeman of the Royal Burgh. At the same ceremony, he was presented with a gold wristwatch by the Boys' Brigade Company in which he had served. In a modest reply, he studiously avoided any mention of his actions except to note, with a smile, that he had learned more about his fight on Bellevue spur during the civic reception than he ever knew before.

By the end of the war he had been promoted captain but before returning to Canada he had one last appointment in Scotland – his wedding. In April 1920 the local press in Ayr proudly announced that Capt. Robert Shankland VC, DCM, had married Anna Stobo Haining, daughter of the stationmaster at Prestwick, in St Nicholas' parish church, Prestwick, with hundreds of people waiting outside to catch a glimpse of the couple. They sailed for Canada on 1 May. The couple had two sons, and during the inter-war years Bob Shankland served as secretary-manager with a number of Winnipeg firms.

Five years after his return, the city staged its own unique tribute. In a series of articles on Canadian VC winners, Carolyn Cornell, librarian at the *Winnipeg Tribune*, suggested that in recognition of the honour won by three former residents of Pine Street, the road should be renamed. The Women's Canadian Club of Winnipeg agreed and after much lobbying the city council decided in favour of the new name – Valour Road. A plaque displayed on a lamp-post in the street paid tribute to Fred Hall, Leo Clarke and Bob Shankland. Eighty years later, the gallant triumvirate were further honoured by the opening of Valour Plaza, with a monument in the shape of the Victoria Cross as its centrepiece, five blocks north of where they lived.

By 1939 Shankland had moved to Vancouver where, in June, he was one of six VC holders pre-sented to King George VI and Queen Elizabeth during their Canadian tour. They were destined to meet again four years later in England, by which time Shankland would be back in uniform.

At the outbreak of the Second World War, Shankland, by then aged 51, re-enlisted in the Queen's Own Cameron Highlanders of Canada. Promoted major in January 1940, he was subsequently appointed camp commandant of the Canadian HQ in England with the rank of lieutenant-colonel. However, he was denied the chance to serve in France on account of his age. In 1946 he left the Army to take a post as secretary of a securities corporation in Vancouver. Ten years later Shankland, who had been a widower for four years, returned to Britain to attend the Victoria Cross centenary celebrations in Hyde Park.

Bob Shankland died on 20 January 1968 in Shaughnessy Hospital, Vancouver. His body was cremated and his ashes scattered in the grounds of Mountain View cemetery. To the very end, he sought to play down his role in the capture of Bellevue spur. When pushed on the subject during a visit to his home town of Ayr, he simply remarked: 'All I did was play poker with the Hun!' That others knew better was evidenced in the C$240,000 paid by the Canadian War Museum in 2009 to ensure his outstanding medal group was saved for the nation as a lasting memorial to courage in adversity.

C.J. KINROSS, H. McKENZIE AND G.H. MULLIN

Near Furst Farm and Meetcheele Spur,
30 October 1917

It was a clear moonlit night and as the freezing wind whipped across the exposed heights of Bellevue Spur shadowy figures lay huddled, numb with cold, waiting for the first grey streaks of dawn and the roar of heavy artillery that would send them on their way. Near Furst Farm, two green flares shot into the sky. Shells had been falling among the leading companies of the Princess Patricia's Canadian Light Infantry and the 49th Edmontons most of the night, but now the bombardment grew more intense. It was a little after 4.30 am on 30 October, the day selected by General Currie for the second stage of his advance on Passchendaele.

The men of the 7th Brigade were taking over where the 9th Brigade had left off. The Princess Pats, on the right, and the 49th, on the left, were to clear the pillboxes scattered across the narrow spur, carrying the line beyond Meetcheele Spur and Furst Farm to the north-western fringes of Passchendaele, an advance varying in depth from 850 to 1,100yd. On their left, the 5th Canadian Mounted Rifles (8th Brigade) were to seize the strongpoints from Source Farm to Vine Cottage, thus securing a foothold on Goudberg spur.

Day broke cold and stormy. The gusting wind had done little to dry the drenched ground. According to Lt-Col Agar Adamson, the Princess Pats' CO, although it did not rain heavily in the early morning 'it might just as well as done so far as the ground was concerned'. Not for the first time, the British barrage scheduled for 5.50 am was less than effective. Lt-Col R.H. Palmer, commanding the 49th Edmontons, described it as 'very light' and inaccurate with 'shorts' falling on his right flank. Worse still, he complained, it was 2 minutes early, an error which had tragic consequences for the men of B and C Company. Even before they clambered out of their shell-holes, a counter-barrage broke around them,

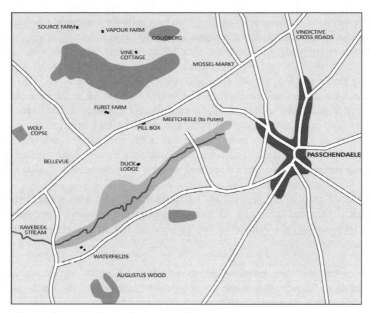

The road to Passchendaele, scene of the Canadians' epic struggle, October–November 1917

machine-guns quickly joining in. Palmer bitterly noted: 'The line slowly advanced at Zero but suffered casualties immediately ... My right front company lost practically all its effective strength before it crossed the road.' The road, running from Wallemolen to Bellevue, was barely 35yd beyond the 49th's start line.

The barrage was timed to creep forward in 50yd bounds at 1 minute intervals, but even this proved too much for the Canadians, battered by wind and pelted by machine-gun fire. At 5.52 am, A and D Companies, forming the second and third waves, moved off, 'suffering heavy casualties'. The attacking waves split into smaller parties, advancing in short rushes. Eventually even these tactics became impossible in the face of fierce resistance from machine-guns near Furst Farm. Around 6.30 am the remnants of B Company lay trapped in shell-holes in front of a well-sited pillbox firing into them at almost point-blank range. Any forward movement appeared suicidal. But Private Cec Kinross, an unorthodox individual from No. 15 Platoon, who was known throughout the battalion by his nickname 'Hoodoo', saw things differently. The young D Company runner, whose reputation as a fighting soldier was matched only by his unruly behaviour out of the line, decided to put his own plan into action.

It meant stripping off anything that might impede him. The men going into action that day were weighed down by up to 170 rounds of ammunition, three sandbags, two rifle grenades, an aeroplane flare, two iron rations, one day's fresh rations, one or two waterbottles, a Tommy cooker or a tin of solidified alcohol and, in certain cases, a shovel. But 'Hoodoo' Kinross had little use for any of these for what he had in mind. Lt Alfred E. McKay of D Company later reported that the men were being machine-gunned, sniped and shelled, when he suddenly saw a lone figure dart towards the strongpoint. In an account written on 6 November, he stated:

> Private Kinross ... threw off his equipment and advanced single-handed, with a rifle and bandolier to attack the gun. On reaching their position he jumped into the Post, shot and clubbed all the crew and destroyed the machine-gun ...

None of the six men manning the gun survived Kinross' ruthless assault. According to McKay, this single act of heroism transformed the battle, allowing the company to advance 300yd.

While the 49th Edmontons were engaged in their bitter struggle, the Princess Pats, on the right, were also being severely tested. Their line of advance led past the strongpoint at Duck Lodge and on to the crest of Meetcheele Spur, where a large pillbox dominated all approaches. Col Adamson wrote: 'It was useless to lay down any mode of attack to troops going over unknown and swamped lands, pitted with shell-holes filled with water.' Much would depend on the initiative of section leaders and individual soldiers.

The Princess Pats attacked with No. 2 Company on the right and No. 3 on the left. Behind them came two platoons of moppers-up with No. 4 and No. 1 Companies, forming a third wave. Accompanying the infantry was a small detachment of the 7th Canadian Machine-Gun Company, under the command of 31-year-old Lt Hugh McKenzie DCM, who had served more than two years in the ranks of the Princess Pats. He knew many of the infantrymen personally, particularly those in No. 3 Company with whom he had served.

McKenzie had four Vickers guns and a force of twenty-seven men, divided between the 49th Edmontons and the Princess Pats. Their orders were to move forward with the infantry at zero hour, advancing 200–300yd at a time and pausing for 10–15 minutes between each bound. Few plans, however, survive contact with the enemy and this was no exception.

Like the 49th the Princess Pats suffered fearful losses at the opening of the assault. Caught by the enemy's counter-bombardment, they then waded into a hail of fire from machine-guns at Duck Lodge and the pill-box on Meetcheele Spur. By 7 am almost every subaltern was either dead or wounded. Nos 3 and 1 Companies, on the left, had only two surviving officers between them. The losses among NCOs was almost as severe. To make matters worse, the battle was fought for long periods in a vacuum. Enemy shelling had ripped up telephone cables, leaving runners to brave galling fire to maintain communication with headquarters.

Despite the confusion, however, progress was made. Duck Lodge fell after a sharp struggle and the advance along the Bellevue–Mosselmarkt road carried the Canadians remorselessly towards what the Princess Pats' historian called 'the most dramatic and fateful incident of the day'. Nos 3 and 1 Companies had already been roughly treated. Only forty men survived in No. 3, and they had been led, in turn, by a company sergeant-major and an acting sergeant. Now they faced their greatest test. Directly ahead, bordering the road on the right, lay the massive fortification dominating Meetcheele Spur, a modest eminence little more than 50ft high. Machine-guns firing from the pillbox swept the entire ridge, inflicting casualties among troops advancing almost half a mile away. Mixed parties of Nos 3 and 1 Companies succeeded in reaching the foot of the slope, but could get no further. Casualties began to mount and it seemed only a matter of time before the Canadians would be compelled to give ground. It was at this critical moment that Lt McKenzie made his way forward, accompanied by Lt J.M. Christie DCM and Sgt Harry Mullin MM, a 25-year-old American-born scout who was one of the Princess Pats' snipers.

McKenzie's passage across the ridge had been a difficult one. Only one man had been lost in the early stages, but thereafter his two gun teams had taken a hammering. As they approached the huge pillbox, however, McKenzie realised that somone needed to kickstart the stalled attack. Cpl T. Hampson, second-in-command of the machine-gun detachment, recorded:

There seemed to be a lull or complete stop. Mac was a lieutenant and I was a corporal. We talked the situation over for seemingly some time. I suggested something had to be done. A minute or so after, Mac got out of the shell-hole that we were resting in, got what men we had left going again (I won't mention how) but sorry to have to say he hadn't gone more than 200yd or so when he was hit through the head with a bullet.

McKenzie's death, however, was not in vain. With Christie providing accurate covering fire, the machine-gun subaltern had rallied the survivors, in some cases by forcible means, and organised them for one last effort. Whether by design or not, and his subsequent VC citation claimed it was, the desperate frontal attack which McKenzie led took the form of a forlorn hope, diverting attention away from a flank attack. If this was McKenzie's plan, it worked, though only at the cost of his own life and as a result of the fearlessness of Sgt Mullin.

Taking advantage of McKenzie's gallant charge, Mullin crawled close to an enemy post beside the pillbox. A well-placed grenade disposed of the occupants and then Mullin jumped up and raced for the pillbox. Capt. Theodore Roberts, of the Canadian War Records Office, described the climax of the fight:

Sgt G.H. Mullin

> Mullin climbed to the top of the pillbox. Crawling to the centre, he fired down upon the German machine-gunners inside, laying them out across their weapons. Then, sliding down the roof, he landed beside the entrance in time to receive the surrender of the thoroughly demoralised garrison.

Ten prisoners were taken by the sergeant armed only with a revolver. Mullin's action had been widely witnessed and, miraculously, although his clothes were riddled by bullets, he was unharmed. Just as Kinross' action had influenced the outcome of the 49th's battle, so Mullin's feat of daring galvanised the Princess Pats.

First news of the vital capture did not reach Battalion HQ until 9.25 am. The message simply read: 'Crest of hill taken. Large pillbox surrendered. Our machine-guns established.' A little over an hour later, Mullin reported personally to Col Adamson, giving him full and accurate details of the location of the blockhouse, the extent of the advance and the strength of the unit, which he estimated fairly accurately at 225 from the 600 men who had set out less than 5 hours earlier.

By the time Mullin returned to the fray, two counter-attacks had been repulsed; a third, from the direction of Vindictive Crossroads, was similarly dealt with before noon and brought a slackening of enemy fire. A line of shell-hole posts running roughly level with the blockhouse was established and consolidated, the Princess Pats making contact with the right flank of the 49th Edmontons. It was not until midnight on the following day that the two shattered battalions were able to quit the gruesome battlefield. Even then the Germans made it difficult, drenching the Gravenstafel ridge with poison gas.

The 7th Brigade's assault, like that of the 9th Brigade four days earlier, had failed to achieve all its objectives, but it had edged the Canadians closer to their main goal. Once again, the casualty lists made harrowing reading. The Princess Pats lost twenty out of twenty-five officers, nine of them killed, and 343 men, of whom 150 were either killed, reported 'missing believed killed' or died of wounds. The 49th's losses were still greater. They had suffered 443 casualties, including 126 dead. The loss among Lt McKenzie's small party from the 7th Canadian Machine-Gun Corps was proportionately grim: seventeen casualties out of twenty-eight who had started.

Almost ten weeks later, the *London Gazette* of 11 January 1918 announced the awards of the Victoria Cross to No. 437793 Pte Cecil Kinross and No. 51339 Sgt Harry Mullin. Kinross, who had been seriously wounded in the arm and head towards the end of the day's fighting, was said to have fought 'with the utmost aggressiveness against heavy odds'. It was no over-statement, although the official dates of his award, 28–29 October until 31 October–1 November, are misleading, for he ended his greatest day in a Casualty Clearing Station. The long list of honours for the battle also included MCs for Lts McKay of the 49th and Christie of the Princess Pats. Unaccountably, the posthumous award to Lt Hugh McKenzie (erroneously spelt MacKenzie) was delayed until 13 February. He had been buried close by the pillbox he died attacking, although his grave was later destroyed. His death made a deep impression on the pitifully few men of his detachment who survived the fight. Many years later, Cpl Hampson remembered:

> We put a cross up where we buried him. Came up after we were relieved and did this. Just showing how much we thought of him. You know, it was 6 miles of duckboards to do this. Seems crazy but we did it. Yes, Mac was blunt, said little, meant what he said, have a good laugh after. A man among men.

Although often claimed as a Scottish-born VC winner, Hugh McKenzie was actually born in Liverpool on 5 December 1885, the second son of James and Jane McKenzie, both of whom came originally from Inverness. His father, a sugar boiler in a confectionery factory, had moved south in search of work, eventually joining the Merchant Navy as an engineer. McKenzie spent the first two years of his life on Merseyside, but moved back to Inverness with his mother, three brothers and three sisters in 1887 when his father was lost at sea.

Educated at Leachkin School, he joined the Highland Railway Company as a cleaner. Around 1905 the family uprooted again and moved to Dundee, although they maintained their connections with Inverness, spending their annual holidays there. McKenzie found work with Messrs Watson & Sons of Seagate, and then the Caledonian Railway Company as a carter. A noted sportsman, he was a fine athlete and a founder member of the Dundee Amateur Boxing and Wrestling Club. As a wrestler, he was crowned North Scotland champion, won a clutch of trophies and became a club instructor.

He immigrated to Montreal, Canada, in 1912, and around this time married Marjory McGuigan, who came from Dundee. They had two children, Alexander and Elizabeth, and there is some suggestion that Elizabeth may have remained in Scotland with relatives, presumably until her parents were settled. By 1914 the McKenzies were living at 297 Gertrude Avenue, Verdun. McKenzie may have gained work on the railways, although on joining the Army he gave gave his trade as machinist.

He enlisted on 21 August 1914 as a private (Regimental No. 1158) in the Princess Patricia's Canadian Light Infantry, a newly raised battalion named after the daughter of the Duke of Connaught, Canada's Governor-General. On his attestation papers he was described as being 5ft 7in tall, with grey eyes, brown hair and a fresh complexion. His only identifying mark was a tattoo in the form of a heart on his right wrist. Two days after his enlistment, in a display rich in imperial pageantry, Pat's Pets, as they were soon dubbed, were presented with their Colours in front of a huge crowd in Lansdowne Park, Ottawa. McKenzie was a member of No. 3 Company which proceeded to England in October and was selected to become the first Canadian unit to serve on the Western Front, arriving in France before Christmas as reinforcements for the British 80th Brigade (27th Division). They took their places in the line near St Eloi mound, the scene of much fighting in the winter of 1914–15. Hugh McKenzie's war, however, was soon interrupted by a bout of dysentery. He was admitted to hospital on 22 January, returning to his unit eleven days later.

April found the Pats in the Salient, south of the Canadian Division. They missed the first poison gas attack, but the following month at Bellewaarde spur fought a costly defensive action which has become enshrined in regimental legend. McKenzie, by then a corporal in the machine-gun section, figured prominently in the four-day battle. His numerous acts of gallantry began on 4 May when the Pats' crude trenches were pounded by shells which wiped out his gun team and went on until 8 May when he led fresh troops to their relief. In twenty-five days, the Pats had lost 700 men. McKenzie was awarded the Distinguished Conduct Medal (*London Gazette*, 14 January 1916):

For conspicuous gallantry. His machine-gun having been blown up by a shell and the whole crew killed or wounded, Cpl McKenzie displayed the utmost coolness in stripping the wrecked gun of all undamaged parts and bringing them safely out of the trench, which by then had been absolutely demolished. Having no machine-gun, he volunteered to carry messages to and from Brigade Headquarters under terrific fire and succeeded. His devotion to duty has always been most marked.

The same list of awards featured the DCM to L/Cpl J.M. Christie, who as the unit's sniping officer, would play a key role in McKenzie's final action.

The following month, McKenzie, who had been promoted sergeant on 11 September, was awarded the French Croix de Guerre (*London Gazette*, 24 February) 'for gallant and distinguished service in the field'. His active service with the Princess Pats ended in September 1916 when, as a result of his machine-gun experience, he was transferred to the 7th Canadian Machine-Gun Company as company sergeant-major, a rank confirmed on 18 November. Almost his entire military service had been spent with machine-guns, and his proficiency, already recognised in his selection for a special course at St Omer, was further reflected in his being promoted temporary lieutenant on 28 January 1917. Although commissioned into the Princess Pats, he never served as an officer with them, being immediately seconded to the 7th Brigade's machine-gunners.

While his army career went from strength to strength, his private life was a mess. His marriage had hit trouble and on 6 February 1917 he applied to stop his monthly $20 payments to his wife on the grounds of her 'infidelity'. Around this time, he asked a friend, Clement Hayward to 'look into his family'. What Hayward found was shocking, and he referred to it years later as a 'sordid story'. He discovered that his wife had placed their son in a Montreal 'infants home' for young Protestant children. Hayward wrote back but could not bring himself to mention this, and after McKenzie's death travelled back to Montreal only to find that his estranged wife had reclaimed her son.

Whether or not any of this was known to McKenzie is not clear, although it may be significant that he left both his DCM and his Croix de Guerre with his mother, who was still living in Dundee. At that time, his elder brother Robert was serving in the Army Service Corps and a younger brother Alexander, a reservist in the Cameron Highlanders, was a prisoner of war. Throughout the war, McKenzie had paid several visits to his relatives in Scotland, the last time during a ten-day spell of leave in October 1917. Rejoining his unit on 17 October, he was killed in action thirteen days later.

On 5 November a telegram informed his widow, then living at 1021 Clarke Street, Montreal, that he was reported 'missing, believed killed'. A second wire confirming his death followed a week later. In his will, scribbled out while in Flanders on 14 March 1915 and apparently unaltered before his death, he left all his back pay and wristwatch to his mother and the remainder of his personal effects to his wife. His widow later received his Victoria Cross and other campaign medals, but it would not be for another fifty-two years before his complete group was brought together in unusual circumstances.

Marjory McKenzie, who had settled in North Bay, Ontario, remarried on 6 January 1920. According to a regimental account, her daughter came out to Canada after her husband's death and stayed with her until she died. Their son Alex later served in the Canadian Army during the Second World War, and was killed in a road accident shortly after being demobbed.

Tragedy continued to stalk the McKenzies. In May 1955 a fire ripped through the daughter's house in Amherstburg, on the shores of Lake Erie, killing her sister-in-law and three children. All her possessions were destroyed in the blaze, including her father's VC. Unaware of the medal's fate, staff at the Princess Pats' regimental museum embarked on a quest to locate the McKenzie VC and any surviving relatives. Appeals were published in Canada and Scotland which eventually resulted with contact being made with his daughter in 1970. She had just returned from Scotland, bringing with her the DCM and Croix de Guerre that her father had left with relatives during the First World War. On learning about the loss of the VC, the regiment organised an official replacement to be presented which she in turn donated to the Canadian War Museum.

Today, the VC, DCM, Croix de Guerre and service medals are on extended loan to the PPCLI museum in Calgary, a fitting memorial to one of the bravest of Princess Pat's 'originals'.

One of the war's most unconventional heroes, Cecil John Kinross was born on 17 February 1896 at Dews Farm, Harefield, near Uxbridge in Middlesex, the third of five children to James Stirling Kinross and his wife Emily (née Hull). His father was a Scot from Ardoch in Perthshire and, according to family records, had led him as a teenager to the United States where he was said to have worked as a cowboy in Texas. Returning to England to run a farm in Hurley, Warwickshire, owned by his brother, he met his wife-to-be before heading south to Dews Farm. At some point, the family decided to move back to Warwickshire and it was there Cec Kinross was educated, at Hurley School and Lea Marston Boys School before progressing to Coleshill Grammar School.

In 1912 James Kinross uprooted his family again and travelled once more across the Atlantic, only this time he chose to settle not in the United States but in Canada at the year-old township of Lougheed, Alberta. Situated south of the Iron River valley and some 90 miles east of Edmonton, Lougheed lay astride the Canadian Pacific Railway and was ideal country for growing cereal crops. The small prairie town remained Cec Kinross' home for the rest of his life. He was working as a farmer when war broke out and the following year he travelled to Calgary where he enlisted on 21 October as a private in the 51st Battalion, Canadian Expeditionary Force. His army papers show him to have been almost 6ft tall, with blue eyes, dark brown hair and scars on both shins caused by a ploughing accident.

He embarked for England on 18 December 1915 as a member of the 3rd Reinforcing Draft. Posted, on landing, to the 9th Reserve Battalion at Shorncliffe, he proceeded to France to join the 49th (Edmontons) Battalion on 6 March 1916, reaching his new unit, which was in divisional reserve near Kemmel, ten days later. Cec Kinross quickly became known as something of an oddball character and proved a hard man to control. A former sergeant-major in the unit later insisted no officer ever got the better of him:

> His appearance on parade, even after several days in reserve and at rest was, as often told him by his platoon officer, 'a disgrace to the platoon, Kinross', which always brought forth a queer smirk on his dial, only not enough for a charge of dumb insolence. Of course, the next parade he would be good-and-spruced-up, by reason of a chunk or two of trench mud having fallen off his clothes while moving around, and to that extent he was regarded as incorrigible.

As time went by, the young private, who was made runner of 'Steady D' Company, acquired a reputation as being something of a jinx for his officers, resulting in his nickname 'Hoodoo', by which he would forever be remembered by veterans of the 49th. A comrade recalled:

> He had in the short space of a few months about umpteen officers pass through his hands. All the shells, etc, that Fritz threw round him and his follow the leader seemed to have the other fellow's moniker on them, and never his 'Hoodooship's'. It happened so often in this manner that when he was given charge of another 'Puppy' to follow his trail, the boys used to start betting as to how long the new tourist would last ... It never struck them that if only one came back from a line trip it would be any other than Hoodoo.

His legendary cussedness allied to his reputation for being a harbinger of misfortune may account for two spells away from the battalion. From 23 May to 25 August 1916 he was attached to the 7th Canadian Trench Mortar Battery and the following year from 18 May to 24 July he served with the 7th Field Company, Canadian Engineers. In between, he went through the fighting on the Somme, being wounded during the disastrous attack on Regina Trench on 8 October 1916 when the 49th suffered 50 per cent losses. Admitted to No. 3 Canadian General Hospital in Boulogne on 10 October with shrapnel wounds to his right arm and body, he was discharged to a convalescent depot three days later, rejoining his unit on 6 November.

He took part in the attack on Vimy Ridge, where the Canadian Corps gained its greatest victory, and after an interlude with the brigade engineers rejoined the 49th Battalion in time for the August fighting around Lens. His next major action on the outskirts of Passchendaele was also his last. The shrapnel wounds to his head, left arm and body resulted in him being hospitalised for three months. Evacuated to England, he was a patient at No. 16 Canadian General Hospital in Orpington when a photographer visited his ward to take his picture. The young Canadian only discovered the reason when he read of his VC award in a newspaper a few days later. According to a medical report, his wound was 'progressing satisfactorily' and in February 1918 he was posted to the 21st (Reserve) Battalion at the Alberta Regimental Depot in Bramshott.

Trouble, however, never seemed far away when Kinross was around. Within hours of receiving his Cross at Buckingham Palace on 6 April 1918, he was arrested by military policemen who accused him of wearing a VC ribbon to which they thought he was not entitled. They were only convinced after Kinross had taken his medal from his pocket and showed them the inscription on the back. As a tribute to his heroism, on 14 July 1918, Maj. C.Y. Weaver, commanding the 49th Battalion, ordered that 'Hoodoo' Kinross' old platoon would be renamed No. 15 (Kinross) Platoon.

Ruled medically unfit in December 1918, he returned to Canada the following month, still suffering from the legacy of his injuries sustained in the fighting near Passchendaele. A medical examination carried out at Edmonton on 27 January 1919 found that he had lost all sensation in two fingers on his left hand and had only partial feeling in his left arm which made it difficult to hold farm implements such as forks and spades. The subsequent report also noted that since being wounded he suffered 'headaches about once a month which last two or three days'. It concluded that he might take up to a year to recover from his partial paralysis and was unable to fully resume his old job in farming. The following month he was honourably discharged from the Army.

At a civic reception in Edmonton, he was presented with a purse of gold and granted 160 acres of prime farmland some 8 miles west of Lougheed. Perhaps as a result of his injuries, he appears not to have worked the land, preferring instead to rent it out while taking jobs with neighbouring farms. Variously described as 'wild and crazy', 'happy go lucky' and 'everybody's friend', Cec Kinross was a gregarious man noted for his eccentricities. People recalled the time in 1934 he went into hospital to have his tonsils removed and refused to have anaesthetic. And they remembered his reaction to being teased about which required the greater courage: charging a German machine-post single handed or jumping into a frozen stream. He settled the argument by taking off his coat, walking over to a hole in the ice-bound stream and plunging in!

A confirmed bachelor, Kinross travelled to Britain in 1929 to attend the Prince of Wales banquet for VC holders and again twenty-seven years later for the Victoria Cross centenary celebrations. Having taken early retirement, he moved into the Lougheed Hotel which had long been his second home and lived there cheerfully on his army pension until his sudden death on 21 June 1957.

Such was his popularity, people turned out in their droves to witness the passing of a great, albeit thoroughly unorthodox, Albertan. In the largest funeral ever seen in Lougheed, the community hall was filled to overflowing with hundreds more listening to the service relayed over a public address system. Among the pallbearers were a holder of the DCM, three Military Medallists and another Albertan VC holder, Alex Brereton. Cec Kinross was buried with military honours in the soldiers' plot of Lougheed cemetery with pipers playing a lament.

More than six decades on, he is still proudly remembered on both sides of the Atlantic. In his home town, both the local branch of the Royal Canadian Legion and a children's playground bear his name, while in his English birthplace a blue plaque unveiled in 2011 near to Dews Road, Harefield, commemorates his association with the borough of Hillingdon. But his most spectacular memorial resides in Jasper National Park, in the Rockies, in the shape of a 2,731m peak overlooking Pyramid Lake. Mount Kinross stands as a towering salute to a towering personality. As fellow Lougheed farmer Thomas Barton once remarked: 'You couldn't get him to talk about the VC or what happened. He was a very proud man. But he didn't give a damn for anything.'

One of a handful of American-born winners of the Victoria Cross, George Harry Mullin was born in Portland, Oregon, on 15 August 1891, the son of Harry and Effie Mullin. The family moved to Canada when he was two years old and homesteaded at Moosomin, Saskatchewan. Mullin attended the Moosomin Public School and later the Moosomin Collegiate. At the outbreak of war, he was farming at Kamloops, British Columbia, where he lived with his mother.

He enlisted in the 32nd Battalion at Winnipeg on 14 December 1914, and was one of a draft transferred to the Princess Patricia's Canadian Light

Infantry in February 1915. He became a battalion sniper and was wounded at Sanctuary Wood in June 1916. Evacuated to England for hospital treatment, he rejoined the unit in September 1916 on the Somme, where his brother Roy was killed.

He joined the battalion's sniper section and was awarded a Military Medal (gazetted 19 February 1917) for an act of gallantry carried out on 16 December 1916 opposite Vimy Ridge. The recommendation stated:

> In the La Folie Sector as a sniper [he] assisted Sgt Dow in his reconnaissance of an enemy post. At 3.20 am [he] accompanied Lt McDougall's party to the same spot, killed the sentry, threw bombs down the communication trench to block the enemy supports and assisted in carrying his officer out of the crater. He has on many occasions examined enemy wire after an artillery bombardment under very dangerous circumstances and his reports have always been accurate.

Sgt N.D. Dow received a Military Medal and Lt A.A. McDougall a Military Cross for this action.

Mullin was promoted corporal in the field on 16 March, made acting sergeant on 9 April, the day of the assault on Vimy Ridge, and by July was a full sergeant, commanding the battalion's scouts and snipers. It was while serving in this role that he won his Victoria Cross at Meetcheele Spur. He left the Princess Pats in March 1918 and was attached to the 6th Reserve Battalion prior to attending the Canadian Officers' Training School at Bexhill. Commissioned temporary lieutenant on 6 August 1918, he was posted to the 6th Reserve Battalion and saw out the rest of the war as battalion bombing instructor.

He had married in April 1918 and before returning to Canada in June 1919 he helped to coach and lead the 6th Reserve Battalion baseball team. After the war he returned to farming, but maintained his military associations. He served in the 4th South Saskatchewan Regiment, the 1st Assiniboia Militia and 110 Field Battery (Howitzers). During the Second World War, he again volunteered for service and spent six years as an officer in the Veterans' Guard of Canada, including a spell in command of an internment camp.

The war interrupted his ceremonial duties as sergeant-of-arms at the Saskatchewan Legislature, a post he had held since 1934. But in 1953 he donned full regalia as one of Saskatchewan's representatives at the coronation of Queen Elizabeth II.

Major Harry Mullin died in Regina, Saskatchewan, on 5 April 1963 aged 70, and was buried in the South Cemetery Legion Plot, at Moosomin, where his parents had first settled in Canada over sixty years earlier. His

Victoria Cross group, including the Military Medal and a Mention in Despatches, is now displayed alongside Hugh McKenzie's awards in the Princess Patricia's Canadian Light Infantry Museum at Calgary, having been purchased by the Canadian War Museum for an undisclosed sum in 1975.

G.R. PEARKES

Vapour Farm, 30–31 October 1917

As Maj. George Pearkes clambered out of his muddy shell-hole at around 5.54 am on 30 October, he could barely make out the dark shapes of his men, indistinct in the dim early morning light. Flares and rockets shot through the grey gloom, followed by the enemy counter-bombardment, shattering in its intensity as it exploded around them. Pearkes, OC C Company, 5th Canadian Mounted Rifles, would remember that moment well. Many years later, he said:

We'd hardly got out ... when that barrage came down. At that time I was hit in the thigh [by shrapnel] and was knocked down. I rather thought: 'Now I've got it!' There seemed to be a little uncertainty among the men immediately alongside me, whether they should go on when I'd been hit. For a moment I had visions of going back wounded and I said to myself: 'This can't be. I've got to go on for a while anyway, wounded or not.' So I clambered to my feet and I found a stiffness in my left thigh but I was able to move forward and then the rest of the company all came forward.

The ground fell away towards a swamp speckled with the stumps of Woodland Plantation. Beyond it, roughly 1,000yd from the start line, lay their objective, the fortified Vapour Farm strongpoint on the edge of Goudberg Spur. Parallel to his company, and skirting the other side of the mire, was A Company, headed for the strongpoint at Vine Cottage. Behind came D and B Companies to consolidate the ground won. Together, they represented 8th Canadian Brigade's attacking force, squeezed, because of the dreadful nature of the ground, into a two-platoon front between the 49th Edmontons and the 28th Londons (Artists' Rifles). As we have seen, the enemy's barrage took a fearful toll of the 49th. The 5th CMR were similarly hard hit. Worst affected of all, however, were the Artists' Rifles. Caught in the open, they suffered crippling losses which stopped their advance on Source Farm almost before it had begun. Ignorant of the disaster which had befallen their flanking unit, C Company pushed on. It soon became clear something was wrong. As well as fire from the strongpoints in front, they found themselves exposed to fire from untouched pillboxes on the left. Pearkes began losing men at an alarming rate:

> We found that the barrage ran away from us; we couldn't begin to keep up with it [even though] it was moving at the rate of 100yd every eight minutes ... I was carrying a rifle and I remember turning around and help-ing men who were not wounded but who had got stuck in shell-holes. I'm certain that there were men who, wounded, fell into the shell-holes and were drowned. If you got in you just couldn't climb out by yourself ... because the sides all kept oozing down if you reached out to help yourself.

Despite everything, C Company had reached its intermediate objective by 6.30 am. During a lull in the barrage, the German defenders were seen scurrying back towards their main defences around Vapour and Source Farms. During that last effort, the Canadians were assailed by machine-guns ranged to the left and to the front. Yet Pearkes managed to maintain some semblance of order. Realising the danger represented by the Source Farm strongpoint, he sent a platoon to take it, while pressing on towards Vapour Farm with just thirty-six men.

At 7.55 am Pearkes signalled his success. The fate of A Company's advance was more obscure. A pall of smoke blotted out much of the bat-tlefield. Observers thought they had seen A Company on the intermediate objective. Later, flares were reported on the right and were taken to mean they too had reached their final objective. But it was not so. So heavy were their losses that they were unable to make an attempt on Vine Cottage. Instead, they veered left, reinforcing Pearkes' small garrison. It was not until 8.30 am that a message from Pearkes, scribbled 45 minutes earlier, apprised Battalion HQ of the true position. It read: 'We hold source, vapour and vanity, both flanks in the air. Have about 50 men from "C" and "D". We must have help from both sides. Hun about 100 yards away.'

Attempts to support them were hampered by enfilading fire and heavy shell-ing. Pearkes' men had achieved the near-impossible. But their grip was tenuous. Almost a mile ahead of the 28th Londons, they had advanced way beyond any other unit. But without support it seemed their sacrifices would be in vain.

Pearkes sent off another urgent appeal for help, this time via one of the company's two pigeons. The man carrying the message clips had been killed, so Pearkes ingeniously attached his note to the bird's leg using a strand of sandbag fibre. In the hours that followed, a trickle of reinforcements, including men sent up from the 2nd CMR, arrived, but they were still all too few in number. An attempt to take Vine Cottage was driven off and the swaying fortunes were revealed in a brief report sent by Pearkes at 10.50 am:

> Am holding line of shell holes ... VAPOUR and SOURCE FARMS inclusive. Have about 30 men and Lts ANDREWS, GIFFORD and OTTY, 5th CMR Bn. Strong counter-attack by enemy en masse successfully beaten back. 50 men 2nd CMR arrived. Both my flanks in the air. Bde on left must endeavour to come up. Am short SAA but will hold on. VANITY HOUSE now held by enemy.

The garrison's two Lewis guns exacted a heavy toll, but on the debit side the party sent against Vine Cottage was overwhelmed. Later, around eight to ten men of the 2nd CMR, all that remained of a company of reinforcements, staggered in. Throughout, Pearkes had been the life and soul of the defence. Although in great discomfort from his leg wound, he seemed to be everywhere, crawling from shell-hole to shell-hole, cracking jokes, directing fire, even taking a few pot-shots at the enemy. But after nearly 8 hours of continuous fighting exhaustion was setting in. At 1.45 pm, he informed Battalion HQ: 'Germans are digging in on top of ridge about 200 yards away. Are in force. I have 8 2nd CMR and 19 5th CMR. All very much exhausted. Ammunition running short. Do not think we can hold out much longer without being relieved. Both flanks still in the air.'

Years later he admitted, 'it looked a pretty hopeless position'. But there was nothing for it but to stand and fight. Pearkes recalled: 'To have gone back and given up everything we had gained that morning didn't seemed very sensible as, if we had started to drift back there would have been more casualties.' A British unit was ordered to form a defensive flank towards Source Farm, but unaccountably it never budged, leaving Pearkes to form his own fragile perimeter. In a message which reached Battalion HQ at 5.45 pm via a wounded officer, he reported:

> About 10 men 'A' Coy 2nd CMR Bn have got through. Huns counter-attacking again. We have had some more casualties. Have formed a defensive flank on the left and continued a short distance past SOURCE FARM with right flank resting on WOODLAND PLANTATION. Reinforcements might get through after dark. They are most urgently needed, also SAA. Men of 5th CMR Bn all in. Do not think I can hold out until morning.

But as darkness fell, first ammunition and then relief reached the defiant Canadians in the form of two companies of the 2nd CMR. Of all the attacking units, only the 5th CMR had captured and held any of its final objectives. Fewer than forty men struggled back from Vapour Farm and Source Farm. The last to leave was George Pearkes, his trouser leg caked in blood and mud. In his post-battle report, the Battalion CO, Lt-Col D.C. Draper, recorded:

> The boldness, initiative and skill displayed by Maj G.R. Pearkes cannot be too highly commented upon. It was entirely due to his leadership that the operation of this battalion was so successful. For a considerable time he held Vapour and Source Farms with a mere handful of men, beating off the first German counter attack without any other assistance. His appreciation of the situation was most accurate and his reports at all times were clear, concise and invaluable.

Pearkes' own assessment, recorded years later, was more prosaic: 'We had got on when nobody else had got on; we had survived ... and we were all thankful.' There can have been little surprise when, on 11 January 1918, the *London Gazette* announced the award of the Victoria Cross to Maj. George Pearkes 'for most conspicuous bravery'.

George Randolph Pearkes, destined to become the most distinguished Canadian holder of the Victoria Cross, was born in Watford, Hertfordshire, on 26 February 1888, the eldest son of George and Louise Pearkes. After a spell being taught by governesses, he went to Berkhamsted School where he remained for the next ten years. Although an intelligent boy, academic study took second place to outdoor pursuits, most notably horse riding. A member of the school cadet force, his ambition was to become a cavalry officer. But all that changed when his father's business slumped.

Instead of joining the Army, Pearkes immigrated to Canada, and in May 1906 he headed west for Red Deer, Alberta, where his ex-headmaster owned a farm. It was nicknamed Baby Farm because it served as a kind of practical agricultural college, teaching youngsters the way of the land. At 21, Pearkes had his own homestead, consisting of 160 acres of untamed Albertan wilderness on which he built his own makeshift shelter. Within a little over a year, he had been joined by his brother (who in true pioneering spirit helped build a log cabin), his mother, who had separated from her husband, and his sister.

In 1913, having already ventured to the far north as a member of a land survey expedition, he joined the Royal North-West Mounted Police, being stationed at White Horse, in the Yukon, while his brother looked after the farm. At the outbreak of war, he immediately applied to buy himself out to enlist. But it was not until early 1915 that the authorities relented and on 2 March 1915 he joined the 2nd Canadian Mounted Rifles at Victoria, British Columbia, as a trooper. His skills as a horseman brought him swift promotion. He was made a rough-riding corporal but when they sailed for France in September 1915 it was as a dismounted cavalry unit later to be fully converted to infantrymen.

Pearkes was among the first party from the 2nd CMR to go into the trenches. He later recalled his tour of the line near Ploegsteert: 'There was a sort of strangeness to it all which, at the same time, keyed one up and I was excited.' His first brush with the enemy came near Messines in December. Selected for specialist bombing training, he was kept on as an instructor. By the time he returned it was as sergeant of the bombing platoon. Shortly afterwards, he was wounded during a fight near Hooge on 26 March 1916. He was quickly back with his unit and on 30 April, his platoon officer having been wounded, he was commissioned in the field.

His career had begun to assume a pattern that would continue for the rest of the war. Astoundingly successful and blessed with good fortune, it was punctuated by promotions, injuries and awards for gallantry. Wounded and temporarily blinded on 20 May, he lied about the extent of his wounds in order to return to his unit. Within a matter of a few weeks he had won his first award, a Mention in Despatches, for destroying an enemy listening post. An appointment as 8th Brigade bombing officer proved short-lived. On 27 September he was transferred to the 5th CMR to take command of C Company. Four days later, he led them in an attack on Regina Trench on the Somme. Wounded again, his fearless leadership resulted in his award of the Military Cross (*London Gazette*, 21 December 1916): 'He led a bombing party with great courage and determination, clearing 600yd of trench and capturing 18 prisoners.' That same month and within the space of two days he rose from lieutenant to acting major.

The unit, and his company in particular, came to represent his universe. By the close of the Passchendaele campaign, he had made up his mind to make the Army his life. The injury sustained at Vapour Farm quickly healed and by mid-November he was back with the 'Fighting Fifth'. His stay, however, was brief. Posted as senior major to the 116th Battalion, he was promoted lieutenant-colonel in command of the unit in January 1918. During the Allied offensive at Amiens on 8 August, his new unit featured prominently, resulting in his third decoration. The citation for his DSO noted:

He handled his battalion in a masterly manner and with an enveloping movement completely baffled and overcame the enemy, who were in a very strong position. He then captured a wood, the final objective, which was about 5,000yd from the start. Before this, however, the men were becoming exhausted, on observing which he at once went into the attack himself, and by his splendid and fearless example, put new life into the whole attack, which went forward with a rush and captured 16 enemy guns of all calibres up to eight inches.

Pearkes' outstanding war record ended on 17 September at Guemappe, France. During a bombardment of his unit's billets, he was seriously wounded in the arm and side. His life hung in the balance, and it was only the surgeons' skill that saved him. He was convalescing in London when the war ended. On New Year's Eve he was Mentioned in Despatches again and shortly afterwards awarded the French Croix de Guerre.

He returned to Canada in March 1919 and for the next nine years served as a staff officer in the western provinces. During that time he married Constance Blytha Copeman, whose family originally came from Norfolk. They had two children. His career continued to flourish. By 1935 he was serving as Director of Military Training and Staff Duties, and in 1938 he took command of Military District No. 13 based at Calgary on promotion to brigadier. Shortly after the outbreak of the Second World War, he was appointed to command the 2nd Brigade, 1st Canadian Division, and proceeded with it to England in December 1939. Two months later, following a visit to the BEF in France, he was struck down by spinal meningitis. Despite fears that he might not survive, he pulled through and in the aftermath of Dunkirk was promoted major-general in command of 1st Canadian Division.

Pearkes proved an excellent commander. Thoroughly professional and greatly respected, he brought the division up to a high level of efficiency. But there was friction with other commanders, and in the wake of the Dieppe débâcle, in which his division was not involved but which he had strongly opposed, he was sent back to Canada to take over Pacific Command, with responsibility for protecting the western provinces in the unlikely event of a Japanese attack. He held the post until 1945, retiring from the Army with a Companion of the Most Honourable Order of the Bath (CB) and the United States Order of Merit.

In June 1945 he embarked on a new career as a politician. He was elected a Progressive Conservative MP for Nanaimo, British Columbia, and when his party was returned to office in 1957, Pearkes was appointed Minister of Defence and became a Canadian Privy Councillor. At the time, he was the only Cabinet minister in the Commonwealth to hold a VC. He eventually stepped down in 1960 to become one of the most popular lieutenant-governors in the history of British Columbia. During his eight years in office, he also served as grand president of the Royal Canadian Legion, retiring from the post in its golden anniversary year of 1976.

A man revered by ex-servicemen and respected by politicians and ordinary citizens alike, he retained a desire to serve his fellow Canadians. 'I took an interest in my soldiers and in the Legion,' he once said. 'I have concern for people rather than just the favoured few.' George Pearkes, whose extraordinary life took him from cadet to major-general and from homesteader to lieutenant-governor, died in a Victoria rest home on 30 May 1984, aged 96, after suffering a stroke. The man of whom it was said he merited the phrase '*Chevalier sans peur et sans reproche*' was given a state and military funeral as befitted his dual career. The funeral parade was led by thirty-two Mounties followed by units of the Princess Pats, a guard of the Canadian Scottish and a black, riderless horse with saddle draped in black and riding boots reversed in the stirrups.

C.F. BARRON AND
J.P. ROBERTSON

Vine Cottage and Passchendaele,
6 November 1917

On the morning of 6 November Philip Gibbs, the distinguished British war correspondent, picked his way towards a line of captured pillboxes on the approaches to the Steenbeek. From there, 'through the smoke of gun-fire and the wet mist' he saw Passchendaele. Or what was left of it. As he scanned the crest of the ridge that 'curved round black and grim below the clouds, right round to Polygon Wood and the heights of Broodseinde', he could see only one ruin poking through the murk. It was the church, 'a black mass of slaughtered masonry'.

No more than a speck on any but the most detailed of maps, Passchendaele and its formidable ridge, an objective in the early stages of a campaign designed to break the deadlock of three years' fighting, had become the vainglorious *raison d'être* for the continuation of a struggle in which hope of a breakthrough had long since vanished. The Germans, however, had no intention of giving up the ridge without a fight. As Gibbs looked on, the damp air was filled with 'the savage whine' of the enemy's artillery 'and all below the Passchendaele Ridge monstrous shells were flinging up masses of earth and water'. After four months of fighting, the village that would give its name to the campaign and all its futile carnage had become the day's main target. It was not, however, the only one.

On the left, the Canadians of the 1st Division had the task of clearing the enemy strongpoints along the spurs feeding on to the main ridge north-west of Passchendaele. As always, the lines of attack were governed by the swamp. The entire divisional frontage was constricted into the 380yd width of the Bellevue-Meetcheele Spur, along which the 1st (Western Ontario) and 2nd (Eastern Ontario) Battalions were to advance in conjunction with a flank attack by the 3rd (Toronto) Battalion to the east astride the Goudberg spur. The latter operation was a continuation of the efforts made by the

5th Canadian Mounted Rifles to capture the Vine Cottage strongpoint. The ruined farmhouse sheltered one of the largest pillboxes in the sector, with walls reckoned to be 18in thick and machine-guns covering every conceivable approach. The defenders also had another ally – the mud. The rain and relentless shelling had created a glutinous barrier guaranteed to restrict any assault.

Conscious of the difficulties, Lt-Col J.B. 'Bart' Rogers DSO, MC, drew up a plan which concentrated on dealing with Vine Cottage. His attacking force consisted of C and D Companies and two platoons from A Company, under the command of Maj. D.H.C. Mason DSO. The spearhead, led by Capt. J.K. Crawford, comprised C Company and the elements of A Company, attacking on a three-platoon front with three platoons in close support. Lt H.T. Lord's platoon was given the job of seizing Vine Cottage. At 6 am, the two most northerly platoons of Crawford's force slipped out of their shell-holes near Vanity House and crept as close to the barrage as they dared. An anxious ten-minute pause followed before the bombardment ranged on to their objective, and then they moved off. The swampy ground made it impossible to approach Vine Cottage due eastwards from the jumping-off line. Lord had no choice but to attack south-eastwards, maintaining shape and direction under trying conditions, before swinging left to reach the battalion's final objective facing due north. Hardly surprisingly, the attack did not run smoothly.

It was soon apparent that the barrage had made little impression. The defences consisted of two intact pillboxes, of which the largest was at Vine Cottage, and 'a multitude of two or three man "funk holes" dug into the side of deep shell-holes'. From these burst a withering fire which combined with the mud to delay both Crawford's and Lord's advance. Each machine-gun had to be assaulted in turn, leading to heavy losses. Retribution, however, was severe. Lt-Col Rogers candidly reported:

> When our men got to within about 20 yards of them they ceased firing and the crews attempted to surrender but in the majority of cases they were given no quarter and the bayonet was used to good effect as our men were infuriated at the casualties which had been caused by them.

Slowly, and at considerable loss, Lord's depleted platoon closed in on Vine Cottage and the outlying posts. A persistent drizzle was falling as they divided into smaller parties, hoping to confuse the defenders by rushing from three directions at once. But every time they were driven back before they could get within bombing range. As casualties mounted in proportion to the number of failures, it appeared as though Lord's attack would go much the same way as that of 5th CMR on 30 October. That it did not do so was due to the resolution and initiative of Cpl Colin Barron, a Scots-Canadian member of D Company.

Barron, who was commanding one of the battalion's Lewis gun sections, had grown frustrated by the repeated reverses. So he decided to show the way. Worming his way round the flank, lugging his weapon with him, he somehow managed to reach a position close by the strongpoint without being seen. Then, he opened fire at 'point-blank range' with devastating results. Two of Vine Cottage's three machine-gun crews were annihilated

Cpl C.F. Barron

one after the other by his deadly fire. According to Rogers, they were put 'absolutely out of action'. The third gun, blocked from Barron's view, continued to fire, but even before the pillbox's startled garrison had time to react, their nemesis was among them, followed by the remnants of his platoon bent on revenge. According to one account: 'There was a wild melee in the confined space ... for a few moments, with Barron using the bayonet and clubbed butt of an old rifle he had picked up, with terrible effect.'

Four men fell to Barron and the remainder, according to his VC citation, were taken prisoner, although given Rogers' earlier comments this must be a matter for some conjecture. In his own account, he makes no mention of prisoners, merely stating that 'at least a dozen of the enemy' were bayoneted in the final assault. Barron, meanwhile, rounded off his whirlwind attack by turning one of the captured machine-guns on to those members of the garrison who had escaped his frenzied charge.

Much behind time and greatly reduced in number, Lord's platoon had nevertheless accomplished their mission, and succeeded in linking up with Captain Crawford's force. Enemy machine-guns continued to play havoc along the Canadian lines of communications and, although reports of Vine Cottage's capture had been made shortly after 11 am, it was not until 12.30 pm that Battalion HQ received confirmation of their success.

Eventually, at 6.52 pm, after an afternoon spent consolidating and recovering the wounded, a fuller report arrived from Maj. Mason in which he stated that 'C Company continue to hold objectives ... and are digging in ... Estimated strength of C Company 150 ... 40 prisoners taken and are being held at Vine Cottages [sic] until dusk, so they can take stretcher cases out.' All told, Crawford's platoons had taken fifty-nine prisoners, including one officer, and captured five machine-guns, three of them taken by Cpl Barron at Vine Cottage. The price, as always, was a heavy one: sixty-four men, including three officers, dead, 154 wounded and twenty-two missing. Among the wounded were Capt. Crawford, whose leadership was recognised by the award of the DSO, and Lt Lord who received a Bar to his MC. According to Lt-Col Rogers, only the determination of his men had saved the day and prevented the 'serious stumbling blocks' around Vine Cottage from defeating his attack. And of them all none had displayed greater determination than Colin Barron.

While the 3rd (Toronto) Battalion had been slugging it out across the Goudberg Spur, the main effort had been focused 1,500yd further south-east on the high ground from which the 2nd Division, employing the 6th Brigade, launched its attack on Passchendaele. Behind a creeping barrage, described as 'splendid' by the Canadians, the 27th (City of Winnipeg), 31st (Alberta) and 28th (North West) Battalions advanced at a rapid rate. The 27th's objective was the village itself, and so swiftly did they follow the barrage on to their first objective that the enemy scarcely had a chance to resist. It was textbook stuff, but the nearer they came to the village the fiercer the opposition grew.

By adopting the newly devised tactics of single file sections leap-frogging one another on to the strongpoints, they gradually whittled away the enemy defences. But one machine-gun, on the left, proved particularly stubborn. Barring the Canadians' entry into the main street, the position was ringed by uncut wire and broken, reinforced walls. Three times the 27th's flanking platoon had charged it, only to be driven back by point-blank fire and a shower of bullets from marksmen hidden in nearby houses. It was at this cheerless moment, with the toll of casualties mounting and hopes fading, that Pte Peter Robertson intervened.

Standing 6ft 3in tall, Robertson, a locomotive engineer known as 'Singing Pete', was a good-humoured giant of a man who had refused all offers of promotion. He was highly regarded as a fighting soldier, but few could have anticipated that one man could succeed where an entire platoon had failed, not once but on three occasions. Robertson, however, was apparently undaunted by the odds. A man noted for his willingness to take risks was about to take one of the greatest gambles of his life. While his comrades blazed away at the machine-gun post with Lewis guns and rifles, he leapt up and sprinted alone across the line of fire. With the bullets from marksmen kicking the ground around his feet, he dashed round the flank, hurdled the barbed-wire fence and set about the gun team with his bayonet. It was all over within seconds. Four men lay dead around the gun and as the remainder bolted back towards the houses Robertson turned their own gun on them. Few survived to reach the sanctuary of the ruins.

By 7.10 am the Canadians 'were streaming through and either side of Passchendaele in large numbers, bayoneting Germans in the ruins and along the main street'. Foremost among them was Peter Robertson. Not content with merely capturing the machine-gun, he had decided to employ it against its former owners. With his comrades trailing after him, he advanced through the village, setting up his captured weapon and using it to great effect whenever targets presented themselves. House-to-house fighting continued until 7.40 am when the 27th reported Passchendaele cleared. A little over an hour later, the eastern crest of the ridge beyond the village had been secured. The rest of the day was spent consolidating the ground so spectacularly won. The Germans retaliated with sporadic shelling and a few disorganised counter-attacks which were easily beaten back. But minor fire-fights amid the ruined village continued throughout the day. It was during one of these that Robertson, displaying courage in a different cause, lost his life. From his position on the eastern edge of the village, he saw two snipers from his battalion lying wounded well in advance of the Canadian line. Without hesitation, he set out across the open to bring them in. He rescued one, but the enemy were closing in, infiltrating more men forward, raising the stakes considerably. Robertson, however, ignored the risks. Capt. Theodore Roberts, of the Canadian War Records Office, wrote:

In spite of a veritable storm of bullets, Robertson went out again. He fell before reaching the second man – he was probably hit – but picking himself up, he continued on his way, and secured his second comrade. Slipping on the sticky mud, nearly exhausted, he stuck to his man, and had put him down close to our line, when an unlucky shell exploded near by, killing him instantly.

In the gathering darkness, a heavy bombardment fell on the Canadian positions. Enemy patrols were sighted, but an anticipated German counter-attack never materialised. It had taken Haig's army ninety-nine days to cover 5 miles, but now, at least, the fight for Passchendaele was over.

Nine weeks later, the *London Gazette* of 11 January 1918 announced the award of Victoria Crosses to Cpl Colin Barron and Pte Peter Robertson, the latter sadly posthumously.

Colin Fraser Barron was born at Baldavie, Boyndie in Banffshire, Scotland, on 20 September 1893, the son of Joseph Barron, a farmer. He was educated at Blairmaud, Boyndie, and immigrated to Canada in March 1910. Settling in Toronto, he became a railway worker. In keeping with his Scottish roots, he enlisted in the 48th Highlanders, a militia unit, on 16 May 1913, and was posted to H Company.

It is unclear if he was still serving with this unit at the outbreak of war, but his attestation papers have him volunteering for the Canadian Expeditionary Force on 11 January 1915, giving his occupation as teamster and his father, living in Mill of Boynde, Banffshire, as next-of-kin. A medical examination revealed that a shoulder bone, broken in an accident in 1913, had still not set, but this was not deemed sufficient to reject him for military service and he was posted to D Company, 35th Battalion. Shortly before heading out to France in July, 1915, he forfeited a day's pay for going absent without leave. On July 31, he joined the 3rd (Toronto) Battalion, the unit with which he was to remain throughout the rest of the war. Promoted lance-corporal on 9 April 1917, the day the Canadian Corps captured Vimy Ridge, and was confirmed in the rank of corporal on 11 January 1918, the same day his VC was gazetted. The following month he was made acting sergeant and assigned to the Canadian Corps Lewis Gun School as an instructor. It was from there, in March 1918, he returned to his native Scotland to attend a ceremony at which the Duke of Richmond and Gordon presented him with a gold watch and a wallet of Treasury notes raised by public appeal. Given an extension to his leave to deal with family affairs, he eventually returned to his training duties in May.

He returned to Canada a sergeant and was demobilised on 23 April 1919. Between the wars, he continued to soldier in the militia, re-enlisting in the 48th Highlanders of Canada on 4 November 1921. He served until 22 May 1931, rising to CSM. He married and had two daughters, but like many veterans he was forced to endure an uphill struggle to support his family. For a time, he served with the Provincial Police at Kitchener, Orangeville and Niagara Falls. According to his daughter, Marjory Thompson, he had been rejected by the national force as he was not tall enough. In between running his own transport business, working for the Ontario Department of Highways and a job at Don Jail, there were periodic bouts of unemployment. During the depression, he was out of work for two years, eventually finding work as a guide at the provincial government building before transferring to the staff at Don Jail.

When the Second World War broke out he enlisted again in the Royal Regiment of Canada, successors of the Toronto Regiment. Described at the time as being 'still powerful and built for hand-to-hand fighting', Colin Barron was the first Canadian holder of the Victoria Cross who was not a member of the Permanent Force to be sent on active service. He was a member of the Canadian force that took part in the occupation of Iceland and was later made provost sergeant-major at 1st Division HQ in England.

After the war, he returned to his job as a security guard at the Don Jail and later joined the Toronto Corps of Commissionaires, serving at the CBC television studios, Hester How School and Sunnybrook Hospital. He attended

Davenport Presbyterian church and was an honorary member of many Toronto military clubs. His daughter Marjory recalled: 'He enjoyed going to the Legion and he would go on all the parades, but he would never talk about his experiences. He could be quite fearsome when his temper was up, but even now I find it hard to think about what he did.' Barron was among the Commonwealth holders of the Victoria Cross who attended the Coronation of Queen Elizabeth II, reportedly saying he wished he were young enough 'to be in her service as I was in her grandfather's'.

Colin Fraser Barron VC died in Sunnybrook Hospital on 15 August 1958 and was buried in the Veterans' Plot, Prospect cemetery, in Toronto. His VC group was later sold.

His daughter Marjory said of him: 'He was a very proud man; proud of his roots and his award. As a young man, he was a bit of a devil. And he was a fighter too.'

James Peter Robertson, who won the only VC awarded for the fighting in Passchendaele itself, was born at Albion Mines, Pictou, Nova Scotia, on 26 October 1883, the son of Scottish-born parents Alexander and Janet Robertson. One of eleven children, he was educated at Springall, Nova Scotia, where the family moved when he was 4. During their time there, one of his brothers was presented with a gold cross for saving an injured man after a colliery explosion, despite having been injured himself. In 1898 the family relocated to Medicine Hat, Alberta, and it was there that Pete, as he was known, joined the Canadian Pacific Railway. He worked his way up to fireman and was transferred to Lethbridge as a locomotive engineer. A happy-go-lucky character forever telling jokes and with a song for all occasions, he was reputedly known throughout Alberta as 'Singing Pete'.

He enlisted at Macleod on 14 June 1915 and before heading overseas he wrote to 'the best mother in the world': 'The empire needs the very best that's in us.' Joining the 13th Canadian Mounted Rifles, he was based for a time in Medicine Hat, where a delay in being shipped to Europe sparked a mutiny. It also led, on one occasion, to Robertson coming to blows with a civilian who had insulted members of the unit for their lack of action.

He eventually embarked for England on 29 June 1916. Posted initially to the Lord Strathcona's Horse, he served briefly with the 11th Battalion at Shorncliffe before being transferred to the 27th Battalion and proceeding to France on 27 September. His early service with his new unit was blighted by illness. A bout of influenza was followed by treatment for influenza and the more serious matter of a sexually transmitted disease which resulted in him forfeiting allowances and pay during nearly two months spent in hospital. He

Pte J.P. Robertson

rejoined the 27th Battalion in February 1917 and in the months that followed he saw a considerable amount of action in which he enjoyed a number of narrow escapes. Once, he and two comrades had to be rescued after surviving almost a day buried in the wreckage of their collapsed dugout, and on another occasion he was given up for dead after a disastrous attack. However, his fighting qualities and cheery optimism never flagged. Following his final gallant action at Passchendaele, one of his officers wrote of him: 'He was a dandy soldier ... he kept the boys in good spirits under the most trying conditions.'

On 25 April 1918 the citizens of Medicine Hat, Alberta, turned out in great numbers to see Janet Robertson receive her son's Victoria Cross from the lieutenant-governor, Robert G. Brett. In his address, he declared: 'This cross is only a small thing, its cost is very little, but it has engraved on it the words "For Valour", which mean a great deal. Money can do much – with money titles can be bought, but money cannot buy the Victoria Cross. It must be won by valour and service.' Tributes poured in for Canada's first 'Locomotive engineer VC'. In Cleveland, Ohio, 77,000 delegates at an international railway convention saluted his courage. As a mark of respect, the Canadian Pacific Railway displayed his photograph in Montreal station and almost twenty years after his death, the people of Medicine Hat dedicated the Robertson Memorial Park in his honour. Since then, a swimming pool, a street and the local branch of the Royal Canadian Legion together with a 'Hero Class' coastguard vessel have all been named after him.

AFTERWORD

Four days after Passchendaele fell to the Canadians, the final act in this ghastly campaign was played out. Attacking in the midst of a rainstorm, the 7th Canadian Brigade pushed the Allied lines 500yd further along the main ridge. It was an advance rendered worthless by the bloody repulse of a flanking attack to the north. Even Haig was forced to concede that the position won along the ridge was precarious and unlikely to be sustained in the face of serious counter-attack. In the event, he did not wait to find out. Following the Germans' Spring Offensive, the gains of almost four months were abandoned in three days.

The cost of such folly to British morale was incalculable. The final casualty figures are uncertain, but even the most conservative estimate puts them around the quarter of a million mark, with at least 36,000 dead and 29,000 missing. The Canadians had lost 12,000 men in the space of fifteen days. Of those who died, a large number now lie buried on a hill at the highest point of the Salient, less than 2 miles south-west of Passchendaele. In all, 11,500 graves are concentrated in the 35,000 square metres that form Tyne Cot cemetery. Included among their number is the last resting place of the last man to earn the Victoria Cross in the campaign, James Peter Robertson. His mother's inscription below the carved outline of the medal he died winning reads:

Behold
How good and how pleasant
It is for brethren to dwell
Together in unity.

SOURCES

The following collections have been consulted in the course of my research:

The Lummis VC files at the National Army Museum, London
The Victoria Cross files at the Imperial War Museum, London
The National Archives of Canada, Ottawa
Queen Elizabeth II Army Memorial Museum, New Zealand
The Public Record Office, Kew, Surrey
Regimental Museums and Archives
London Gazette, 1914–20 (HMSO)

PUBLISHED WORKS
For reasons of space I have not listed the numerous unit divisional histories
consulted.

Bancroft, J.W., *Devotion to Duty*, Aim High, 1990
Bean, C.E.W., *Official History of Australia in the War: The AIF in France,
    Vol IV*, University of Queensland Press, 1982
Bishop, A., *Our Bravest and Our Best*, McGraw-Hill Ryerson, 1995
Bryant, G., *Where the Prize is Highest*, Collins, 1972
Carton de Wiart VC DSO, *A Happy Odyssey*, Jonathan Cape, 1950
Clayton, A., *Chavasse: Double VC*, Leo Cooper, 1992
Creagh, Sir O'Moore & Humphris, E.M., *The VC and DSO*, Standard Art
    Book Company, 1924
Crook, M.J., *The Evolution of the Victoria Cross*, Midas Books, 1975
Edmonds, Brig.-Gen. Sir J.E., *Official History of the War: Military
    Operation France and Belgium 1917*, HMSO, 1948
Floyd, T.H., *At Ypres With Best-Dunkley*, Bodley Head, 1920
Gummer, Canon S., *The Chavasse Twins*, Hodder & Stoughton, 1963
Kirby, H.L. & Walsh, R.R., *The Four Blackburn VCs*, THCL Books, 1986
Lindsay, S., *Merseyside Heroes: A Collection of Biographical Notes*, pri-
    vately pubd, 1988
Lisle, Sir B. de, *Reminiscences of Sport and War*, Eyre & Spottiswoode, 1939

McCarthy, C., *Passchendaele: The day-by-day account*, Arms & Armour, 1995

McCrery, N., *For Conspicuous Gallantry*, J.H. Hall & Sons, 1990

Macdonald, L., *They Called it Passchendaele*, Michael Joseph, 1978

Pearce, L/Sgt L., *A Short History of the Regiment's VC Holders*, RHQ Coldstream Guards, 1988

Pillinger, D. & Staunton, A., *Victoria Cross Locator*, revised & updated second edition, 1997

Prior, R. & Wilson, T., *Passchendaele: The Untold Story*, Yale University Press, 1996

Roberts, Capt. T.G., *Thirty Canadian VCs*, Skeffington, 1919

Ross, G., *Scotland's Forgotten Valour*, MacLean Press, 1995

Roy, R.H., *For Most Conspicuous Bravery: A Biography of Major Gen George R Pearkes VC Through Two World Wars*, University of British Columbia Press, 1977

Royal Army Medical Corps, *The Medical Victoria Crosses*, RAMC Historical Museum, 1988

Smyth, Sir J., *The Story of the Victoria Cross*, Frederick Muller, 1963

Swettenham, J., *Valiant Men: Canada's Victoria Cross and George Cross winners*, Hakkert, 1973

This England, *Register of the Victoria Cross*, 1981

Torsin, R.H., *They Stayed With Us ... The Victoria Crosses in Belgium*, 1992

Uys, I.S., *For Valour: The History of Southern Africa's Victoria Cross Heroes*, Ian Uys, 1973

Walkinton, M.L., *Twice in a Lifetime*, Samson Books, 1980

Wigmore, L. & Harding, B., *They Dared Mightily*, Australian War Memorial, 1963

Williams, W.A., *The VCs of Wales and the Welsh Regiments*, Bridge Books, 1984

Willis, C.J. & Rogers, D.F., *For Valour HMS Conway & HMS Worcester*, Conway Club & Assn of Old Worcesters, 1984

ARTICLES AND PERIODICALS

Together with numerous newspaper reports, the following have been particularly useful:

Passchendaele 1917, Hubert Essame, War Monthly Issue 27, 1976

An Account of the Life and Achievements of Pte G.I. McIntosh VC, D. Mitchell, Gordon Highlanders Museum, 1995

Captain H. Ackroyd VC, MC, RAMC, E.F. Malet de Carteret, Stand To, No. 44, 1995

Victoria Cross: Story of a Tasmanian. Lewis McGee and his Medals, M. Spohn, 1996

UNPUBLISHED PAPERS

D. Andrew (family papers), Major Gen. The Viscount Monckton of Brenchley (Colyer-Fergusson family papers), W.B. Harrison, M. Giles (Mayson family), J.&K. Edwards (family papers), G. McIntosh (family papers), S.R. Davies (family papers), M. Moody, G. Armstrong (Bye family papers), E.F. Malet de Carteret, Dr C.E. Ackroyd (family papers), A. Loosemore (family papers), J.M. Lockier (Room family), H. Cooper (family papers), W. Ireland, A.J. Skinner (family papers), Major M.S.S. Moore VC, Letters and family papers (IWM), Major J.R. Webster DSO, MC, Diary (IWM), P.A. Feeney (Egerton family papers), J.H. Rogers (Hamilton family papers), M. Goggins (Dwyer family papers), Pte P.J. Bugden, Letters and family papers (Queensland Musuem), B. Newman, G. McGee, S. Kuo, I. Wrankmore (McGee family papers), L.P. Evans VC, DSO, family papers (National Library of Wales), J. Ockendon (family papers), F. Brown (Molyneux family), L/Sgt J.H. Rhodes VC, DCM, letters (family), A. Risley (Rhodes family papers), F. Bromley (Halton family), H. McKenzie VC, DCM, Papers (PPCLI Archives), M.F. Thompson (Barron family papers).

INDEX

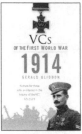

VCs of the First World War: 1914

GERALD GLIDDON

978 0 7524 5908 0

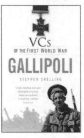

VCs of the First World War: Gallipoli

STEPHEN SNELLING

978 0 7524 5653 9

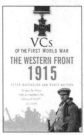

VCs of the First World War: The Western Front 1915

PETER BATCHELOR AND CHRIS MATSON

978 0 7524 6057 4

VCs of the First World War: Somme 1916

GERALD GLIDDON

978 0 7524 6303 2

Visit our website and discover thousands of other History Press books.

www.thehistorypress.co.uk